Ishwar Chandra Vidyasagar

Iswer Chandra Vidyasagar

Series Editor

Dr. M.H. Syed

Editor

R.K. Singh **P.K. Choudhry**

hbpl

Himalaya Books Pvt. Ltd.

'Ramdoot', Dr. Bhalerao Marg, Girgaon, Mumbai - 400 004
Tel : (022) 23863863, Fax : (022) 23877178
Email : himpub@vsnl.com

First Edition : 2011

Published by : H.B.P.L.
"Pooja Apartments", 4-B, Murari Lal Street, Ansari Road,
Darya Ganj, New Delhi-110 002
Phones : 23270392, 23278631 Reliance : 30180392 to 396
Fax : 011-23256286 Email : hphdel@vsnl.com

Sole Distributers : HIMALAYA PUBLISHING HOUSE PVT. LTD.

Branch Offices

Mumbai : "Ramdoot", Dr. Bhalerao Marg, Girgaon, Mumbai-400 004.
Phones : 23860170/23863863 Fax : 022-23877178
Email : himpub@vsnl.com
Website : www.himpub.com

Nagpur : Kundanlal Chandak Industrial Estate, Ghat Road, **Nagpur 440-018.**
Phone: 2738731, 3296733 Telefax : 0712-2721215

Bengaluru : No. 16/1 (Old 12/1), 1st Floor, Next to Hotel Highlands, Madhava Nagar, Race Course Road, **Bengaluru - 560 001.**
Phone : 22281541, 22385461, Telefax: 080-22286611

Hyderabad : No. 3-4-184, Lingampally, Besides Raghavendra Swamy Matham, Kachiguda, **Hyderabad - 500 027.** Phone: 040-27560041, 27550139, Mobile:- 09848130433 Telefax: 040-27560041

Chennai : No. 85/50, Bazullah Road, T. Nagar, **Chennai - 600 017.**
Phone: 044-28344020, 32463737, 42124860

Pune : No. 527, "Laksha" Apartment, First Floor, Mehunpura, Shaniwarpeth, (Near Prabhat Theatre), **Pune - 411 030.**
Phone: 020-24496323/24496333/32326733

Lucknow : Jai Baba Bhawan, Near Dr. Sanjiv Awasthi, Church Road, Kurshi Road, Aliganj, **Lucknow - 226 024.**
Phone: 9305302158, 9415349385

Ahmedabad : No. 114, "SHAIL", 1st Floor, Opp. Madhu Sudan House, C.G.Road, Navrang Pura, **Ahmedabad – 380 009.**
Phone: 079-26560126, Mobiles: 09327324149,09314679413

Ernakulam : No. 39/104 A, Lakshmi Apartment, Karikkamuri Cross Rd., Ernakulam, **Cochin – 682011**, Kerala.
Phone: 0484-2378012, 2378016, Mob.: 09344199799

Bhubaneswar : 5 Station Square, **Bhubaneswar (Orissa) - 751 001.**
Mobile: 9861046007, E-mail:-orissa@himpub.com

Indore : Kesardeep Avenue Extension, 73, Narayan Bagh, Flat No. 302, IIIrd Floor, Near Humpty Dumpty School, Narayan Bagh, **Indore (M.P.) 452 007** Mobile: 09301386468

Kolkata : 108/4, Beliaghata, Main Road, Near ID Hospital, Opp. SBI Bank **Kolkata - 700 010.** Mobile: 09910440956

Printed at : Shri Krishna offset Press Delhi-93

Preface

Biography, is now a form of literature, very much in vogue. In fact, biography is a description or account of someone's life and the times, which is usually published in the form of a book. A biography is more than a mention of personal facts (life, education, work, relationships and death), it also portrays the subject's experience of events. Technically speaking, a work is biographical, if it covers, all of a person's life. Biography writing has a long history. A biography is real. Ancient Greeks developed the biographical tradition, which we have inherited, although until the 5th century AD, when the word 'biographia' first appeared, in Damascius' "Life of Isodorus," biographical pieces were called simply "lives". It is quite likely that the Greeks were drawing on a pre-existing eastern tradition. Certainly Herodotus' "Histories" contains more detailed biographical information on Persian kings and subjects. The earliest surviving pieces, which we would identify as biographical are Isocrates' "Life of Evagoras" and Xenophon's "Life of Agesilaos," both from the fifth century BC. "Parallel Lives" by Plutarch, a Greek writing under the Roman empire, is a series of short biographies of eminent men.

The Golden Age of English biography emerged in late eighteenth century, the century in which the terms "biography" and "autobiography" entered English lexicon. The classic works of the period were Samuel Johnson's "Critical Lives of the Poets" and James Boswell's "Massive Life of Johnson". Generally American biography followed English model. By World War I, cheap hardcover reprints had become popular. The decade of the 1920s witnessed a biographical 'boom'. Later, biographical writings developed a lot and today biographies are written and compiled in the finest form of the genre. In India too, biography, as a form of literature has been evolved, cultivated and polished over the years. Here is an effort to promote this tradition further.

This series of biographies of great men, great women and celebrities in all walks of life is an adventurous academic endeavour, in its own right. A team of researchers and compilers has worked for a good period of time to accomplish the project. For this purpose, hundreds of books by eminent authors and editors have been consulted and referred to. We have benefited from various works, liberally, in order to illustrate and enrich this effort of ours. Present book is devoted to the great personality of Ishwar Chandra Vidyasagar.

Ishwar Chandra Vidyasagar is considered as one of the pillars of Bengal renaissance. He managed to continue the reforms movement that was started by Raja Rammohan Roy. Vidyasagar was a well-known author, intellectual and above all a staunch believer in humanity. He brought a revolution in the education system of Bengal. In his book, "Barno-Porichoy" (Introduction to the Letter), Vidyasagar refined the Bengali language and made it accessible to the common strata of the society. The title 'Vidyasagar', (ocean of knowledge) was given to him, due to his vast knowledge in almost all areas. Ishwar Chandra Vidyasagar initiated the concept of widow remarriage and raised concern for the abolition of child-marriage and polygamy. He also opened the doors of the colleges and other educational institutions to lower caste students, which were earlier reserved only for the upper castes. For his immense generosity and kind-heartedness, people started addressing him as "Daya Sagar" (ocean of kindness).

This is a compact and comprehensive account of the above mentioned great life, which is bound to attract the attention of scholars, researchers, students and the general readers alike. Let's hope this humble effort would receive a warm welcome and due applause.

— ***Editors***

Contents

1

An Illustrious Life

Birth and Ancestry

Great educationist and social reformer, Ishwar Chandra Vidyasagar was born on the 26th day of September, in the year 1820, corresponding with the twelfth of Ashwin, 1227, Bengali Era, of a poor, but respectable Brahmin family, at Birsingha, a small village in the district of Midnapore, in the lower provinces of Bengal. His father's name was Thakurdas Bandyopadhyay. Ishwar Chandra was his first-born son. The village Bir-singha is 52 miles to the west of Calcutta, the metropolis of India, and is only 5 miles from Ghatal, which is one of the subdivisions of the Midnapore district. But Birsingha was not the original home of the family. Vidyasagar's grandfather had removed there from Banamalipur, where the family had been living for several generations. Banamalipur is a village in the Hooghly district, lying to the west of Tarakesvar, a sacred place with the Hindus, where thousands of pilgrims from different parts of India assemble annually to offer their *puja* (prayer and offerings) to their god Tarakesvar or *Siva*. The life 'and character of a man are greatly influenced by his surroundings. This was amply verified in Vidyasagar. We should therefore begin with a brief description of the family, he was born in. His pedigree may uncontrovertibly be traced to his great grandfather. In this respect it would be better to quote what Vidyasagar himself has said in his autobiography:

"My paternal great-grandfather, Bhuvanesvar Vidyalankar, had five sons, of whom the eldest was Nrisingha Ram, the second, gangadhar, the third, Ramjay, the fourth, Panchanan, and the fifth, Ramcharan. The third, Ramjay Tarkabhushan, was my grandfather. After the death of my great-grandfather (father's grandfather), his first and second sons managed the family affairs. In a short time, my grandfather, Ramjay Tarkabhushan, had some dispute with his elder brothers about the family property, and soon the dispute rose into downright quarrel and breach of brotherly friendship. Ultimately, my grandfather left the village in disgust.

"There lived, at that time, in the village of Birsingha, a famous Pandit (profound Sanskrit scholar) named Umapati Tarkasiddhanta. My grandfather, Ramjay Tarkabhushan, was married to Durga Devi, the third daughter of Umapati Tarkasiddhanta, Ramjay Tarkabhushan, had by this wife, two sons and four daughters. Of the two sons, Thakurdas was the first, and Kalidas, the second. Of the four daughters, the eldest was Mangala, the second, Kamala, the third, Govindamani, and the fourth, Annapurna. Thakurdas was my father.

"After Ramjay Tarkabhushan, my grandfather, had left his native village; his wife Durga Devi was living with the family at Banamalipur. But, unfortunately, the brother's of her husband, in a short time, began to look down upon and; neglect her and her children; and the neglect soon rose to such a height that she was compelled to leave the village, and take shelter in her father's house at Birsingha. For a few days she lived here comfortably, but presently her misfortune began anew, for she soon saw that she could not live peacefully in her father's house, as she had imagined.

"Umapati Tarkasiddhanta, the father of Durga Devi, had grown too old to look to the management of the family affairs, which had consequently to be left in the hands of his son, Ram Sundar Viclyabhushan. This Vidyabhushan and his wife were not well disposed towards Durga Devi and her children, and were always a source of oppression and terror to them. The husband and wife treated them with such disdain and inhumanity that Durga Devi had no other alternative than to leave at once this dreadful shelter, namely her father's house. Her father, Umapati

Tarka-siddhanta, was deeply and sincerely pained at the conduct of his son and daughter-in-law, but he was now quite helpless himself. He, therefore, had a hut built for his daughter in the neighbourhood, not very far off from his own house; and here Durga Devi began to live with her children, and passed her days in a most wretched state.

"At that time, many poor, helpless women of Bengal earned their livelihood by spinning cotton into thread by means of a spinning wheel, known by the name of *Charka,* and by selling them to the weavers. Durga Devi was now compelled to take to this industry. But the income from this source was too small to maintain herself and her six children. Her father helped her now and then, but even this, added to her own income, was barely sufficient to feed and clothe them. As a matter of fact, Durga Devi was most miserably circumstanced, and she always shed tears at the sight of her barely-fed children, Her eldest son, Thakurdas, was at this time fourteen or fifteen years old. At this young age, he, with his mother's permission, left her cottage, and proceeded to Calcutta in search of livelihood.

"Sabharam Vachaspati, a near kinsman of whom he had left in a most deplorable situation, made him forego this design. At last, it was definitely settled that he should attend to such education! as would soon enable him to earn some money.

"At that time, a little knowledge of English easily procured berths in European mercantile firms; and it was, therefore, thought advisable for Thakurdas to have a little English instruction, instead of Sanskrit. But English education was not easily obtainable then, because there were only a limited number of English schools, and these were resorted to only by the rich, as they were very costly, and the poor could not afford to pay for such education. Under the circumstances, it was quite impossible for poor, helpless Thakurdas to obtain his English education in a school. It was finally settled that he should read English with a friend of Jaganmohan Nyayalankar's, who had a tolerable knowledge of English, and who, at the request of his friend, the famous Sanskrit professor, consented to give Thakurdas, lessons in English. This gentleman was employed in a mercantile office, and so he had no time during the day to impart his gratuitous instruction to

Thakurdas. He told the boy to come to him after nightfall, and the poor pupil daily attended the night school and received lessons free of cost.

"It has been said before, that Jaganmohan Nyaylankar used to give food and lodging to many poor outsiders, who had very little or no relation with him. In the evening, the feeding of these poor people was finished immediately after sunset. And this was the time when Thakurdas had to leave Nyaylankar's house and go to his teacher for the sake of a little English education; and when he returned from his teacher's house, it was too late, and he had to pass the night without food. This happened to him every night, and he thus grew thinner and weaker day by day. One day, his teacher asked him the cause, and he, with tearful eyes, explained to him the real cause of this sad change. While this conversation was going on, a kind-hearted gentleman of the *Sudra* caste was sitting there. He was deeply moved at the sad tale, and he told Thakurdas that he should no longer lodge in the house of Jaganmohan Nyayalankar, and that if he could cook his food, he was ready to give him (Thakurdas) food and shelter. As was expected, Thakurdas was highly delighted at the proposal, and readily accepted the kind offer. The next day he left his former refuge, and took shelter in the house of his new benevolent patron.

"But the earnings of this kind-hearted benevolent gentleman were not equal to his generosity. He was an ordinary broker, and earned a very scanty livelihood. He lived from hand to mouth, yet his kind heart always melted at the tale of other people's distress. Thakurdas considered him-self very fortunate that he now had two belly full meals every day. But this happy state of things did not last long. As ill luck would have it, in a short time, the paltry income of this benevolent benefactor was still reduced, and what he daily earned, was not always sufficient to maintain two persons with comfort. He used to leave his house early in the morning, and toiled hard to earn a few piece, not only for his own sake, but also for the sake of the poor Brahmin boy, whom he had kindly taken under his protection. But, unfortunately, many a day he could not return to his house in time, and consequently, on those days, Thakurdas had to remain without mid-day meal.

"Thakurdas had no other property than a small brass *thala* (shallow dish) and a *lota* (waterpot) of the same metal He used to eat his rice from the *thala,* and drink his water from the *lota.* In some parts of India, even in Calcutta, a few teak leaves stitched together are used by the poor to eat their rice from. Now, Thakurdas thought within himself thus: 'The purposes of a *thala* may be well-served by teak-leaves, I shall be able to manage the eating of my rice even without a *thala.* So if I part with it I shall not feel its want. Let me sell this *thala* and retain the *lota.* The sale proceeds shall be my pocket money, I shall use this money in cases of upmost emergency. The day I shall be deprived of my midday meal, I shall lay out a piece in buying something to eat, and thus save myself from starvation". Having thus be thought himself, he went one day to a brazier's shop, and offered the *thdla* for sale. But the brazier declined to buy the *thala,* saying that purchase of old plates and utensils sometimes threw them into great difficulties, as most of the articles thus purchased were stolen property, Thakurdas entreated the brazier earnestly, but he turned a deaf ear. He then went to the other braziers, one after another, but none of them yielded to his request. Greatly dejected at the disappointment, he returned to his lodging, quite as helpless as ever.

"One noon, when the sun was in its zenith, Thakurdas Under intense pressure of hunger, began to pace up and down the street, in the hope that his: mind would ' thereby be diverted from the thoughts of want of food, and he would thus forget the pangs of hunger. Unconsciously, by slow movements, he walked - from Barabazar to Thanthania, a distance of nearly two miles. But far from the results he had anticipated, the physical labour caused by his pedestrianism, kindled his appetite more fiercely, and he was so much over Come with hunger and thirst, that he was quite unable to move farther. Presently, he found him-self standing before a shop, where a middle-aged widow was selling such poor victuals, as *Muri* (fried husked rice) and *mtirki* (fried paddy soaked in molasses). On seeing him thus standing, the woman asked him kindly, "Why are you standing here, my boy?" Thakurdas answered that he was thirsty, and begged for a little water to drink, The kind woman very affectionately told him to sit down, and thinking that it would not be proper to give the Brahmin boy only a little water with nothing to eat, gave hint some *murki* and some water. She gazed at him as he greedily devoured the *murki,* and asked him whether he had eaten any food that day. Thakurdas replied, 'No, mother, I have had nothing to eat today till now. Thereupon the kind-hearted woman told him to desist from drinking water, and to wait a little. She at once hastened to a milk man's shop, and came back with some curd, which she graciously placed before Thakurdas, and presenting him with some more *murki,* pressed him to make a belly full meal of the curd and *murku* After the meal had been over, the benevolent woman, by kind and affectionate words, drew out from Thakurdas all particulars of his circumstances, and at last told him to come to her, whenever he would be in want of food.

"Henceforth whenever he felt the pangs of hunger, and could not procure food in the daytime, he used to go to the kind-hearted woman, and she was always very glad to feed him heartily in the manner related before.

"Some time after this, Thakurdas, with the help of his protector, secured a berth worth two Rupees a month. He was highly delighted at this appointment, but did not leave the protection of his benefactor, who had given him shelter in times of dire need. He lived in the same house with his protector as before, and without minding in the least his own privations, began to regularly send the two rupees every month to his mother to mitigate her sufferings. He was very intelligent and industrious, and performed his duties most willingly and cheerfully. For this reason, his employers, whereinsoever he was employed, were all highly satisfied with him.

"In two or three years, Thakurdas had a pay of five rupees a month. The sufferings of his mother, brother, and sisters were now much relieved. At this time, my grandfather (Thakurdas's father) returned to his native place. At first, he went to Banamalipur, but not finding his wife and children there, he came to Birsingha, and there joined his family, At his return home after an interval of seven or eight years, every one was delighted. He considered it humiliating to live *in* his father-in-law's house or in its neighbourhood. He, therefore, designed to remove with his family to Banamalipur, his paternal home. But when Durga *Devi* his wife, related with tears in her eyes, the inhuman conduct of his brothers, he gave up his design, and most reluctantly consented to settle down permanently in Birsingha. It was in this wise that Birsingha became our place of abode.

"After a short stay at Birsingha, Ramjay Tarkabhushan, my grandfather, came down to Calcutta, to see his son, Thakurdas. When he heard from Thakurdas's benefactor and protector of his son's patience, forbearance, and diligence, he was highly delighted, and showered upon his son his choicest blessings. At this time, there lived, in the Barabazar quarter of Calcutta, a certain well-to-do gentleman of the *Uttar Rarhiya Raya-stha* family, by name Bhagavat Charan Sinha. My grandfather had a great intimacy with this gentleman, who was a perfect pattern of a Hindu householder. He was very kind and benevolent. On hearing from my grandfather everything connected with him, from the time of his leaving his native place, he was deeply touched, and proposed that henceforth Thakurdas should put up with him in his house, and that he would undertake to provide him with proper meals, adding, at the same time, that when Thakurdas was able to cook his food, there was not the slightest chance of any inconvenience.

"My grandfather, Ramjay Tarkabhushan, was very pleased at the offer, and readily accepted it. He placed Thakurdas under the care of this kind gentleman, and then returned to Birsingjia. From this time forward, the troubles of Thakurdas with respect to his meals were over. On receiving regularly the necessary belly full meals twice a day, he considered himself entering into a new life. This happy combination did not only put an end to his troubles of proper food, but was also the means of providing him with a better appointment. Bhagavat Babu secured for him a situation worth eight rupees a month. When his mother came to learn that her son, Thakurdas, had got an appointment bringing a monthly salary of eight rupees, her delight knew no bounds.

> "Thakurdas was, at this time, twenty-three or twenty-four years old. My grandfather considering this a marriageable age, married him to Bhagavati Devi, second daughter of Ramkanta Tarkavagis of Goghat. This Bhagavati Devi was my mother. In her childhood, she had been brought up with the family of her maternal grandfather".

Ratnkanta Tarkavagis had, in the prime of his youth, lost the sanity of his mind. His father-in-law, Panchanan Vidyavagis of village Patul, therefore, took him with his wife and children to his own house, and housed them there. In spite of medical treatment of different kinds, for a long time, by experts, Ramkanta did not recover from his malady, and he died quite insane. It was for this reason that Vidyasagar's mother, Bhagavati Devi, had been brought up in the house of her maternal grandfather. Ramkanta Tarkavagis had two daughters, of whom Bhagavati Devi was the younger, Her mother's name was Ganga Devi who again was the eldest daughter of Panchanan Vidyavagis. He had five other children, four sons and one daughter, besides Garga Devi.

Vidyasagar was famous for his spiritedness, truthfulness, frankness and love of independence. It appears that he imbibed these virtues from his father and grandfather. Ramjay Tarkabhushan, his grandfather, was a man of independent spirit. He never flattered anybody, nor was he ever daunted by the threats of malicious persons. It was this love of independence and spiritedness that turned his brother-in-law (wife's brother) and his partisans to be his enemies. His idea was that the country, at that time, was devoid of men (i.e. good men) and that it was full of blasts: His amiability, modesty and truthfulness were equal to his spiritedness. It is said that while he was travelling to the different pilgrimages after leaving his home, one night he heard somebody say to him in dream:— Your wife has left your native village, Banamalipur, and has been living in Birsingha". At this, he returned to Birsirgha, and once again took charge of his family.

The land-owner of the village, Birsingha, offered to him his homestead land free of rent, and his friends and relations urged him to accept the offer. But he thankfully declined it. Ishwar Chandra Vidyasagar, in his autobiography, thus speaks of his grandfather:

He never depended upon, or flattered, any body. It was his firm conviction that death was preferable to dependence on another person. He was a vegetarian, and ate only one meal a day. His character was stainless and purer, and he always took great care to devote most of his time and attention, to the worship of his hevenly father.

Ramjay Tarkasiddharita's bodily strength was equal to the strength of his mind. Body and mind are so very closely connected that the strength or weakness of the one is generally followed by the strength or weakness of the other. We have seen, with our own eyes, the truth of this verified in Ishwar Chandra Vidyasagar, and we have heard of it in his grandfather, Ramjay Tarkasiddhanta. Ramjay always travelled fearlessly with an iron cudgel in his hand. One day, on his way to Midnapore from Birsingha, a bear came upon him. At the sight of the animal, he took his stand behind a tree. The bear tried to seize him with its fore paws. No sooner had the beast stretched out its paws to catch hold of Ramsay, than he seized it by its out-stretched paws, and began to rub the ugly beast against the tree. Soon the bear was nearly dead. Seeing that the brute was completely overpowered and almost dead, Ramjay left it really and proceeded on his-journey. But the beast, was not dead, and no sooner was his back turned, than it rose, and tore his back with its sharp nails. Ramjay had now no other alternative than to let fall his iron cudgel on the bear's head, which killed it on the spot. He had to suffer for upwards of a month from the effects of the wound, and the sore mark was visible on his back as long as he lived.

When Thakurdas was able to- work well and take good care of the family, his father, Ramjay Tarkasiddhanta, again went out on a pilgrimage, and returned home a second time, when his grand-Son, Ishwar Chandra Vidyasagar, was in the womb of his mother. It is said that, one night, when he was staying on the top of a hill, Ratrijay dreamed that a good male child, who was destined to do "much real good to the country and to win a world-wide renown, was going to take its birth in his family. This dream made him forsake his ascetic life and return again to his home. This child was Ishwar Chandra Vidyasagar.

When Ramjay returned a second time to Birsingha, he saw that his daughter-in-law, Bhagavati Devi, was really pregnant, but at the same time quite insane. She had lost her sanity from the moment she had conceived the child in her womb. This insanity lasted throughout the whole period of her pregnancy. Strange to say, that although with continued treatment of different kinds for tea months failed to cure her, yet no sooner was she delivered of the child, Ishwar Chandra, than she began to regain her sanity even without any medical help. In a short time, she was as sane as ever, and continued so to the last day of her life. Kind-hearted as she naturally was, she was ever after-wards seen to feed and clothe the poor. As is the custom with unallowed Hindu women, she cooked food with her own hands, and took great delight in distributing it to the guests and the needy, without distinction of caste or creed. Her generosity, kindness and benevolence Were unparalleled. We shall try to give a more detailed description of her character later on, But we may mention here, in passing, that kindness of heart, which figured so conspicuously in Vidyasagar's character, and encleared him to all classes of people, and which caused his name to be lovingly cherished in memory by everybody, was due mostly to his ever-kind and bounteous mother. George Herbert used to say: "One good mother is worth a hundred school masters". The truth of this saying has been verified in all such great men, as Ishwar Chandra Vidyasagar, Napoleon Bonaparte, and others.

Formerly in India, the science of astronomy, palmistry, and fortune-telling, generally known by the name of astrology, like all other sciences, had risen to perfection. Even at the time of Vidyasagar's birth, there -were many astrologers, palmisters and fortune-tellers, who could by the help of their occult science, foretell the future of a new-born child. Before Vidyasagar's birth, Bhavananda Bhaltacharya, a great astrologer of the time, had predicted that Bhagavati Devi (Vidyasagar's mother) would give birth to a child, who would be a bodily incarnation of humanity, and that after the birth of the baby, she would recover her former sanity. This prediction of Bhavananda Bhattacharya was fulfilled to the letter. It was for this, or some similar, reason that Ishwar Chandra Vidyasagar was a great admirer and advocate of this occult science.

Childhood

It was noon when Ishwar Chandra took his birth. His father, Thakurdas, was not at home, at that time. He had gone to the neighbouring *Hat* (market) of Kumargaiija, which was nearly a mile off from his village. On his way back from the market, he met his father Ramjay, who told him that a bull-calf was born that day in their house. By this he alluded to his newly born grandchild by way of joke, but in this jest he darkly hinted at the future character of Vidyasagar. What he really meant by this joke, was that the child would be as stubborn as a bull-calf; and, most probably, he foresaw this from the marks on the child's fore-head and the lines on the palm of his hand. Besides, the science of astrology showed that the child was born at the moment when the moon was connected with the *bull* (one of the signs of the zodiac). Those, who are born at such a time, must be stubborn and strong-minded like a bull, The *Sastras* say:

> "One, born at a time when the master of the night *(i.e.* the moon) is at the *bull,* must be righteous, ever-pleased, complaisant, true to his word, fer-famed, large-eyed, strong-bodied, and of amiable appearance".

Stubbornness was one of the principal features of Ishwar Chandra Vidyasagar's character, and it was conspicuously visible in most of his acts. Stubbornness generates fixedness of purpose. It was for this reason that Stephen Gerard employed under him men of stubborn character. Ishwar Chandra had a great fixedness of purpose. Whatever he handled, whether good or bad, he never left undone or half-done.

Thakurdas could not grasp the real purport of his father's jest. He understand the simple meaning that a bull-calf was actually born in their house, as at that time one of their cows was pregnant and her delivery was expected every moment. Both father and son soon returned home. Thakurdas went into the cow-shed, and found that the cow was not yet delivered. Thakurdas's father then took him to the nursery, and showed him the child, saying, at the same time, that this was the bull-calf he referred to, and then explained its real meaning.

Sambhu Chandra Vidyaratna, one of the young-er brothers of Ishwar Chandra, says in his, Life of Vidyasagar:

"Our grandfather, Ramjay Bandyopadhyay, who had then returned from his pilgrimage, wrote with lac-dye a few words in the lower part of the newly-born child's tongue, before the severance of its umbilical cord, and then told his wife, Durga

Devi, that as an effect of this writing the child would be incapacitated for a little while from sucking the breast of its mother. He also said that the infant's delicate tongue, being handled by his hard, rough hand, the child would stammer for a time; but that, being born at a most auspicious moment, the child would in future become a great man, and that his fame would spread far and wide". All this, Sambhu Chandra says, he heard from his father and from his paternal and maternal grandmothers. But Vidyasagar himself has made no mention of this in his autobiography.

Shortly after Ishwar Chandra's birth, Kenaram Acharyya, a great astrologer of the time, prepared his horoscope, and he was greatly surprised at the indications, He foresaw that the future of Vidyasagar was very auspicious, and that he would become a great man. That the Hindu astrology is no myth, but a well-founded science, is clearly proved from Vidyasagar's horoscope. At its predictions were fulfilled to the letter. As the subject is very abstruse and incomprehensible without a careful study of the science, we forbear entering into a discussion of Ishwar Chandra's horoscope.

As we have said before, Ishwar Chandra was born at a propitious moment, and this was verified by the surrounding circumstances. Slowly, but surely, his father's troubles lessened. He began to have a larger income, and soon there was a sudden change, on all sides, for the better. There was a general talk in the neighbourhood that a most fortunate child was born to Thakurdas Bandyopadhyay. Hence Ishwar Chandra was a great favourite with the neighbours. The grandfather, Ranvijay Tarkasiddhanta, gave the child the name, Ishwar (which means *Lord*).

Early Education

The village Birsirigha was not in a very flourishing state at that time. It had no English-teaching school. There was only a vernacular *pathasata* (primary school) for giving little boys an elementary education in reading and writing the Bengali language. After a few year's training in this school, the sons of comparatively well-to-do Brahmins were sent to *tols* (seats of Sanskrit education), where they had to study hard for several years, and then undergo a set of examinations held by the professor himself. After the final examination, the professor gave the pupils each a degree or title, and then dismissed them, who; in their turn, then opened *Tots* and set themselves up as independent professors of Sanskrit.

Ishwar Chandra was now five years old, and it was time, according to the Hindu Sastras, that he should begin to read and write. At this time, there was a primary *pathsala* in Birsingha under the teachership of Sanatan Sarkar, School-masters of this class were generally rigorous and fond of using their rods freely. They were strict followers of the ancient proverb,—'Spare the rod and spoil the child.' Sanatan Sarkar, the village school-master of Birsingha, used to beat mercilessly the tender-aged boys under his care, and he was an object of terror to them. Ishwar Chandra's father, Thakurdas, disapproved of this harsh dealing, and he heartily disliked Sanatan. He was, therefore, in great anxiety with respect to his little boy's education, and began to look out for a more humane teacher, who would use his rod less freely, and in whose hands he could safely place his little son.

His choice fell on a Kulin Brahmin, by name Kalikanta Chattopadhyay, who had formerly been a native of Birsingha, but had subsequently removed to his father-in-law's at Garuti, a small village close to Bhadresvar in the district of Hooghly, This Kalikanta had many wives in different places, as was the custom with the Kulin Brahmins of those days. Thakurdas sent for him at his father-in-law's, and on his arrival, set up another *pathsala* at Birsingha with Kalikanta as its teacher. Kalikanta, unlike his fellow-brother Sanatan, was a man of amiable disposition and considerable humanity. His treatment of his pupils was mild, decent and genial. He very seldom gave them corporal punishment. He tried, by gentle and soothing words, to rectify their mistakes, and to impart to them educational and moral lesson.

He secured the warmest love and esteem of his pupils, and sincere friendship and patronage of their guardians. Such was the village school-master, who was introduced into Birsingha, and into the hands of this worthy teacher; was Ishwar Chandra placed by his father, at the early age of five years.

The boy, Ishwar Chandra, had uncommon parts, which began to develop early in this elementary school. He finished the course of study taught in this kind of school in three year's time, and at this early age of eight, he wrote a very good hand. Good handwriting had a very high place at that time, and was taken to be the best recommendation, a bride could have, The teacher, Kalikanta, was greatly surprised at the degree of intelligence and memory displayed by young Ishwar Chandra, and he was often heard to say that this boy would become a great man in his after-life.

After he had been one year with Kalikanta, Ishwar Chandra was seriously ill with Enlargement Spleen and Dysentery. He had, therefore, to be removed to the house of his maternal uncle at village *Patul,* for treatment. His younger brother, Dinabaṇdhu, accompanied him. Here he was placed under the treatment of Ram Lochan *Kaviraj, a* native physician of Kothra, which is a village, close to Khanakul Krishnanagar in the Hooghly district. Under the treatment of this able physician, he was soon cured perfectly. When he regained strength enough to be able to undertake a journey, he came to his native village, Birsingha, and he was again placed under the tuition of the worthy teacher, Kalikanta, who loved his young pupil, Ishwar Chandra, exceedingly.. In the evening, after he had dismissed his school, Kalikanta used daily to give him seperate lessons in native Arithmetic, Mensuration, and other subjects, which formed the curriculum, of study in elementary vernacular schools of those days, and then, when the lessons were over, he used to carry the boy to his home. For this reason Ishwar Chandra adored him ever after.

In his early years, Ishwar Chandra was very naughty, and many stories are told of his childish waywardness and mischievous freaks. Surely enough, most boys are naughty and mischievous in their early years, but their naughtiness is never called to mind, nor does it ever appear in the pages of immortal history. But one feels a sort of curiousity to hear, with thrilling pleasure, the tales of mischievous freaks of those who, in after years, led a glorious life, and left a good name. Chaitanya, otherwise known as Gauranga, the great Hindu reformer of *Vazsknatsm,* while a young boy, used to steal and eat up fruit and other articles of divine worship offered by his compatriot Brahmins. Shakespeare, in his early days, associated himself with some other wicked boys, and stole deer. The famous poet Wordsworth, in his boyhood, exceedingly tortured his mother. It is said that, one day, young Wordsworth, on looking at an old picture hanging from the walls, suddenly caught hold of his elder brother's arms, and requested him to lash the picture. His elder brother declining to comply with his inhuman request, he himself took up a whip, and with it lashed the picture several times. The rever-end Doctor Peli was very naughty in his early years. He was a terror to his neighbours, who could not rest peacefully at night, for his depreciations. Robert (afterwards *Lord)* Clive, the founder of the British Empire in India, while only a little boy, used to ascend on the steeple of a very high church, and sit there composedly. Instances of such childish naughtiness on the part of men, who in after-life attained superiority and greatness, tend in a great measure to excite curious pleasurable feelings. The early part of the lives of many of these great men is conspicuously marked by freaks of childish naughtiness.

During his latter days, on one occasion, a gentleman paid Vidyasagar a friendly visit, accompanied with his young boy, Vidaysagar remarked that the boy would become a great man, at which the visitor smiled, saying that the boy was very naughty. Vidyasagar retorted as follows:. 'Never mind, my friend, I too was very naughty in early days. I *used* to steal fruits from the orchards of my neighbours, and defile with soil other people's clothes left to dry in the sun. I was an object of terror *to* my neighbours.

Ishwar Chandra Vidyasagar was often heard to frankly admit his childish haughtiness. One Mathur Mandal was his near neighbour. Almost every day, on his way to or from school, he eased himself in front of Mathur Mandal's outer gates. Mathur's mother and wife removed "the soil with their own hands. Mathur's wife, now and then lost her temper, and wanted to punish the culprit, but her mother-in-law prevented her, saying that she had heard from the boy's grandfather that he would become a great man. Whenever he passed by a rice or other corn field, of which there are plenty in Bengal, he used to tear away the ears of the newly-ripe corn and trample them under foot, or scatter them to the winds, thus causing a great mischief to his neighbours. Now and then he chewed and devoured a few of the unhusked grains. On one of these occasions, the awn of a barley stuck into his throat, and he was in danger of his life. His grandmother drew it out with great dexterity, and thus saved the boy from imminent death. This wicked boy, in after-life, became a most inoffensive, humble, peaceful, pious man. In fact, such was the case with many men, who though very naughty *in* their early years, turned afterwards to be good and great men.

Further Studies

While still in the Belles-lettres class, little Ishwar Chandra had acquired a great proficiency in grammar and language. He could at this early age, for he was then only thirteen years old, compose beautiful verses, elegant both in style and rhetoric. His *slokas* won admiration from all classes. On occasions of his visits to his native village, Birsingha, during College-vacations, he used to compose *Sraddha slokas* (invitation letters in Sanskrit verse). On one of these occasions, at the *Sraddha* of a rich man, Ishwar Chandra was asked to compose an invitation *sleka* for the householder. The *sloka*, he composed, was so beauti-ful that the Brahmin pundits from different parts of the country, assembled on invitation, admired the *sloka,* and wondered who the writer was. And when little Ishwar Chandra, who was also present in the assembly, was pointed out as the author of the *sloka,* their wonder waxed hundred-fold. They blessed the lad with all their heart, and remarked, that the boy, in time, would be the best pundit, surpassed, nay equalled, by none.

Was not Ishwar Chandra gifted with genius? Milton was considered a genius, because at an early age, he simply attempted at poetical composition in English, his mother language, and a language spoken in nearly every part of the world. But young Ishwar Chandra wrote elegant, poetry in a dead, classical language, spoken nowhere. Which of the two was greater, we leave the readers to decide.

To Calcutta for Higher Studies

One day, after Ishwar Chandra had finished his preliminary education in the primary school of his native village, his teacher, Kalikanta, came to his father, Thakurdas, and said:—"This boy is very intelligent. He has finished his curriculum here. You should now take him to Calcutta, and place him in a good English school there so that he might receive proper English education. Thakurdas agreed, and resolved to take the boy to Calcutta. But their departure had to be deferred for a few days, owing to the death of Ishwar Chandra's grandfather, Ramjay Tarkasiddhanta, who had been suffering for some time from dysentery. After the funeral and *Sraddka* ceremonies (last rites in honour and memory of the dead in accordance with the Hindu *Sasifas*) had been over, Thakurdks, accompanied with his little son; Ishwar Chandra, started' for Calcutta, one day in the month of November, 1829. Ishwar Chandra's beloved teacher Kalikanta, and Atiandaram Guti, a menial servant, were their sole companions; Ishwar Chandra's affectionate mother, Bhagavati Devi, began to cry bitterly and loudly when she heard that her dear little boy of eight years was going to Calcutta where he would have to put up with many troubles.

The journey, at that time, from Birsingha to Calcutta was very difficult and tedious. There was no railway or anything of the kind. In fact, there was no good road, properly so called. The communication between the two places by water also was not very easy. The new Uluberia canal was not then dug, and it was not considered safe to pass the rivers by boat. There was the fear of storms, which rose quite suddenly, over and above the dread of pirates, who were always in search of prey, and plundered and killed the passengers whenever opportunity presented itself. Boats belonging to traders and merchants journeyed on in company during day-light, and took shelter before dusk at some convenient, safe harbour. Ordinary passengers dared not travel by the rivers.

These considerations led Thakurdas to prefer the land route. So he followed by his son, the village schoolmaster, and the servant, started for Calcutta on foot. At the end of the first day's journey, they came to the house of the maternal uncle of Ishwar Chandra's mother in the village of Patul, and there lodged for that day. The next day, they travelled twenty miles, and about sunset, arrived at the residence of a gentleman, who was nearly related to Thakurdas, and here they rested for the night. The third day, they were on the metalled road from Sheakhala to Salkea.

The extraordinary intellect and memory, with which Ishwar Chandra was gifted, and which raised him to such eminence, showed themselves in the little boy on this Salkea road. Here way visible the sprout which subsequently grew into a big tree, with, spreading branches bearing nice fruit and sweet-smelling flowers, under which many a wearied traveller found shelter, and ate of the fruit, and smelt of the flowers. There were milestones on the road, and the boy, Ishwar Chandra, with childish inquisitiveness, enquired of his father what these stones were for; His father smiled at the simplicity of the boy, and replied that these were called *mile-stones,* explaining, at the same time, that they were placed at intervals of a distance of mile, which was nearly equalled to half a Joengali krosh, to indicate the length of the road. The boy learned the English figures (1 to 10) from the numbers engraved on the mile-stones, Presently, a little farther on the road, a milestone was not shown *to* the boy purposely, in order to test the boy's knowledge. When they came to the next milestone, Ishwar Chandra remarked that they had omitted to notice a mile-stone, upon which his teacher, Kalikanta, said that the omission was intentional and made on purpose to see whether he (Ishwar Chandra) had been able to learn the English figures.

They walked the whole day, and, at about sunset, reached Salkea. Here they crossed the river Hooghly; and arrived at Barabazar, Calcutta,' where they repaired to the house of Babu Jagaddurlabh Singha, son of Babu Bhagdvat Charan Singha, who had formerly given shelter to Ishwar Chandra's father, Thakurdas. Bhagavat Charan had died sometime before this. "Jagaddurlabh Babu was, at this time, only twenty-five years old. He knew Thakurdas from his early years, and revered him as his own father. His mother, who was the mistress of the house, an elder sister and her husband and two sons, a widowed sister and her only son—these were the sole members of Jagaddurlabh Babu's family.

The boy, Ishwar Chandra, was a great favourite with every one of the members of this household, He surprised them all by his wonderful memory; On the second clay of their arrival at Calcutta, his father, Taakurdas, was engaged in ad ling up the amounts of several bills written *in* English, belonging to Jagaddurlabh Babu. Ishwar Chandra was sitting close to his father, and looking at the bills. Presently, he whispered in his father's ears that he could, if permitted, sum up the figures. With this, he began to add the figures, and in a few minutes summed up the amounts of the several bills correctly, without a single mistake. Every one present was amazed at the marvellous parts" of the little boy. His teacher, Kalikanta, who was sitting by him, was exceedingly delighted, having, affectionately kissed him, said:

> "Well done, my dear boy, may God give you a long life. The love I bestowed on you has not been in vain". The reader may laugh at the story with incredulity; but this is not very incredible. When we study the lives of great men, we find many instances of extraordinary power in every one of them. All talented men, endowed with extraordinary powers of the mind, are known to have given clear indications, in their early years, of their future greatness. The germs of their future eminence put forth their sprouts at an early age, and indicated the place they were to occupy in their after-life. Milton used to say:—"The child shows the man, as morning shows the day".

It is said of the famous Bengali poet, Ishwar Chandra Gupta, that when he first came to Calcutta he was only seven or eight years old. Shortly after his arrival, one of his father's acquaintances asked him, one day, how he was faring in Calcutta. The future poet, at once replied in verse, that he was living in Calcutta with mosquitoes in the night and flies in the day.

Bankim Chandra Chattopadhyay, the best novel-writer of Bengal, is said to have learnt the Bengali alphabet in one day.

Johnson was known to be the possessor of many qualities. He had a superior memory. One day, when he was only a little boy, and had only begun to read and write, his mother asked him to learn a prayer-book by heart, and leaving the boy with the task, went upstairs. The little boy ran after his mother, and scarcely had she reached her room, when Johnson appeared before her and repeated the prayer-book from the Beginning to the end, without missing a single syllable. His mother was quite surprised and delighted at the marvellous memory of her little son. To tell the truth, he read the book only twice and learnt it all.

The famous poet, Pope, wrote his "Ode on Solitude" when he was only twelve years old. He used to compose verses at a still earlier age, but his father did not approve of this, He told Pope Hot to waste his time in writing poems, but the boy would not hear him, and when his father, one day, gave him a severe beating, he cried out in verse:

> Papa; papa, pity take,
> I will no more verses make".

Milton composed verses at a very early age, and the famous writers of the time were amazed at the beauty of his poems, Such instances are not rare.

Everyone admired the extraordinary powers" of the little boy Ishwar Chandra, and earnestly requested his father to place him in a good. English school. Thakurdas was highly delighted at the praise bestowed on his son, and expressed his desire that he would send him to the Hindu College. Those present suggested that he could not aspire to that, as he was getting a pay of only ten rupees a month, out of which he would have to pay a school-fee of five rupees every month, if he sent his son to the Hindu College. Thakurdas-replied that he would somehow or other manage to defray his household expenses at five rupees. Thakurdas's mind was then full of aspirations, and was animated with the ardour of giving his son a decent education. He called to mind his little son's extraordinary talents, and, encouraged with the prospects of Ishwar Chandra's future greatness, wholly lost sight of his pecuniary difficulties.

Although he had resolved to send his son immediately to the Hindu College, Thakurdas could not carry out the project for three succeeding months. These three months Ishwar Chandra devoted in obtaining a little more preliminary instruction in a neighbouring vernacular *pathsala* under the tuition of a veteran teacher, Svarup Chandra Das, of whom Vidyasagar thus speaks in his autobiography.—'The teacher of the *pathsala,* Svarup Chandra Das was perhaps more skilful in the art of teaching than my former teacher, Kalikanta'. Ishwar Chandra must have considered himself very fortunate in finding shelter with Babu Jagaddurlabh Singha, whose kindness of heart was equal to his means. Not only did he give the boy and his father shelter, but he provided them also with food and clothing, and treated them most kindly and affictionately. The female members of his household were equally kind and lovely. Jagaddurlabh Babu's younger sister. Raimani, loved the boy, Ishwar Chandra, dearer than her own son. In his autobiography Vidyasagar thus describes her:—I have never seen a woman equal to Raimani in kindness, affection, amiability, loveliness, and openness of heart. The image of this noble woman has been indelibly engraved in my mind. She was a goddess to me. I adored her as my mother. Even at this old age I cannot help shedding grateful tears at the recollection of her amiable appearance and noble qualities, whenever her name is mentioned in passing.'

In fact, without the affectionate kindness of this motherly, noble woman, it would have been very difficult for young Ishwar Chandra to live *in* Calcutta. For a few days after his arrival at Calcutta, he was much pained at the recollection of his affectionate mother and grandmother. His father could not always remain with him. Thakurdas used to go out daily to his place of employment at nine O'clock in the morning and came back in the evening at the same hour. He was thus absent from his son continuously for twelve long hours. All this time, Raimani and the other inmates of Jagaddurlabh Babu's house, tried their best to divert his mind by kind and gentle words. They gave him food and drink whenever the boy required, and comforted him. In this way they won over Ishwar Chandra's heart.

In India many such poor boys have found shelter with kind-hearted noblemen, who have taken great care to bring up and train these helpless boys. Some of these poor boys are known to have become great men and to have left an everlasting name. Who is there in Bengal who has not heard the name of Ramdulal Sarkar, the then great millionaire of Calcutta? And what was he in his early years? He was only a poor, helpless urchin, wandering in the streets of the large city, with no one to care for him. But how did he then succeed in amassing such immense wealth, and rising to such eminence? He found shelter with the benevolent Dattas of Hatkhola, a highly noble family in Calcutta, who not only fed and clothed him, but also brought him up as the son of a gentleman. He was then provided by them with a suitable employment, and, gradually, by dint of his honesty, truthfulness, and business capacity, he soon became one of the foremost and wealthiest native merchants of Calcutta. When we think of the utter destitute and helpless state of the poor boy, Ramdulal, and the kind and generous treatment he received from the Dattas, we forget that the world, we live in, is wicked. On the contrary, it appears to be a heaven, and its inmates, angels.

After Ishwar Chandra had been three months in Calcutta, he had a sudden attack of acute dysentery of a very severe type. The stools were too frequent and bloody. His father, Thakurdas, nursed him, and removed the soil with his own hands. He was placed under the treatment of Durgadas Kaviraj, a neighbouring native physician of great repute. But the foul disease grew more serious every day, and, at last, his life was despaired of. No sooner did the news of his illness reach Bir Singha, than his old grandmother hurried to Calcutta, and was soon by the bedside of her dear, little grandson. She nursed him tenderly for a few days, but when she saw that the disease was growing worse every day, she took him away to his native village, Bir Singha, where he soon re-covered even without any medical help.

To regain his former health, Ishwar Chandra had to stay at his home for three months. By the end of May he returned to Calcutta in company with his father, who had gone home to bring him back. They resolved to travel by land as before. On the former occasion, they were accompanied by a menial servant, Ananda Ram Guti, who, at intervals, bore the boy Ishwar Chandra on his shoulders. Thakurdas now asked Ishwar Chandra whether he would be able to walk such a long distance, or Ananda Ram should accompany them, to which the bey replied with great enthusiasm that he would be able to walk, and that Ananda Ram would be an unnecessary accompaniment. Ishwar Chandra was fearless and enthusiastic from his very childhood.

Both father and son started on foot, and after walking a distance of more than twelve miles, came to village Patul, where they lodged for that day, This first day Ishwar Chandra felt no difficulty. The next morning, they started for Ramnagar, a village twelve miles off from Patul. Annapurna, a younger sister of Thakurdas's, had been married to a respectable Brahmin of Ramnagar, At the time, of which we are speaking, she was living with her husband, but was ill. Thakurdas and Ishwar Chandra were going to Ramnagar to see her, on their way to Calcutta. When they had walked only six miles from Patul, Ishwar Chandra was quite disabled to move farther. His legs and feet were swollen and painful. It was a hot and sultry day of Indian May, and the sun was then in its zenith. Thakurdas was in great peril, What was he to do now? How was he to help his son on? The path was lonely. There was no conveyance available. Thakurdas showed the boy a yonder field of melons, saying that he would feed him with a belly-full of melons, if he would only walk to the field. Thus encouraged, Ishwar Chandra limped slowly towards the field, which he reached with great difficulty. He ate nylons there, and appeased his appetite, but his feet became more painful and refused their office, Thakurdas was now exceedingly annoyed. In great vexation he left Ishwar Chandra on the spot, and walked on, at which the little boy began to cry. Thakurdas came back to his son, and took him up on his shoulders, but he was a feeble man himself and quite unable to carry a stout lad *of* eight years.. He then set down the boy on the ground, and began to upbraid him for not allowing Ananda Ram to bear them company. The father, who had never before laid hands on Ishwar Chandra, now smote him in the face, Ishwar Chandra renewed his cries more loudly. But all this would not do. Anyhow the boy must be borne, or he would die on the road. The father again took up the child, and moved slowly on. In this way he carried the boy with utmost difficulty, and, at about sun-set, arrived at Ramnagar. Here they rested for that night and the next day. On the fourth day they came to Baidyabati, and from thence by boat to Calcutta.

Now was the time to send young Ishwar Chandra to school. This time Thakurdas thought of giving him Sanskrit education. His idea was that if Ishwar Chandra learnt Sanskrit well, he would be able to open a *tol* (Sanskrit school) and set up as a Sanskrit professor. Madhusudan Vachaspati, a not very distant relation of Ishwar Chandra's was then a student of the Sanskrit College, Calcutta. This Madhusudan was cousin to Radha Mohan Vidyabhushan, who was maternal uncle to Ishwar Chandra's mother. Madhusudan advised Thakurdas to send his son to the Sanskrit College, where the system of imparting instruction was more perfect. Besides, he said, there were plenty of paths open for the successful students of this school. There were good prospects even for him, who would aspire to a respectable situation. The post of *Judge-Pandit* (legal adviser to a District civil Judge on Hindu law) was reserved for those brilliant scholars who, after passing the course of training in the other branches of the Sanskrit Literature, also passed the Law-Committee examination.

Madhu Sudan delivered this advice in a most impressive manner, and Thakurdas, convinced of its propriety, approved of it. Pandit Gangadhar Tarkavagis was, at that time, one of the professors of Grammar in the Sanskrit College. Thakurdas consulted also the learned professor on the subject and the latter was of the same opinion as Madhu Sudan. Ultimately, it was definitely settled that Ishwar Chandra should be placed in the Sanskrit College.

Admission in Sanskrit College

Ishwar Chandra was admitted into the Sanskrit College on the first day of June, 1829. The chief aim of the College till then, and some time after, since its establishment, was to diffuse Sanskrit education. English was not then compulsory. It was optional. Very few boys took up English as a second language, and it was taught only meagrely. From this, it seems that the authorities had Sanskrit most at heart and that their object was to impart Sanskrit education to the exclusion of English, Whatever their object might be, practically English was excluded from the curriculum of the College.

The mode of imparting instruction, too, adopted in this seminary, at that time, was wholly indigenous. There were no benches for the pupils, no chairs for the teachers. Only Brahmin and other *Dvija* (twice-born) boys were allowed to enter the College. The pupils had to sit on mats spread upon the floor, and their teachers sat opposite to them, reclining on heavy pillows, as is the practice in *tols*.

The Sanskrit College of Calcutta was established in the year 1824. At the time of its foundation, Raja Ram Mohan Ray, the founder of the modern Brahma faith, and the first Hindu native of Bengal, who dared leave the shores of India and cross the ocean, and who has immortalised himself in the pages of history as the first Hindu native of India, who raised his hand against the practice, then obtaining in this country, of burning living *Satish* in the funeral pyres of their dead husbands, and some other influential men of the time, who had got English education and imbibed Western notions and civilisation, raised many objections in its way. Their chief contentions were that what the country needed, was not a separate Sanskrit College, but an English College on a sound basis for instruction of European Arts and Sciences, In as much as there were a good many *tols* in Bengal, where Sanskrit was well taught. On the other hand, the other party argued that there was already the Hindu College for English instruction, that there was no good institution for Sanskrit education, and that the Hindus were in urgent need of such a seminary as would teach Sanskrit in all its branches more systematically. Raja Ram Mohan was deeply disappointed at the failure of his attempts.

The Hindu College, of which mention has been made before, was seven years older than the Sanskrit College, No doubt, the students of the Hindu College learnt English well, and gained a good knowledge of the Arts and Sciences of Europe, but they had one great failing. They saw that the English were a most powerful and civilised nation, and were masters of the soil. Their idea, therefore, was that whatever the English did, was good. Most surely, the English possess many good qualities, but they are men, and have their faults too. In their endeavours to imitate the English and other Europeans, the students of the Hindu College failed to imbibe any of their good qualities, but merely copied their frailties and evil practices. They forsook their national customs, and took to European manners in many respect. They cast aside *Dhuti* and *Ckadar*, their national dress, and dressed themselves in trousers and coats. They even took pride in drinking wine and spirits, and in eating beef, the restricted food of the Hindus. They considered their fathers no better than barbarians, and treated them accordingly. They were thus an eyesore to the orthodox Hindu community, who were deeply pained at this state of things, and yearned for a school, where Hindu boys might obtain a decent education, without losing their nationality. Thus originated the Sanskrit College, and, perhaps, this was one of the reasons, which led the orthodox Hindu, Thakurdas, to alter his mind, and forego his former design of sending his son, Ishwar Chandra, to the Hindu College.

Ishwar Chandra was admitted to the third form of the Vyakaran (Grammar) class of the Sanskrit College, Sanskrit grammar is the door to Sanskrit knowledge. Without a perfect mastery of this subject, one can have no sound knowledge of the Sanskrit literature, It is, therefore, that a Student of this ancient tongue has first of all to apply himself to the study of Grammar, There are many books on the subject, of which *Mugdha-bodha, Kalap, Sankshiptasar,* and *Panini* stand foremost, and a student of Sanskrit must take up any one of these. *Sankshiptasor* was selected for Ishwar Chandra, because his father, Thakurdas, bad some knowledge Of the book, as he had read a great part of it in his early years, and, he thought, he would thus be able to give some help to his son in his home study, Ishwar Chandra had to repeat, every night, to his father what he had learnt of Grammar in his college-class in the day. As we have said before, Pandit Gangadhar Tarkavagis of Kumarhatta was one of the professors of Grammar in the Sanskrit College, and Ishwar Chandra was placed in his hands. We give below, in passing, a full list of the learned professors, then engaged on the instructive staff of the College. *Grammar*— Gangadhar Tarkavagis, Hari Prasad Tarkalankar, and Haranath Tarkabhushan. *Rhetoric*—Nathu Ram Shastri; *Smriti* (Hindu law) Ram Chandra Vidyavagis; *Philosophy*— Nimchand Siromani; *Vedanta*— (Theology) Sambhu Chandra Vachaspati; *Belles-lettres* —-Jay Gopal Tarkalankar; *Astronomy*—Yogadhyan Misra; *Ayurved* (Hindu medicine)—Kshudiram Visarad. These were the best Sanskrit scholars of the time, and were selected by Professor Wilson for the Sanskrit College at the time of its foundation Gangadhar Tarkavagis was exceedingly pleased at the uncommon intelligence displayed by young Ishwar Chandra, and loved his little pupil dearly. In addition to the usual daily lessons in grammar, the professor used to teach him, every day, some *Udbhat Slokas* (extempore verses composed at different times by different bards), of which there are an infinite number in the Sanskrit language.

To attend his school, Ishwar Chandra had to walk from Barabazar, the residence of Jagaddurlabh Babu, where he was putting up, to Pataldanga, where the Sanskrit College was located, a distance of over two miles. For the first six months, his father, Thakurdas, used daily to accompany him to school at nine o'clock in the morning, and again bring him back at four in the evening, for fear lest the little boy should miss his way. This had also the effect of preventing him from mixing with bad boys, who loitered on their way, or wasted time in seeing sights, or doing mischievous deeds of different kinds. At the end of the six months, he won a scholarship of five rupees a month. When he was familiar with the roads he had to pass, and had a sufficient knowledge of the boys he was to keep from, he was left to walk to the College by himself.

In his early years, Ishwar Chandra was a dwarf, that is to say, he was not tall to his age. His stature was diminutive, but his head was larger in proportion to the other limbs. His school-fellows, therefore, humorously gave him the nickname of *Jasure Kai* (i.e. the *Kai* fish of Jessore), at which Ishwar Chandra used to be greatly annoyed. The boys were much amused at his futile rage. Sometimes, by a wilful misplacement of the sounds *J* and *K*, they called him *Kasure Jai,* instead of *Jasure Kai,* and then he was provoked to the extreme. But he could not give utterance to a single syllable, as he was a great stammerer, at that time. Had the boys been able to foresee that this little large-headed dwarf, whom they thus nicknamed jocosely, would become such a great man in after years, they would never have ventured to tease and annoy him in this fashion.

Thakurdas was a man of rigour and irritable temperament. It has been mentioned before, that what Ishwar Chandra read in his class in the day, he had to repeat, every night, to his father. If he ever missed a single word or syllable, he had to receive a good thrashing from the hands of Thakurdas. Even at this young age he had to sit up a great part of the night. His father returned home from his place of business at nine o'clock in the evening, and after that, he cooked food for himself and his son. All this time Ishwar Chandra had to read his lessons, or repeat them to his father, If accidentally he fell asleep, either from exhaustion, or any other cause, his father was sure to thrash him. The beating was sometimes so severe, that the other inmates of the house were aroused by the loud, pitiful cries of the little boy, when the kind Raimani, Jagaddurlabh Babu's sister, mentioned above, hastened from her inner apartments, and saved Ishwar Chandra from further chastisement, It is said that, on one occasion, Thakurdas beat his son so severely with a huge fire-wood, that lay close by, that Ishwar Chandra fled from the house, and took shelter with Babu Ramdhan Ganguli, the then clerk of the Sanskrit College. Ramdhan Babu comforted the boy by kind and gentle words, and after feeding him, took him to his father. When the tale of this incident reached Jagaddurlabh Babu's ears, he was very sorry and displeased with Thakurdas. He remonstrated with Ishwar Chandra's father on the impropriety of his conduct, and even threatened to remove him from his house, if he continued to beat the little boy so heavily. This had the desired chastening effect on the father, who henceforth lessened the severity of his treatment to wards the boy. Ishwar Chandra, too, grew every day more careful. He took great care to keep himself awake till his father slept. For this purpose, he poured into his eyes mustard-oil, which caused them a great irritation, and prevented them from closing their lids.

Ishwar Chandra studied in the Grammar department for three years. In the first two years, he stood first at the annual examinations, and won prizes. But, in the third year, he neither topped the list, nor secured any prizes. Ishwar Chandra was so much disappointed and dejected at this, that he even thought of quitting the College and prosecuting his studies in a *Tol*. No wonder. Every one knew that he was the best boy in the class, and toiled hard, day and night, for the examination. What was then the cause of his failure? Some say, that Mr. Price, a European, was appointed examiner of Grammar for that year. The examination was conducted orally. Whatever questions were put to Ishwar Chandra, he took time to weigh them carefully in his mind, and then made answers slowly, but correctly, without committing a single blunder. But this was a fault in the eyes of Mr. Price, or he himself was unable to grasp the full meaning of what Ishwar Chandra said. Whatever that might be, the examiner gave more marks to those boys, who answered the questions with readiness and promptness, though their answers were defective or wrong.

After much persuasion, Ishwar Chandra was induced to come back to the College. The next six months he devoted to the study of *Amarkosh* (a Sanskrit Dictionary, which every student of Sanskrit must learn by heart, before he begins the Belles-lettres). At this time, Ishwar Chandra's waywardness and obstinateness showed themselves clearly. What is considered to be a fault in ordinary men, turns to good account in the case of those who are gifted with extraordinary talents. Such was the case with Ishwar Chandra. He was zealous, enthusiastic, and obstinate. He chose to be guided by nobody but his own will. He did not care for what other people said or would say. Menaces and threats, or even punishment, could not move him a single step from his design. If his father told him to change his dirty clothes and put on clean ones, he would act quite the contrary. If his father told him to bathe, he would never do it. In short, if his father told him to go one way, Ishwar Chandra was sure to take the other.

Thakurdas was very much annoyed at this wilful waywardness of the boy, and beat him severely; but Ishwar Chandra would have his own way. Thakurdas then devised other means. He gave out in words directions quite contrary to what he really meant. If he wished that the boy should bathe, he directed him not to bathe, and Ishwar Chandra would be sure to wash himself. If the father wished his son to change his dirty clothes, he told him not to change them, and Ishwar Chandra at once put on a clean dress. But, at last, the boy found out the tricks played upon him by his father, and then he very carefully weighed the directions, and tried to discover what the father really wished determining always to go against his wishes. This stubbornness of mind, which formed a principal element of his character, ripening with age, was productive of many noble deeds, for which Ishwar Chandra Vidyasagar's name will be ever remembered with grateful reverence.

The stubbornness of Ishwar Chandra reminds us of the stubbornness of Johnson in his early years. It is said of Jhonson that in his childhood, a servant used daily to accompany him to and from school. One day, the servant was a little too late, and

Johnson walked out of the school by himself. The governess being apprised of this, ran after the child, for fear lest he should miss his way and fall into some trouble. When Johnson found, that he was followed by the governess, his pride was touched, that she must have been doubtful of his powers. He was so much provoked at what he considered to be a deliberate affront on the part of the governess, that he retraced his steps, came back to school, and struck her. This stubbornness was very conspicuous in Johnson's after-life.

When Ishwar Chandra entered the Belles-lettres class, he was only eleven years old. Besides, he was not suffciently tall for his age. The teacher of this class, Jay Gopal Tarkalankar objected to take him into his class, and stated that so little a boy would not be able to comprehend the meaning of the Sanskrit poems. The pride of Ishwar Chandra was touched. He requested the teacher to examine him on the subject, and then to take him if he was considered fit, as otherwise he must leave the College. Jay Gopal Tarkalankar gave him a few *Slokas* (stanzas) from *Bhatti* (a very difficult poem) to explain, which the *boy* paraphrased and explained very creditably. There could now be no objection to take the little boy. He was accordingly admitted into this class.

We have forgotten to mention, that in the second year of his Grammar class, Ishwar Chandra had also enrolled himself as a student of English. We have already noticed briefly what the state of English instruction was, at that time, in the Sanskrit College. Very few students applied to it with due diligence, Ishwar Chandra read in the English class for only six months, and then gave it over. But Ishwar Chandra repented of it in after years, and he had to toil hard to obtain a little knowledge of the English language.

Now, let us see how he fared in the Belles-lettres department. In the first year, he studied *Raghu-vangsa, Kumxr-sainbhava* and *Rdgkava-Pandaviya.* At the annual examination of this class, he headed the list of successful students, and won the first prize. In the second year, he read *Magha, Bharavi, Sakuntala, Meghduta, Uttaracharita, Vikramorvvasi, Kadambari, Dasakumarchrita, Mudrarakshasa* and other poetical and dramatical works, At the annual examination of this class, he stood first and won the best prizes. Most of these works, both poetical and dramatical, he had learnt *by* heart and could repeat with wonderful accuracy. He was best at *Translation.* Even at this early age of twelve, he could speak Sanskrit and Prakrita correctly and fluently. Not only his teachers and class-fellows, but all the pundits of the time were amazed at the wonderful powers of the intelligent, little boy. Was not Ishwar Chandra talented?

We have already stated that from his childhood, Ishwar Chandra wrote a very good hand. He was one of the best writers in the College. Every year, he won prizes for good hand-writing, Everybody admired his penmanship. He copied, with his Own hand, many Sanskrit books for himself, and the penmanship of these books, even to the present day, appears as if it were a fine wool-work executed by some skilful hand. Very few literary men have been able to win such universal praise in all respects.

We now come to that part of little Ishwar Chandra's life, where he had to struggle hard to be able to keep pace with, nay to excel, his College rivals. The adverse circumstances, under which he had to carry his point would, no doubt, damp the spirit of Ordinary people, and make them forego their design. But Ishwar Chandra was far above the ordinary rank; He had an uncommon strength of mind and fixedness of purpose. He had many obstacles in his way, but he overcame them with manly spirit and easy alacrity. The difficulties and troubles rather served to encourage him the more. He has shown to the world that poverty is no hindrance to the attainment of an object. He has left an unparalleled example of noble heroism for the poverty-stricken. With such a precedent before one's eyes, one cannot lose heart, even under most adverse circumstances.

When Ishwar Chandra was reading in the second year class of the Bsllesletteres department, his younger brother, Dina Bandhu, came to Calcutta to prosecute his studies in the Sanskrit College.

Now there were thus three members- of Thakurdas's family in Calcutta, for him to maintain with his slender means, besides those that were living in Birsingha. We have already said, that Thakurdas had a very limited income. It was not, there-fore, possible for him to retain a domestic or cook, Poor Ishwar Chandra had to do everything. He did all the marketing and cooking. Coal had not then come into use in Calcutta for purposes of cooking, which was done by fire-wood. Little Ishwar Chandra chopped the fuel-wood with his own hands. He cooked food, and distributed it to his father *and* brother. He did all the cleaning. In short, Ishwar Chandra was both a domestic and a cook. He did not feel tired with all these daily house-hold works, but rather performed them with *his* usual cheerfulness. He felt a sort of inward pride and exultation at being able to show to the world, that he was above the ordinary rank and could beat down his compeers in every respect, even under such discouraging circmustances. But the question now is, how could he make time for his studies? After all, Ishwar Chandra was a man, and to learn, he must read. Mere talents would not do. Ishwar Chandra was not only talented, but also industrious to the extreme, He was very assiduous, and toiled hard at his lessons, and being possessed of a retentive memory, could easily make up for lost time. He never wasted a minute. He read his books even while he was engaged in cooking, In the night, he slept only two hours. After performing the usual household duties and feeding his father and brother, he used to go to bed at 10 P. M. requesting his father, who sat up on business till 12 P. M. to arouse him (Ishwar Chandra) at that hour. He read from mid-night to day-break, when he had to put aside his books, to apply himself again to the domestic duties. It is also said, that on his way to and from College, he used to read his books and ponder over his lessons.

Nor did Ishwar Chandra's troubles end here. He had patiently to put up with difficulties most trying and painful. The readers of the present day can have no idea of the city of Calcutta of those days. The conservancy was most defective, particularly in the native quarters. The uncovered drains on two sides of the lanes were full of dirt and foul water, appearing like cesspools, with worms of various descriptions rolling about in their midst, and mosquitoes filling the air with their peculiar songs. The houses standing in rows by the sides of these drains, shut out the sun throughout the year, and they were therefore always damp, especially their lowest floors. The privies and cook-rooms for the tenants of the lowest floors were, for want of space, located side by side. Cockroaches and other insects and worms abounded in them; The very sight of them was loathsome.

The lowest floor of Jagaddurlabh Babu's house, where Thakurdas lived with his sons, was not an exception to this. It was as filthy, as damp. The air in it was filled with a most offensive smell. The worms and cockroaches from the neighbouring privies moved about freely in Ishwar Chandra's cook-room. To keep the worms away, he kept a jug of water ready at hand, and whenever they approached him, he poured down some water upon them, making them recede with the water. But it was not so easy to keep back the cockroaches. These were particularly troublesome in the night.

On one occasion, it so happened that when Ishwar Chandra was eating his supper in company with his father and brothers, but upon different seats on the floor, as is the custom with the Hindus of Bengal, he discovered a dead cockroach in one of his prepared dishes. Most probably, the insect had flown into the dish while it was in the process Of being cooked, and *died* there. What was Ishwar Chandra to do now? He foresaw, that if his father and brothers should see the loathsome insect, or hear of its existence in the dish, they would certainly give up eating, and throw their meals away. Clever Ishwar Chandra, therefore, very carefully and dexterously took the insect out, and, at great risk, devoured it whole, along with a mouthful of vice. His father and brothers, quite unconscious of the matter, ate their meals a usual.

After the me was over, Ishwar Chandra related the story, and every body, who heard it, was amazed at the little boy's wonderful forbearance and presence of mind. The manner of Ishwar Chandra's sleeping was not less difficult. The room in Jagaddurlabh Babu's house, where Thakurdas lodged with his sons, had a veranda attached to it, three feet in length by two feet in breadth. Ishwar Chandra used to sleep in this veranda upon a mat of the same size, procured by him for the purpose. Later on, when his third brother, Sambhu Chandra, came to Calcutta to prosecute his studies, Ishwar Chandra obtained permission to sleep in one of the lowest floor rooms of a neighbouring gentleman, by name Tilak Chandra Ghosh, His brother, Sambhu Chandra, slept in the same bed with him, but being much younger, he was usually permitted to go to bed, immediately after the night-meal. One night, Sambhu Chandra having a little ailment of his bowels, eased himself on the bed and lay there sleeping, without apprising anybody of it Later in the night, Ishwar Chandra, quite unconscious of his brother's indisposition, lay down on the bed, and quite exhausted with hard labour, both physical and mental, fell fast asleep. When he awoke early in the morning, he found, to his utter astonishment and disgust, that his back and sides were besmeared with night-soil. He immediately removed the dirt with his own hands, and washed himself and the bedding. He did neither mention this to anybody, nor rebuke the offender, Sambhu Chandra. He was as much devoted to his brothers, as to his parents.

We have not yet noticed Ishwar Chandra's clothing. India had not then been overflooded with foreign cloths turned out from machine-looms, Neither were there any weaving-machines imported from the West, set up in the country. The "native weavers used the hand-looms of their progenitors, and manufactured cloths of different kinds, both fine and coarse. There was a time, and that not long ago, when the fine muslin of Dacca, and the silk of Murshidabad and Rajsahi found favour with the fashionable of the West, and were exported to a large extent, thereby greatly generating the country. But, alas! those days are gone, and the sons of the former weavers have parted with the looms of their forefathers, and taken to agriculture or other means of livelihood.

Thakurdas's limited means would not permit him to give his sons fine dress. He could not afford to pay for any luxury. He was content to be able to provide them with coarse clothing. Ishwar Chandra wore a coarse *Dhuti* and a *Chadar* of similar texture. He never grumbled at this. He was always averse to luxury. Even in later years, then he became a great and rich man, he never indulged in luxuries. A coarse *Dhuti* and *Chadar* and a pair of slippers constituted his complete dress. The simplicity of his dress and manners was derived from the habits, he had formed in his «early years under poverty. With such a noble example before us, we cannot but admit that poverty does not necessarily generate meanness, as some people are apt to think, but, on the contrary, in not a few cases, it has been known to be the generator of many noble qualities. The victims of poverty are electrified, as it were, by their hardships, and are incited to work with zeal and ardour. Their very privations tend to make them hard-working, painstaking, persevering, patient and ever-cheerful. Ritcher said:— "I cannot but choose to say to poverty,—V welcome, so thou come not too late in life."

Speaking of the great Spanish writer, Servantes, one man remarked that the world had been enriched by his poverty, meaning, that he had done an immense good to the world by his books.

Carlyle said:— "He who has battled, were it only with poverty and hard toil, will be found stronger and more expert than he, who would stay at home from the battle, concealed among the pro-vision waggons, or even rest unwatchfully, abiding by the stuff".

Ishwar Chandra bore his hardships with patience and cheerfulness. But even this would not save him from his rigorous father, The slightest accidental failing on his part was sure to bring down on his head his parent's wrath. He looked upon his father with the greatest awe and dread. It so happened, that Ishwar Chandra, had forgotten the *Sandhya-Mantras* (prayers to be told at different parts of the day). He merely feigned the *Sandhya* by making an apparent show of the outward for Vnalitioe and gestures. When Thakurdas came to know, that his dear son, Ishwar Chandra, was such a hypocrite, his rage knew no bounds, and he gave the little boy a sound thrashing. Ishwar Chandra was then made to re-learn the *Mantras* on the which he did in a very short time. So sharp was his memory!

Completion of School Education

Shortly after he had passed the Law Committee examination, the post of the Judge-Pandit of Tippera, a district in East Bengal, fell vacant. Young Ishwar Chandra applied for the situation, and was favoured with the appointment. But his father would not permit him to go to such a distance. He was therefore, obliged to decline the offer. He had toiled hard to pass the law examination, and then had applied for the post, simply to help his father in his pecuniary difficulties. But when that father wished him not to go, how could Ishwar Chandra accept the post, against his father's will? He was so much devoted to his parents, that he considered them to be his only objects of worship. He had no other gods or goddesses before them. He could not act against their wishes.

He had still two subjects to learn,— *Vedanta* (Theology) and *Philosophy.* He entered the *Vedanta* class at the age of nineteen. Sambhu Chandra Vachaspati, the learned professor ot that class, was highly amazed at the merits of Ishwar Chandra, and loved him as dearly as if he was his own son.

According to the practice then obtaining in the Sanskrit College, a separate examination on essay-writing, both prose and poetry, was held every year at the annual examinations of the, *Vedanta* and *Philosophy* classes, and a prize of one hundred rupees in cash was given to each of the best essayists. Three hours were allowed for each essay,—10 A.M. to 1 P.M. for prose, and 1 P.M. to 4 P.M. for poetry, Ishwar Chandra, fancying his inability, was absent from this examination, Premchand Tarkavagis, the teacher of the *Rhetoric* class, not finding Ishwar Chandra among the examinees, began to look for him. The teacher, at last, discovered him sitting in a corner of his class-room. He remonstrated with his favourite pupil on his shyness, and after much persuasion and pressure, induced him to appear at the examination at 12 O'clock. The subject for that year's proso composition was *Truthfulness,* Ishwar Chandra's essay was considered the bast, and he own the prize of one hundred rupees. He had now the satisfaction to see the tree of his hard toil fruitful. Sooner or later, honest labour must have its fruits. Such is God's dispensation. Ishwar Chandra's second composition in poetry too was considered one of the test, and he won a prize for that also.

Here, again, at this young age, we find in Ishwar Chandra a noble instance of strength of mind, independence of opinion, firmness of purpose, soundness of judgement, and gentleness of heart. While *in* the Vedanta class, his teacher Sambhu Chandra Vachaspati, like all his former teachers, was greatly attached to him- for his merits, and consulted him on all points. He was a widower at this time, and was grown old and infirm; but he had a great mind to enter again into married life. He consulted Ishwar Chandra, seeking his advice on the point. The young pupil heard the arguments of his teacher patiently, but could discover nothing important in them. He thought the professors proposal extremely unreasonable and selfish, and openly expostulated with the old man on the impropriety of his resolution. Vachaspati was greatly offended with his pupil at his strong protests, and made strenuous attempts to bring him to his opinion, but in vain, Ishwar Chandra was as fixed and immovable as the Himalayas Sambhu Chandra was, at that time, the family Pandit of Chhatu Babu and Latu Babu, sons of the late Ram Dulal Sarkar, the well-known self-trade millionaire of Calcutta, Through the influence of these two rich men and of Babu Ram Ratan Ray, the wealthy Zamindar of Narail, the old and decrepit Sambhu Chandra was married *to* a beautiful little girl of Barasat.

Ishwar Chandra was greatly displeased with his teacher for making such an unreasonable alliance, but being affectionately attached to each other, he could not cut off all communications with him. After the marriage was over, the old professor, one day, took his pupil to see his young bride, Ishwar Chandra went with his teacher reluctantly, and placed two rupees at his wife's feet as a present of honour. He was then receding back without looking at the unfortunate girl's face, when his teacher caught hold of his arms, and did not leave him till he had a full sight of his new wife. Ishwar Chandra only cast a glance at the beautiful girl's face, and immediately left the place. The sight move his gentle heart, and drew tears from his eyes. He foresaw the miserable, wretched life which the unfortunate, little girl robust live in a very short time, and he sobbed and wept like a child. It is superfluous to say that Sambhu Chandra died not long after the unfortunate alliance, leaving the little girl to live the austere, ascetic life of a Hindu widow.

It has already been mentioned, that his third brother, Sambhuchandra, had joined Thakurdas's little family *in* Calcutta, and the number of members had risen from three to four. Moreover, Thakurdas having, at this time, married his second son, Dinabandhu, he had contracted some debts, He was, therefore constrained to considerably reduce his family expenses, which had never been very liberal. It is said that only *one* pice was now allowed for the tiffin of the four members, The dishes prepared for the daily meals were very poor, and hardly fit for eating. Nor did their troubles end here, Jagaddurlabh Babu, who had so long given them shelter, was also deeply immersed in debts. The room in the third floor of his house, where Thakurdas slept with his sons, Jagaddurlabh Babu had let to a tenant. Thakurdas was, therefore, obliged to remove with his son to a room In the lowest floor, quite unfit for a gentleman's lodging. What trying difficulties! In later years, Ishwar Chandra Vidyasagar, alluding to the painful situation of these days, thus spoke to one of his friends:— 'I suffered many troubles in my early years, but I never minded them far my own sake. They rather served to heighten my zeal—to invigorate me—to incite *me* to action, But the sufferings and privations of my brothers rent my heart. The very sight of their dejected,' mournful faces drew tears from my eyes.' Such was the depth of Ishwar Chandra's fraternal love. It was not at all strange that the universal philanthropist, whose heart melted at the very tale of other people's distress, should love: his own brothers so affectionately and sincerely.

After finishing the *Vedanta* (Theology) course, Ishwar Chandra entered the *Nyaya* (Philosophy) class. The great pundit Nimchand Siromani was, at that time, the teacher of this class. But shortly after this, he died, and Pandit Jay Narayan Tarkaratna was, at the instance of Ishwar Chandra, appointed to the post. Was it not a glory to a pupil, that he could nominate his professor? At the second year's examination of this class, he stood first and won the first prize of one hundred rupees. His paper on poetical composition was also the best, and he won a further sum of one hundred-rupees as prize far that composition. These two hundred rupees went a great way to help his father in the clearance of his debts. What wonderful talents did Ishwar Chandra possess! During the period of his studies in this class, he used now and then to visit his native village, Birsingha, and there enter into debates on this difficult subject with the learned Pandits of the neighbourhood. It is said that, on one occasion, he had an Earnest debate on old *Nyaya* with Ram Mohan Tarkasiddhanta, one of the greatest philosophers if the time. Tarkasid Jhanta was defeated, When Thakurdas heard of the indent, he ran to the scene, and laid the dust of the vanquished pandit's feet on Ishwar Chandra's head, because the latter was much younger in age.

While still-reading in the *Nyaya* dass, he was appointed for two months as officiating second teacher of Grammar on a monthly salary of forty rupees. He placed the whole of the eighty rupees of his first earning Into the hands of his father, and requested him to go on a pilgrimage, which the father very gladly did. When he returned from the pilgrimage, he found that his son, Ishwar Chandra, had wan one hundred rupees as first prize for the *Nyaya* examination, a further sum of one hnndred rupees, as prize for the best poetical composition, twenty-five rupees as prize for proficiency in Law, and eight rupees for good hand-writing, making in all two hundred and thirty-three rupees. This sum the devoted son made over to his father, who paid it off to clear a part of his debts.

When Ishwar Chandra passed the final examnation of the Sanskrit College, he won the title of *Vjdyasagar* from the College. He was then only twenty years old. How many are there who can attain to such eminence at such an early age? Surely, Ishwar Chandra must have been uncommonly gifted. Every one of his teachers, from the village schoolmaster, Kalikanta Chattopadhyay, to the professor, of the College, was highly satisfied with his proficiency, and thought it a pride to have had Ishwar Chandra for his pupil. Besides the government certificate, the learned professors of the College granted him a separate certificate of his brilliant success, countersigned by Babu Rassomay Dutta, the then Ṣecretary to the College.

Before bringing this chapter to its conclusion, we will try to notice briefly Ishwar Chandra's attempts at essay-writing.

Essay-writing is a great help to the acquisition of knowledge in a language. A piece of written composition is one of the best tests of one's command of a tongue. When Ishwar Chandra was a student of the Sanskrit College, both the teachers and the authorities of the College as well as the pupils, paid great attention to original composition. To encourage the students in this respect, prizes were awarded to the best essayists, Every student essayed at good composition. The pupils, as well as their teachers, had a great earnest zeal for this. The. present University system had not then been introduced. The students were not forced to pay equal attention to the different branches. Every one was free to take up a particular branch according to his own inclination. He could thus devote his whole time and attention to that branch, and make a good progress in it. The present system of cramming leaves no room for culture of a particular branch.

Although there were nice arrangements in the Sanskrit College for award of prizes to the best essay-writers, Ishwar Chandra had no mind to attempt at these prizes. His impression was that, in this age of degeneration, no one was capable of writing good Sanskrit. He had formed that impression from the composition of several of his colleagues. It was, therefore, that he did not appear at his first examination on Sanskrit composition, We have seen, however, that he was pressed to attend the examination. He finished his essay on *Truthfulness* which was the subject for that year, in one hour's time, and won the first prize of one hundred rupees.

It is true that Ishwar Chandra was not very eager to appear at these examinations, but when ever he did appear, his essay was considered the best, and he won prizes. Essay-writing is not practised in *Tols,* nor had there been any such practice in the Sanskrit College till 1838, when it was ruled that students of *Sinriti, Nyaya and Vedanta* must undergo a separate examination on essay-writing.

The subject of essay for the second year was *Knowledge,* and Ishwar Chandra won this prise too.

During the first two years of this examination, Mr. G. T. Marshall was Secretary to the Sanskrit College. In the third year, Babu Rassamay Dutta was the Secretary. This year, the subject of essay was "The Penance of Raja Agnidhra," Rassamay Babu gave a few words, and required the examinees to write on them a poetical composition. Ishwar Chandra's composition won the admiration of Rassamay Babu.

In the year 1838, Mr. John Mayor, a civilian, offered a prize of one hundred rupees in cash for the best poetical essay in one hundred *Slokas* on a description of this globe of the earth and the celestial globe, according to the ancient Hindu Puran, Suryyasiddhanta, and the modern European notions. Ishwar Chandra's poem was considered the best, and he won the prize, These *Slokas* were under publication in the form of a booklet, while Vidyasagar was still alive, but were not out of press then.

The publication has since been complete. The book now contains 408 *Slokas.* Most probably, the additional *Slokas* in excess of Mr. Mayor's requisition, were added in his later years. In the beginning: of this book, there is ample evidence of Ishwar Chandra Vidyasagar's belief in God, devotion to his preceptor, and humility of heart.

Marital Bond

The fame of Ishwar Chandra's extraordinary talents, uncommon powers, and great proficiency in Sanskrit, soon spread throughout the length and breadth of the country, and many persons came forward with proposals of marriage, offering their daughters as brides to Ishwar Chandra. At last, the marriage was definitely settled with a daughter of one Satrughna Bhattacharya, a well-to-do Brahmin of Khirpai, It was at that time an important village. It was a great market of country-made cloth. Dealers in cloth from different parts of Bengal, nay from remote corners of western and northwestern India, resorted to this mart. Satrughana Bhattacharya was one of the most respect-able men of this large village. He considered Ishwar Chandra the best bridegroom for his daughter, and he resolved on marrying her to him.

Ishwar Chandra was thus married, at the early age of fourteen, to Satrughna Bhattacharya's daughter, Dinamayi Devi, a most beautiful girl of eight years. Satrughna said to Thakurdas: 'You see, Bandyopadhyay, I present my daughter to your son, not for the sake of your riches, for you are not a rich man, I know, but simply because your son, Ishwar Chandra, has won a great reputation for his profound erudition. At first, Ishwar Chandra had no mind to enter into such an early marriage, but he had to yield to his father's requisition, for fear of his parent's great disappointment and displeasure, We have already said, that Ishwar Chandra had always a great reverence for his father, and he now unhesitatingly submitted to his direction, Ishwar Chandra must have considered himself fortunate in having Dinamayi for his wife. Without her aid, much of his future noble deeds might have remained undone. She was as noble-minded and generous, as she was kind and forgiving. To understand her character fully, the reader should be acquainted with her father.

Satrughna Bhattacharya was a robust Brahmin of great strength, both of body and mind, of irritable temper, but, at the same time, generous, liberal and forgiving. His co-villagers dreaded him for his uncommon prowess and strength, but its escape. Satrughna then caught hold of the car, and, with -a sudden jerk, overturned it, and threw it aside, thus clearing the way for the procession. The enemy, daunted at the sight of his prowess, dispersed and ran with their lives. Satrughna was, by this time, greatly enraged, and he followed the *enemyj* unaccompanied by his followers. The leader of the antiparty, Haldar, ran into his house and shut the outer gates. Satrughna began to kick violently with his bare legs against the spiked doors, which, unable to bear the heavy blows, gave way, and he entered the house of his enemy. He then went in search of his rival, upon which some of his opponents struck him with brick-bats in the delicate parts of his body, which deprived him of his senses. He was then carried off, from the scene, by his followers.

The antiparty now fancied, that Satrughna would prosecute them, and take the matter into lawcourt, for the unwarranted heavy assault and outrage, he had received at their hands. They, therefore, sent a messenger to him, the next morning, to ascertain the truth. Satrughna said:— 'I see, why you have come. Haldar fancies, I shall see him; does he? Oh! no, I am not so fool as to fill the pockets of lawyers and bailiffs with my money. This year he has beaten me, the next year I shall beat him. If we resort to lawcourt, our *Gafan* festival, for which we have been so much at daggers, will come to an end for ever.' So saying, he dismissed the messenger, who delivered the message faithfully. The antiparty were touched at their enemy's generosity, and at once repaired to-his house, and earnestly prayed for him forgiveness, Haldar said: 'Bhattacharya, I did all this simply to put your prowess to test. It has been proved beyond doubt, that you possess not only strength, but also manliness. Your valour is equal to your forethought. I crave your forgiveness. Will you not forgive me?' Bhattacharya replied:— 'You need not talk in this fashion. But none of you shall leave my house, without partaking of my poor meal. I invite you today to dinner.' The other party gladly accepted the invitation. The reconciliation was perfect.

On another occasion, as he was sitting, one day, with some of his co-villagers in a grocer's shop, a dealer appeared with a sack of pulse, weighing four "maunds, for sale. His compatriots said:— 'Bhattacharya, if you can carry the sack of pulse home, it is yours; we make you a present of it'. Satrughna replied:— No doubt, I can carry it, but not walking erect; to carry the sack, I must walk on all fours, like a beast of burden; you will only place a quilt on my back, and then lay the sack upon it.' The heavy sack was laid on his back as directed, and Satrughna, to the utter astonishment of all present, walked on all fours, with the sack of pulse on his back, to his home, a distance of more than a mile, Some two or three hundred spectators followed him to his house, enjoying the sight. On being offered the sack of pulse, Satrughna Bhattacharya declined to accept it as a bet won. He said that he had nothing to do with the pulse, but that if they would procure the necessary fed and other vegetables, he was ready to feed the Whole assembly with rice and *Dal,* prepared front the staked pulse. This was accordingly done.

A certain Ghosh of Khirpai of the *Sadgop* caste had taken to robbery. He lay in ambush in a; thicket of reed or other long grass by the side of a canal, and, as opportunity presented itself, way-laid and plundered wayfarers, whom he sometimes killed, when necessity arose. He was a man of considerable physical strength, and the residents of Khirpai stood in terror of this dreadful robber. Once on a time, Satrugbna Bhattacharya's elder brother said to him:— "Satu, it is strange indeed, that Ghosh is still a terror to the village, and you do not bring him to his senses; "at which, Satrughna promised to his brother to bring round Ghosh in a very short time.. One morning, Satrugbna went out in the direction of the canal, and hid himself in a thicket, lying, in wait for the robber. Presently he heard a rustling sound, and saw a movement of the thicket on the other side. He guessed that Ghosh had caught his prey. And he was right for the robber had fallen on an up country man, who was not much inferior to Ghosh in strength. Both of them were engaged in deadly struggle.

Satrughna Bhattacharya now issued from his covert, and suddenly appeared before them. No sooner did the robber recognise the Herculean Bhattacharya, than he ran for his life, and ascended on the top of a big *Simul* tree. The wayfarer had lost his sense, and Satrughna applied himself first to revive the man by sprinkling water on his face and head. He then went to the tree, where the robber had taken shelter, but could not ascend it, as he was a plump man himself, and the tree was thorny. He lay waiting below the tree for the robber, whom he asked to come down. But the robber dared not do his bidding. When Satrughna saw, that Ghosh would not descend from the tree, he thus addressed him:— 'Come down, Ghosh, swear by my feet, that you will not commit robbery any more, and I will forgive you this time.' Ghosh replied from the top of the tree:— 'If you swear by your holy thread, that you will not molest me if I come down, I may do your bidding.' Bhattacharya smiled and rejoined:— 'Will you believe me, if I say that I swear by my holy thread?' Ghosh answered:— 'You are prepared to believe me, if I swear by your feet; and is it possible, that I shall not believe you, when you, a Brahmin, will suffer by your holy thread?' At this Satrughna swore by his holy thread that he would not molest the robber; whereupon the latter came down from the tree, and swore by the Brahmin's feet, that he would never more engage himself in robbery, Satrughna now forgave the robber, and dismissed him. He then returned home with the tip-countryman, whom he had saved from the hands of the robber. He fed the wayfarer with kind care, and then let him go on his way.

Satrughna had once a painful, carbuncle, which required surgical operation. The surgeon in attendance was ready with chloroform for his inhalation to induce his insensibilty. But the patient very composedly said to the doctor:— 'you need not apply chloroform; you may operate upon me, and take it for granted that I am insensible. The surgeon threw aside the phial of chloroform and applied lancet. At the first attempt, the instrument broke in two, so tough was the patient's skin. The operation was carried through with a defecting instrument, and the patient bore it with perfect composure.

Such was Satrughna Bhattacharya, the father of the fair girl, Dinamayi, who was married to Ishwar Chandra. But we have digressed too long, and it is now proper, that we should resume the thread of our narrative.

At the age of fifteen, Ishwar Chandra entered the *Rhetoric* class. Premchand Tarkavagis was the teacher of this class. He was equally erudite in grammar, language, and rhetoric, and taught the three subjects equally well. Most of his pupils attained great proficiency in Sanskrit. Of all the Students of this class, Ishwar Chandra was the youngest in age, but the best in proficiency. He won the admiration of all. In one year, he finished the *Sahityadarpana, Kavyaprakasa, Rasagangadkar,* and other works on *rhetoric.* At the annual examination, he stood first and won the highest prizes, both in books and money. The *Raghuvansa, Sahityadarpand, Ratnabali, Malatim adhava, Mudrarakshasa Vikramorvvasi Mrich chatika*— these were the prize books, he was awarded this year.

But, for this examination, he had to work very hard. He had to sit up night after night, and read his books, for in the day-time, he had to do every-thing of the household work, as we have said before. He had not a wink of sleep for several nights in succession. After the examination was over, he fell ill with acute dysentery of a very severe type. The stools were very frequent and bloody. All sorts of treatment in Calcutta failed, and he was removed to Birsingha, as on the former occasion. No sooner did he recover from his illness, than he again returned to Calcutta, and took over charge of the usual household duties.

Previous to this, Ishwar Chandra, on his way home from the College, used daily to visit Pandit Taranath Tarkavachaspati's house, and there read the *Sahityadarpana.* One day, the then famous philosopher, Jaynarayan Tarkapanchanan, who had called there, saw Ishwar Chandra reading the historical book The philosopher asked the boy if he understood the book, and at once began to examine him. He was greatly surprised that the little boy had mastered the book thoroughly, and Remarked that the boy would, in time, be the best pundit in Bengal. Such was the praise young Ishwar Chandra won, at an early age, from the greatest philosopher of the day.

At this time, Ishwar Chandra got a monthly Scholarship of eight rupees, which he made over to his father every month. As has been said before, Thakurdas had a great mind from the beginning to set up a *tol,* in his native village, with Ishwar Chandra as professor. He therefore laid out a part of his son's scholarship funds in purchasing lands for the site of the *tol* and for the maintenance of students. After the acquisition of the lands, he would not receive Ishwar Chandra's stipend money, but directed his son to spend a portion of it in buying manuscript copies of rare and valuable Sanskrit books. Ishwar Chandra procured many such manuscripts, and they are still to be found in his library.

Nor was this all. The heart of Ishwar Chandra was as soft, as his mind was strong. He was kind and sympathetic, and always eager to relieve the distrest. He was a lover of mankind. His smart heart was the seat of unbounded love and kindness. The slightest mention of affliction and suffering was sure to awaken his universal benevolence. Even at this early age, whenever he saw, or heard of, any fellow-creature in distress, he ran forward with eagerness with a helping hand. He had not much means at his command, but still he spent his last piece in succouring the poor and afflicted. What remained after his charities, he spent in a little tiffin after the school hours. When there were others present at his tiffin, he was sure to divide it with them.

If he saw a poor man with ragged clothes, and happened not to have sufficient funds at his disposal at the time, he would borrow the required money from the porter of the College, and give the poor man a new piece of cloth. Whenever any of his school-fellows fell ill, Ishwar Chandra was always at his bedside, attending and nursing him with great care and affection, If anybody had a contagious disease, and no one dared approach him, Ishwar Chandra at all hazards was sure to attend his sick-bed, and nurse him gladly and fearlessly.

Whenever young Ishwar Chandra visited his native village Birsingha, he, first of all, went to his former teacher, Kalikanta Chattopadhyay, and paid him his best respects. He then called at the houses of all his neighbours, one after the other, enquired after their health and affairs. When any of them was ill, he never failed to attend the sick-bed. He thus endeared himself to his villagers, who looked upon him as their best friend and benefactor. Even the sufferings of such lower animals, as cats and dogs, drew tears from his eyes. What a fountain of universal love and sympathy was hidden in the small heart of the young boy.

Ishwar Chandra always regarded his elders with great esteem. His respect for them depened with his age. Even in later years, when he had attained great knowledge and eminence, he never treated them with arrogance or disrespect, though they were much inferior to him in every respect. On the contrary, if his elders tried to forget their former tender love for him and to show signs of honour to him, he shrank from them with bashfulness. When he rose to be the Principal of the Sanskrit College, the then clerk of the College, Ramdhan Gangopadhyay, who loved Ishwar Chandra dearly, and to whom he had, one night, fled from his father for protection, as has been narrated before, rose from his seat, *in* honour of Ishwar Chandra, at which the latter was greatly abashed, and said:— 'You see, my dear sir, I am still your beloved Ishwar Chandra; please do not put me to shame in this way. Ramdhan Babu was quite astonished at his superior's goodness find modesty.

The reader may remember that, soon after his recovery from the severe dysentery, he was ill with, Ishwar Chandra had returned to Calcutta and taken over the charge of his usual domestic duties. But being still too weak, his younger brother, Dinabandhu, helped him now and then. One evening, Dinabandhu having gone out to market, did not return till ten O'clock in the night. Ishwar Chandra was greatly anxious for his brother, and began to search for him from one bazar to the other. At last, he was found sleeping in the veranda of a small shop in Nutanbazar. The elder brother gently awoke him, and brought him back. It is said, that Dinabandhu was never afterwards allowed to go out by himself.

After finishing the Rhetoric course, Ishwar Chandra entered the *Smriti* (Law) class in the year 1837. The general practice, at that time, was that students had to pass through the *Philosophy* and *Vedanta* classes before they could be admitted into the *Smriti* class. But Ishwar Chandra resolved to study *Smriti* first, for he had a great mind to pass the Law committee examination and become a *fudge-Pandit,* and unless ope passed this examination one could not aspire to that post. He had, therefore, applied to the authorities and obtained permission from them to study *Smriti* before *Philosophy* and *Vedanta.* So difficult was the subject, that ordinary students, who had already passed through the *Philosophy* and

Vedanta classes, took two to three years to study such books, as the *Mitakshara, Dayabhag* and *Manusanghita,* and then to obtain a tolerable knowledge of *Smriti.* But how wondrous! Young, unbearded Ishwar Chandra, for he was then a mere lad of seventeen years, mastered the subject in six months' time; at the end of which, he underwent the Law-Committee Examination, and came out successful. Of course, these six months he neither cooked his food, nor performed other functions of a domestic, and slept daily for two or three hours only. So powerful were his memory and intellect, that in six months he learned the whole *Smriti by* heart, and could easily repeat, and give a lucid explanation of, every line in it. All his teachers, colleagues, and contemporary pundits were wonder-struck at his extraordinary abilities. Was not Ishwar Chandra a genius?

The wonderful talents of Ishwar Chandr remind us of what the great Indian poet Bhava Bhuti has very justly sung on the subject:

> 'The preceptor imparts instructions equally to the sharp and the dull; but he can neither increase nor decrease their powers of comprehension. The great difference in the extent of their knowledge is due to their own merits. It is a pure, transparent gem, and not a lump of clay, that Iras the power of reflection.'

Ancestral Home Destroyed

In March 1869, Vidyasagar's house at Birsingha with everything in it was destroyed by fire. His mother and second brother were in sound sleep at the time, but most fortunately they escaped from the fire and not a single life was lost. No sooner did the news of the sad accident reach Vidyasagar, than he hastened to Birsingha and made provisions for the re-erection of the house. He wanted to take away his mother with him to Calcutta, but she declined on the ostensible plea that without her, there would be nobody to look after the comfort of the school-boys, whom Vidyasagar had been giving food and shelter, and look after her poor neighbours. In the same year, he published a correct edition of the Sanskrit *Meghadoota* with Mallinatha's annotations.

We now come to a most painful scene—the desertion of his ancestral home. The main cause of this abandonment is attributed to a sad incident in connection with widow marriage. One Muchiram Bandyopadhyay of Khirpai, Head Pandit of the Kenchkapur School, had settled to take to his wife a Brahmin widow named Manomohini of Kasiganja. He came to Vidyasagar and implored his help in the affair. Vidyasagar at once proceeded to Birsingha to celebrate the marriage.

But the Haldars of Khirpai, a respectable body, accompanied with some advocates of widow marriage, called upon Vidyasagar, and entreated him most earnestly to prevent the alliance. The father of the widow marriage movement was so moved by their urgent entreaties, that he promised to them that he would not allow the marriage to be consummated, and told them that they might take away with them the bride and bridegroom, who had been already brought to Birsingha for the alliance. The Haldars were satisfied at the word given by the truthful Vidyasagar, and they went their way. But in the dead of the very night, his second brother, Dinabandhu, and third brother, Sambhu Chandra, with the help of some other villagers, celebrated the marriage, without the knowledge of their eldest brother. Early in the next morning, as he was sitting in his verandah smoking his hookah, he heard a conch sounded. The sound took him by surprise, but he could make neither head nor tail of it. At this moment, Gopinath Sinha, a respectable co-villager made his appearance. Vidyasagar asked him the cause of the sounding of the shell. The visitor replied—'You are not aware? Muchiram's marriage has been consummated.' At the news, his face was flushed with rage.

He spoke not a word, but began incessant inhaling and exhaling of tobacco smoke. This was an indication of his serious displeasure. He had some peculiar modes of signifying his in-ward rage. His unusual reserve with gravity of countenancs, and respectful addresses applied to his inferiors, signified that he had found cause of displeasure. After a long silence, he asked Gopinath Sinha whether he knew anything of the' affair. Gopinath swore by his feet that he was quite ignorant of it At length, Vidyasagar said,— 'I gave word to those gentlemen, but I have failed to keep my word. I therefore quit Birsingha once for all. I shall never more come here. The truthful Vidyasagar, though the father of the widow marriage movement, was so grieved at the breach of his promise, that he deserted his fatherland for good, never more to return to it. Although he kept his word and never more visited Birsingha personally, he could not efface it wholly from his mind. The very recollection of his early scenes often drew tears from his eyes. The monthly stipends, that he had settled upon his relations and other poor families of the village, and the expenses of the charitable institutions, that he had established there, he paid regularly up "to the end of his life. It is said, that some 20 years after this sad incident, one day he received by post a pamphlet in Bengali, styled Birsingha Jananir Patra" (*i.e.* a letter from mother Birsingha). The pitiful appeals of the paper moved him to a flood of tears, and he resolved to pay a visit to Birsingha, if it was only for once. Accordingly he gave orders for repairs to his house, but ill-health prevented him from carrying out his plan. His illness grew serious, which ultimately carried him off this wicked world, and thus saved him from committing a breach of promise.

In August 1869, he made a gift of the Sanskrit Press Depository to Braja Nath Mukhopadhyay of Krishnaghar. He had been highly dissatisfied with the working and conduct of his officials. As he was sitting one day surrounded by some of his friends and dependents, in course of conversation, he expressed a desire to give away his Depository to any body, who should come forward to receive the gift. Braja Nath, who was one of the company, said that he was prepared to receive the gift, if the donor should gladly and voluntarily give it to him. Vidyasagar at once made him the gift. It is said, that on the next day, some people offered him 10,000 rupees for the property, but he declined the offers, saying that when he had once given his word, he could not retract it even for a *crore* of rupees.

At 3 O'clock in the afternoon of the 20th February, 1870, Durga Charan Banarji breathed his last. He was one of the best friends of Vidyasagar. He was exceedingly generous and benevolent, He was a great help to our hero in relieving the sufferings of the diseased poor. It is needless to say, that the tender-hearted Vidyasagar was heartily grieved at the loss of such a sincere, intimate friend and cooperator.' The two were so

Intimately connected, that as Durga Charan helped Vidyasagar in many of his works of love and benevolence, so the latter aided him with all his heart and soul in all his difficulties. Some time before his death, his eldest son, the Hon'ble Surendra Nath Banarji, the greatest Indian orator of the day, had passed the Competitive Civil Service Examination in England in the year 1869, but the Medical Board had disqualified him as having gone beyond the restriction of the limit of age. Surendra Nath wired to his father of the difficulty, and Durga Charan implored Vidyasagar's assistance in the matter. The latter, in his turn, consulted his friend, Dwarka Nath Mitter, and sent Surendra Nath's horoscope to England, which settled the question of age. Surendra Nath was declared an Indian Civil servant, but his father had not the good luck to hear the glad tidings, as it reached India shortly after his death. Vidyasagar was often seen to shed tears at the mention of Durga Charan's name. Subsequently when Surendra 'Nath was dismissed the Civil Service, Vidyasagar made him a professor of his own College.

Durga Charan's family were indebted to Vidyasagar on, many accounts. After his death, his wife and children entered into a serious quarrel about his assets, and went to lawcourt for the settlement of the dispute Vidyasagar stood up as an umpire and settled the question out of court. Not only was he a man of great learning and kindness of heart, but he was also the possessor of good business capacities. He had a great tact of settling disputes. Whenever there was a quarrel in a rich family, he was invited to settle it. Oil the death of Babu Asutosh Dev, generally known by the name of Chhatu Babu, son of the renowned Ram Dulat Sarkar, the self-made great millionaire of Calcutta, when the state of his affairs ran into disorder, Vidyasagar was entrusted with their management. He made his best exertions to settle the matter without asking for any remuneration, but he was so displeased at the conduct of the relations and officers of the deceased, that he was constrained to give over the charge of his own accord.

Vidyasagar had three sincere friends among men of the medical profession, who were his great helps in most of his works of benevolence, namely Durga Charan Banarji, Nil Madhav Mukharji, and Mahendra Lal Sarkar. He had on irrevocable loss in the death of the first two, Nil Madhav having died some time before Durga Charan. He had only one left to him—Dr. Mahendra Lal, who is now on the "top of the temple of fame in his profession. In, Vidyasagar contributed one thousand rupees to the aid of Mahendra Lal's Science Association. But latterly the two had a great difference. It is said, that it originated on the occasion of the illness of Vidyasagar's youngest daughter, Vidyasagar wrote to the Doctor requesting his attendance to the girl; but the latter put aside the letter without opening it at the moment. After the lapse of several hours, he opened the note and called. When Vidyasagar heard from him the cause of his unusual delay in attending to such a serious case, he was deeply pained and a little offended. Thus origianated the difference, which ultimately grew so serious, that the two hardly met, and if ever they met by accident, their four eyes never met. They met only again for the last few days of Vidyasagar's life, when Mahendra Lal willingly forgot the difference and called to see the great man in his sick-bed.

In the year 1874, Vidyasagar lost one of his greatest friends and supporters in the demise of Maharaja Mahatap Chand Bahadur of Burdwan. He was a staunch advocate of all of Vidyasagar's movements.

About this time, he displayed a noble, heroism which showed to the world that he was no hypocrite. Some people had been insinuating that Vidyasagar was a double shuffler—that he, who was the father of the widow marriage movement and was forward to consummate such alliance in others, had not yet given any member of his own family in such marriage—had not yet shown to the world that "example is better than precept" But every candid man, who knew Vidyasagar personally, must admit that he had no duplicity, in him. It is true that his opinions and convictions in many cases, particularly in matters of social reform, were wrongly formed, but there pan be no doubt that he always acted up to those ideas and beliefs with sincerity. That he had not so long given any member of his family in widow marriage was because he had not had an opportunity for it. What could he do? He and his brothers had already been married; he could not make either himself or any of his brothers lose his wife. He could neither make his married daughter a widow, in order to be able to give her in remarriage—to set an example to the public. No sooner had he this opportunity than he availed of it with most eager promptness. He gave his only son in widow marriage.

On Thursday, the 9th of August, 1870, Narayan Chandra was married to Bhava Sundari Devi, a widowed daughter of Sambhu Chandra Mukhopdhyay of Khanakul Krishnanagar. The bride's age at that time was 16 years. Some time after the death of her first husband, her mother took her away to Birsingha, and there requested Vidyasagar's third brother, Sambhu Chandra, to give her widowed daughter in remarriage, Sambhu Chandra wrote to Vidyasagar, who there-upon settled a bridegroom for the girl. In the meantime, Narayan Chandra, who was at home then, fell in love with the fair girl, and expressed a desire to marry her himself. Information of this proposal was sent to Vidyasagar, and he received the news with utmost delight and rejoicing. He sent for the bride and bridegroom, and when they arrived, he performed the ceremony with great eclat.

The marriage was celebrated in the house of Kali Charan Ghosh of Mirzapore in Calcutta. Narayan Chandra was, at this time, aged 21 years. Vidyasagar had not fetched his wife at the nuptials, for fear lest she should stand in the way and prevent the alliance. All the members of his family, particularly his brother Sambhu Chandra, were against the union. Before the celebration of the marriage, Narayan Chandra had said to his father —'Sir, I have no such merit, whereby I could add to the glory of your name. I know full well that your life-long aim is to relieve the miseries of virgin widows by giving them away in remarriage; in the achievement of that aim you have the chiefest pleasure. That lies in the power of this unworthy son. I shall never turn my back to that. If I can there-by contribute my small mite to minister to your pleasure of heart, I shall consider myself most fortunate; and your opponents will then have no cause to cast innuendoes at your honest, benevolent intentions. It is needless to say, that Vidyasagar's heart bounded with delight to hear his son speak in this strain.

We have already said, that Narayan Chandra's mother was not present at the nuptials. Vidyasagar was afraid, that she would oppose the marriage. It was this fear which led him to provide for a separate rented house for the accomodation of the married couple. But Narayan Chandra said to us that had no objection to the alliance, and she declared it openly after the marriage. The truth of Narayan Chandra's saying is evident from the fact that when she came down to Calcutta, she lived in the same mess with her son and his wife, She was quite illiterate and a devout follower of the orthodox Hindu faith, and yet it was her love for her husband and dear child, that made her live with them in the same mess and look to their comfort. It may not be out of place to mention here, that Vidyasagar's father, Thakurdas, was opposed to female education, and he bad not allowed his daughters-in-law to learn to read and write.

That Sambhu Chandra was quite against this marriage and had written to his brother to prevent the union, is evident from the letter, which Vidyasagar addressed to him after the celebration of the marriage. The letter was in Bengali; we will *try* to give its purport here in English.

My dear brother, on Thursday, the 27th Sravan, Narayan Chandra was married to Bhava Sundsri. Communicate the news to my dear mother and others. "You wrote to say, that if Naravan Chandra married a widow, our kinsfolk and relations would not eat with us and would have no intercourse with us. On this point I have only to say that Narayan Chandra has entered into this alliance out of his own motion, and not at my instance. When I heard that he was determined on marrying a widow and that his bride was also come, what could I do but gladly approve of it; I ought not to have opposed it. I am the originator of the widow marriage movement; we have already given many widows in marriage. Under such circumstance, if my son had taken to wife an unmarried girl instead of a widow, I could not have appeal in public; I would have been an object of hatred and aversion in higher society. By entering into this alliance of his own accord, he has added to the glory of my name; he has made himself worthy to call me his father. I consider the inauguration of widow marriage into Hindu Society the most virtuous deed of my life. I don't think I shall be able to do anything more pious in this life. For the furtherance of this cause I have given my last piece, and if necessity arises, I am prepared to sacrifice my life. In comparing to this, the severance by our kinsfolk and relations of their intercourse with us is of very little consequence. Had I, on this consideration, prevented my son from contracting widow marriage, which he did from the impulse of his own heart, I would have been the basest of men. In fine, I consider myself fortunate that Narayan Chandra entered into this alliance out of his own motion, I am not a slave to the customs of my country. Whatever I may deem proper or necessary for the good of the country or myself I will do at all risks. I will never shrink from it for fear of society or of my kinsfolk. In conclusion, I have to say that those, who will not have the courage or will dislike to keep festal or other intercourse with Narayan Chandra for fear of society or for any other reason, may easily refrain from such communication. I don't think, Narayan Chandra will be sorry on that account; and as for me, I too will not be offended or displeased. In my opinion, in these matters every one is at liberty to act according to his or her own free will; no one should follow our instance or act up to our wishes. 31st Sravan.

Your well-wisher (Sd). ' Ishwar Chandra Sharma.' The letter clearly shows that Vidyasagar was no double-dealer. His advocasy of the remarriage of Hindu widows was sincere, though it must be said that his conviction was based on wrong arguments. The Hindu Society has nothing to fear from men like Ram Mohan Ray or Ishwar Chandra Vidyasagar, who never concealed their real motives under false disguises. There is every fear of danger from those hypcocrites, who proclaim themselves true Hindus in public but act quite the contrary in their private life. These non-Hindus are a pest to Society, and the sooner they are shorn off their false guise, the better for the country.

Mother's Death

In the month of August, 1870, Vidyasagar's mother set out on pilgrimage. First of all, she went to the holy shrine of Banaras to see her husband. After a short stay there, she again proceeded on her journey, and after travelling in the different shrines of India, she again came back to Banaras. She requested her husband to accompany her to Birsingha. But he declined, and pressed her to live with him in Banaras. The benevolent matron replied;—'Let us go home now; you have still some years to live. My poor neighbours will miss me very keenly. My first duty is to succour the distrest and feed the hungry. I must go to do that now. But know this for certain, that wherever I may remain, I will come here in time, and die before you.' The prediction of this honest, faithful woman was fulfilled to the letter. It is generally found that honest, virtuous, and religious persons foresee the disolution of their life in distant future and sometimes predict the exact day and hour of their death. We do not see how they are enabled to do so, but nevertheless it is a fact and quite inexphacable. How inscrutable are the ways of Providence!

Vidyasagar's mother left her husband to live in Banaras, she herself returning to Birsiugha. In February following: (1871), information reached Vidyasagar that his father was seriously ill at the sanctum. He at once proceeded to Banaras, and was soon joined by his mother and his second and third brothers, in a few days, Thakurdas recovered from his illness. Vidyasagar returned to Calcutta, leaving his mother and brothers to took after his father. Bhagavati Devi lived with her husband for two months, and on the last day of the Bengali year (which is a sacred day with the Hindus), she was seized with Cholera, and expired in a few hours at the feet of her husband, as She had predicted. Before her death, she had begged for the blessings of her husband, whereupon Thakurdas said:—How shall I bless you? You are a most pious woman; it is your own piety that fakes you away before me: yours the victory. It is needless to say, that he was deeply grieved at the loss of such a virtuous Wife.

On his return from Banaras, Vidyasagar had taken his lodgings in a rented house by the river-side at Kasipore, a little north to Calcutta, when the sad intelligence reached him. The news came upon him like a thunder-bolt. How shall we describe the intensity of his grief? Words are too inadequate to express the sufferings of his heart. He was quite disconsolate, and wept bitterly like a child. The reader is aware how devotedly attached he was to his mother. Alas ! that mother, to obey whose word he had encountered the perils of a long pedestrian journey amidst thunder-storms and rains, and had plunged into the impassable stream of the terrific Damodar, was no more! Oh! the pangs of his heart—the more so, as he had not been able to attend to her death-bed and to have a last look of her face!

He performed the Sraddha ceremonials on the shores of the Bhagirathi at Kasipore; after which he led a secluded life for several months together, during which time his main business was to shed incessant tears at his dear mother's memory. He observed the mourning rites in accordance with the tenets of the Sastras for one complete, year. These twelve months he led the rigidly ascetic life of a true Hindu; he gave up fish and meat; he ate only one meal a day, and that 'composed of only rice and vegetables and cooked with his own hands, permitting nobody to help him in preparing the food save his wife, Dinamayi Devi, and that very rarely, only on occasions of his illness, when he was too weak to do the cooking himself; he gave up wearing shoes; he did not use umbrella; he slept on a rug on the floor; in short, he renounced all luxuries and comforts of life. He did not visit Banaras, the scene of her last days, for two years after the mournful incident.

In November 1873, Thakurdas was again ill. No sooner did the news reach Vidyasagar, than he hurried to Banaras. He nursed his father most tenderly, who recovered in a fortnight. Every morning he walked about the holy city with a purseful of silver coins of all values, which he gave away in alms to the poor and the needy. He had a great aversion for the Bengali Brahmins of Banaras; but he had a very high opinion of the Mahratta Brahmins, whom he treated with much respect. He even washed their feet with his own hands.

Whenever he had an occasion for feeding Brahmins, it was the Brahmins of Mahratta whom he entertained most sumptuously. He never feasted those of his own country. His main duty in Banaras was to do the marketing and cooking for his father with his own hands, and to eat the *Prasad* (the remains of a meal) left by his parent. The reader is aware that in his early years want made him do all the cooking himself. He had thus acquired a great proficiency in the art of preparing food. Not only did he cook his father's meal, but he took a great delight in feeding people with food of his own cooking. This self-imposed task was very agreeable to him.

During this sojourn at the sacred place of the Hindus, a gentleman one day called at Thakurdas's lodgings. Both the father and the son were present then. Vidyasagar thought that the new-comer was his father's acquaintance, while Thakurdas thought that the visitor must be known to his son. In the meantime, a piece of business called Vidyasagar away. When he returned to the lodgings, he found that the visitor had departed. He then enquired of his father about the man's personality. Thakurdas said,—I don't know him. I believed that he was known to you, and that you would come back and talk to him. I myself was too deeply engaged on an important matter to attend to him. 'Everything was now clear to Vidyasagar, and he was deeply sorry for what had passed. He at once set out in the direction of *Bangalitola* (that quarter of Banaras where the Bengalis reside) to find out the unknown visitor. After a diligent search of some time, he at last discovered the man. He apologised to the stranger for the apparent slight shown to him; the man was satisfied.

Vidyasagar then asked him why he had called. The stranger replied,—'I heard that you were come, and therefore called to see you. Besides, I wanted to ask you a question about religion.' Vidyasagar desired him to put his question. The gentleman wanted to know our hero's religious faith. Vidyasagar replied,—'I have never declared to anybody my faith, nor will I ever declare it; but this much I can say, that if you believe that the bath in the Bhagirathi purifies you and the worship of *Siva* brings sanctity to your heart, there is your religion.' With this, he return to his own quarters.

On a previous occasion, while his mother was still living, the Brahmins of Banaras asked him whether he believed in *Visvesvara* (the god Siva of Banaras). Vidyasagar replied,— 'I have no faith in *your* Visvesvara.' The Brahmins were highly offended at such a reply from a Hindu, and asked him,— 'What do you believe in then?' Vidyasagar answered,—'*My* Visvesvara and Annapurna (another name of goddess Durga, Siva's wife) are my *father and mother*, present here in flesh. Here was some indication of his religious faith. It might not be much amiss to infer, that his feeding of Brahmins was for the satisfaction of his parents, who were his sole objects of worship.

The Hindu Wills Act was passed on the 1st September, 1870. The Draft Bill had been introduced into the Legislative Council in the previous year The purposes of this Law had hitherto been served by the Indian Succession Act, which operated equally on the Indians and non-Indians. Previously, since the establishment of the Supreme Court, the wealthy residents of Calcutta used to leave their testamentary Wills at their own option, which gave rise to serious litigations, consequent on frauds with respect to the deeds. Thus arose the necessity for a fresh legislation to prevent these evil practices. The Bill, introduced in 1869, was framed by the alteration of some of the sections of the Indian Succession Act. The movement caused a great agitation throughout the country.

The government asked for the opinions of all the influential, leading members of society and some of the Sastrik Pandits. Vidyasagar was also called upon to give his opinion. He bestowed his best thoughts on the subject, and opposed two points: first, according to the Hindu Sastras, the gift of something to an unborn person is un-lawful—both the donor and the donee of a gift must be cognisant of it; but in this Act, such gifts have been considered lawful in certain cases: secondly, what has been termed as Rules against Perpetuity is also opposed to the Hindu Sastras. Vidyasagar's arguments were founded on sound bases. But the government paid no heed to them, and the Bill was passed into a law applicable to the Hindus, including Buddhists and Jains.

In the course of this year, Vidyasagar had *to* encounter another serious calamity in the death of Maharaja Satish Chandra Rai Bahadur of Nuddea, who breathed his last on the 25th day of October, 1870. Vidyasagar was intimately connected with the Nuddea Raj family. He had a friendly intercourse with Satish Chandra's father, Maharaja Sris Chandra. The acquaintance first began when Vidyasagar had gone to the Nuddea palace for the manuscript of Bharat Chandra's works, and it gradually grew into familiar friendship in the course of his subsequent visits to Krishnaghar for inspection of schools, while he was an Inspector of Schools. Sris Chandra had such a high regard for him on account of his vast erudition and noble conduct, that whenever Vidyasagar called on him, he rose from his throne, and clasped the poorly dressed visitor in his arms. In fact, he was so enamoured of our hero, that he supported his widow marriage movement and even subscribed his own name to the petition submitted to government for legislation on the subject. We have already noticed briefly, in the chapter on Widow Marriage, how one of his ancestors, Maharaja Krishna Chandra, had baffled the attempts of Raja Rajaballabh of Dacca to introduce widow marriage into Hindu Society. But the descendant of the same Krishna Chandra felt no compunction in advocating the uncanonical renovation and lending his aid to the furtherance of the cause, though highly injurious to society and repugnant to orthodox Hindu feelings—he was so charmed and led away by Vidyasagar's arguments and by his own Western education.

Sris Chandra died on the very day that the first widow marriage of his name sake under the new Law was celebrated with eclat in Calcutta, his son, Satish Chandra, looked upon Vidyasagar with the same regard and esteem as his father. The reader is aware how our noble hero made over to him 1800 rupees deposited by his father in Vidyasagar's care. Even after Satish Chandra's death, Vidyasagar often visited Krishnaghar to provide for the proper management of the Nuddea Raj Estate at great personal sacrifice. It was quite natural for our grateful hero to suffer losses for the good of a benefactor's descendants and heirs, from whom he had himself received so much benefit.

With respect to Vidyasagar's grateful benevolence and kindness to the near relations of a deceased friend and benefactor, Jogendra Nath Bandyopadhyay, mentioned before, has tried to condemn the conduct of our hero in connection with the family of his father-in-law Madan Mohan Tarkalankar. We would ask the reader to recall the circumstances under which our hero acquired the sole right of the Sanskrit Press and the copyright of the three parts of Madan Mohan's *Sisu-Siksha.* On the death of Tarkalankar, when his family were miserably circumstanced, Vidyasagar *very* kindly settled on the deceased friend's mother, wife and widowed daughters a monthly allowance of ten rupees each. But that stipend was not sufficient for their comfortable living. Madan Mohan's son-in-law, Jogendra Nath aforesaid, therefore begged Vidyasagar for the copy right of the three parts of *Sisu-Sikska* in the name of Kunda Mala, Tarkalankar's second widowed daughter, Vidyasagar accepted the proposal and consented to make her a present of the copyright. But subsequently he was so offended at somebody's behaviour, that he was constrained to withdraw his promise. Surely, this unusual conduct on the part of the truthful Vidyasagar is by no means to be justified, and has brought down some discredit on his unsoiled character. However offensive other people's behaviour might have been, or under any circumstances, however displeasing, Vidyasagar ought not to have retracted his word of gift, once pledged by him.

Maharaja Satish Chandra had married two wives. He had left a Will. One of the provisions of the testament was that if neither of his wives had any male issue, then on his demise, the younger widowed Maharani should take an adopted son, and that if she did not take to that course, the elder Maharani should adopt a son. The elder one had already died in the lifetime of Satish Chandra. On his demise, the younger Maharani, Bhuvanesvari, expressed a wish to keep the Estate in her own hands.

The Raj-Dewan, Kartik Chandra Ray, saw that the Estate was already in an embarrassed state, and that if the Maharani should keep it in her own hands, it would grow more deplorable still. He, therefore, called On Vidyasagar, and consulted him on the point The latter decided upon placing the Estate in the hands of the Court of Wards. Kartik Chandra thereupon requested him to persuade the Maharani to take that course.

Vidyasagar did as he was desired. He went to Krishnaghar and waited upon Bhuvanesvari. After much persuasion, he succeeded in convincing her of the advisability of the step. The Estate was accordingly made over to the Court of Wards on the 6th January, 1871. It soon prospered under the able management of the Court; all its former debts were cleared off.

The present Maharaja Kshitis Chandra Ray Bahadur, when he attained his majority and took over charge of the Estate in his own hands, received from the Court of Wards, a sum of two *lakhs* and ten thousand rupees in ready money. Kshitis Chandra had been placed in the Wards' Institution, where he received his training.

Publications

In 1871, Vidyasagar published new editions of the Sanskrit "Uttara-Charita" and "Abhijnana-Sakuntala" with his annotations. The two prefaces of these publications are very good pieces of Bengali prose reading, displaying his powers of the same sweet, serious language, the same melodious flow of elegant style, as in his former works, and discussing concisely, in a short compass, the high talents and abilities of the two immortal poets, Bhavabhuti and Kalidas.

Besides these two publications) he issued correct editions of the Sanskrit "Sisupala-Badha," "Kadambari," "Kiratarjjuniya," "Raghu-Vansa," and "Harsha-Charita," without annotations. He also published, for the students of the lower forms, three Selection-books from standard English authors, namely, "Selections from the writings of Gold-smith," "Selections from English Literature"' and "Poetical Selections".

Vidyasagar was a great appreciator of merits. His heart was always drawn to a spirited, amiable, kind, truthful and honest man, be he a Hindu, Brahma, Christian, or Mussulman—be he a native of his father-land or of a foreign country. Whatever might be his course, if Vidyasagar believed that he was working sincerely for the good of his country, he would clasp him in his fond embraces. Keshab Chander Sen, the famous orator of Bengal, was a great favourite with him, although the opinions of the two widely diverged on many points, simply because Vidyasagar believed that the orator wished well of the country. Keshab Chander also had a great fond regard for him. The two often met in Vidyasagar's house, and whenever they were together, they had no other talk than the device of means for the good of the country.

Raj Narayan Basu, though a Brahma, had, by his honesty and truthfulness, won over Vidyasagar's intimate friendship. The two reciprocated feelings of affectionate esteem for each other. Raj Narayan believed that if Vidyasagar had turned a missionary and preacher, he could have done a great good to the people. He even went so far as to declare his idea to Vidyasagar. The latter gave a somewhat humorous reply. He said, 'I don't want to be a preacher. If I have to suffer punishment for what I am and what I have been doing, I must take the consequences. Suppose, I turn a missionary and convert some people to my faith. If they should be asked who converted them, *they* must point to me, and supposing' that they are punishable for their acts, it is 1 on whose back the punishment is sure to fall. I can suffer for my own sins; but how can I receive stripes for others?'

Raj Narayan consulted Vidyasagar on all important matters. He once asked for his friend's advice on the subject of his daughter's marriage. Vidyasagar conveyed his instructions by a long letter couched in respectful terms. The letter was written in Bengali; we will give here its purport in English:

'Accept my best compliments—

'It is some days that your letter reached, me; but I was very busy with different matters, and could not therefore reply to your letter in time. Please excuse me the delay.

'I have bestowed my best thoughts on the subject of your daughter's marriage, but have failed to decide upon the advice that I am to give you.

To speak the truth, it is very difficult to advise on these matters. In the first place, you are a Brahma. As you are a strict follower of that faith, you' should by all means pursue the course adopted by Babu Devendra Nath Tagore on the occasion of his daughter's marriage, if you think, that course was in consonance with the Brahma religion. In the second place, if you do not pursue the course adopted by Devendra Babu, and celebrate the marriage of your daughter in accordance with the old practice, there will arise a great obstacle to the propagation of Brahma marriage. In the third place, it is most doubtful whether the celebration of your daughter's marriage according to the Brahma practice should be considered valid on all points. For these reasons I am unable and unwilling to lend you any advice on this point But this much I can say, that you should not jump at once into any side.

'What I really mean to say on this subject is, that it is not proper to ask for other people's advice in these matters. In such cases one ought to ask one's own heart for instructions, and act up to its dictates. For whomever you will consult on this point, will deliver his counsels according to his own opinions and wishes; he will never consult your good or duty.

'In my opinion, you would do well to think over the matter seriously, and then determine for yourself which course to pursue.

The reader is, no doubt, familiar with the name of the saintly Ram Krishna Paramahansa, whose purity of manners, honesty of purpose, and pious conduct had drawn to him many disciples. He was fond of the company of pious and honest persons. One day he said to his disciples that he wanted to have an interview with the famous Vidyasagar, his disciples asked him why he so wished. He replied, because without God's love and divine grace, Vidyasagar could not have been so great. Accordingly he presented himself one evening before our hero. No sooner did he appear, than Vidyasagar rose from his seat and advanced to receive him; but before he could approach the Paramahansa, the latter sat down before him upon the floor of the room, and said,—'I have crossed drains and ditches, pools and tanks, and at last I am come to the *Sagar* (sea).' Vidyasagar replied,— 'As you are already come, there is no help; you may take out some salt water, if you like, or if you cast your net, you will fish only shells; there is nothing in this sea but salt water and shells.' The Paramahansa said,—'Why should 1 take out salt water? There is not merely a sea of salt; there are a sea of milk, a sea of curd, a sea of honey, and so forth. You are not a sea of ignorance; you are one of knowledge. When I have come to you, I will fish out pearls; you are full of pearls.' After such humorous talks for some time, they fell to serious conversation on different topics, and each was highly delighted at the other's conduct and manner of speech. In the meantime, arrived a quantity of the well-known delicious confectionary of Burdwan presented to Vidyasagar by one of his friends. He requested the Paramahansa to partake of the dainty sweets. The saintly visitor accepted the invitation and ate of the sweetmeats. Henceforth the two had a great fond regard and esteem for each other.

In June, 1872, Vidyasagar's second daughter, Kumudini Devi, was married to Aghor Naih Chattopadhyay of Rudrapur in the district of 24 Pergunnas. He was Sub-Registrar of Purulia in Manbhum.

About this time, arose some incidents, which led Vidyasagar to be highly offended with his only son, Narayan Chandra. By degrees, the displeasure grew to such a fearful height, that he was constrained to estrange him. There was thus a wide gulf between the two. God alone knew what his heart suffered at the unnatural separation, but to all external appearance he had perfect composure, which showed that he was not dissatisfied with the step he had taken. Narayan Chandra's mother was, of course, most sincerely grieved at the estrangement of her only, dear son. She never afterwards felt ease or comfort. She often remonstrated with her husband on his uncompromising conduct towards the son, but Vidyasagar was as firm as a rock. Narayan Chandra's enemies found an opportunity to be revenged upon; they brought on serious complaints against him. They added fuel to the fire, and kept Vidyasagar's feelings of displeasure against him always wide awake, thereby preventing the reconciliation so heartily desired by the mother.

Narayan Chandra, by his own efforts, became a Sub-Registrar of Assurances. He was, at that time, as spirited and self-reliant as his father. He visited his father's house now and then, but no talk passed between the two.

Instances of a father's estrangement of his child for the latter's failing in duty or improper conduct are very rare in this world Although Vidyasagar had been constrained to be separated from his son to all outward appearance, he could not wholly efface his love for him. The ties of natural affection are too strong to be easily cut asunder. It is said, that on one occasion, a look at the son's photograph moved him to a flood of tears. Narayan Chandra's wife and children were very dear to his heart. He kept up epistolary communication with them, and aided them by remittances of money.

On the 15th June, 1872, the "Hindu Family Annuity Fund" was established. It was started with very laudable objects. The natives of Bengal, with a limited income, can leave no provision *tot* the maintenance of their parents, wives, children, or other relations. The Fund was created with a view to provide for such means. If one wished that one's wife or any other relative should have a monthly allowance of 5 rupees, after one's death, one had to deposit two rupees and a quarter every month till the last day of his life, if one wished for a monthly provision of 10 rupees, one had to deposit a proportionate amount. In this way one might make provisions for a monthly allowance up to the limit of 30 rupees.

The necessity for the establishment of such a Fund was first determined at a meeting of some respectable and influential native gentlemen held on the 23rd February, 1872, in the premises of the Metropolitan Institution. The Fund was first opened at No. 32, College Street, with 10 subscribers. Besides, a few benevolent, wealthy persons paid considerable amounts as donations to begin, with. The Paikpara Raj family contributed 2,500 rupees. For the first and second years, Ishwar Chandra Vidyasagar and the Hon'ble Dwarka Nath Mitter were Trustees of the Fund. On Dwarka Nath Mitter's death, Maharaja Jatindra Mohan Tagore, the Hon'ble Ramesh Chandra Mitra, and Vidyasagar were Trustees for the third year. At the outset, the following gentlemen were office-bearers of the Fund. Chairman—Syama Charan De. Deputy-Chairman—Muralidhar Sen. Directors—Ray Dina Bandhu Mitra Bahadur, Rajendra Nath Mitra, Govinda Chandra Dhar, Nabin, Chandra Sen, Isan Chandra Mukhopadhyay, Prasanna Kumar Sarvvadhikari, Nanda Lal Mitra, Rajendra Nath Bandyopadhyay, Narendra Nath Sen, and Panchanan Chaudhuri. Medical Officer and Health Examiner of the Subscribers—Dr. Mahendra Lal Sarkar.

Sometimes after the foundation of the Hind Family Annuity Fund, the "Albert Life Assurance Company" was started with the same object; but the latter business failed, to the great loss of many poor persons. Vidyasagar was connected with the Annuity! Fund till the end of 1875. In his opinion, the Fund worked well in an organised way for years since its establishment. On the 27th December, 1875, he addressed a letter to the Directors intimating his design to sever his connection with the Fund. On the 2nd January, 1876, the Directors held a special meeting and called on Vidyasagar to give his reasons, for his intended separation. He communicated his reasons in a very long letter, dated 21st February, 1876. The letter was subsequently printed, covering over 20 pages Foolscap. The language of the letter is vigorous, and may be given a high place as a very good piece of literary composition in Bengali. The reasons set forth therein were not groundless. The gist of what he said was, that the Secretary and most of the Directors had combined themselves into a party and had mustered strong to thwart Vidyasagar's measures and to humiliate him, and that they had brought about much irregularity in the management of the Fund. He, therefore, thought it advisable to withdraw himself from its connection.

He charged the Directors with disregard of the rules and neglect of the true interests of the Fund, and the Subscribers with indifference to its affairs. His idea was that the natives of Bengal had not yet learned to work in conjunction and cooperation. He stated it distinctly in his letter, when referring to the ill-management of the Fund. It was this conviction of his that had led him to decline to join the Fund at the outset. Groat persuasions had afterwards induced him to join it.

That the Secretary and the Directors of his party had mustered strong and brought about great irregularities in the management of the Fund, Vidyasagar demonstrated very clearly. The main charges brought against them were, that the accounts had not been properly kept, that the rules had not been altered v.hen necessary, that the name of the Chairman had been put down in the Annual Report of the Fund without his cognisance when the latter had declined to sign it for irregular proceedings, that unnecessary withdrawals of money had been made from the Fund's Bank, and so forth. He brought another very serious charge. A clerk Toeing required for the office of the Fund, Vidyasagar had been urgently requested by the Directors to find a competent man for the post. He had at first declined to take the responsibility, but at the pressing solicitations of the Directors, he gave a fully qualified man. This man had already been holding an office in the East Indian Railway Company's service, and Vidyasagar made him resign that place, and appointed him as clerk to the Fund. But shortly afterwards, the Secretary dismissed the man, without even consulting the Directors, and thus placed Vidyasagar in a false position. The reasons set forth by Vidyasagar were most distressingly painful. He stated in clear and plain but pitiful words how sincerely he was pained at the severance of his connection with the Fund. The purport of what he said in the concluding portion of his letter was:

'I lent my utmost exertions and attention to the foundation and improvement of this Fund. you have expectations of the enjoyment of the fruits of this tree, but I do not entertain such hopes. My idea is, that every one should try his best to do good to his native country. It was with this conviction, that I bestowed my best thoughts and endeavours on this subject I had no other motive of furthering my self-interest. I do not know whether you will believe me when I say, but still I must say, that I have a greater affection for the Fund than any of you. My inmost heart alone knows what pangs it suffers to forget that affection wholly. Those whom you have intrusted with the charge of management, do not walk in a straight path. These circumstances have led me to be afraid that my further continuance in the business of the Fund will in future bring a" great censure on my head, and I shall be made answerable before God. It is this fear only that makes me cut off my connection with the Fund, though most reluctantly and painfully.

'At your special meeting of the 2nd January, you have expressed a wish and request that I should retain my connection with the Fund; but it has become very difficult for me to comply with your request Numbers 'of people, come to consult me whether they should subscribe to the Fund, I am then put to a great dilemma. Under the present state of the Fund, I think, it would be wrong to advise any one to subscribe to it; while it would be equally wrong to deter any body from subscribing to it. The reason is, that it would be deceiving a man to induce him to subscribe to it, when a conviction has grown upon me that in future the Fund might be in a state of disorder; while to deter him would be acting in opposition to the Fund. To deceive a man wilfully, and to act in opposition to it while continuing in its connection, both are equally very wrong. If I keep any further connection with the Fund, I must commit either of the wrongs. It is this dilemma that disables me to comply with your request, for which I crave your indulgence.

'In fact, I am an unimportant person; yet you relied on me and charged me with such an important trust; I therefore pour forth my heartfelt gratitude to you. In the course of the period I held the important trust, I must have committed some errors; you will, please, be good enough to excuse me for them. So long that I was one of your trustees, I tried my best to do good to the Fund.

I never cognisantly or wilfully showed the slightest disregard, indifference or inattention to it. I hope, you would be graciously pleased to give me leave to retire.'

From this time forward he had no connection with the Annuity Fund. Some time afterwards, Maharaja Jatindra Mohan Tagore and the Hon'ble Ramesh Chandra Mitra also withdrew their names from the Fund. Consequently, the Directors had to seek the help of the government in the affair.

Vidyasagar had put forth all his energies—had devoted himself, heart and soul, to the establishment of the Hindu Family Annuity Fund. As he was the principal starter, he was nominated one of the trustees. For one year he worked with full vigour. At the end of the first year, the enthusiasm diminished a little; in the second year, it slackened still more; and, in the third year, his independent spirit revolted at the idea of acting in subordination to others, who had in consequence of mustering strong, had the upper hand in every-thing. After all, Vidyasagar was a native of unfortunate Bengal, particularly of this degenerated age. The Bengalees of the present age have no unity among themselves; they cannot act in union and conjunction. Every one is independent; every one is arbitrary; every body follows his own opinions. It was with a view to remove this slur of his countrymen that Vidyasagar attempted to exhibit a different scenery on the stage of the Annuity Fund. But he had to yield *to* the overpowering influence of the opponents. In the short space of three years he was obliged to quit his post In giving up the helm of the Fund, he charged others with want of unity and with in-capacity to work in conjunction; but others laid the blame on his shoulders. They said that in many cases Vidyasagar had proved his own in capacity to work in conjunction, with other people. No doubt, he joined them, at the outset, with great enthusiasm, but he could never keep to the end. This was Vidyasagar's peculiarity. Such peculiarity is undoubtedly an indication of spiritedness; but does it not sometimes lead to arbitrariness?

The letter, referred to above, clearly showed that Vidyasagar was not a double-dealer; he was never afraid to open his mmd for fear of incurring one's displeasure, or to suppress his feelings for the satisfaction of another. He firmly believed that it was wrong not to declare frankly one's own mind or opinions. As he never shrank from giving out freely his own convictions, so he was highly pleased, when he found others doing the same. We will illustrate this by an incident of his previous life.

On 'one occasion, Mahamahopadhyay Rakhal Das Nyayratna, Pandit Sibchandra Sarvvabhauma. Madhu Sudan Smritiratna, and Panchanan Tarkaratna called upon him. The last-named visitor was, at that time, still a pupil but had nearly finished his course of instruction. In course of conversation, they fell to discussing religious topics. Vidyasagar said that religion was nothing but formation of parties. 'Take for instance the following *Sloka* of Manu:

> 'You should take an honest course, and follow the track of your fathers and grandfathers; it would not be wrong to pursue that track,' Vidyasagar continued,—'Now, what is the meaning of this? If you would take an honest course, why then should you go to follow the track of your fore-fathers? The simple meaning is, that unless the two ways are indicated at the same time, the screw of your party becomes slack. Manu was afraid that if he indicated only the honest course and let it alone, the members of his party might quit his side, and pursue the honest course of other nations. It was this fear, that led him to bestow his best thoughts on the subject and indicate two ways at the same time.'

Panchanan Tarkaratna very humbly and politely suggested,—'My interpretation is quite different. But, under the circumstances, it is not a very difficult thing to give such a signification of the Manu's passage as may be somewhat gratifying to you.'

Vidyasagar,—'How can you give that signification to it?

Tarkaratna.—In the expression there might be a clerical error; it might very conveniently be read; and then, the meaning would be,—'To follow the track of forefathers is the true course for virtuous people.

Vidyasagar.—'Nyayratna, this youth is very sharp, indeed!'

Rakhal Das Nyayratna and the other visitors unanimously complimented the young Tarkaratna in eloquent terms. At last,

Vidyasagar said,— 'What is the end of all this praise? Nothing, but beggary. At this young age, he has finished the *Nyaya* and other philosophies; it is a high compliment, no doubt. But what will he do? Let him go home and starve.

In the beginning of 1873 Vidyasagar had to face a most dire calamity. On the 4th February of that year, his eldest son-in-law, Gopal Chandra Samajpati, died of cholera at Benares, where he had gone in company with Vidyasagar's nephew, (sister's son), Beni Madhav Mukhopadhyay, for a change, as his health had already been much impaired. The news came upon our hero like a thunder-bolt. He loved the son-in-law most dearly. Gopal Chandra was a young man of handsome and lovely, appearance. He had a profound scholastic education and a poetic genius. His manners were most affable and courteous. Vidyasagar was most grievously afflicted at the loss of such a beloved relation. But to console his dear, widowed daughter, he had to assume the appearance of external composure, which served to rend his tender heart the more. He sympathised with his daughter most sincerely. She led a rigidly austere life; Vidyasagar also did the same. She had to give up fish and flesh and to eat only one meal a day; Vidyasagar did the same. She fasted on the *Ekadasi* day; her father also observed fasting on that day. This state of things continued for a considerable period. At last, at the urgent solicitations of the daughter, he had to give up the austerities.

He made Hemlata (which was the name of the eldest widowed daughter) the sole mistress of his house-hold. She also did her best to improve the affairs of her father. Her house-wife and affectionate treatment pleased everybody. The busy, active life that she led to feed and tend her father and generally to bring ease and comfort to all the inmates of the house left her no leisure to openly shed tears for her dear husband. In fact, she was the goddess of the house-hold. Would the advocates of widow marriage open their eyes and see how a true Hindu widow can pass her days virtuously without pining away at the loss of one husband and eagerly looking out for another? Hemlata had two little boys, whose sole charge fell on the shoulders of her father. Vidyasagar brought them up with the tenderest care. He made the best provisions possible for their education. The two boys, Suresh Chandra

Samajpati and Jatis Chandra Samajpati, read English and Sanskrit at home. Vidyasagar did not think fit to send his grandsons to school. He himself taught them Sanskrit, and engaged competent teachers to instruct them in English, There was nothing in the world that he would not give them or do for them. If he ever heard them lament the loss of their father, it would pierce his heart like a poisoned dagger. The elder grandson once expressed a desire to go to England, but his grandfather and mother, both prevented him. One day, when sitting to dinner, Suresh Chandra said to his mother;—'Had *my* father been living now, I would never have gone to *ask your* father.' Vidyasagar overheard this, and was moved to a flood of tears. If he saw them undertake or carry out a noble and benevolent deed, his delight knew no bounds. On one occasion, the younger boy, Jatis Chandra, found a poor man suffering from Dysentery, lying on the road. He brought home the helpless sufferer, Vidyasagar was highly pleased at his young grandchild's humanity. He provided for the patient's treatment and nursing, and took great care of him. But, unfortunately, the poor man's days were numbered; nothing could save him from the hands of death. Suresh Chandra's abilities for good composition were a source of great delight to the grandfather. The two boys were dearer to him than his own begotten children. Suresh Chandra is, at present, the editor of the *Sahitya,* a well conducted monthly. Vidyasagar took charge not only of his own grandsons, but also of the mother, brothers, and sisters of the deceased son-in-law. He housed them in a separate rented house, and provided for their comfortable living.

In spite of these dire catastrophes, the thoughts of his educational institutions were always vivid in his mind. He never for a moment lost sight of them. The anxieties for their welfare and success made him sometimes forget "his afflictions. Even under such distressing circumstances, he opened, in 1874, a Branch Metropolitan School at Syaropukur. Like them other institution, it soon rose to high eminence and success.

Differences with the Authority

Vidyasagar had some difference with Sir George Campbell, the then Lieutenant Governor of Bengal, with respect to the *Smriti* branch of the Sanskrit College. Campbell was a man of highly enthusiastic and revolutionary spirit and rather chary of expenditure on high education. He revolutionised almost every department of the government under him.

The Hon'ble C. E. Buckland in his 'Bengal under the Lieutenant-Governers,' says: 'Reform was the principal feature of Sir G. Campbell's government The experiment of appointing a Lieutenant-Governor who had not graduated in Lower Bengal certainly led to great changes, and it seemed as if every department and institution had to justify its method of working. It would have been impossible for any one, in such a postition and bent on such a mission as Sir G. Campbell, to avoid running counter to many cherished ideas in conservative Bengal: and it was no wonder that the pressure he applied on all officers and classes tended to render him unpopular".

A contemporary writer thus described Sir George Campbell:—"That he was more than a mere executive officer every one knows who knows India. His Governorship represented a virtual revolution, succeeding that of Sir William Grey. It was a change from desk management to root-and-branch administration, resting on fixed and matured views as to political principles underlying action. As a statesman, Sir G. Campbell stands foremost among the lieutenant-Governors, and it is unpleasant to add that he was the least popular".

He was a great enemy of the high education of the natives of the soil; he lowered the status of the Berhampur, the Krishnaghar and the Sanskrit Colleges from the first to the second grade.

The Hon'ble C. E. Buckland, in his 'Bengal under the Lieutenant-Governors,' says: "Reductions were carried out in the Berhampore, Krishnagar and Sanskrit Colleges, which provoked some expression of dissatisfaction among the upper and literate classes of Bengal. Sir G. Campbell's policy was to reduce the number of Colleges educating up to the highest point, concentrating in the remainder improved means of the highest education. The reduced Colleges were not abolished, but were still efficiently maintained to teach to the point to which experience proved that the greatest demand existed, i.e. up to the First Arts standard".

It was this too excessive economical policy of his government that led him to resolve upon making a monthly saving of 650 rupees from the establishment charges of the Sanskrit College by the abolition of the posts of the Professors of *Smriti* and two professors of English. This resolution threw the whole country in a state of great agitation. Protests and oppositions were raised from every quarter, but without the desired success. It was, however, finally settled that the *Smriti* department should be placed under the tuition of the Professor of Rhetoric. The Bengal Government had previously asked Vidyasagar for his opinion on the point, and he had opposed the retrenching policy. But still, it was stated in "government resolution published in the Calcutta Gazette, that in this matter Vidyasagar's opinion had been taken. The people of the country very naturally, suspected that Vidyasagar must have supported the policy of government He was, therefore, obliged to address a letter to Luttman Johnson, Private Secretary to the Lieutenant Governor, contradicting the statement of government, The letter ran as follows:

"Calcutta, 23rd May 1872

"To

"He Luttman Johnson Esq.

"Private Secretary to his Honour, the
"Lieutenant Governor of Bengal".

"My Dear Sir,

"Adverting to the government order on the reorganisation of the Sanskrit College, published in the last Calcutta Gazette, I find that reference has been made to me and the Principal of the Sanskrit College as the persons among others with whom his Honour the Lieutenant Governor was pleased to discuss the subject, and his Honour considers their suggestions 'to be so moderate and reasonable that he has much pleasure in being able substantially to comply with their wishes pending further trial of the arrangements now to be made.' These arrangements are that the first Arts classes should be revived and that the Professorship of Hindu Law should be merged in that of Rheotric and Philosophy by giving an increment of Rs. 50 to the present incumbent for this additional duty.

"As I was asked by you under instructions his Honour to consult the leading members of the Hindu community, who take interest in Sanskrit studies before meeting. His honour, and as it might lead to an impression that the above suggestions emanated from me, I think it my duty to remind his Honour that so far as the proposed arrangement for instruction in Hindu Law is concerned, it did not come from me. Indeed I told his Honour distinctly that the importance of the subject demanded a separate chair, and I still entertain the same opinion. Hindu Law, as his honour is aware, *is* a vast subject— it forms the life-study of a man. It is true that there may be versatile persons, who may combine a thorough knowledge of Sanskrit literature with a profound acquaintance with Hindu Law, but such versatility is rare. To merge the chair of Hindu Law with other chairs is to give it a secondary rank and to reduce its practical usefulness, for a professor who will teach it at his leisure moments as it were can-not be expected to devote that attention to it, which the vastness of the subject demands. I find it stated in the government letter that according to the Principal of the College "Smriti or Hindu Law is now taught in a most satisfactory manner by the professor in addition to some other duties". From my experience of the working of the college as ex-principal I cannot however persuade myself to subscribe to this opinion. Perhaps his Honour would form a clear idea of the anomaly of the proposed arrangement if he would consider the effect of calling upon a Professor of Literature, Philosophy or Mathematics in the Presidency College, who may have attended Law lectures but who has not made law his special study, to fill the chair of Law in addition to other duties; I have no doubt that the legal profession would scout such an idea, and yet this is exactly the arrangement proposed for giving instruction in Hindu Law in the Sanskrit College. I have high respect for the attainments and scholarship of Pundit Mahesh Chandra, but I fear that the union of so many duties in his hands will not only result in a falling off in the study of Law but also of those branches, which he is prominently qualified to teach. His Honour observes, 'it was and is in-tended that the teaching of Hindu Law shall be fully maintained', but as I have endeavoured to show above His Honour's intention will be but ill-fulfilled by the arrangement proposed. I would therefore earnestly and respectfully solicit his Honour to consider this part of his recent orders. The saving which the absorption of the chair effects is so small, *vis.* Rs. 100 a month, that I earnestly trust that his Honour will see the propriety of making this concession to the Hindu community, particularly as his Honour has shown a commendable spirit of moderation and conciliation in these orders.

"As it might be inferred from the tenour of the government letter referred to that I have advised his Honour the proposed arrangement for filling the chair on Hindu Law, and as I am consequently liable to be misunderstood by the Hindu community, whose feeling is very strong on the subject of the chair of the Hindu Law, I would respect fully request that in justice to me his Honour may think fit to remove the erroneous impression which his too general allusion to my suggestions regarding the reorganisation of the Sanskrit College is calculated to produce on the public mind.

"I remain &c. "Ishwar Chandra Sharma".

To this letter Luttman Johnson the Private Secretary replied, as follows:—

"Belvedere Alipore. "The 25th May 1872 "My dear Pundit,

"I have laid your letter of the 23rd current about the recent orders for reorganisation of the Sanskrit College before his Honour the Lieutenant Governor. His honour has no doubt that you are correct in saying that you did not Individually recommend the absorption of the Professorship of Hindu Law. His honour desires me to assure you that he proposes to make the Hindu Law the primary and not a mere secondary object of one of the chairs. He has every reason for believing that Pundit Mahesh Chandra is at least as qualified for the duty of teaching Hindu Law as any other gentleman whom he could have selected to succeed the late Professor, and he has fie distinct assurance of the Principal that the Pundit Is teaching the subject in the most satisfactory manner. Upon the whole, therefore, his honour thinks that he has been well advised in the orders which he has passed. He must in the present experiment sufficiently before he can consent to make another change.

"I remain,

Dear Sir,

"Yours faithfully Sd. "H. Luttman Johnson

"Private Secretary".

With a view to remove the erroneous impression from the minds of the public, Vidyasagar afterwards addressed a letter to the Hindu Patriot, which was published in its issue of the loth June, 1872. The letter is quoted below:—

To

The Editor of the Hindu Patriot

Dear Sir,

As considerable misapprehension prevails among my countrymen as to the opinion I expressed to his honour the Lieutenant-Governor, when he did me the honour of consulting me regarding the Sanskrit College, particularly in reference to' the Constitution of the Chair of Hindu Law, I deem it due to lay before the public through the medium of your paper the accompanying correspondence which I hope will remove the erroneous impression entertained on the subject. I am always reluctant to rush into print, but when I find myself actually abused and looked upon as the individual, who has advised the Lieutenant-Governor the arrangement about the Chair of Hindu Law, which is unhappily regarded as a piece of downright jobbery, I cannot in justice to myself refrain from letting the public know the part I have taken in this business. I need hardly add that I am compelled to resort to this step by the equivocal terms used in the letter of Mr. Bernard, Secretary to the Director of Public Instruction, on the subject. I however feel much indebted to his honour for completely exonerating me in the last letter of his Private Secretary to my address.

'Yours faithfully

"The 8th June 1872. Sd. "Ishwar Chandra Sharma". His relations with Sir George Compbell being thus much strained some of his publications were excluded by government from the list of textbooks prescribed for schools in Bengal. As a matter of consequence, his income from books, which formed the main portion of his means, was considerably diminished. He was therefore obliged, though most painfully, to curtail some of the stipends which he had kindly settled on poor families. But as soon as he again found sufficient means for it, he raised the allowances to their former rate, which he had been constrained to retrench.

In this connection, we will notice here, in passing, the appointment of Pandit Mahesh Chandra Nyayratna as a Professor of the Sanskrit College. On the retirement of the old professor, Pandit Premchand Tarkavagis, his place in the College fell vacant. There were two candidates for the post—Rammay Bhattacharyya, a brother of the retired professor, and Mahesh Chandra Nyayratna. Both were qualified men; the people naturally expected that the first-named Pandit would get the appointment. Although the second candidate was not a student of the Sanskrit College, yet he was highly proficient in Bellesletters and Rhetoric, and had acquired a great reputation as the most learned man in the six *Darsuvt* (Philosophy). Mr. Cowell, the Principal of the college, found a difficulty in making the choice. At last, he asked for Vidyasagar's opinion in the matter. Vidyasagar said,—'To teach the Kavyaprakash to the students of the Rhetoric class, the professor should have a sound knowledge of the *Nyaya* philosophy. Pandit Mahesh Chandra Nyayratna has mastered the whole Nyaya Sastra; I therefore think him to be duly qualified for the post.' Nyayratna was accordingly appointed to the vacant place.

The continued physical and mental sufferings combined with intense afflictions and griefs at the lots of his nearest and dearest relations and friends completely broke down his already impaired health.

A secluded and retired life in some salubrious climate was now absolutely necessary for him. About this time, a Bungalow was notified for sale at Deoghur, a most healthy place in upper Bengal. He offered to purchase it, but the terms being immoderately high, he gave up the idea. He then rented a plot of land, very close to Karmatar, a Station midway between Jamtara and Madhupur on the East Indian Railway Line. The place lies in the Santhal Pergunnas. It had, at that time, a somewhat jungly appearance, being covered on all sides with dense woods, and was, in consequence, very well suited to the purpose. He laid out the land, and erected there a nice Bungalow to his mind. In its compound he planted flower plants and fruit trees, and thus turned it to a most comfortable habitation. The poor, savage Santhals were his only neighbours. The Santhals are believed to be one of the aboriginal tribes of India. They are honest and truthful They soon perceived the flow of natural kindness and benevolence of their new neighbour, and became his objects of love and endearment—his friends and relations. In fact, some of them addressed him father, some brother, some uncle, and so forth. Their poor huts of leaves were overflooded with the flow of Vidyasagar's genial kindness and assumed a gay, cheerful aspect Vidyasagar supplied them with food in hunger, clothes in nudity, medicine in sickness. He fed them with delicious fruits and confectionery. In winter, he gave them warm clothes. He was by their sick-bed, drenching them with physic, dieting them with light food, and nursing them with the tenderest care. He kept with him a large supply of Homoepathic drags for their treatment. The reader is aware that he had acquired a great proficiency in the healing art of Hahnemann. His heart was a fountain of universal love and kindness. Wheresoever he was, there was nothing but love and kindness. In his daily morning walks, he visited the hut of every one of his Santhal neighbours, and very cheerily accepted their little presents of gourd, cucumber, or brinjal. He then returned to his neat and clean villa, accompanied with some of his honest, savage friends, to whom he gave whatever they required. He made them dance their barbarous dances, which gave him an infinite pleasure. In fact, in this country seat he felt a heavenly tranquility and happiness. Not only did he minister to their external improvement and physical comfort, but he also provided for their internal advancement, intellectual culture, and moral correction. For the education of their children, he founded a vernacular school at his own expense.

There were no fish-mongers in the vicinity of the place, as there were very few purchasers of fish. Vidyasagar proclaimed that he would boy all the fish that would be brought to him. The poor Santhals now found a fresh source of income. They brought to him very large quantities of fish, for which he gave them the price they demanded. He then distributed the fish among the

Bengalee gentlemen—officers and servants of the Railway Station and the Post Office. He now and then invited the Babus to dinner, and passed the days that he stayed at the place in merriment. When-ever he went to Karmatar, one of his own children or grandchildren always accompanied him. Sometimes his friends resorted to the place for a change. Vidyasagar received and entertained them hospitably. On one occasion, Pandit Nilmani Nyayalankar being seriously ill, went to Karmatar for restoration of his health. Vidyasagar tended and nursed him with affectionate care. He used to remove the discharges of the patient's bowels and kidneys with his own hands. Nyayalankar felt awkward and ashamed that so great a man should trouble himself with such menial services. But the noble-minded Vidyasagar smiled and said,—'Never mind, my dear, I pay you in earnest,' meaning that Nyayalankar would serve him similarly, in case he himself should fall ill. We have already said, that Vidyasagar was very witty, and whenever an opportunity presented itself, he would be sure to give expression to his merry humour. On one occasion, he attended the Governor's *Darbar*, accompanied by four other Pandits. The Pandits saw that all ether Indians had their heads covered with turbans, except the Bengalees. They enquired of Vidyasagar the cause of it. He smiled, and replied,—'When the Bengalees failed to do any-thing for their father-land, they gave up wearing turbans and thus lightened the weight of its burden.' This, was, no doubt, a merry joke, but very cutting indeed.

One Abhiram Mandal, a Santbal, was employed by Vidyasagar as his chief gardener at Karmatar. The poor savage was a great favourite with his master on account of his truthfulness and honesty. Vidyasagar sometimes sent to him clothes for distribution and cash remittances for payment of monthly allowances to the poor Santhals.

The Santhals were quite enamoured of him Whenever they heard a report of his intended visit, they looked out anxiously for his arrival, and as soon as he arrived, they flocked to him with their little presents—some with gourds, some with cucumbers, some with brinjals, and some with other vegetables of the like nature. A poor Santhal having nothing else to offer to his dear benefactor, brought a cock-fowl for him. Vidyasagar smiled, and producing his holy thread, said to the innocent savage,— 'You see

I am a Brahmin. I cannot accept your present The poor Santhal at once burst into tears, and insisted on his acceptance of the fowl Vidyasagar's tender heart was moved at the sad disappointment of his poor neighbour, and for his satisfaction received it from his hands. The Santhal felt highly delighted. When he was gone, Vidyasagar set free the fowl. On one occasion, another Santhal came to him, accompanied by a woman of his race. He said to Vidyasagar, -—'Would you give this woman a piece of cloth?' The latter replied by way of joke,—'I have no cloth; and why should I give her?' Santhal.—'That won't do; you mast give her a piece of cloth.'

Vidyasagar,—'No. I have none.'

Santhal.—'Let me have your key. I will open your trunk, and see whether you have got cloth.'

Vidyasagar laughed at the simple familiarity of the savage, and handed his key over to him. The; Santhal opened the cheat, and cried out *in* great delight,—'Why, there is an abundance of cloth here.' With this, he drew out a piece of nice cloth, and gave it to the woman.

About this time, Vidyasagar had to suffer a most heart-rending affliction at the loss of his most sincere friend, the Hon'ble Dwarka Nath Mitter, a Judge of the Calcutta High Court, who passed away on the 35th February, 1874. The *Englishman*, a leading Anglo-Indian newspaper, in its issue of the 3rd March of the same year, in noticing the lamented death of the deceased Justice, thus said of him:—"Amongst his more brilliant qualities was his surprising command of the English language; the readiness, the precision and the force with which he used that language are not common even among those who speak it as their mother tongue and were the theme of constant admiration".

The two friends were fellow-workers and co-adjustors in many affairs. They consulted each other on all difficult points. The two were generally of the same opinion. Their opinions diverged only in one case—on the question of the right of inheritance of a fallen woman. The case had been instituted in the High Court before Dwarka Nath's death. Before the decision of the case, Pandits Ishwar Chandra Vidyasagar, Mahesh Chandra Nyayratna, and

Bharat Chandra Siromani were called upon for their opinions. The point at Issue was—if a Hindu widow, who had once inherited a property, subsequently loses her character—whether that fallen woman should be deprived of her inheritance. Vidyasagar was for the inheritance, whilst the other two Pandits were against it. Dwarka Nath was also of opinion that the fallen woman should be deprived of her inheritance, but he could not carry his point. A full bench consisting of ten justices sat to decide the case. Out of the ten, only Mr. Phear agreed with Dwarka Nath. The Hon'ble C. E. Buckland, in his 'Bengal under the Lieutenant-Governors,' says: "The Hindu widow's unchastity case, in which it was contended that property once vested in a widow can never be divested on the ground of subsequent immorality, had a very strong opponent in Mr. Justice Dwarka Nath, with whom Mr. Justice Phear concurred. But the opinion of the majority prevailed, and the widows were left un-disturbed in their course of life".

In this connection, Vidyasagar said to one of his friends, "How could I give a wrong opinion? Supposing I gave one, who should hear me? Of course, I am not a supporter of lewd character; but when one had already inherited a property, how could I say, that one should be divested of it?" In that case, there would be no end of litigations on this plea.' It must be said, that in this case Vidyasagar wanted in foresight, and the whole Hindu community was disappointed in him; but It should be borne *in* mind, that he gave his opinion according to his own conviction. Some insinuate that Vidyasagar was afraid, that if a fallen widow were deprived of her inheritance, obstacles might rise in the way of the furtherance of his widow marriage cause, and he therefore gave his opinion in favour of the inheritance. But such insinuation is quite baseless. Vidyasagar was not a hypocrite—he was not a man to go astray or to designedly mislead others for the sake of his self-interest.

Dwarka Nath often said,—'Vidyasagar is the root of my prosperity. It was he who advised me to appear at the Law Examination. But for his advice, I might have taken a different course.' He had a great fond regard and esteem for Vidyasagar. He is said to have acquired a drinking habit; but he was always very cautious not to offend his friend by giving him occasion to be aware of his intemperance. He often visited Vidyasagar at the latter's residence after Court hours. When he was a pleader, he appeared before him in his professional dress, and even when he became a Judge, he never felt degrading to present himself before his old friend in his gown. Now and then he passed his nights with Vidyasagar. He was a great help to our benevolent hero in many of his noble deeds, particularly in rescuing the poor tenants from the hands of the oppressive zamindars. When Dwarka Nath was still a pleader, some Brahmins one day came to Vidyasagar and charged their Zamindar, Babu Jaykrishna Mukharji of Uttarpara, with usurpation of their Brahmotra (rent-free) lands. Vidyasagar aided them in their law-suits against their Zamindar. At his instance, Dwarka Nath conducted these cases without fee or remuneration.

On one occasion, Dwarka Nath aid to his friend,—'Lest you should think, that 1 return these cases simply because I am not paid for them, I come to offer my explanation. These people have no title to the lands in dispute. Had there been the slightest evidence in their favour, I would surely have given my life for them.' Vidyasagar now saw that Jay Krishna was quite blameless in the matter. He had entertained very different views of the Zamindar, and his esteem for the latter had also lessened a little; but what he heard from Dwarka Nath served to rekindle his former feelings for the wealthy gentleman. He was afterwards heard to say, that he came to learn subsequently that Jay Krishna never usurped the lands of those who could produce evidence in support of their title.

Vidyasagar often praised him for his manly exertions by which he rose to such eminence, and for his very liberal charities. The two had a great intimate familiarity. Vidyasagar always kept himself aloof from politics and political meetings, but he now and then entered the rooms of the British Indian Association, only to have an interview with Jay Krishna Babu.

2

A Scholarly Career

First Steps in Practical Life

Completing his education, Ishwar Chandra Vidyasagar, entered the practical life and proceeded step by step, to that part of his life, where the qualities of his early years developed themselves to their full extent, bringing in, their train, other qualities, equally noble and fascinating. He was now standing on the threshold of his worldly life, which was full of events displaying his intrepidity in danger, vivacity in despondency, love for mankind, disinterestedness in every undertaking, and modesty in prosperity. These qualities were conspicuous in his life at all times, from the very first day of his entrance into the world to the last day of his life. His infinite kindness and unbounded love for all creatures were prominent in almost all his acts.

Unfortunately, his deeds did not meet with general approbation. But this was not Vidyasagar's fault (we shall henceforth call him by this name, which he so gloriously obtained from his College). As men are of different opinions, so they must differ in the appreciation of a deed. However that might be, there is not an iota of doubt, that he was always actuated by unselfish motives and a strong impulse of universal good-will. Whatever he thought good, he tried to accomplish, in spite of every obstacle,

He was never dejected by failures, nor daunted by menaces. He was always untiring in perseverance. He detested laziness. Want of occupation was a source of great annoyance to him. He was never fatigued with toils. Time unemployed hang heavily on him. Occupation was his best recreation. What the famous writer Seadon Smith said on this point, has been amply verified in Vidyasagar's life: "Let every man be occupied, and occupied in the highest employment of which he is capable, and die with the consciousness that he has done the best".

Appointment at Fort William College

Vidyasagar's first appointment was under Mr. Marshall in the Fort William College. This college had been established in Calcutta in the year 1800 for the education of those civilians, who came out from the Halibury College for employment in India, in the different vernaculars of the country. The competitive Civil Service examination had not then been introduced. The students of the Halibury College had to pass an examination in Bengali, Hindi, Urdu, Persian before their appointment, and those that failed to pass it, had to go back to Europe. These civilians were then called the 'Writers of the East India Company, and the house where they lodged were called after them, the 'Writers' Building.' In the midst of this building, there was the Fort William College with its office. In this office were employed a 'Head Writer' or 'Cashier', and under him, two to three clerks to do clerical work. Besides these, a Hindu Pandit and a Mahomedan Maulavi were employed as teachers. The former Head Pandit, Madhusudan Tarkalankar having died, the post was vacant. Mr. Marshall, the Secretary to the College, was on the look-out for a qualified man. He set his eyes on Ishwar Chandra Vidyasagar, whom he had known for many years, while he was Secretary to the Sanskrit College, to be uncommonly intelligent, exceedingly laborious, highly persevering, and generally proficient in every branch. He called personally at the Sanskrit College, and enquired for Vidyasagar of Jay Narayan Tarkapanchanan, who, in his turn, informed Thakurdas, Vidyasagar's father, of everything. Vidyasagar was, at this time in his native village, Birsingha, enjoying the sweet pleasures of a country seat and the happiness of his mother's company.

Thakurdas at once dent for him. He soon reached Calcutta, and was appointed to the vacant post *in* December, 1841, on a salary of fifty rupees a month.

In this connection, we may note here, in passing, that Mr. Marshall was a great appreciator of merits. When the post of the Head Pandit of the Fort William College fell vacant, there were many candidates for the situation. Babu Kalidas Datta, a resident of Bowbazar, was in terms of great intimacy with Mr. Marshall. They had' a great affection for each other. Kalidas Babu earnestly recommended a particular Pandit, a friend of his, tor the post. But Mr. Marshall rejected his earnest solicitations, saying that he had already selected Vidyasagar for the post When Kalidas Babu heard Vidyasagar's name mentioned, he approved of the choice, for he had also known Ishwar Chandra for a long time.

During his employment in the Fort William College, which was his first appointment, Vidyasagar displayed an independence of spirit and love of justice, which were conspicuous throughout his life. We have mentioned before, that those would be civilians, who failed at the vernacular examinations, had to go back to, England disappointed. Mr. Marshall felt a great pity for them, and, to avoid their disappointment, he requested Vidyasagar to soften the stiffness of the examinations and to take a somewhat lenient view of their answers, on which Vidyasagar openly declared in unequivocal terms, that he would rather resign his post than act dishonourably. Mr. Marshall, who was an upright man himself, and a great lover of justice, was highly pleased, rather than annoyed, at the honesty of his young subordinate. Here was only the beginning of that noble heroism which was so-conspicuous,- throughout his after-life; He was a poor man, bred and brought up amidst the privations and troubles of indigence. He had no one to back him. A post of fifty rupees of those days was more than a valuable property to a man of his circumstances. But still even for the sake of that, he was not prepared to sacrifice his conscience, and condescend to meanness and foul play. The reader will find many such instances in his later-life.

Shortly after his installation to this post, Vidyasagar began to learn English and Hindi simultaneously. The would-be civilians of the Fort William College had to undergo monthly examianations.

Vidyasagar's main duty was to examine their answer papers. Besides this, he had to teach Mr. Marshall Sanskrit. He had thus to come always in contact with the British. Hence was the necessity of his learning English. He had moreover, to see the Hindi answer papers. A knowledge of Hindi was, therefore, absolutely necessary for him. Hindi, like Bengali, has its origin in Sanskrit, and bears much similarity to Bengali as well as to Sanskrit. So Hindi was not difficult for him to learn. He engaged a Hindi teacher on a monthly salary of ten rupees, and learned the Hindi language in a short time. But the acquisition of English, which was a foreign tongue, was not so easy. He had to spend a great deal of time and labour, and even some money, on it. Nothing was impossible with the persevering Vidyasagar.

Most of those that have been reputed as great geniuses, and who have immortalised their names by noble' deeds, were bred and brought up in poverty. Nay, some of them were, in their early life employed in humble occupations, But they were, always far superior to the ordinary rank. No-dififculty was insurmountable to them. They never gave up a task, simply because it was difficult. Had they not bean endowed with this superior merit, they could never have left such indelible conspicuous footmarks for the guidance of their descendants. Garfield, one of the late Presidents of the United States of America, was the son of a farmer. The great Napoleon, who rose to be Emperor of France, was at first employed as a private. Benjamin Franklin was a printed.

The great poet Chaucer was an ordinary soldier. Shakspeare was an actor. But why seek other countries? What was Keshab Chander Sen, the great Bengali orator? Be was at first a mere clerk of twenty rupees. Harish Chander Mukharji, the first independent-spirited Editor of the "Hindu Patriot" was an humble clerk. Lord Clive, the Founder of the British Empire in India, came out to this country as a clerk to the East India Company. The great Vidyasagar, of whom we are speaking, and who, by dint of perseverance, assiduity and honesty, rose to such eminence, began with a post of fifty rupees. It was not, therefore, very strange that he should apply himself to learn English with his usual zeal and earnestness, and be able to master it soon. The famous Doctor Durga Charan Banarji, father of Babu Surendranath Banarji, the present great orator of Bengal, and renowned Editor of "The Ben-galee," was his first English teacher. Durga Charan Babu was not a doctor (medical practitioner) then. He was, at that time, a teacher in the Hare School. He used daily to visit Vidyasagar's house, and there engage himself in various pastimes. The post of the Head Writer in the Fort William College havings at this time, fallen vacant, Durga Charan Babu was appointed to the post, on a monthly salary of eighty rupees, by Mr. Marshall, on the recommendation of Vidyasagar, There was thus a great intinriacy between the two. "While employed in this office, Durga Charan Babu attended the Medical College lectures as an Out-student,' and afterwards adopted the profession of an independent medical practitioner, in which he was eminently successful He was a great help to Vidyasagar in his many acts of philanthropy.

Vidyasagar's second teacher was Raj Narayan Basu, with whom he read English for a short time. In this connection the two gentlemen formed and intimate friendship, which lasted to life. His next teacher was Babu Nil Madhav Mukharji, pupil of Babu Durga Charan Banarji, of whom mention has been made before. At last, he entertained the services of Babu Raj Narayan Gupta then a student of the Hindu College, as his private English teacher on a stipend of fifteen rupees a months To learn European Mathematics he used to go to Ananda Krishna Basu, Amrita Lal Mitra, and Srinath Ghosh at the Sobhabazar Raj house. He made some attempts to learn the subject, but it did; not suit his taste. Besides, he considered the subject dry, and at last gave it up.

He now pursued the course of his natural taste, and made great self-advancement. When one devotes himself to the study of a particular subject, which is agreeable to his taste, one can make much improvement in it. On the contrary, when one is forced to take up a subject, which one has no liking for, one cannot devote all his energies to it, and, consequently, can make no progress in it. As is the case with one's education, so is the case with one's calling. In this connection one writer says;— "It is often seen that many persons do not succeed in their business, simply because they could not, or were not allowed, to make a proper selection, They have not the particular capacity for the occupations they have been engaged in. For instance, one who has no capacity for the Law, but for Medicine, has taken up the Law for one's profession; or, one who has no taste for Medicine, but only for Engineering, has been made to adopt the Medical profession. How can such a one expect success?"

Surely, one ought to be allowed to follow his Own inclinations. The above writer also says, that a man's bodily and mental marks clearly indicate what business he is fit for. Some European philosophers are of the same opinion too. But this is not always true. Doctor Gilbert has come to the Conclusion, that a large head is the seat of intellect and genius. But, when we take into account the heads of such intelligent and talented great men, as Alexander, Julius Caesar, Frederick the Great, Byron, Bacon, Plato, Aristotle, and others, we arrive at a different conclusion. Would it not be batter then if, instead of relying on these. doubtful conclusions, every one had tried to follow and better the calling of his forefathers. The ancient Hindus bestowed their bast thoughts on the subject, and apportioned a particular occupation for each, to be strictly adhered to, by his descendants. Thus originated the Hindu caste system, the propriety or otherwise of which we leave the reader to judge.

After giving up Mathematics, Vidyasagar began to read Shakspeare with Babu Ananda Krishna Basu. For this purpose, he often frequented the Sobhabazar Raj house, which, in a few days, had also the effect of making him acquainted with Raja Radha Kanta Dev Bahadur. It so happened that, one day, when Raja Bahadur was washing his face and hands after dinner, Vidyasagar passed, by him, on his way to Ananda Krishna Babu. Raja Bahadur caught a glimpse of him, and enquired of a relation who was near by;— 'Who is that stout and strong, handsome Brahmin youth who passed by us? His very appearance indicate that he is a man of uncommon genius, Send for him at once.' Vidyasagar immediately appeared before the Raja Bahadur, who heard, from him, everything connected with his life. The Raja was highly delighted at his conversation, and at once knew him to be a highly talented man. Ishwar Chandra was, at that time, an ordinary youth with only the title *Vzdyasagar* recently obtained from his College. He was not then the famous, great Vidyasagar of later years.

It was in this Sobhabazar Raj house that Vidyasagar was acquainted with Babu Akshay Kumar Dutt, one of the greatest Bengali writers, and formed an intimacy with him. Akshay Babu was not then the Editor of the *Tattvabodhini Patrika.* An association called the *Tattvabodhini Sabha* had been formed in connection with the Brahmo Samaj in the month of October, 1839. From the year. 1843, this association began to publish a Bengali monthly magazine, called the *Tattvabodhini Patrika,* under the care and patronage of Babu Devendra Nath Tagore and some other eminent men of the time. Akshay Babu had been a member of this association from the beginning, and he was afterwards intrusted with the edition of this magazine, which he did honestly and creditably for twelve years, up to 1855.

All the contributions to the Tattvabodhini Patrika passed through the hands of Ananda Krishna Babu and some other educated men of the time, who had to go through the articles, and make necessary corrections. One day, when Vidyasagar was sitting with Ananda Krishna Babu in the latter's house, a messenger appeared with a piece of Akshay Babu's composition intended for the periodical. Ananda Krishna Babu read out the article to Vidyasagar, and asked his opinion about it. It was a piece of translation from English, impregnated with European ideas and notions. The former translations of Akshay Babu were all of this sort. In reply to Ananda Krishna Babu's query, Vidyasagar said that the style of the composition was not bad, but that it was somewhat impregnated with European ideas. He then made some alterations and corrections in it, at the request of Ananda Krishna Babu, Subsequent to this, Vidyasagar had to make such corrections on several occasions, Akshay Babu saw that these corrections were far superior to the usual ones, and wondered who could be the author of them. To satisfy his curiosity he, one day, appeared in person before Ananda Krishna Babu, and learned that they were Vidyasagar's doings. It was thus that Akshay Babu came in contact with the young pundit and formed his acquaintance. By degrees, this acquaintance grew into sincere friendship, which ripened with their age.

This was a happy combination for the newly-born Bengali language. Every native of Bengal should commemorate the eventful period in his heart of hearts, and rejoice in the fortunate union. Both Ishwar Chandra Vidyasagar and Akshay Kumar Datta may be said to have laid down their lives for the development of their mother language. The combination of Addison and Steel is considered by the English to be the origin of the progress and spread of modern English, and they still congratulate on the happy event. Many educated Bengalees too look upon the day of the union of Addison and Steel as a day of their national festival But how many Bengalees are there who ever call to mind the fortunate combination of Ishwar Chandra Vidyasagar and Askhay Kumar Datta? How ungrateful we are!

For some time, a sub-commitee, styled the "Paper-committee," was formed in connection with the *Tattvabodhini Sabha.* Ananda Krishna Basu, Raj Narayan Basu, Rajendra Lai Mitra, Ishwar Chandra Vidyasagar, Radha Ballabh Ray, Syama Charan Mukharji, Prasanna Kumar Sarvvadhikari, and Ananda Chandra Vedantavagis were elected members for this Sub-committee. These members were designated paper-examiners, and Akshay Babu was paper-editor. The *Tattvabodhini Sabka* was Devendra Nath Babu's beloved object. He had always the association at his heart. If he found anywhere anything new and useful, he tried to bring it in. He had introduced the "paper-committee," in imitation of a committee of the same name in the Asiatic Society. The business of the newly formed committee was to examine and correct all the books and writings intended to be published by the *Tattvabodhini Sabha.* No such writing or book could be published unless and until approved of by this committee. Great benifits were derived from this system. Nothing incorrect or unchaste, either in language or sense, even if it were from the pen of a paper-examiner, was; printed. Akshay Babu himself admitted that he was greatly benefited by his being associated with Vidyasagar in this way.

Proposed by Babu Akshay Kumar Datta, and Seconded by all other members, Vidyasagar was nominated a member for the "Paper-Committee" In this connection he came in touch with Babu Devendra Nath Tagore, who since that time bore a great respect for him. It may not be out of place to note here, in passing, that Vidyasagar had no connection with the then *Brahma Samaj.*

He was connected only with the "Paper-Committee". Even Akshay Babu, who edited the Tattvabodhini Patrika, had to seek the opinion and permission of the "Paper-Committee" on his own compositions, before they could be published in the periodical. In support of this, we quote below a copy of some correspondence on the subject, which passed between editor and some of the examiners;

"I beg to send herewith a copy of an article on the "History of the Kavirpanthis". Please do the needful.

Tattvabodhini Sabha, Sd Akshay Kumar Datta
177O Sak, 14 Asharh Paper-editor.'

> "1 am glad to read the copy sent by you. It been nicely got up and written *in* easy, chaste language. I, therefore, gladly approve of its publication in the Patrika (magazine). *Sd. Ishwar Chandra Sharma*"

> "The corrections and alterations made by Ishwar Chandra Vidyasagar here and there have been *very* nice. *Sd Syama Charan Mukhopadhyay*".

It was at the instance of Babu Akshay Kumar Datta, that Vidyasagar commenced publishing his translation of the Mahabharat in February, 1848, in the sixty-seventh issue of the *Tattvabodhini Patrika.* Some portions of its Adiparva had only been brought into publication, when Babu. Kali Prasanna Singha requested him to desist, and, with his permission, began to publish his translation of the great epic. Kali Prasanna Babu himself has acknowledged it:

> "In the translation of the Mahabharat I have had to seek and obtain much assistance from many learned men. I am, therefore, under a deep debt of obligation and gratefulness to them. Of these, my venerable friend, Ishwar Chandra Vidyasagar, was the foremost. He had himself begun a translation of the Mahabharat and already published a part of it, in several issues of the *Tattvabodhini Patrika,* as well as in the form of pamphlets; But when he came to learn that I was; endeavouring to issue a translation of the great poem,

> he very kindly desisted from his translation, If he had not done so, I could never have finished my version. Not only did he forego his desire of translating the Mahabharat, but took the trouble of going through my translation whenever he had leisure for it, and even personally attended my printing press and superintended the translation of the Mahabharat, when business called me away from' Calcutta, now and then. In fact, language, written or spoken, cannot express the extent of benefits I have obtained from Vidyasagar in different forms at different times, since I was a student".

Before he commenced the translation of the Mahabharat, Vidyasagar had written two other Bengali books, *Basudeva Charita* and *Vetala Panchavingsatu* In the language of these two books-he has amply proved his powers of translation, of which hereafter.

Babu Akshay Kumar Datta, the worthy editor of the "Tattvabodhini Patrika," having resigned his post for ill-health, a motion moved by Babu Kanai Lal Pain and seconded by Ishwar Chandra Vidyasagar, was brought forward before a meeting of the *Tattvabodkini Sabka* for award of some pension to the able editor. Babu Devendra Nath Tagore opposed the motion. His argument was that the pension was allowable, if the income of the "Tattva-bodhini Patrika" left a margin for it; but that when the income of the "Tattvabodhini Sabha" and that of the "Tattvabodhini Patrika" were combined, no such pension was judiciously and rightly allowable. Btit the motion was carried by a majority of votes, and a monthly pension of twenty-five rupees was granted to Babu Akshay Kumar Datta. There can be no doubt, that the pension was granted chiefly through the exertions of Ishwar Chandra Vidyasagar.

Some time after the resignation of Babu Askhay Kumar Datta, Vidyasagar also cut off his connection with the *Tattvabodhini Sabka*. This was owing to difference of opinion with Babu Devendra Nath Tagore in some respects. No wonder that a conflict of the opinions of two such independent-spirited men should bring about their separation. The friction of two pieces of dry, hard wood, or |he collision of a piece of steel against a piece of flint is sure to produce sparkles of fire. It was for a similar reason, that Keshab Chander Sen and some of his associates severed their connection with the *Brahma Santaj.*

When Vidyasagar was himself engaged in learning English privately at his own residence, he had, in his turn, to give private lessons in Sanskrit to a number of elderly scholars. Syama Charan Sarkar, one of the translators of the Sudder Court, Ramratan Mukharji, Nilmani Mukharji, Raj Krishna Banarji, and some other gentlemen were among his pupils. His mode of imparting instruction was so ingenious, that he could make his pupils easily master even a difficult subject The learned professors of the Sanskrit College were quite amazed at his novel mode of instruction. He took great pains for the education of his pupils. To enable the reader to form some idea of his mode of instruction, we- will try to describe briefly how Raj Krishna Babu acquired his knowledge in Sanskrit from Pandit Ishwar Chandra Vidyasagar.

Raj Krishna Babu was a grandson of the late famous Hriday Ram Bandyopadhyay of Bow-bazar. He was; at this time, only 15 or 16 years old. His house stood in front of that of Ishwar Chandra Vidyasagar. He had studied English for some time in the Hindu College, but had given it up at this early age. He had formed an acquaintance of Vidyasagar, and used to visit his house every morning and evening. One day, he heard Dinabandhu (Vidyasagar's younger brother) reading Kalidas's *Meghadnta* in tones of music. Raj Krishna Babu was fascinated by the young boy's sweet recital of the elegant poem, and he felt a strong desire to learn Sanskrit. He gave out his mind to Vidyasagar, who promised to teach him the ancient language. But Vidyasagar was afraid, that Raj Krishna Babu was now grown too old to begin with the *Mugdhabodha* or any other Sanskrit grammar, and that he might lose his patience, and give it up as a mere waste of time. Vidyasagar, therefore, thought of devising some method, by which he could make the learning of Sanskrit attractive, as well as easy, to his pupil. So he dismissed Raj Krishna Babu for that day, and set himself on thinking of a novel mode of teaching, Grammar. When Raj Krishna Babu called the next morning, he found to his utter astonishment, that a Short abridgments the Sanskrit grammar, *Mugdhabodha,* in Bengali characters, from the Alphabet to the

Inflexion of Verbs,·composed by Vidyasagar, Was ready for his use. This was the basis of Vidyasagar's *Upakramanika,* a brief Sanskrit Grammar in Bengali. *Upukramanika* has opened a new, easy way to the Sanskrit Literature. This single treatise is sufficient to clearly demonstrate Vidyasagar's superior intellect and ingenuity.

With the aid of this manuscript, abridged gram-mar and an elementary Sanskrit book printed at the Baptist Press, Raj. Krishna Babu began to learn Sanskrit. In three months, he acquired a little knowledge of the language, and had some conception of its grammar. At the end of this period, he began to read the *Mugdhabodha,* which he, by dint of his indefatigable zeal and toil, and unremitting, perseverance, and through Vidyasagar's ingenious mode of instruction, mastered in six months. He then applied himself to the study of the Sanskrit Literature. Vidyasagar now urged Raj Krishna Babu to prepare himself for the Junior Scholarship 'examination of the Sanskrit College.

The system of Junior and Senior Scholarship examinations had been introduced into Sanskrit College by Mr, Marshall. Raj Krishna Babu applied himself in right carnest, and was fully prepared for the examination, when Vidyasagar suddenly heard that a poor Brahmin boy was getting the Junior Scholarship of eight rupees. Vidyasagar was afraid that if Raj Krishna Babu should appear at the examination and succeed in winning the scholarship, the poor boy would be deprived of his only means. He informed Raj Krishna Babu of everything, and told him to desist, for the present, from his attempts at the Junior Scholarship examination. He then urged his apt pupil to prepare himself for the Senior Scholarship examination; at which Raj Krishna Babu said: 'Do you think, I shall be able to qualify myself for that?'

Vidyasagar replied: 'Why not; but, mind, you shall have to take more pains. Only if you accompany me every day to the Fort William College, I believe, I shall be able to make you fit for the examination.' Raj Krishna Babu agreed to this, and accompanied him daily to the Fort William College. Vidyasagar was occupied in teaching' the Civilians and in doing other duties up to 3 P.M. after which he devoted himself wholly in giving lessons to Raj

Krishna Babu till sun-set. They then returned to their houses, and after supper, again applied themselves *in* giving and receiving instruction to a late hour in the night. By such unremitting toil and perseverance, both on the part of the pupil and the teacher, Raj Krishna Babu was fully instructed in Sanskrit Grammar, Belles-lettres and Smriti, in two years and a halt. He appeared at the Senior Scholarship examination of 1843-44, and passed creditably with a second grade scholarship of fifteen rupees a month. Two years after this, he won a first grade scholarship of twenty rupees. He had a great mind to appear at the next higher (i.e. final) examination, but, Unfortunately, his health having been very much impaired by his excessive toils, he was obliged to forego his design, and remove to' a sanitarium' tor recruit his broken health.

The news of this unparalleled success soon spread like bonfire; and surprised even the learned professors of the' Sanskrit College. People of all' classes daily crowded Vidyasagar's house, with an eager desire to have a sight of the unusually intelligent and hardworking pupil and of his ingenious and clever teacher. In fact, the mode of instruction adopted by Vidyasagar was quite novel, and was a' conspicuous proof of his inventive genius; Was it very strange then, that the people were so curious about it? When the famous Scotch author Carlyle devised his new plan, and books were published under the novel device, many learned and wise men of the time hurried to the farm' of Dumfrey in the' hilly tracts of far Scotland to have a sight of the famous author. Even Emterson, the great philosophical writer of America', visited Scotland, and satisfied his curiosity by seeing Carlyle with his own eyes. Such is the fascinating attraction of all novel, ingenious plans and methods.

Madan Mohan Tarkalankar was one of Vidyasagar's early friends. They had been acquainted since both of then; were in the Grammar class, and they were slowly drawn to each other. By degrees, they formed an intimate friendship, which ripened with their age and made them very closely united. In later years, whenever Vidyasagar attemped at, or began, a noble, benevolent deed, Madan Mohan was always by his side, lending a helping hand with all his zeal and ardpur. In some cases the two were found to be equally eager and interested, and it would then be very difficult to distinguish the principal from the assistant, Vidyasagar's friendship was always sincere and uniform. He could never be apathetic to one whom he had once loved. Vidyasagar regarded Madan Mohan as if he was his own brother, and always sought for opportunities to do him a good turn. It was mainly through Vidyasagar's exertions that his friend, Madan Mohan, obtained the situation of Head Pandit in the Calcutta Bengali Pathsala, After this, when the latter was acting as Head Pandit of the Barasat Government School, a teacher was required in the Fort William College to teach Hindu Law to the civilians. At the instance of Vidyasagar, Madan Mohan Tarkalankar was appointed to the post on a monthly salary of forty rupees.

Pandit Ityaraka Nath Vidyabhushan and Giris Chandra Vidyaratna, were two of his friends. At the time of which we are speaking, the post of the Second Teacher of the Grammar class, and that of the Librarian of the Sanskrit College, fell vacant, The salaries attached to the posts were 50 and 30 rupees respectively. Babu Rassomoy Dutt was then the Secretary to the College. There were many candidates for the two situations, and, at the suggestion of Vidyasagar, it was decided upon to hold an examination to fill up the vacancies. At this examination, Dvaraka Nath Vidyabhushan and Giris Chandra Vidyaratna stood first and second respectively.

But Rassomoy Babu, for reasons best known to himself, instead of conferring the post of the Second Teacher on Vidyabhushan, precipitately appointed him to the post of the Librarian, Vidyabhushan felt himself aggrieved, and Vidyasagar lost no time in informing Mr. Marshall of the injustice. Mr. Marshall brought the matter to the notice of Dr. Mouett the then secretary to the Educataion Council. Dr. Mouett, overturned Rassonpy Babu's arrangement, and appointed Dvaraka Nath Vidyabhushan as Second Teacher of Grammar, and Giris Chandra Vidyaratna as Librarian.

It may be still fresh in the reader's mind, how through the exertions of Ishwar Chandra Vidyasagar, then a mere student of the Sanskrit College, Pandit Jay Narayan Tarkapanchanan had been appointed to the post vacated by the death of Nim Chand Siromani. The reader will find many such in-stances in Vidyasagar's life.

Continuance in the Fort William College

We have stated before, that Mr. Marshall used to read Sanskrit with Vidyasagar, and receive from him lessons in that language. He had already acquired a tolerable knowledge of Bengali, and he preferred to converse with Vidyasagar in that tongue. The latter, therefore, wrote to him letters in Bengali, as occasion needed. One day, he was unable to attend his office on account of the illness of one of his relations living in his house. He informed Mr. Marshall of this, in a letter written in Bengali. Thus by degrees Vidyasagar rose in influence and eminence, while still in the Fort William College.

The more Mr. Marshall came in contact with Vidyasagar, the more was he led to be pleased at the latter's keen intellect, sound knowledge, excellent character, intrepid spirit, dignified manners, and noble generosity. He had a firm trust in whatever Vidyasagar said or did. He never did anything without consulting Vidyasagar. Whenever Dr. Mouett, the Secretary to the Education council, had a necessity for some information on the Sanskrit Literature or Hindu Religion, he used to go to Mr. Marshall for the information. The latter, in his turn, had the matter decided by reference to Vidyasagar. It was in this way, that Dr. Mouett came to know Vidyasagar, whom he henceforth regarded with much esteem and trust. Gradually he had a great affection for Vidyasagar, and was ever his well-wisher and benefactor.

Shortly after he had entered the Fort William College, Vidyasagar had to witness a great change in the educational policy of this country. He was intimately connected with the education department, and under this department, he had to bring about many alterations, and introduce new plans, We will, therefore, try to notice them briefly.

When Ishwar Chandra first entered the Sanskrit College, as a student, in 1829, English education had not much spread in this country. Some respect-able residents of Calcutta and its neighbourhood were the first to begin to appreciate English education, and try to introduce it into this country. Through the exertions of Hare, Harrington, East, and some other generous Europeans and a number of influential natives of this country, a school was set up in the premises of Gora Chand Basak of

Garanhata on Monday, the 20th of January, 1817. It was the groundwork of the Hindu College of after years. There was also another party who were in favour of diffusing Sanskrit education throughout the country, and the government of the time sided with them. But ultimately, on the petition of Raja Ram Mohan Ray, backed by Hare and Wilson, Government altered its former policy and resolved to propagate Western education in this land of the Hindus. After much efforts, a building for the accomodation of the Hindu and Sanskrit Colleges was erected at a cost of one lac and twenty-four thousand rupees an a plot of land presented for the purpose by the well-renowned, munificent David Hare. Hare is no more, but his name will be ever cherished very dearly in the heart of every English-educated Bengali. But for his indefatigable exertions and munificent gifts, the current of education in this country would have taken a very different course. In 1825, the two Colleges were set up in this new building.

Heretofore, the administration of the education department was in the hands of a Committee known by the name of "General Committee of Public Instruction". This committee had been started *in* 1823. The dispute of the two parties as to whether Western or Eastern education was beneficial to this country, alluded to before, continued for twelve years even" after the foundation of this committee. At last, by the decision of Lord Macaulay, the promoters of Western education gained the victory. In the year 1839, Lord Auckland, the then Governor-General of India, declared in his Minute that English should be the medium of imparting Instruction in the Arts, Sciences, and Philosophy of Europe, that the Vernacular Schools already existing in the country should be placed in a more perfect working order, that equal encouragements should be given to the students of English and Vernacular, and that the vernacular languages should be; taught along with English.

From this time forward the Committee of Public Instruction began to supervise the working of the new system, and the current of English education began to flow vigorously: The liberty of the Press had already been dealared in 1835. The use of Persian as Court language was interdicted in the year 1837. The native judicial officers of the country were entrusted with more powers. Consequently the working of the new system found fresh fields of expansion. The Committee of Public Instruction divided Bengal into nine divisions. A college was; started in each of these divisions, and an Anglo-Bengali school was set up in each district of these divisions. In the year 1852, the Committee of Public Instruction made over charge of the education department to a more powerful association, viz. "The Education Council". Vidyasagar had to bring about many revisions under this Council, of which hereafter.

While Vidyasagar was employed as a teacher in the Fort William College, Lord Hardinge, the then Governor-General of India, came to visit the College, one day, on inspection duty, and had a long talk with Vidyasagar on various topics. In course of conversation, Vidyasagar complained of the hard lot of the students of the Sanskrit College. He said that they had now no prospects. The post *of Judge-Pandit,* which had so long been reserved for them", had been abolished. The numerical strength of the College was, in consequence, falling off. It was, therefore, proper that government should do something for them. It was finally settled that a number of vernacular schools should be established in the country, and the teachers for these schools should be taken from among the students of the Sanskrit College, 101 such schools were established in the different parts of the country from 1844 to I846, and they were styled "Hardinge Schools" after the name of their founder. These schools were set up in imitation of Western schools for the propagation of Bengali education, and Vidyasagar was not wholly unconnected with them. He took great pains for their advancement.

The selection of teachers for these schools by examination, and their appointment were entrusted to Mr. Marshall and Vidyasagar. The latter had now to face difficulties of a strange sort. The elderly professors of the Sanskrit College and some other private Pandits turned to be his bitter enemies. The professors grudged his influence with the authorities that young Vidyasagar was charged with the examination of the new teachers in preference to them, who were Car superior to him both in age and experience. The other Pandits were highly displeased with: him, because merit, and no favour, was his maxim. He gave away the posts to the more worthy candidates. He showed, neither favour nor bias. No consideration of any kind, either of friendship, relationship, or recommendation, found place in his conscientious heart. The disappointed Pandits began to indulge in vile slanders of Vidyasagar. But the just and heroic Vidyasagar, who had not shown the slightest favour to the civilians even at the recommendation of Mr. Marshall, his official superior and patron, was not a man to be intimidated, and to lose heart, by such mean slanders and envy. He acted up to the dictates of his own conscience. It was quite against his nature to do any thing which in his judgement, was not right and proper.

Immediately after his appointment in the Fort William College, Vidyasagar's first impulse was to relieve his father from the troubles of his toil-some servitude. Some say, that shortly after he had got his first appointment, his father had an accident on his way to office, and that this led Vidyasagar to urge him to give up his office. But we have no authority on that point. However that might be, Vidyasagar said to his father one day:— 'You see, father, I now earn 50 rupees a month, and this would be quite sufficient to cover our expenses. Why should you then work? I shall give you 20 rupees every month. Please, go home and enjoy rest. His father hesitated a little, but, at the earnest importunity of his son, was fain to accede to his terms. He resigned his situation and went to Birsingha, where Vidyasagar used to remit his promised 20 rupees regularly, month after month.

The remaining 30 rupees he spent on his house in Calcutta. He had, at this time, his two younger brothers and five cousins living with him, besides a menial servant, by name Sriram, and by caste, a barber. Of the five cousins, two were sons of his father's brother, two were sons of his father's sister, and the other was a son of his mother's sister. There were thus nine members (including, himself) in Calcutta, to maintain with 30 rupees. Besides, several outsiders and visitors had to be fed almost daily. There was no cook in the establishment. All the inmates of his house, not excepting Vidyasagar himself, had, by turns, to do the cooking. Dear reader, do you see wherein Vidyasagar's greatness lay? He was the master of the house, earning 50 rupees a month. He could indulge in luxuries. He could engage a cook. But he did nothing of the kind. As soon as he had the means at his command, his first impulse was to relieve his parent's troubles. In his childhood he had heard from his father the tales of his early distress; When a student in Calcutta, he had witnessed, with his own eyes, the pains and sufferings of his father. He had seen him remove and cleanse his sons' soil with his own hands. How could then a man of Vidyasagar's character act otherwise than what he did? What else did he do? Quite regardless of his own inconvenience, he defrayed the maintenance of distant relations and some other persons wholly unconnected with him, and divided with them? equally the domestic works of his household. Was this not greatness of heart? How many men of means are there now, who would consent to act like Vidyasagar under similar circumstances?

We have already seen, that while a scholar in the Sanskrit College he showed his kindness of heart by giving food and clothing to the needy, and by succourirg the poor and distrest, out of his paltry scholarship funds; He was now earning 50 rupees a month, out of which he gave 20 rupees to his father, and reserved the rest for his establisment expenditure in Calcutta, He defrayed the expenses most economically, and what he could thus save out of the 30 rupees, he spent gladly in feeding the hungry and in succouring, the distrest. In 1843, Gangadhar Tarkavagis, one of the professors of the Sanskrit College, had an attack of Cholera.

No sooner did the news reach Vidyasagar, than he hastened to the spot, accompanied with his friend, Doctor Durga Charan Banarji, of whom' mention has been made before. Durga Charan Babu was engaged in the treatment of the patient, and Vidyasagar removed the discharges with his own hands; He paid for the medicines out of his own pocket. Whenever he saw or heard of a poor, helpless man suffering from illness, he hurried to him, and nursed him tenderly, and supplied him with medicines and diet out of his own funds.

On one occasion, Vidyasagar was told that *one* Isan Chandra Bhattacharya, nephew (sister's son) of Professor Jay Narayan Tarkapanchanan of Narikeldanga, was saffering from Cholera. He presented himself there in the night, and provided for the patient's treatment. He took articles of bedding from his own house, and with them", made a comfortable bed for the sufferer. His favourite disciple, Raj Krishna Babu, said to one of his friends:— 'He (*i.e.* Vidyasagar) had often to act similarly. It is not possible for me to recollect all the deeds of his unfeigned, disinterested benevolence. They are too many for me to en umferafe; and for you to hear patiently. The recollection of the benevolent acts of that incarnation of kindness calls his noble image vividly to mind'. The very thought of him: rends my heart and makes tears flow down in torrents. Alas! We shall no more find a man, equal to him in charitableness and kindness.'

On another occasion, a domestic in the employ of a well-to-do householder, who lived in a house in front of Vidyasagar's lodgings, having been seized with Cholera, was sent away by his master and abandoned in the streets. The poor sufferer had no one to look after him, or to give him a drop of water. No sooner did Vidyasagar hear of it, than he hastened to the spot. He carried the unfortunate man on his shoulders to his lodgings, and gently laid him down on his own bed. He placed the poor man under the medical treatment of his friend, Doctor Durga Charan Banarji, paid for his medicines out of his own pocket, and nursed hint faith great care and tenderness. He thus saved the life of the helpless man, who recovered *in* a few days. But for his kindness, the unfortunate man must have died in the streets. Gentle reader, was not Vidyasagar a truly great and benevolent man?

Allusion has already been made of Vidyasagar's disinterested forwardness in' securing, situations for has friends, relations and acquaintances, of worth' and ability. The reader has seen how he secured appointments for Jay Narayan Tarkapanchanan, Madan Mohan Tarkalankar, Dvaraka Nath Vidyabhushan and Giris Chandra Vidyaratna. In this unselfish work of benevolence, he had sometimes to suffer pecuniary losses and even undergo physical pains. While he was still employed in the Fort William Collet on a salary of 50 rupees, the post of the fast teacher of the Grammar class in the Sanskrit College fell vacant. The post carried a monthly salary of 90 rupees. Here was a great chance of vidyasagar's own promotion. Dr. Mouett, Secretary to the Education Council, called on Mr. Marshall to consult on the selection of a competent man for the post. Mr. Marshall recommended Vidyasagar. The situation was accordingly offered him, but he declined the offer. The real cause of his refusal was, that he had already given word to the famous professor, Taranath Tarkavachaspati that he would secure him a suitable situation. He knew Tarkavachaspati to be a most worthy man versed in all the diffèrent branches of the Sanskrit literature, and he now took this opportunity to fulfil his promise. He recommended Tarkavachaspati to Mr. Marshall, saying that Vachaspati was the best grammarian of the time, which he sincerely believed.

This was Saturday, and the appointment was to be made on Monday, Taranath Tarkavachaspati was, at this time, at Kalna, somè 50 miles away from Calcutta, The postal system then was not so well organised as at present. There was no railway. *A* great difficulty now faced Vidyasagar. How was he to inform Tarkavachaspaty of this happy news? He could not communicate it by a letter, as it would not reach him in time; and even if it should reach him, what certainty was there, that he would accept the post? Tarkavachaspati had already opened a *Tol* at a, and engaged himself in money-lendingness. What was Vidyasagar to do now? He was not long in thinking. That very night he started on foot for Kalna, accompanied with a relation of his.

They walked the whole night, and at noon of the next day (Sunday), reached Tarka-vachàspati's house. Both Vachaspati and his father were wonder-struck, when they heard from Vidyasagar the cause of his advent, and they knew not bow to thank him for such disinterested benevolence. When they saw, that he had walked such a long distance in the night, merely to keep his promise, without at all caring for his own interest, they were touched to the very core of their heart, and poured forth their choicest blessings on the young hero's head. They declared in one voice;—'Glory to you, Vidyasagar! You are not a man, but a heavenly god in human form. He started again for Calcutta the same day, on foot as before, with Tarkavachaspati's application and testimonials, leaving his relation behind to return by boat, who was too much exhausted to be able to walk a step farther. But Vidyasagar felt no uneasiness or difficulty. He reached Calcutta the next day (Monday) in time only to be able to hand over Vachaspati's application and testimonials to Mr. Marshal}, who in his turn, recommended Tarkavachaspati to government. In a few days, Vachaspati arrived at Calcutta and received his appointment letter.

Vidyasagar was not only a strong man mentally and morally, but physically also. He was a good pedestrian.

Many stories are told of his abilities at pedestrianism. At first sight, these stories seem incredible, but they are as true as anything. It is said, that even in his declining years, when he was quite broken down by ill health, stout and strong young-men could not match him in walking. The journey to and from his native village, Birsingha, Vidyasagar performed on foot *in* one day. In the course of the whole journey, he ate or drank nothing but a raw cocoanut at Masat, a village some 24 miles from Birsingha. Even in later days, when he was Principal of the Sanskrit College, he used to perform the journey on foot, as before. If any of his co-travellers or companions had a load or luggage too heavy, he would divide it with him, and carry it on his own head or shoulders. On one occasion, it so happened, that two *Darwans* (porters) of the Sanskrit College came in his way, and saw him walking with a burden on his head. They were quite surprised at the sight, and offered to *carry* the load for him. But he dismissed them with kind and gentle words, and went on with the burden.

It is said, that while Vidyasagar was employed in the Sanskrit College, he had unexpectedly a very, urgent necessity to return to Calcutta from Birsingha, and make the journey on foot, as usual, in less than one day's time. As he started on his journey, one Madan Mahdal, one of his servants, came to him, and expressed his willingness to. accompany him, Vidyasagar doubted his ability, and asked him whether he would be able to walk with him at the same rate. The man replied in the affirmative. They then proceeded on their way. For 9 or 10 miles, Madan Mandal followed Vidyasagar closely, but presently he fell back. He soon saw that his master, had outpassed him nearly 200 yards. Madan Mandal was a *lathial* (clubman). He gave himself and his *lathi* (club) several whirls in the air. He then ran forward as fast as his legs permitted, and was soon at his master's heels. Again they proceeded together. As soon as they reached an inn, 24 miles from Birsingha, Madan Mandal said to his master,—'Let us stay here for this day. We need not go to Calcutta today; at which Vidyasagar smiled, and replied,—"I must go today. You may put up here for this day, and go to Calcutta tomorrow. Here are some pice to pay your hotel-bill. With this, he left Madan Mandal to rest at the inn, and reached Calcutta by nightfall.

During his tenure of employment in the Fort William College he found opportunities of visiting Birsingha more frequently. When at home, his main business was to call on, and enquire after his neighbours, attend and nurse the diseased, help and succour the distressed, and divert himself by various athletic sports and amusements. One of his chief amusements at that time was to attend dinner-parties in company with his brothers and other relations. If, on such occasions, a ditch would lie on his way, he would leap across it by way of sport, and then ask his second brother, Dinabandhu, to follow his example. In trying to do so, Dinabandhu often threw himself down into the ditch, which raised a roar of laughter from the company. Vidyasagar engaged himself in various sportive monuiments of this nature with his younger brothers.

It is said, that on one occasion, he was walking to Calcutta, as usual, from Birsingha. When he reached a field, he saw an old cultivator standing there with a load on his head. The load was too heavy for the old man, and the old man was too weak to walk with the load. On enquiry, Vidyasagar learned from him that his house was 5 or 6 miles from the place, and that his son, who was a young man, had charged him to carry the load home. The sight of the poor, old man's condition, and the tale of his son's conduct moved Vidyasagar's kind heart, and tears flowed in torrents from his eyes. He at once took over the load from the old man's head on his own head, and, thus equipped, followed the aged cultivator, with slow steps, to his home. He then retraced his steps, and reached Calcutta rather later than usual.

Whenever there was an occasion of presenting winter-cloth to any body, the charge of purchasing the cloth was intrusted to Babu Braja Nath De, the Suprintendent of the Metropolitan Institution. One day, Vidyasagar said to him,— "You see Braja Nath, whenever there is any necessity for cloth, it is you whom I send to the shawl-merchants". It does not look well that one man should trouble himself on all occasions with this affair. If you will once show me the shop tomorrow, I may occasionally call at the place and make purchases by myself. Please, come tomorrow, and

I will accompany you to the shop". The next day, Braja Nath Babu made his appearance at the proper time, and both started together for Barabazar, the chief place of native traders, especially cloth-merchants. But Braja Nath Babu was ill at ease to keep pace with Vidyasagar. The latter was always in much advance of the former. Vidyasagar had every now and then to stop on the way to let his follower come up to him. When they were again together for the fourth time, he said to Braja Nath Babu,—'I have acquired a habit of walking rather a little too fast. My followers, as a rule, cannot keep pace with me. Never mind, Braja Nath, let us do one thing. This time you walk foremost, and I will follow you.' Braja Nath Babu now felt himself at ease. On the way Vidyasagar warned his friend not to let the mer-chant know his (Vidyasagar's) personality. But it was of no avail. As soon as Vidyasagar entered the shop, followed by his friend, the merchant rose from his seat, and received him respectfully, saying,—'Welcome venerable *Panditji,* good morning; surely, I am very fortunate today.' Vidyasagar whispered into the ears of his friend, that he wondered how the merchant could identify him. The shrewd, witty merchant replied, that fire must proclaim itself by its heat, even when put under cover.

Even in later years, when he was enfeebled by age and disease, no one could match him in pedestrianism. It is said, that when he was staying at Karmatar for change of climate, he was out one day to take a walking excursion accompanied with some of his friends and a grown-up grandson. The grandson said to him,—'Let us see, if you can outpace us today.' The feeble grandfather smiled, and said,—'Very good, let it be so *V* So saying, he proceeded on his way, and the others followed. Shortly, all others save the grandson fell much behind. Soon afterwards, the grandson saw that his dear grandpapa, with his usual slippers on, had much outpaced him. He tried his best, to overtake him, but could approach him no nearer. The grandfather enjoyed the fun from a distance, and smiled at the futile attempts of his grandson, who was now quite abashed and dumbfounded with amazement.

Dear reader, you see what wonderfully expert walker Vidyasagar was. Was not his strength of body equal to his strength of mind, and his strength of mind equal to his strength of heart?

What happy combination ! How many were or are there in this world, who were or are endowed with the three strengths in equal proportion? Very few, we believe. The reader will, by and by, see how strong Vidyasagar was in every respect.

The depth of Vidyasagar's affection for his mother was equal to, if not more than, that for his father. He idolised his mother. We will give the reader an illustration of the strong affection and esteem, he felt for his dear mamma.

One day, when he was working in the Fort William College, information reached him that the marriage of his third brother, Sambhu Chandra, had been settled at Birsingha. In a few days, he received a letter from his mother asking him to be unavoidably present at the nuptials. He was eagerly anxious to obey the command of his mother. He at once called on Mr. Marshall, and applied for leave, but the application was rejected. He was very sorry, and thought within himself thus:—'Mother will miss me very keenly. What pangs she will suffer ! Without me she will be half-dead. How ungrateful I am, not to obey her commands; What shame ! Fie to me.' After office hours, he returned to his lodgings, and, to his great disappointment, found that the other inmates of his house had already left for Birsingha in accordance with previous arrangements. He was now quite alone, and felt the disappointment very keenly. He sat up the whole night, crying and weeping for his mother. He had not a wink of sleep that night.

The next morning, he resolved that he would renew his application for leave, and that if the leave should be again refused, he would resign his appointment. Go home he must, at all risks. Accordingly, he called again on Mr. Mar-shall, and renewed his application. With great emphasis he said;- 'Sir, if you do not grant me leave to go home, I resign my post. Please, accept my resignation.

For the sake of my service, I can not suffer my mother to shed tears. Mr, Marshall was wonder-struck at the uncommon feelings of filial devotion. Vidyasagar felt for his mother. He could not utter a single word of protest, but very gladly granted the leave. Vidyasagar at once repaired to his lodgings; and accompanied with his faithful servant, Sriram, started for Birsingha at 3 P.M. in the afternoon.

This was in the month of July,—the rainy season of tropical Bengal. The sky was overcast, clouds thundering dreadfully with flashes of lightning every now and then, winds roaring incessantly, rains pouring in incessant torrents. The roads were all slippery and muddy. Quite regardless of these, Vidyasagar moved on as fast as his legs permitted, and he was not a slow walker, as the reader is already aware. At nightfall he reached Krishnarampur, and it being too dark to find his way, he was, at his servant's request, compelled to stay there for the night in an inn. He had still to journey 25 miles, before he could reach his home.

The next morning he rose very early, and proceeded on his way, followed by his servant. When he had travelled some distance, he found that Sriram was quite wearied with fatigue and hunger. The servant's home was not very far from this place. Vidyasagar, therefore, provided for the servant's breakfast in a neighbouring inn, and giving him a few pice, said;—'Here is some money to pay your hotel-bill; you may now go home. With this, he left him, and ran on like an arrow. Sriram could no more follow him, and was obliged to go to his own home. Vidyasagar soon reached the banks of the Damodar.

The river Damodar was very wide, and full to its brinks on both sides, and there was a very strong current flowing in the dry season, the water in the Damodar is very shallow, and the river is fordable in many places; but during the rains, the water swells to its banks, and sometimes overflows them. Vidyasagar saw, that the river was not only full to its brinks, but also rough and turbulent, with a strong current flowing vigorously. The ferry boat was, unfortunately, on the other side of the river. What was Vidyasagar to do now? What means would he adopt to cross the river? He was not long in thinking. He was now inspirated with a heavenly animation,—an eager longing to see his dear mother. In the name of God and his mother, he plunged precipitately into the stream. He swum across the river, and reached the other bank safe. What a good swimmer 1 He then proceeded on his way with running speed, and was soon on the banks of the Dvarakesvar. Here was the, same difficulty again. The river was as swollen and turbulent as the Damodar. There was no ferry boat. He was now quite exhausted. He had nothing to eat the whole day. But he aid not care for all this. He was animated with divine inspiration. He plunged into the river, and with God's grace, who is ever ready to help those that help themselves, swam across safely to the other side He now ran apace, for it was growing dark. When he came to the *Kuran-Khal*, the sun had already set, and it was quite dark. The place was very dreadful. It was notorious as the chief haunt of robbers, who lay in wait, concealed under some covert, and as opportunity presented itself, fell on and plundered wayfarers, occasionally killing them. But Vidyasagar had no room in his mind for fear or anything of the kind, save the thought of his mother. He proceeded on fearlessly, and when he reached home, it was past nine O'clock in the night. He found, that the marriage procession had already left for the bride's. He looked for his mother, but could not find her, for she had shut the doors of her room, and lay there weeping for her dear child, Vidyasagar called aloud, "Mamma, where are you, mamma, 1 am come". The mother knew her son's voice, and instantly ran out and clasped him in her arms, and pressed kisses on his forehead. Then mother and child both fell a-crying. When the outbursts of their feeling had somewhat subsided, they sat down to their meals. None of them had eaten any food that day till then.

The readers have, no doubt, heard and read many anecdotes of children's love for their mothers. The affectionate, filial devotion of Napoleon, Washington, Johnson, and some other great men are reputed to be unparalleled in the annals of history. But, sweet reader, can you conscientiously say, that the filial love of any of these men could approach the filial love of this poor Indian? We think, not. It is said of Julius Caesar that when, with a view to conquer England, he had shipped his army, and was ready to weigh anchor, a great storm arose, threatening to sink all his ships laden with the army and himself. Every one of his followers importuned him not to dare his valuable life, and tried to dissuade him, but he headed them not. When Vidyasagar was about to plunge into the Dainodar, some men, who were working in the neighbouring fields, tried to dissuade him from his attempts, which they considered to be nothing but rash and foolish. There is a good deal of similarity between the acts of these two great men. Both were heroes, though of different sorts. Both risked their valuable lives, the one for conquest of another's kingdom, and the other, for worship of his own mother. May we now" ask you, dear reader, which of the two was the nobler hero? Which of the two was more admirable? Which of the two should have his name engraved in our hearts? Which of the two ought to be our model for imitation? We leave the thoughtful reader to answer the questions for himself. This is only one illustration of Vidyasagar's filial love. The reader will, by and by, find many such instances in his life.

Before concluding, we will once more notice his powers of versification. We have seen his abilities at composition of beautiful Sanskrit poems, when a student,—winning prizes for them. In his maturer years those powers had not lost their vigour. His abilities at versification were always the same. But, unfortunately, he did not cultivate them. During his tenure of office in the Fort William College, Mr. Cost, a Civilian, re-quested Vidyasagar to compose a *sloka* (a very short stanza) about him.

Vidyasagar composed the *sloka* extemporaneously. Mr. Cost had some knowledge of Sanskrit, and he thought the *sloka* beautiful. He admired it, and was so pleased, that he at once offered him a reward of 200 rupees. Vidyasagar would not take the money himself. He proposed that the money should be deposited in the Sanskrit College and out of it a prize of 50 rupees should be given each year to the best Sanskrit essayist. Mr. Cost agreed to Vidyasagar's proposal, and the money was funded accordingly. Vidyasagar was thus the means of awarding four prizes to four pundits of his country, thereby encouraging the culture of Sanskrit composition.

These prizes were called Cost-prizes, after the name of the donor. What disinterested self-sacrifice Vidyasagar was never known to have any greed of gain. On the contrary, it is well known that in many cases, when he had good opportunities of getting money, Vidyasagar, poor as he was, instead of receiving the money himself, gladly provided for the award of that money, however large the amount might be, to some other person or persons. He had such greatness of heart. It was for this, that respectable Europeans cherished a great esteem for Vidyasagar.

We will notice here briefly, in passing, another instance of his self-sacrifice, in connection with one of the Cost-prizes.

Vidyasagar was appointed examiner of the Cost-prize essays. At the second year's examination for this prize, the essays of one Srischandra Vidyaratna and Dinabandhu Nyayratna, Vidyasagar's younger brother, were superior to the others. The style and diction of both the essays were beautiful. In Srischandra's essay there were a few grammatical mistakes, but in that of Dinabandhu there was none. But Dinabandhu had a great misfortunate in that his elder brother, Vidyasagar, was charged with the examination of the papers. Though Dinabandhu's essay was the best in every respect, he did not get the prize. It was awarded to Srischandra Vidyaratna. The chief cause of this seeming injustice was, that Vidyasagar feared, that if he should award the prize to Dinabandhu, people might think, though unjustly, that when the two essays were of equal quality, Vidyasagar had shown undue favour to his brother. He was also afraid that when he was indirectly interested in the affair, he might unconsciously have been biassed on his brother's side. But, in fact, there was no cause of fear in that respect, as it was universally known that he had weighed the balance evenly. Anyhow, Vidyasagar judged it best to be on the safe side, and he sacrificed self for the sake of another. What a brilliant example of noble self-sacrifice!

When Mr. Cost passed the vernacular examination, he was posted in the Punjab, where he worked as a civilian for many years. Subsequently when he retired from the service, and was about to return home, he came to Calcutta, and paid a visit to Ishwar Chandra Vidyasagar. In course of conversation, he recalled Vidyasagar's powers of versification, and asked him to compose a few *slokas* about himself. Vidyasagar then and there wrote five beautiful, sweet *slokas*, Mr. Cost was highly delighted, and thanked him profusely.

There can be no doubt that Vidyasagar's powers of writing Sanskrit prose and poetry were equally great But he never cultivated those powers. He devoted himself to the cultivation of his mother language. Yet, he now and then composed Sanskrit verses at leisure. He wrote several elegant poems on "Travel", "Contentment", "Anger", "Cloud'" and some other subjects. He composed 408 *slokas* on *Sahnalidvip, Kusadvip, Sakadvip* and other names of countries according to the ancient *Pauranic* geography of the Hindus, and on America, England, France, Africa and Asia, modern names according to the Westerners. He also wrote brief annotations on *Uttara-Charita, Meghduta* and *Sakuntala.* It is not known whether, after this, he made any more attempts at Sanskrit composition, either prose or poetry. When writing the annotations on *Meghaduta,* he remarked, one day, with a smile, to one of his grandsons, who was sitting by;—'You see, my dear, I have written very good Sanskrit, indeed V But this was merely a joke, as he had been heard to observe on many occasions, that in this age of degeneration, it was not possible for any one to write good Sanskrit.

New Responsibilities

Principal of the Sanskrit College, as well as, Special Inspector of Schools

In 1855, when the authorities resolved to start government-aided English and Vernacular schools in the different parts of the country, they called on Vidyasagar for a report on the mode of instruction to be followed in these schools, and the scheme under which they were to be worked. Vidyasagar submitted an able report on the subject, which met with the approbation of the authorities. They then appointed him a Special Inspector of Schools on a monthly pay of 200 rupees in addition to his pay of 300 rupees for holding the post of the Principal of the Sanskrit College. He had thus a monthly salary of 500 rupees now. He was entrusted with the establishment and inspection of schools under the new scheme in the interior of the districts, Nuddea, Midnapore, Hooghly and Burdwan.

In his second report, Vidyasagar had suggested the opening of a Normal School to train up teachers for the newly established schools. The authorities saw the propriety of his suggestion, and, in the same year, a Normal School was opened in the premises of the Sanksrit College. Vidyasagar was charged with its management. At his instance, his dear friend, the famous author, Akshay Kumar Dutta was appointed its first Head Master. Not long after this appointment, Akshay Babu was afflicted with a severe head disease, which grew so serious, that he was compelled to resign his office. Vidyasagar's great favourite, Ram Kamal Bhattacharyya, was then appointed to the post Madhu Sudan Vachaspati, one of

Vidyasagar's early playmate, was also another teacher of the Normal School.

As Inspector of Schools, he had usually to travel into the interior of the Hooghly, Burdwan, Midnapore and Nuddea districts, and to come in contact with many wealthy and influential persons of the places he visited. He advised these respectable men to establish schools in their localities and estates. In this way, he made an acquaintance of Babu Jay Krishna Mukharji, the learned Zamindar of Uttarpara.

During these tours, Vidyasagar generally travelled in palanquins, and if he found any sick person, faint and feeble, lying on the way, he used to alight from his vehicle and take the poor sufferer into it. He then walked on foot himself to the next inn, where he placed the poor man under the care of the innkeeper, giving him sufficient money to feed, and take care of, the sufferer. He never travelled without money in his purse. He always kept with him a stock of a sufficient quantity of coins of different values. Whenever a poor person presented himself, he was sure to give him some money in proportion to his need. He never sent away a bragger displeased.

Vidyasagar's heart was a fountain of sympathy and kindness. The tale of distress moved his naturally gentle heart, and he tried his utmost to relieve the distrest. There is no reckoning how many orphans he helped with food, books and school-fees. Whenever the tale of a poor boy reached his ears, that for want of means, the boy was prevented from obtaining education, he never failed to take the boy to his own house^, and make proper arrangements for his education. It is said, that on, one occasion, when he had gone on business to the house of Kali Krishna Datta of Dattapukur, a village in the district of 24 Pergannas, a poor Brahmin orphan appeared before him, and, with tears in his eyes. narrated his sad story. Vidyasagar was so much touched at the tale of distress-, that he wept like a child. He then took the poor *boy* with him to his own residence, and provided for his education. At this time, nearly one hundred persons were daily fed by him, both in Calcutta and at Birsingha.

We have said, that Vidyasagar never sent away a beggar without giving him or her some alms. The reader has already seen how fondly devoted he was to his mother. When a beggar appeared before him, and said that he was motherless, the very thought of the loss of mother drew tears from Vidyasagar's eyes, and: he was sure to give the mendicant something more than he expected. On one occasion, it so happened that a beggar came to him, and represented falsely that he was mother-less, under instructions of a neighbouring grocer-Vidyasagar came to know that his statement was untrue, and that he had, in reality, his mother living. He did not, however, send the beggar away, but gave him some alms, and advised him not to tell lies again. In fact, many poor persons thus deceived him with false representations that they were motherless, and drew out from his purse, money more than they expected.

Vidyasagar was, as if, spell-bound with the word 'mother'. He had never a very great taste for music. But whenever he heard any one sing a song, containing pitiful addresses of 'mamma', he was moved to the very core of his heart. He clasped the singer to his bosom, and did not know how to satisfy him. A poor, blind Mussulman beggar was in the habit of wandering in the streets a-begging and singing *Syama-Sangits* to his violin. These songs contained in them pitiful addresses of 'mamma,' which moved the filial heart of Vidyasagar. He used to send for this beggar, and hear his songs. As he heard the pitiful cries of 'mamma', tears flew in torrents from his eyes. He helped the Mussulman beggar liberally. When the poor, blind man's hut was destroyed by fire, Vidyasagar paid the whole cost of his new hut.

As was the son, so were the parents. Vidyasagar's father and mother, both were liberal to the core. They felt a great delight in feeding guests and hungry people. The father personally used to go to market and make purchases for the daily feast, and the mother took equal delight in doing the cooking and distributing the food to the guests and the hungry. Many stories are told of their liberalities. Vidyasagar's parents lived to a good old age and enjoyed the happiness of their con-jugal love. But it is usually seen in the world, where there is excessive love between two persons, especially between husband and wife, the fancied slightest disregard of one, either in words or acts, wounds the pride of the other, who- takes- it to be an affront offered, and enters into dispute with the fancied opponent. Such was the usual occurrence with Vidyasagar's father, Thakurdas, and his mother, Bhagavati

Devi. The reader is already aware that the husband, Thakurdas, was of a peevish temperament. His wife, Bhagavati Devi, also easily lost her temper. Consequently, their conjugal dispute was almost a daily occurrence, but it never had a long duration. When the quarrel' grew rather serious, Bhagavati Devi used to shut the doors of her room, and lay there, giving, vent to her pent up passion by angry words mixed with tears.

Thakurdas would then be in great peril, but he had always a remedy, ready at hand. As soon as his beloved consort entered the room, he left the house and went out in search of a big bash. Having procured one to his mind, he returned home with it, and, with a heavy bang, threw it down, with great force, on the ground in front of his wife's room. No sooner did the sound of the big fish-reach her ears, than Bhagavati Devi, at once ran out of the room, and with a large fish-knife began dividing the fish, with a smile in her tearful eyes. How beautiful was the admixture of tears with mirth! Thakurdas, with wilful wickedness, would peremptorily tell her not to touch the fish, but his wife would not pay the slightest heed to his inter and thus won the victory.

The other female inmates of the house were greatly amused, and smiled at the happy, speedy termination of the old couple's quarrel. Referring to this, Vidyasagar's son, Narayan Babu, said to us: "My grandmother (Vidyasagar's mother) used to lend money to the lower class people of the village. When any of these poor persons could not repay their debts, she would go to their houses, and sometimes demand repayment in angry' tones. She would say to them,—'If you do not repay your debts, how can I carry on the money lending business?' When *the* creditors saw her *in* such passion, they tried to pacify her with gentle, flattering words. Some would relate, with tearful eyes, the tales of their distress; while others blessed her son, Vidyasagar, in her presence, and prayed to God for his welfare. My grandmother's passion would vanish in an instant; she would then say,— 'Very good, never mind, pay your debts, when you" find convenience. Rut today you- must have *Pnisad* (eat your rice) at mine.' The female inmates of their house sometimes gave her *Muri* (fried rice), cocoanut, *Batasa* (light sugar-cake) and other eatables. She would bring them home wrapped in a corner of her cloth. At noon, after she had done the cooking and fed the guests and dependents", she took her stand daily by the outer gates of her house. As a wayfarer or a peddler passed by her, she would take him in, and feed him with satiety. If she saw any one with a pale face, she would say to him. 'Oh! you have had nothing to eat today. Come, come to my house, I will feed you. Whenever she got a big fish, her delight knew no bounds. She was very happy to divide large fishes with her own hands, and to feed people with them.

The reader has already seen that Vidyasagar was a great appreciator of merits. Besides, he was ever prepared to help the deserving in the way which would best suit the helped. He had known Babu Prasanna Kumar Sarvvadhikari for a long time. Prasanna Kumar had been a student of the Hindu College, where he had won a gold medal, besides a monthly scholarship of 40 rupees. He had gone to Dacca on appointment, which not suiting him, he had come back to Calcutta without the permission of the authorities, who were consequently highly dissatisfied with him. At last, at the earliest request of Vidyasagar, he was appointed as one of the lower teachers of the Hindu College on a monthly salary of 40 rupees. Subsequently, when the scheme of English instruction in the Sanskrit College was approved by the Education Council, and English was made a compulsory subject, Prasanna Kumar Sarvvadhikari, at the instance of Vidyasagar, was appointed first teacher of English in the Sanskrit College, and after him Babus Srinath Das, Kali Prasanna Chatarji, Tarini Charan Chatarji and Prasanna Kumar Ray were appointed teachers of English. This Prasanna Kumar Sarvvadhikari afterwards became Principal of the Sanskrit College, and ultimately, one of the professors of the Presidency College, Calcutta.

We will notice here, in passsing, the incident connected with Prasanna Kumar Sarvvadhikari's resignation of his office as Principal of the Sanskrit College. Some malicious persons insinuate that he resigned the post at the instigation of Vidyasagar. We will show that he had nothing to -do with the resignation. On the contrary, he tried his best to induce Prasanna Kumar to withdraw his resignation.

Shortly after Prasanna Kumar Sarvvadhikari had been installed as Principal of the Sanskrit College, he had a dispute with the Principal of the Presidency College on official matters. The Library of the Sanskrit College had all along been in a room on the second floor of the College-building. But the Principal of the Presidency College requiring it on urgent business, he directed the Library of the Sanskrit College to be removed to a damp, dark room in the lowest floor. The Library contained a good collection of valuable and rare books and manuscripts. Prasanna Kumar Sarvvadhikari objected to the removal of the Library, on the score that the damp might cause a great injury to the rare collection. The Principal of the Presidency College was a white European. He referred the matter to the higher authorities, who decided in his favour, as is the usual occurrence in cases of dispute between a black native and a white European. The Library was removed to the damp, dark room. Prasanna' Kumar naturally took this to be a downright insult, and highly resented it From his long connection with Vidyasagar, he had acquired much of his habits and spirit He at once sent on his resignation letter. We will now quote some portions of the letters that passed between Vidyasagar and the then Lieutenant-Governor of Bengal, which speak for themselves:

(1)

"My Dear Sir

"When I had the pleasure of waiting upon you lest, you were pleased to allude to the resignation of the officiating Principal of the Sanskrit College. But as I was not aware of all the circumstances connected with the affair, I could not tell you anything regarding the matter. I have since made myself acquainted with the facts of the case, and am inclined to think that the treatment of the Principal by has been unnecessarily and unbecomingly harsh, as will, I believe, appear to you also on perusal of the papers enclosed.

"I have, therefore, tried my best to persuade him to withdraw his letter of resignation. But he says "Ishwar Chandra Sharma".

Special Inspector of Schools.

(2)

'My Dear Pundit,

"I am sorry you have not been able to induce P. C. Sarbadhicari to withdraw his resignation, because I feel sure it is a step which he will regret, and I am always sorry to lose the services of good officers, especially if it be for an inadequate cause.

As to the fitness of the room for the reception of the Sanskrit Miss. I will make enquiry. "Believe me yours sincerely,

(Sd). "Cecil Beadon":

(3)

"My Dear Sir,

'As I am inclined to suspect that he may have also represented the matter to you in the same light, I beg to assure you that I had no hand whatever in inducing Babu P. C. Sarbadhicari in forming his resolution. On the contrary, as I was under the impression that the severance of his connection with the Sanskrit College would be injurious to that institution, I tried my best to make him withdraw his resignation, though without the desired effect.

(Sd.) "Ishwar Chandra Sharma"

(4)

"My Dear Sir,

"You may be quite sure that if I had the least suspicion that Babu P. C. Sarbadhicari had acted under your advice in resigning his appointment in the Sanskrit College, I should not have asked you to try and induce him to reconsider what I thought a hasty and unasked for step.

'Yours Sincerely (Sd.) "C. Beadon"

Shortly after English had been made a compulsory subject, and the students had been compelled to keep pass-marks in English as well, the Calcutta University was instituted, and along with it, the system of Entrance and Arts examinations was introduced. Some more English teachers were, therefore, appointed in the Sanskrit College. About this time, one Kali Charan Ghosh, a mere youth, became Vidyasagar's especial favourite. Though he was young in age, he had acquired a good English education. Vidyasagar, therefore, apointed him temporarily as teacher of English, on probation.

But, when the boys saw that their teacher was of the same age with them, they refused to take lessons from him. Besides, some of them tried to treat him with, unbecoming contumacy and contumely. When Vidyasagar was apprised of the misbehaviour of the refractory boys, he was greatly annoyed, and called for the names the ringleaders and instigators. But no one ventured to give names. No one admitted the offence. Vidyasagar was a great enemy of untruth. He knew that the boys were actually guilty, but he could not discover the leaders. He therefore, drove the whole class away. The boys, in a body, complained against him to the higher authorities, who called on him for an explanation. He wrote in reply that in these small matters, the Principal ought to have the sole control, and that if, in such cases, the boys were permitted to bring complaints against the Principal, it would be very difficult to keep them in check. The authorities concurred with him, and returned to him all the papers connected with the case. The boys had been in great glee that they toad complained against Vidyasagar, who in con-sequence would soon be taken to task. Some of them even ventured to declare openly, that he was sure to lose his appointment, and conseqnently would have to turn a petty chapman. But when they heard that the authorities had returned the case to him, they were, as if, struck by a thunderbolt. By and by, the guardians of the boys came to know of their wickedness, and upbraided them severely. The guardians then went to Vidyasagar, and requested him to forget and forgive. He instructed them to send their wards to Kali Charan Babu.

The boys had now no other alternative left, than to go to Kali Charan, whom they had so unreasonably insulted, and ask his forgiveness. Kali Charan took the boys with him to Vidyasagar, who now asked the ringleaders that were in front, who Should turn a chapman, whether they or he? The boys hung down their heads in shame, and could not utter a word. He then asked Kali Charan, if they had asked forgiveness of him. The latter replied, that he had at first declined to come with them, but at their earnest solicitation, after admission of their guilt, he had brought them to him (Vidyasagar), and that he could now do with them as he pleased. Vidyasagar then said to Kali Charan,—' If you request me to forgive them, I will forgive them, otherwise not.' Kali Charan was now put on the horns of a dilemma. After much reflection, he said,—They have committed a greater offence against you than against me. Please, do as you think fit. Do not throw it on my head. The boys fell to Vidyasagar's feet, and with tear-ful eyes, craved his forgiveness, promising never to do so again.

Vidyasagar now forgave them, and told them to go to school. Dear reader, do you see the beauty when strength of mind is combined with kind forgiveness?

It is not very difficult to forgive an offender, when he admits his guilt and repents of it, and it is almost a daily occurrence. But it is not so easy for a man of influence to ask forgiveness of his inferior, for the superior thinks it beneath his dignity to do so, and his pride is wounded. But one, who can do so, must be considered to be truly great. On One occasion, it so happened that Vidyasagar, relying on the misrepresentation of a man, whom he had believed to be a trustworthy person, did, Pandit Tatrakumar Kaviratna a piece of injustice".

Bat he subsequently found out that he had been circumvented by malicious reports. He at once called upon the injured person at the latter's residence, and with tearful eyes and pitiful tones, implored his forgiveness, saying,—' Kaviratna. I have un-justly done you a great wrong. Please, tell me how can I redress it?' What greatness of heart!

Vidyasagar was kind and affectionate, equally to his family, relations and friends. Babu Syama Charan Bisvas, one of the late Vice-Chairmen of the Calcutta Municipal Corporation, was among Vidyasagar's particular friends. In Calcutta, his house stood in front of that of Vidyasagar; but his ancestral home was at village Paintel, in the Hooghly district, some 19 or 20 miles off Calcutta. At the urgent request of his dear friend, Vidyasagar once visited Paintel. Many poor people of the locality came to him to beg for assistance, and he distributed his charities liberally. The people of that place, even to the present day, remember his name with grateful tears. After his return from Paintel, he had an attack of Fever, accompanied with polypus and bleeding of the nose, which, neessitated the use of snuff for some time, but, in a short time, he gave it up, It is said, that he acquired the habit of smoking tobacco, when he was 31 or 32 years old, under the following circumstances.

Doctor Navin Chandra Mitra of Barasat, who lived in Jhamapukur, Calcutta, was in terms, of intimate friendship with Vidyasagar. His brother, Kali Krishna Mitra, was also familiar with him, Vidyasagar used now and then to visit Navin Babu. The doctor was a great smoker of tobacco. One day, as he was engaged in conversation with Vidyasagar, the page presented a hookah to smoke from. The host requested his visitor to smoke, but the latter declined. At last, at the earnest solicitations of his friend, he drew in a little smoke to oblige him. The next day, when he called again, he himself ordered the page to get tobacco ready. The boy presented the hookah, and he consumed the tobacco to ashes, without offering his friend to smoke out of it. He thus formed his habit of smoking tobacco. But he never disturbed his servants and maids in their sleep or when they were busy with some other work, either for tobacco or betel. Sometimes he prepared both, for his use, with his own hands. He used to have small bits of divided betel-nuts and other spices ready at hand, and he prepared and chewed betels at pleasure, without any body's assistance. He never threw away surplus bits of nuts or other spices, but put them into phials for future use. Though he was very liberal in charities, yet in his own house, he was most economical. His maxim was 'Waste not, want not.

Babu Nilambar Mukharji, late minister of the Cashmere Raj, and present Vice-Chairman of the Calcutta Municipality, was one of the scholars of the Sanskrit College in Vidyasagar's time, and was a great favourite with him. Vidyasagar's impression was, that he would become a great man, which was eventually fulfilled. Nilambar Babu had always a great reverence for Vidyasagar. Even when he rose to the highest post in' Cashmere, he consulted him (Vidyasagar) on important State affairs. Be-fore he threw up the high office, he had consulted the learned Pandit and obtained his permission. Since his appointment as Principal of the Sanskrit College, Vidyasagar had made provisions for monthly stated allowances for several poor, but respectable families. It is said, that he had settled upon Bhuvan Mohon Singha, son of Babu Jagaddurlabh Singha of Barabazar, who had, in former days, given shelter to Vidyasagar and his father, a monthly allowance of 30 rupees. After Bhuvan Mohan's death, his wife used to receive the stipend. His son-in-law was also one of Vidyasagar's favourites, and obtained from him pecuniary helps now and then. About this time, he settled upon Syama Charan Ghoshal, a relation of his, a monthly allowance of ten rupees. Besides these fixed stipends, he helped occasionally many poor, high-class people with gifts of money. We have no means of knowing all his charities; because, to avoid exposure and humiliation of the recipients, he made the gifts most privately. In this respect, he followed Christ's precept,—'Let not thy left hand know what thy right hand do'.

Before Vidyasagar's time, Sanskrit Lilavati and Vijaganita (Algebra) were used in the Sanskrit College, but he introduced, in their stead, European Mathematical works. Pandit Priya Nath Bhattacharyya was a professor of Mathematics at that time. He subsequently studied the civil law under Vidyasgar's instructions, and, at his instance, obtained the post of a Munsiff.

An association, called the "Bethune Society', had been formed in memory of the late J. E. D. Bethune, one of the greatest friends the country ever had, mainly through Vidyasagsr's exertions. It was at a meeting of this Society that his essay on "Sanskrit Language and Belles-lettres" was read. It is said, that Prasanna Kumar Sarvvadhikari read an English translation of the essay. However that might be, there can be no doubt, that it is a most learned dissertation. It was first published on the 18th April, 1856. The pamphlet contains 89 pages, demy 12 mo. Considering die weight and importance of the subject, it must be asserted, that the discussion has been very brief and limited. The author has admitted it himself. He says:

> 'This essay was first read at a meeting of the Bethune Society. At the earnest request of many of my friends, I, under the permission of the President, published at that time 200 copies of the book, and distributed them gratis.
>
> 'I am well aware, that the compilation is not as perfect as it ought to be, considering the importance of the subject discussed. In fact, out of the vast number of Sanskrit Literary works, only the names of a few have been mentioned. But it must be borne in mind, that only one hour's time is allowed by the Bethune Society for the reading of an essay. Consequently, keeping in view the shortness of the time allowed, the briefest method possible has been adopted.'

Vidyasagar had a great mind to discuss the subject at great length, and present it to the public, but, to the misfortune of

Bengal, he could not carry out the project for want of time. The language of the short treatise, however, is very plain and elegant.

On the 9th December 1854, appeared his *Sakuntala,* a Bengali version of the Sanskrit "Abhijnan-Sakuntalam" It is not written in a dramatic form, though the original is one of the best dramas in Sanskrit. Some portion of the original text has been translated literally; while of others, the purport only has been taken. It is superfluous to say that, in excellence and beauty, it surpassed all its predecessors.

Last Days

After the submission of his Note on the Age of Consent Bill, he went back again to Chander-Tagore, where he was comparatively fetter, if it might be called so, up to the middle of April, when he was able to take even rice for two days. But, unfortunately, by the end of the month, his illness again took a bad turn, which made his eldest daughter, Hemlata, who had accompanied officers, were called in. They suspected Cancer in the abdomen. They thought the case hopeless, and refused to take charge of the patient For a few days more, he remained under the treatment of Hira Lal and Amulya Charan. But there was no relief. Some times the symptoms—hiccup, costiveness, pain—showed signs of improvement, but that was only for a short duration; they again set in with redoubled force. This state of things continued up to the 14th July. On the next day, Dr. Salzer, the best Homeopathist, was called in. For the first few days, Dr. Salzer's Homeopathic treatment seemed to give the patient a little relief. Previously, his bowels had to be moved by the application of enema, but they now had a free motion. Dr. Salzer suspected Ulcer. He said: 'The jaundice, which has set in, may lessen in a short time. If it should not so lessen, the patient may die in seven days; and even if it should lessen, still there is very little chance of the life being prolonged for more than a month. For diet, ass's milk was prescribed. Even this 'milk he could not assimilate. His vitality began to decline day by day. The hiccup increased and decreased by turns. He could not bear the rattling of carriages. To prevent it, straw was spread over the adjacent streets and lanes. The Calcutta Municipality sympathised with him by interdicting their Scavenger carts passing by those streets. On the 19th July, Dr. Mahendralal Sarkar paid the patient a visit. He was of opinion that the chronic Dysentery was the root of all The other medical attendants used to call at regular Intervals, see the patient, and then go away to their respective business; but Amulya Chara attended the sick man day and night, nursed him with great care and watched the course of the disease with the keenest Interest. Vidyasagar loved him very dearly like his own son. He also looked upon him with filial regard as if the patient was his own father. We have said, that Narayan Chandra was permitted by his father to tend him in his last days. He also attended the sickbed with the tenderest care.

Fever, which had already set in, gradually increased day by day. The temperature rose on and On, till at last complete prostration came over the patient on the 20th July, 1901. He could no more rise from his *bed*. He suffered from intense pain accompanied by incessant hiccup, being apparently ameliorated at distant intervals by occasional slight reliefs. This state continued up to the 26th July.

On the 24th July, suggestions were made for a fresh will Babu Golap Chandra Shastri, a renowned pleader of the High Court, drew up a draft of the last Testament. But Vidyasagar could not subscribe to it. He took time to think over his educational institutions, which he intended placing under a committee of management. In the meantime, the malady grew more serious, and deprived of his senses.

On Sunday, the 27th July, the condition of the patient became most alarming. The temperature rose on and on; drowsiness and stupor set in with redoubled force; difficulty of breathing was observed at short intervals, Kaviraj Brajendra Kumar Sen, a well-known native physician of Calcutta (since deceased), who was attending and watching the patient for the last few days; become hopeless. Kviraj Bijay Ratna Sen, another reputed physician, was called in. He saw the patient for the first time. His opinion was, he said, that the internal state of the sufferer was not so bad as it appeared outwardly. But alas! Oh cruel destiny! The disease became worse and worse. On the next day, Monday, the patient was in a state of insensibility. With the disease increased also its concomitant agonies. But the sufferer bore with them patiently. His face was as placid and calm as ever. He never gave expression to his internal physical pains. *So* long that he had not lost his consciousness, who would not allow any one else to remove his evacuations and if ever anybody tried to do it, he showed, signs of displeasure. His tender heart was easily moved at the distress of others, but he never gave expression to even his own excruciating pains; he put up with them with calm fortitude.

On one occasion, he had gone to a Book seller, accompanied by his younger grandson (daughter's son), Jatis Chandra. Quite unexpectedly, a long, heavy iron bar fell upon one of his feet The pain was intense, and would have disabled every other man; but he preserved a stoic silence, and returned home in his palanquin. When Jatis Chandra asked his dear grandpapa, if he felt any pain in the part affected, he smiled, and only said,—'Don't speak of pain; if the accident had occurred to any of you, surely your cries of agony would have resounded through the whole neighbourhood, and there would have been no reckoning how many doctors would have to be called in.' He had once got a very painful carbuncle when he was at Karmatar. He came first of all to Burdwan for treatment, but finding no relief there, he was at last obliged to come down to Calcutta. In a few days, the abscess suppurated and required surgical operation. On the day of performance, he was engaged in conversing with Dina Nath Mallik of Parsibagan respecting the partition of their ancestral property. In the meantime, doctor Chandra Mohan Ghosh, the surgeon in attendance, had opened the carbuncle, evacuated' all the accumulated pus and poisened blood, and dressed the wound. The patient gave not the slightest utterance to his pain; a mustle of his face moved. When the conversation was over, Dina Nath requested the doctor to do the needful, but he was quite surprised to hear that the abscess had already been operated upon and dressed, and that it was in reality a carbuncle. Such was the uncommon fortitude Vidyasagar possessed. Even in the agonised death-bed, he displayed the same extraordinary fortitude.

The Demise

The whole of Tuesday, the 29th July, 1901, was a prolonged period of intense anxiety and fearful suspense. Every hope was extinct. The patient lay in the room, where hung his mother's portrait. He had been laid down with his head on the north side, while his mother's picture was hanging on the eastern wall He was quite speechless and evidently insensible; but, by what enchantment God knows, the dying man in an instant turned himself with his head to the, west, exactly facing the likeness of his beloved mother. He then gazed intently at the portrait, and shed an incessant torrent of tears.

All hopes were gone. Every moment was anticipated to be the last. The son, daughters, grandchildren, brothers, sisters, friends, relations, dependents, all watched the movements of the face with close attention. But it was as calm and tranquil as ever; no expression of internal agonies was visible in it; the countenance was very placid. The morning, noon, afternoon passed in this state of utter suspense, In the evening, the hard breathings which had already begun, became feebler and feebler, till it was almost inaudible. The pulse, which had already begun to fall down, sank and sank and sank, till it was almost imperceptible. The numerous doctors and Kavirajes came in and went out every few minutes, talking in inaudible whispers, with sad despondence depicted in their fates. The great crowd of relatives, friends, and visitors awaited the fatal issue with mournful silence. The thin and feeble wick of the pale, flickering light of life of the ever-merciful, great man was fast dying out. At last, the last symptoms of early dissolution of the body set in; the difficult breathing became more and more rattling and impeded; the pulse quite imperceptible. At 11 P. M. in the night, the breathing could be felt only in the navel. This last struggle continued for upwards of three hours, relaxing every moment, till 2-18 A. M. following, when his last breath was drawn. Not a moan escaped his lips, not a mustle of his feature moved. The friends and relations, particularly the female portion, were frantic with grief. They struck their breasts and foreheads with their fists, loudly bemoaning their fate, and filling the whole neighbourhood with pitiful lamentations, which no body had the heart to prevent. Thus ended the worldly life of the great man, who had struggled manfully with adverse circumstances from his very early years to the last days of his existence.

3

Great Academic

The Backdrop

India produced great individuals in the 19th century: it was a century when the newly awakened social and historical forces were casting persons in various moulds, calling forth their best energies to respond adequately to the challenge of the times. In his response, Vidyasagar was far ahead of his times. It is only today that the social ideals he acted upon a century ago are beginning to emerge as realities.

Most people do not, as individuals, help in the emergence of any new social order, but merely adapt themselves to the existing pattern. But societies have to function in an ever-changing world; and individuals have to work for a change in the pattern when the need arises Vidyasagar emerged as a towering personality in his response to the challenge of his times; his appreciation of the need for social change and his steadfastness of purpose made him a great social reformer.

The great Pandit came of a Rarhiya Kulin Brahmin family of West Bengal. These Brahmins, occupying the highest rank in the caste hierarchy, were proud of their cultural heritage and lineage. From his grandparents and parents Vidyasagar imbibed his pride of tradition. Even the poverty in the midst of which he was born could not efface it. He did not seek to bypass his country's tradition as a shortcut to social progress. He was one of few in India who, in the last century, courageously: the harmonious mingling of the new Western ideas with was best in the Indian tradition.

Vidyasagar has left behind some of the reminiscences of his childhood in the form of an incomplete autobiography in Bengali. He tells us that after the death of his great-grandfather, Bhubaneswar Vidyalankar, the latter's two elder sons took charge of the family, and that the third son, his own grandfather, Ramjoy Tarkabhushan, entered into a dispute with them about the ancestral property. This caused a breach in the joint-family and his grandfather left the ancestral village.

There lived at that time in the village of Birsingha (in the Midnapore district of Bengal) a learned pandit, Umapati Tarkasiddhanta, a good grammarian, of his time, Vidyasagar's grandfather married Durga Devi, the third daughter of this pandit, and had two sons and four daughters, of whom the eldest Thakurdas Bandyopadhyay was Vidyasagar's father.

Soon after his grandfather had left the ancestral village, his grandmother went to her father's house near Birsingha. But the atmosphere there was not happy. Her lather, Pandit Umapati, was deeply grieved to see that his son and daughter-in-law did not properly treat his daughter and grandchildren, but he was helpless in the matter. He had a hut built for his daughter very near his house, and in this hut Durga Devi lived with her six children. Her husband was then wandering from place to place, nursing the injustice meted out to him by his elder brothers. Durga Devi, left alone, had to work hard for bringing up the six children.

Many helpless and poor women in Bengal at that time used to earn their living by spinning and selling the yarn to the weavers. Sitting before the charkha and surrounded by her children, Vidyasagar's grandmother, Durga Devi, had to spin day and night for earning a pittance which was supplemented by some little assistance from her father, Vidyasagar feelingly tells us in his recollections that his father, Thakurdas, grew up in this depressing environment; and when Thakurdas was a boy of fourteen or fifteen, he began to consider seriously if, as the eldest son of the family, he could not do something to help his mother in earning a living. Thakurdas decided to proceed to the city of Calcutta to do so. Durga Devi, finding no other way out, reluctantly agreed to her son's venture.

Thakurdas was not an extraordinary man but he was dutiful, diligent and honest. The story of his struggle for existence In Calcutta, as given in the reminiscences of Vidyasagar, amply bears this out.

In those days, some knowledge of English, the language of the rulers, was the chief qualification for a post in any European firm, or under a sahib. In his preface to the English-Bengali Dictionary, published in 1834, Ramcomul Sen writes: "In 1774 the Supreme Court was established here [in Calcutta], and from this period a knowledge of the English language appeared to be desirable and necessary". The teachers of English at that time were the Bengali clerks of the European advocates and attorneys. They were proud of their stock of English words which was preserved carefully in a pocket notebook. Even those who were known as "complete English scholars" had to master only a small Word Book and a Spelling Book The tuition fee ranged from Rs. 4 to Rs. 16 per student, an unreasonable amount according to 18th century standards. The situation had not changed in the early days of the 19th century when Vidyasagar's father Thakurdas went to Calcutta seeking employment.

It was thought desirable that Thakurdas should acquire some elementary knowledge of English and not waste his energy in learning Sanskrit. The problem of expense, however, was solved for Thakurdas by one of his near relatives, Jagniohan Nyayalankar, who was doing well with his *tol*, a private Sanskrit school. He offered free food and shelter to Thakurdas and asked a friend to teach Thakurdas English free at his night-school. Thakurdas readily availed himself of this opportunity and attended the night-school regularly. To do so he had often to sacrifice his night meal The poor students of the tol, or outsiders, who were allowed to stay in Nyayalankar's house, had to take their evening meal just after sunset by the strict orders of the pandit. If anyone was late, even by chance, he had to go without food for the night. Hence Thakurdas had to frequently forgo his night meal for attending the English night-school.

Soon he secured employment on two rupees a month. Working hard, Thakurdas had it raised to five rupees a month Durga Devi received the news of her son's brightening prospects with joy and celebrated it by offering sweets to the villagers in Birsingjia. More good fortune followed. Thakurdas left Nyayalankar's shelter and came under the care of his father's friend Bhagabat Charan Singha, a well-to-do Kayastha gentleman. It was in his house in Burrabazar that Vidyasagar lived in the early thirties of the 19th century and passed his student days in Calcutta, It was Bhagabat Charan Singha's widowed daughter Raimoni who, by her motherly a Section and care, left an indelible impression on Vidyasagar mind. He remembered her with profound regard to the end of his life. It was possibly the memory of Raimons early widowhood which made him become quite early one of the most ardent champions of the cause of women in India, especially of widows.

Bhagabat Charan secured for Thakurdas a post carrying a pay of eight rupees a month. Thakurdas was then twenty-four years old. He was married to Bhagavati Devi, second daughter of Ramkanta Tarkavagish, a renowned pandit of Goghat in the Hooghly district of West Bengal Iswar Chandra Vidyasagar was born in Birsingha village of this union of the descendants of traditionally high-caste Bengali Brahmin families on September 26, 1820, corresponding to the Bengali year Ashwin 12, 1227.

Bhagavati Devi was an uncommon woman in many ways Vidyasagar's devotion to his mother has inspired many a story in Bengal her catholicity of outlook, quite rare among women of those days, was more remarkable than her kindness She would set aside all injunctions of caste and Shastras with ease, whenever occasion called for it She was as a mother to the villagers She transmitted this blend of kindness and catholicity to her son Iswar Chandra, who cherished it all his life.

Vidyasagar's grandfather, Ramjoy Tarkabhushan, the wanderer, had left his ancestral village, it will be recalled, in protest against the unjust behaviour of his elder brothers. Ramjoy was a very spirited man. He used to move straight, with a big lath! (bamboo rod) in his hand, and always acted on his convictions. At long last he consented to live in his father-in-law's village, Birsingha, so as not to hurt the feelings of his wife Durga Devi.

His brother-in-law, Ramsundar Vidyabhusan, was a prominent man in the local village community and he was a terror to all because of his insolence. Ramjoy did not like this man at all and he refused to truckle to his insolence like the others He often remarked sarcastically that Birsingha was a village like many other villages, where there were many "quadrupeds," but very few "bipeds".

Commenting on the character of Vidyasagar's grandfather, Rabindranath Tagore says in his Vidyasagar-Charit: "This fearless and lofty character of Ramjoy Tarkabhushan is icvealed to us like a mountain peak in the morning: light of the sun. This sort of a witty, spirited and courageous man is hardly produced in the soil of Bengal Had it not been so, the Bengalis would not have been lacking in masculine vigour and vitality. This poor Brahmin could not bequeath any material property to his grandson, except a few precious traits of his noble character".

Vidyasagar inherited a humble mud-hut in Birsingha village and hardly anything else by way of property. But he inherited all the best traits of character of his parents and grandparents—the honesty and dutifulness of his father, the catholicity and deep sense of humanity of his mother, the tenacity and forbearance of his grandmother and the simplicity, courage of conviction and love of truth of his grandfather. In this sense he was a well-endowed heir.

Promising Child

When Iswar Chandra was born, his horoscope was cast It showed that the child would be obdurate like a bull, but famous, honest and truthful. His grandfather jocularly called him erhe-bachur or bull-calf, as also did his father; there was substance in their jest. He had to be told just the opposite of a thing which one would like him to do. To cure Iswar Chandra of his contrariness, his father often had to thrash him.

Never a quiet boy, Iswar Chandra was a source of constant provocation to the villagers. He stole fruits and flowers from their gardens, or outraged their superstitions. Much later in life, when a gentleman came complaining to him about his young son, Tswar Chandra Vidyasagar remarked smilingly: "Don't be disheartened, my friend! Look at me! I was also a problem child, and I was full of pranks just to tease my parents and test the patience of my good neighbours. Now, in spite of all that, I have been able somehow to stand up on my legs, and my future is at least not as dark as was prognosticated by wiseacres at that time. Who knows, your son may have a future in store at least like mine, if not:a-deed something brighter".

In his famous Bengali primer, Vama-parichay, First and Second parts, Vidyasagar has depicted the ideal of a good and obedient boy in the character of Gopal There is another boy Rakhal in the story, held up as an example of a wicked and disobedient boy. Young learners were exhorted by him to follow the example of Gopal and to eschew that of Rakhal. Commenting on this story, Rabmdranath Tagore says in his Vidyasagar-Charit. "In this humble and docile land of ours, there is no dearth of good and submissive boys like Gopal. But if wayward boys like Rakhal and his renowned biographer Vidyasagar were to be born in large numbers in our country, the Bengalis might soon have been able to wipe out the stain of cowardice from their character. Good boys are good for examinations, for dutiful jobs, and at times for commanding handsome dowry in the matrimonial market. But in future our country will need more and more the services of 'disobedient' Rakhals than 'obedient" and 'good" Gopals".

But Iswar Chandra was quite unlike Rakhal in one respect, and that was in the matter of studies. Rakhal used to play truant while Iswar Chandra was never slack in his studies but pursued them against odds.

In those days elementary lessons in reading, writing and simple arithmetic were taught in the village pathsafas, alter which the well-to-do Brahmin boys were sent to tols for higher education in Sanskrit. Birsingha village had its own pathsala, but the gurumahasaya who happened to run it was such a zealous advocate of "spare the rod and spoil the child" maxim that he was a terror to the children. So Thakurdas's choice fell on a Kulra brahmin, Kalikanta Chattopadhyay. Kalikanta was a good and amiable teacher, but the economic advantages of Kulinism were more attractive to him than teaching in a village pathsala. Obviously much against his will, he was at last prevailed upon by Thakurdas to start a pathwla. Iswar Chandra was placed tinder his care at the age of five when according to the Hindu tradition, a child begins to learn.

Kalikanta was greatly impressed with the intelligence of his pupil It was quite unusual, as he often told the father, that Iswar Chandra should have completed his pathsala course in three years. "It is time," said his teacher to Thakurdas, "that Iswar Chandra was sent to a good English school in Calcutta for higher English education". Thakurdas took the same view about the need for sending him to Calcutta for further studies.

The rural atmosphere in which Iswar Chandra passed his childhood was dull and depressing all round. It was a typical backward village of what is now West Bengal, with little sign of education and culture. There was only one important social feature of the village which may be said to have left some impression on Ishwar Chandra's budding mind. The majority of the people in Birsingha and its neighbourhood were either fishermen or small traders. Their social and cultural life, as reflected in village fairs and festivals, still retained some living elements which had not hardened into sterile ritualism The rigid formalism of customs and conventions, widely prevalent among the upper-caste Hindus, was fortunately not part of the rural atmosphere of Birsingha to arrest the growth of Iswar Chandra's active mind.

When he left for Calcutta he was eight years old, small in size, of a frail frame and father timid and shy for his age. It as therefore arrange at a servant should accompany him to Calcutta, along with his father and teacher. When the auspicious day dawned in November, 1828, the four set out on foot from Birsingha to Calcutta, a distance of about sixty miles. It took them three days, walking from dawn to dusk. Iswar Chandra stood the arduous journey very well. Occasionally, his father, teacher, or the old servant had to carry him on back.

On the third day the party reached the new metalled road to Salkca, a village on the western side of the Hooghly river, opposite Calcutta. Iswar Chandra saw milestones on the new road and his curiosity was aroused Thakurdas had to explain to him why they were called "milestones "The boy picked up the English numerals from the numbers engraved on the stones, and he quickly learnt them. Both Kalikanta and Thakurdas were amazed at the quickness of his grasp, and the old servant placed him on his shoulders and danced with joy on the road !

On the third day of their journey, when the sun set in the west, they crossed the river Hooghly on a boat to the east and arrived at the Burrabazar area of Calcutta. From the west of the river Bhagirathi to the east, it was a significant and memorable journey in Iswar Chandra's life, a pilgrimage from an old to a new era.

Advocate of English Education

It was Vidyasagar's firm conviction that English education would be productive of highly beneficial results for this country. He had, therefore, made his best efforts to inaugurate English into the curriculum of the Sanskrit College, and established a free school at his own native village. Even after his retirement from the educational service, he did not give up his project, but founded schools in different parts of the country.

It was at the instance, and through the Untiring exertions of Vidyasagar, that an Anglo-Sanskrit School was established at Kandi in Murshidabad, the native home of the Paikpara Raj family, the brith-place of Raja Pratap Chandra Sinha. Of course, the school was founded at the sole cost of the Rajas, but Vidyasagar was the chief mover He was for some time Honorary Superintendent of the school. At this time, he made an intimate acquaintance of Raja Pratap. The Raj family had once got a great help and benefit from Vidyasagar in other respects. The natural affability and amiability of Vidyasagar's character was so attractive, that his image and goodness were sure to be engraved in the heart of every body he came in contact with.

About this time, he first met at Kandi, after a long separation, Kshetramani Dasi, daughter of Jagaddurlabh Singha, who had formerly given Vidyasagar and his father shelter, Kshetramani had been married to Lal Mohan Ghosh, a nephew (sister's son) of a member of the Kandi Raj family. Unforeseen circumstances had reduced her to a state of indigence. The sight of her after a long period of separation and the tale of her distress' moved his tender heart, and tears flowed in torrents from his eyes. He settled on her a monthly allowance of ten rupees.

As Vidyasagar was a possessor of merits himself, so he was a true appreciator of merits in others. He showed his appreciative faculties in the selection of an Editor for the "Hindu Patriot," one of the ablest native-conducted English news-papers of the day. Haris Chandra Mukharji, the renowned editor and proprietor of the paper, had died at 9 a.m. of the 14 the June, 1861, and its office was removed, on the 25th July of the same year, to Calcutta from Bhowanipore, where it had all along been located, from the day of its birth, in the premises of the late editor and proprietor. Babu Kali Prasanna Sinha purchased the paper at 5,000 rupees and managed it at a loss for some time. But he soon saw the difficulty, and made over its charge to Vidyasagar. Krishto Das Pal was, at this time, employed as a clerk in the office of the British Indian Association. Vidyasagar intrusted him with the editorial charge of the Hindu Patriot. Krishto Das Pal was made not only its editor, but its proprietor also. Krishto Das had not till then acquired any name as a writer. No one could form an idea that he would afterwards become such a great writer. As a matter of consequence, Vidyasagar's nomination of such a person to the responsible post startled all his friends and acquaintances. But soon they found out their mistake, and highly complimented the talented Vidyasagar on his very able selection.

The Hon'ble C. E. Buckland, in his Bengal under the Lieutenant-Governors,' says:—" When Haris Chandra Mukherji, the founder of the Hindu Patriot, died on the 14th June 1861, its new proprietor Babu Kali Prasanna Sinha, after managing it at a loss for some time, made it over to Pandit Ishwar Chandra Vidyasagar, who invited Kristo Das Pal to take the editorial charge in 1861, and subsequently transferred the proprietorship in July 1862 to a body of Trustees. They made over the management to Kristo Das, so that from 1861 to the time of his death, he was in charge, and raised the paper to a position of influence and pecuniary prosperity".

His appreciation of merits in others manifested itself also in the selection of another Editor for the *Soma Prakasa*, a Bengali weekly. Vidyasagar had started the paper, some two years before his retirement from paid public service, solely with the view of providing maintenance for a man quite unconnected with him.

One day, a Brahmin, by name Sarada Prasad Ganguli, came to him, and with tearful eyes, besought him for protection and provision of some means of livelihood. Sarada Prasad had been a student of the Sanskrit College, and had won scholarships for proficiency in both Sanskrit and English, but had, most unfortunately, lost his hearing. Vidyasagar was quite moved at his misfortune, and started the *Soma-Prakasa* with Sarada Prasad for its publisher, solely for the fetter's benefit.

Some time after this, Sarada Prasad was, at the instance of Vidyasagar, appointed Librarian to the Maharaja of Burdwan and Assistant to the Maharaja's translation of the Mahabharat. Maharaja Mahatabchand Bahadur of Burdwan felt a great fond regard and esteem for Vidyasagar, They had met first in 1847, when Vidyasegar had gone to Burdwan in company with Babu Ram Gopal Ghosh, a most celebrated orator of the time, and Raja Satya Saran Ghoshal of Bhukailas to visit the famous city. Vidyasagar had not at that time accepted the articles of food presented by the Maharaja, but boarded with a friend of his. When the Maharaja was apprised of this, he sent for Vidyasagar. He was highly delighted at the latter's conversation, and considered himself fortunate in having been able to make his acquaintance. At the time of farewell, the Maharaja offered him a present of 500 rupees in cash and a pair of *Shawl*. But Vidyasagar declined the offer, and said:—'It is not my practice to accept presents. My pay from the Sanskrit College is sufficient for my maintenance. Such presents might be given to professors of *Tats* to greater advantage.' The Maharaja was quite amazed at Vidyasagar's self-denial. Henceforth he looked upon the young pundit with utmost veneration. After this, whenever Vidyasagar visited Burdwan, the Maharaja received him most cordially and treated him with much respect He bore so much fond regard for the venerable pundit, that on one occasion, he voluntarily offered the latter his native village, Birsingha, as a *Taluk*, but Vidyasagar declined this offer too, saying that he would accept the *Taluk*, when his means would permit him to let lands to the tenants free of rent.

It was this Maharaja Mahatabchand Bahadur, who had backed Vidyasagar in his widow-marriage movement, and had been one of the subscribers to the petition presented to the Government of India, as the under-quoted letter will show:

"My dear sir,

"You will no doubt be glad to hear that his Highness the Maharaja of Burdwan has promised his assistance to the furtherance of the sacred cause of the marriage of Hindu widows. It is really a matter for congratulation, that the first man of Bengal is going to take up the cause.

He entertains such enlightened views that we have every reason to hope for substantial assistance from him. The Maharaja is not a hasty man, nor does he consent to be led by others, but always thinks for himself and forms his opinions of things after mature deliberation. Now that his Highness is convinced of the goodness of the cause, I have no doubt that he will be its staunch friend and champion.

(Sd.) "Ishwar Chandra Sharma.

To the Hon'ble J.P. Grant".

To revert When the *Soma-Prakasa* was first started, Vidyasagar used to write most of its articles. Madan Mohan Tarkalankar also contributed some articles now and then. The paper was issued every Monday, whence its name. By and by, Vidyasagar found it difficult to issue the paper regularly and punctually every week on the appointed day. He could not make time to attend to it with proper care. He was often heard to declare that he was very short of time and the regular publication of the weekly newspaper was harder than another's service. He was, therefore, on the look-out for a competent editor, and he set his eyes on Dvaraka Nath Vidyabhushan, whom he charged with the edition of the paper. Vidyabhushan was made not only editor, but also proprietor of the *Sotna-Prakasa*.

The system, under which newspapers are conducted now-a-days, was first introduced into vernacular journalism by Vidyabhushan. He soon made his paper successful, which reflected great credit on Vidyasagar for his judicious selection. The Bengali papers started prior to the *Soma Prakasa* discussed mostly social and religious matters. Political subjects appeared in them few and far between, and even then they were not dealt with so gravely and elegantly by these papers as by the *Soma Prakasa*. In respect of language too, it was a higher model for the others, Inspite of their many defects, those journals must be complimented upon for their attempts at the development of the Bengali language. It cannot but be admitted that the modern form of Bengali prose originated with these newspapers. We will, therefore, try to notice briefly the principal Bengali newspapers, that were born before the birth of the *Soma Prakasa.*

The general impression is that the Christian missionaries of Serampore were the pioneers of Bengali journalism. But in fact, this notion is mistaken. The missionaries issued their 'Samachara Darpana' in 1817. But before that, Pandit Gangadhar Bhattacharyya had started, in the city of Calcutta, his 'Bengali Gazette' in 1815. So this was the first newspaper in Bengali. In 1820 appeared the ' Sangbada Kaumudi,' edited by Bhavani Charan Banarji, with the help of Raja Ram Mohan Ray and Babu Tarachand Datta. But subsequently when the Raja began writing in it articles against the practice of *Sati,* Bhavani Charan cut off his connection with the paper. In the next year, he started his "Samachara Chandrika," a weekly, which was afterwards made a daily paper, and ultimately incorporated with the 'Dainika of the Bangabasi office. Then followed the 'Timira Nasaka,' also a weekly, edited by Krishna Mohan Das of Mirzapore. This paper lived for a few short years only. After it, appeared the ' Banga Duta,' under the joint management of Raja Ram Mohan Ray and Babus Devendra Nath and Prasanna Kumar Tagores. In the beginning of 1831, Babu Jogendra Mohan Tagore of Pathureaghata started the "Sangbada Prabhakara" under the editorship of Ishwar Chandra Gupta. With the death of the starter in a few years, his paper also lost its life.

Ishwar Chandra then became editor of the "Sangbada Ratnabali," but in a 9hort time, he gave it over. He again revived the "Sangbada Prabhakara" in 1836. It was then made tri-weekly; and in 1839, it was made a daily paper. About the time that this paper was renewed, or a little before it, appeared "Purna Chandrodaya". In the first year, it appeared on every full-moon day, whence its name. In the next year it was made a weekly, and in a few more years, it was also converted to a daily paper. There was also another newspaper, titled the "Sangbada Mrityunjaya". It had one great peculiarity. Everything in the paper, from the advertisements down to the news, appeared in poetry. None of these papers had before been conducted so ably as the *Soma-Prakasa.* It excelled all its predecessors in every respect.

To resume our narrative: on the 13th January 1860, Vidyasagar republished, in pamphlet forms, those portions of his Bengali version of the Mahabharata, which had already appeared in the Tattva Bodhini Patrika. The publication being incomplete, it did not bring him much profits, though the language is very nice.

On the 12th April, 1861, appeared his *Sitar Vanavas (i.e.* The Banishment of Sita), a Bengali version of Bhavabhuti's "Uttara-Charita," but it differs from the original in many respect. Though the original is one of the best dramas in Sanskrit, Vidyasagar has not dramatised his book The original is not a pure tragedy, because the Sanskrit Rhetoric does not permit composition of tragic dramas, but Vidyasagar has made his book purely tragical. Besides these, there are some minor differences too numerous to notice. But the language of the book is very elegant, chaste, refined, and attractive. It is an excellent model for writers of Bengali prose. Vidyasagar wrote the book in four days. Pressure of business would afford him no leisure in the day-time to write. He applied himself to its composition in the morning from 2-30 to 10 O'clock. He could not make even so much time as to revise it.

We will again relate here, in passing, one or two incidents displaying his affability, amiability, generosity and physical strength. The reader may be vexed with us for repeated digressions, but there is no help, and we crave earnestly the reader's indulgence.

On his retirement from the service of the Sanskrit College, when he was free, he visited his native village, Birsingha, oftener than before, and frequented the houses of his neighbours, enquiring after their affairs as previously. Each time he took with him 500 to 600 rupees in coins and cloth to the value of 400 to 500 rupees, which he freely distributed to the poor and helpless. He always gave to the beggars, supplicants, and expectants more than they had expected. He received his visitors cordially and entertained them most generously. He never sent any body away displeased; it was his nature to do his best to please and oblige every body.

On one occasion, when he was at his native place, a man came to him from Patul, the abode of his mother's maternal uncle. The man saluted him, and said; -'Do you know me? We were fellow-pupils of the same *Patksala*. You may recollect, how many times I saved you from the hands of the Guru Mahasay (preceptor).' Vidyasagar at once recognised him, and said;—'O yes, you are Raghav?' The man's name was Raghav Ray, and he belonged to the Bagdi caste, one of the lowest classes in Bengal. Raghav looked displeased, and shut his ears with his fingers. Some body whispered in to Vidyasagar's ears that the man was rather crazed, and considered himself the god Krishna Ray of Bagri. He also said that Raghav did not eat food cooked by other Bagdis or persons of any other caste lower than Brahmins. Vidyasagar now understood the whole affair, He at once stood up and clasped Raghav in his arms, saying: 'You are Krishna Ray.' Raghav's delight now knew no bounds. He took his seat at Vidyasagar's feet, and the two friends of early years fell to talking of reminiscences of their childhood.

On another occasion, as he was sitting in the verandah of his house at Birsingha, one Matuk Ghosh, a Sadgop by caste, called on him. He welcomed the visitor with his usual affability, and asked him to get up on the verandah and to sit by him. The man hesitated. Vidyasagar at once caught hold of his two arms, and lifted him upon the verandah from below it, and made him sit by himself. His physical powers were equal to his powers of the mind.

Some time in 1862, when he was at Birsingha, one day, as he sat to dinner, an aged lady and a young girl appeared before him and began to cry, Vidyasagar was told that the lady was wife of his Guru Mahasay, Kalikanta, and the girl was his daughter. We have already said that Kalikanta was a Kulin Brahmin and had taken to him many wives. Vidyasagar was also told that Kalikanta did not care to provide for the maintenance of this wife and daughter. He at once sent for Kalikanta, whom he had made one of the teachers of his school. When the latter arrived, he requested him to provide for the maintenance of the two females, who were no other than his own wife and daughter, adding, at the same time, that if he did so, his monthly allowance would be raised. Kalikanta agreed to pay them four rupees every month. He at once paid 12 rupees in advance for the first quarter, and promised to make all subsequent payments quarterly in advance. Vidyasagar himself provided for their clothes. But some time afterwards,

Kalikanta drove the two away from his house. When Vidyasagar came to know of it, he was moved to tears, and made provisions for their support.

Raja Ishwar Chandra Sinha of the Paikpara Raj family breathed his last on the 26th February, 1861. Vidyasagar was present by the death-bed, and was deply grieved at the sad catastrophe. The Raja was a great appreciator of Vidyasagar's merits and works, and always sympathised with, and aided, all his movements.

Vidyasagar was a sincere friend of the poor and the rich alike. He never expected a single pice from any one, but spent his all in succouring the distrest. Even when a wealthy man was *in* danger and besought his help, he would spend his last pice in relieving the man. If he happened not to have sufficient funds at the time in his own purse, he would obtain money on loans, and rescue him from the danger. On the other hand, if he saw that any of his friends or relations failed in their duties or tried to damage his respect, he would at once sever all ties of friendship and affection, and cut off his connection with them, even if they were millionaires. It was for some such similar reason, that he on a subsequent date banished his only son from his heart, of which hereafter.

In 1862, he had to meet with another mournful catastrophe in the death of his once dear friend, Rama Prasad Ray, the youngest son of the illustrious Raja Ram Mohan Ray- Rama Prasad was the ablest pleader of the Sudder Adalat of the day. He was the first native of Bengal, who was nominated to be a justice of the said Hon'ble Court. He had received the appointment letter, but before he could take his seat on the bench, he was suddenly ill and died. A few years before this sad event, Vidyasagar had a great difference with Rama Prasad in connection with the remarriage of Hindu widows. It is said, that on the occasion of the marriage of Sris Chandra Vidyaratna, who was the first to come forward to take a widow to his wife, some influential, wealthy persons had subscribed to an agreement to be present at the wedding festivities and promised to contribute largely to the expenses to be incurred on widow marriages. But most of these subscribers did not keep their word, A few days before the marriage, Vidyasagar called on his friend, Rama Prasad, and reminded him of his agreement and promise. The latter replied:—'No doubt, I am in favour of the cause; you may count on my contribution too. But suppose, I do not join the wedding party. Is there any harm?' Vidyasagar was quite disgusted at his friend's conduct.

He was so much offended that for some time he could not utter a single word. After a long silence he pointed to the portrait of Raja Ram Mohan Ray hanging on the walls, and said;— 'Throw it away at once.' With this, he left the place in great haste. After this incident, Vidyasagar never more entered into his friend's house. The two very rarely met. But the mournful news of Rama Prasad Ray's death moved him to a flood of tears. Both were men of great abilities and talents, and naturally had a sincere attraction of their hearts.

In 1862, appeared his *Vyakarana Kaumudi, Part IV* which was his last Sanskrit Grammatical work dressed in Bengali. In the course of this year, there took place several marriages of Hindu widows in different parts of the country. Of these, one was celebrated in Calcutta. The bride and bridegroom both belonged to the highest class of Hindus. All these marriages were celebrated at Vidyasagar's expense. He had now no other income than what accrued from his Press and publications. We have already said that it was quite inadequate to meet his heavy outlays. Consequently he had to obtain money on loans. Besides, he borrowed 10,000 rupees on Michael M. Datta's account, which the latter being unable to repay, Vidyasagar paid off out of his own pocket, which will be noticed.

Age of Consent Issue

In the meantime, Vidyasagar's constitution was gradually sinking, his health was failing him, and he was slowly losing his vitality. You have seen how he had all along struggled manfully with the worries and troubles of life and had always come out victorious. But alas! who has ever won the grim gates of Death? His deep-seated malady was being daily aggravated by heart-rending griefs at the loss of those nearest and dearest to his heart Besides those enumerated before, he had to grieve and mourn over the death of his most beloved friends and relations. His very dear friends, Pyari Charan Sarkar, Syama Charan Biswas, Kristo

Das Pal, Dinabandhu Mitra, and his second brother, Dinabandhu Nyayratna all had departed from this world one by one, leaving him alone to pine away the last days of his existence, Dinabandhu Mitra was a great Bengali writer and" Vidyasagar's most sincere friend. His lodgings stood very close to our hero's house in Sukea's Street. The two families were so intimately connected in friendship, that though they belonged to different castes, they made no distinction in friendly intercourse. When, on Dinabandu Mitra's death, her poor widow with a number of helpless, little children, saw nothing but a blank vacuum all round her, it was only Vidyasagar who comforted her with assurances, and provided for the education of her sons. But for our benevolent hero, God knows what might not have happened to them.

In April, 1890, the looseness of his bowels took an alarmingly serious turn. He had been suffering from its effects for upwards of six years past. He had lost the strength of his digestive" powers. These six years he had taken only one meal a day, composed of a little quantity of boiled rice and some fish-juice. Milk he had to give up altogether. But from the beginning of 1890, his stomach could no more assimilate even such light food, as a small quantity of purboiled rice. A little barley-water or sago was his only diet In the Utter part of the year, he was advised by his medical attendant, doctor Hira Lal Ghosh, to live a retired? secluded life, Vidyasagar said— 'That would be impossible while I am in Calcutta. I cannot refuse to receive visits; nor can I place a *Darwan* (porter) at my gates'. Finally it was settled that he should leave the city. In the month of December, he went to French Chandernagore, in company with his eldest daughter, where a very nice two-storeyed house in a healthy locality by the side of the Bhagirathi had been rented for him. In this house he lived for some times, and showed signs of a little improvement.

Even in this sojourn for purposes of restoration of health, there was no cessation of his acts of benevolence and charity. Wheresoever he would be, the genial flow of his ever tender, ever gentle heart must find its way out. One day, a blind Mussulman beggar, led by his wife, was out in the streets a begging. He wandered over the town for alms, but got nothing. At last, he presented himself before our noble hero. The sad tale of the beggar's misery touched his naturally kind heart, He gave the blind man some pice, and asked, him,—What would you like to eat?' The beggar replied,—'I have not eaten *Luchi* (wheat-flour bread fried in *Ghee)* for some time past I feel a. strong Appetite for it.' Vidyasagar at once had *Luchi* prepared by his daughter, and fed with it the poor, blind man and his wife sumptuously. After the repast had been over, he gave the beggar two, rupees, and asked him to call every Sunday aad partake of *Luchi* at his house.

During his stay it Chandernagbre, he used and then to take 'strolls in the neighbouring places. On one occasion, *he* paid a visit to a *Brahmin* of Bhadresvar, at his earnest reddest, by his third brother, Sambhu Chandra The host's son, who was a leper, offered our hero a hookha prepared with his own hands. Vidyasagar ungrudgingly took the hookha from his hands and smoked it as usual. On their way back, Sambhu Chandra remonstrated with him, and asked him how he could persuade himself to smoke the tobacco prepared by a leper's hands. Vidyasagar very seriously said: 'God forbid, Supposing you or I myself had been a leper what Would I do?' Sambhu Chandra had nothing to say against it.

Some time before this, a Bill had been introduced into the Legislature Council for Amendment of the Indian Pertal Code and the Crimmal Procedure Code on certain sections relating to the Age of Cbnsent on the part of females to sexual inter-course. The government, as all important matters of legislation, asked Vidyasagar for his opinion on the point. In this connection, he had to leave Chandernagbre and return to Calcutta for a week. He studied deeply the differed *Sistras* on religious points, and on the 16th February 1891, gave his opinion Bill in the form in which it had been introduced into the Council, and suggesting a measure consonant to the religious usage of the Hindus. His opinion was that as *Garbkadhana Sanskara* was a religious usage in conformity with the Sastras, binding on every Hindu, and as there was no certainty at what age a female might have her first menses (the period when the *Garbhadhana Sanskara* should be performed), the placing of a restriction on the age limit for the consent of the ferhale would be a direct interference with the religious customs of the country. He, therefore, very wisely indicated a way in accordance with the Sastras, which if adopted would give the desired protection to the child-wives. To enable the reader to form an idea of his opinion on the point, we crave indulgence to quote below some portions of his Note on the subject:

"Though on these grounds I cannot support the Bill as it is, I should like the measure to be so framed as to give something like an adequate protection to child-wives, without in any way conflicting with any religious usage. I would propose that it should be an offence for a man to consummate marriage before his wife has had her first menses. As the majority of girls do not exhibit that symptom before they are thirteen, fourteen or fifteen, the measure I suggest would give larger, more real, and more extensive protection than the Biljj. At the same time, such a measure could not be object-ed to on the ground of interfering with a religious observance.

'From every point of view, therefore, the most reasonable course appears to me, to make a law declaring it penal for a man to have intercourse with his wife, before she has her first menses.

"Such a law would not only serve the interests of humanity by giving reasonable protection to child-wives, but would, so far from interfering with religious usage, enforce a rule laid down in the Sastras. The punishment, which the Sastras prescribe for violation of the rule, is of a spiritual character and is liable to be disregarded. The religious prohibition would be made more effective, if it was embodied in a penal law. I may be permttted to press this consideration most earnestly, on the attention of the government.

Sd. "Isvara Chandra Sharma

The 16th February 1891.!

But this time the government did not accept his views. In spite of his *very* reasonable opposition, the Bill was passed. It is a manner displays the policy of the alien government in the administration of this country. When this Vidyasagar had petitioned for a legislation on the re-marriage of Hindu widows, his prayer had been readity granted Widow-marriage is consonant to the feelings, customs! and policy of the ruling.

The same Vidyasagar proposed a measure on the Age of Consent Bill, which, if adopted, would have saved both sides, but it was rejected, although it was not wholly conflicting with the views of the rulers. Was it because, this time, the government was afraid of losing its prestige?

The 'Hindu Society was glad to find that Vidyasagar did not fall into errors in his discussion of the Age of Consent question, as he had done on the occasion of Widow Marriage movement. Some even weitt so far as to fancy, that it was his own conviction of his former errors that led him to oppose a Bill interfering with the religious usage of the Hindus. Besides, Vidyasagar had kept himself aloof, for some time past, from taking part in the re-marriage of Hindu widows, which also served to make the people draw this portrait in their mind. The advocates of widow marriage, however, attribute his apathy to his own ill-health and to, the want of firmness and faithlessness of his country-men, which might be the more pro-bable cause. We have already said, that he was no hypocrite, and had he been really convinced of his errors, he would never have been afraid to declare i£openly. Moreover, it is said that even so late as a little before his death, he tried to give his own grartdson (daughter's son) in widow marriage. There can be no doubt that he was disappointed at the conduct of some of his followers, who had subsequently forsaken him, which, in his opinion, so much impeded the progress of widow marriage. Perhaps, it was this sad dis-appointment, which led him to exult when the news of Babu Durga Mohan Das's widow marriage reached him, though such an alliance was against his principle, as the woman whom Durga Mohan had taken to be his wife, had been an old widow with several children by her first husband. This marriage took place only two months before Vidyasagar's departure from this world. On the occasion he wrote a letter to Durga Mohan in Bengali to the following effect:

'My dear friend,

'I am glad to hear that your desires have been satisfied. I heartily wish and pray that you may pass the remaining days of your life *in* happiness with your new consort. Communicate my tender compliments and blessings to her.'

East and West

In the thirties of nineteenth century the storm broke out suddenly from more than one quarter It shook many age-old beliefs and customs, causing alarm and confusion in society. The storm raged during Iswar Chandra's student days, from 1829 to 1841.

In the midst of the heated controversy between the Anglicists and the Orientalists, the Hindu College and the Sanskrit College were registering progress In January, 1824, the Managers of the Hindu College applied for financial aid to government, and the Committee of Public Instruction agreed to patronise it in exchange for a share in tibe management of the College. The Bengali Hindu Managers had no alternative but to agree. A new building was erected in 1826 in Galdighi or College Square, wherein both the Hindu College and the Sanskrit College were housed. The Sanskrit College occupied the central part of the building, and the Hindu College its east-west wings. This architectural link between the two institutions went a long way in removing the barriers between classical Indian and modern Western ideas.

But social customs intervened to break up the link. The Sanskrit College was exclusively meant for the boys of the upper-caste Brahmin and Vaidya families The Hindu College excluded the Muslims and the Christians but was meant for Hindu boys of all castes—at least officially The horizons of both East and West learning were thus narrowed down by caste and communal restrictions. The precautions taken in the beginning to check the intermingling of students reading in the two colleges make amusing reading. The two buildings were separated by a wall surmounted by iron railings. The aim was that the two different "classes" of students, the dwijas or "the twice-born" and the sudras or "the once-born," should not come into contact with each other. Similarly, they were permitted to enter by a common gate, provided, of course, it was wide enough for them to pass through without touching one another! The central part of the building was fenced off from the side-wings by an enclosure to prevent the students of one institution from getting into the premises of the other. It was also thought desirable that the out-houses and offices of the two colleges should be kept clearly apart in compliance with "the most inveteiate of Native prejudices".

Ishwar Chandra had to pass his student life in the narrow confines of the enclosure and railings of this otherwise magnificent temple of learning. The conditions were not conducive either to making the Hindu College "the main channel by which... knowledge may be transferred from iti European sources into the intellect of Hindustan' or for effecting in the Sanskrit College "the gradual diffusion of European knowledge" in addition to the cultivation of Sanskrit language and literature.

Yet in this atmosphere Iswar Chandra grew up in his youth and his intellectual horizon widened largely. Standing on the Eastern shore of "the ocean of knowledge," he looked to the West, beyond the "iron rails" and the "enclosure" yearning for the removal of the barriers and for free but critical exchange of ideas between the East and the West.

The whole situation was made worse by the extreme activities of a band of young Hindu College students, called the "Derozians" after their teacher-preceptor, H. L. V. Derozio, a young Eurasian poet, philosopher and teacher. This group of young men was popularly known as "Young Bengal" and "Young Calcutta". Rising in the late twenties, they broke in upon the thirties of the last century with their iconoclastic ideas and exuberant zeal for social reform It all happened in the first half of Iswar Chandra's student life in the Sanskrit College.

Derozio was born in Calcutta on April 10, 1809, and died in 1831, at the age of twenty-two. He was appointed a teacher in the Hindu College sometime in 1827, when he was only 18 years old His charming personality and brilliance of mind drew the senior boys of the College to him, and his biographer, Thomas Edwards, says, "neither before nor since his days has any teacher, within the walls of any native educational establishment in India, ever exercised such an influence over his pupils "The events of the period bear out this tribute.

Between 1827 and 1830 the Young Derozians blossomed forth. In the words of Derozio, they were "expanding like the petals of young flowers," and "like young birds in soft summer hour" they were stretching "their wings to try their strength". They studied under the guidance of their young teacher the works of Bacon, Locke, Berkeley, Hume, Reid, Thomas Paine, Dugald Stewart, and others, and a revolution was taking place in their ideas. They were learning to reason, to question, and to doubt everything round them, and not to acquiesce in any authority, however hoary. They debated weighty subjects in their class-rooms, in the drawing-room of their teacher Derozio, and in their own society, "the Academic Association". The Rev. Lalbehari Dey writes in Ms Recollections that in the weekly meetings of this Association "did the choice spirits of Young Calcutta hold forth, week after week, on the social, moral and religious questions of the day. The general tone of the discussions was a decided revolt against existing religious institutions... The young lions of the Academy roared out, week after week, 'Down with Hinduism,' 'Down with Orthodoxy.' "All this caused consternation in the Hindu society, and the elders deliberated upon the situation.

At this time, stoking the fires already burning, Bentmcb, the Governor-General of India, abolished, after much dillydallying, sati by legislation on December 4, 1829. Many Englishmen were at the time against this piece of legislation as, in their opinion, it was tantamount to interfering with the Hindu religion. The eminent Orientalist, H. H. Wilson, wrote to the Military Secretary to government, in a letter dated November 25, 1826: "One or two individuals in Calcutta, who have signalised themselves by dissenting from many of the practices and principles of the religion, may hold a different persuasion, but the vast body of the population will concur in the same impression, and the government has to legislate not for a handful of sectaries but for the Hindus at large". The "one or two individuals in Calcutta" referred to in Wilson's letter were obviously Rammohan Roy and his handful of associates. Hindu sentiment was outraged by the legislation and it seemed in 1829-30 that the entire Hindu community was in revolt against it The Dharma Sabha was organised on January 17, 1830, by the orthodox Hindus to fight against the legislation and to have it abrogated.

In the midst of the confusion caused by the cries of progress of the ultra-radical Derozians on the one hand and by the loud protests of the orthodox Hindu community on the other, the celebrated missionary, Alexander Duff, arrived at Calcutta on May 27, 1830. He was charged by the Committee of Foreign Missions in Scotland to propagate Christianity and to lay the foundations of Christian education in India. He witnessed the revolution talcing place in the minds of the young intellectuals of Bengal, the extreme nature of their religious and social views, and the spirit of unbounded liberty which characterised their thoughts. In his India and Indian Missions, Duff says. "We hailed the circumstance as indicating the approach of a period for which we had waited, and longed and prayed". He contemplated the scene with mixed feelings of joy and fear. With the co-operation of Rammohan Roy, who was then scheduled to sail for England in November, 1830, he opened the General Assembly's Institution on July 13, 1830, with five students only, at Jorasanko in Calcutta. He also organised a course of lectures on Christianity, to be delivered by himself, the Rev, Mr Adam of the London Missionary Society, the Rev. Mr Hill of the same Society and the Rev. Mr Dealtry, afterwards Bishop of Madras. The introductory lecture, delivered at Calcutta to a large audience of young educated Hindus in August, 1830, fell like a bomb-shell among the Hindu College authorities. They thought that the religion of their forefathers was in danger, and that the students would soon be converted to Christianity. They, therefore, ruled that any student who attended the lectures of the missionaries would be expelled from the College. The young student-reformers raised a loud outcry against this "despotic order" of the College authorities. Debating societies were organised in. which the bigotry, tyranny and orthodoxy of the Hindus weic denounced in unbridled language.

Owing to this agitation Derozio was forced to leave the Hindu College in April, 1831, and he died suddenly the following December, without being able to watch how his young students were "loosening" the "spell" that bound their "intellectual energies and powers". Two leading spirits of the Derozians, Krishna Mohan Banerji and Dakshina-ranjan Mukherji, 17 or 18 years old then, started two periodicals, the English weekly Enquirer and the Bengali weekly Jnananweshan (Search for Knowledge) in May and June, 1831. Week after week, the young editors put the orthodox Hindus in the pillory. The conservative Samachar Chandnka thundered vehemently against the railings of the radicals. The European-owned Indian Gazette and the Bengali Hurkaru, and the Bengali Samachar Datpan of the Baptist missionaries of Serampore tried to steer a middle course between the Right and the Left, admonishing both for their excesses. The English weekly Reformer, edited by Prosunna Coomar Tagore, uncle of

Rabindranath Tagore, set out the liberal point of view dispassionately—this reflected more or less the opinion of the Brahmos, the associates and followers of Rammohan Roy.

Thus the Conservatives (the orthodox Hindus), the Moderates (the Brahmos) and the Radicals (the Derozians) were disposed in the social scene in the thirties of the last century when Iswar Chandra was in the Sanskrit College. The storm-centre of the whole movement was the Hindu College, located in the two wings of the Sanskrit College building As Iswar Chandra was growing up in this decade, the storm did not pass off without leaving some impress upon his growing mind.

Towards the close of the decade and of his student life, the storm clouds were slowly disappearing with some flicker of sunshine on an otherwise gloomy social atmosphere. Two important socio-cultural "groups" were organised by the educated Bengalis—the Society for the Acquisition of General Knowledge, in May, 1838, and the Tattwafaodhini Sabha in October, 1839, to bring under control the chaotic social trends, and to help, as far as possible, the harmonising of the clashing ideals of the East and the West.

This was made possible mainly under the influence of Maharshi Debendra-nath Tagore, father of Rabindranath, and his Tattwabodhinl Sabha. This Sabha took up the cause of Brahmoism, the moral and social influence of which had declined considerably after Rammohan's departure from Bengal in 1830 and his subsequent death in England in 1833. Debendranathfs courage of conviction made the Sabha a powerful and dynamic progressive force before long; and it became the rallying point of a large number of intellectuals of Bengal of varying shades of liberal views Many prominent Derozians of the thirties were attached to it in the forties, and became its most influential members Iswar Chandra was naturally attracted to this group and was gradually drawn into its fold when his student life was over.

The catholicity of the Sabha and the liberal policy of its Bengali organ Tattwabodhini Patrika, with which he became associated, provided him the opportunities for equipping himself for the role he was to play on the social stage in later years.

Traditional System

The traditional tol-chatuspati system of education was till then rigidly pursued in the Sanskrit College of Calcutta. There were no benches for students, no chairs for teachers. They used to sit on mats in rooms and to carry their books and papers wrapped up in a piece of cloth like a bundle. There were very few printed texts, and students had to copy down their lessons from manuscripts. In accordance with age-old custom, Brahmin and Vaidya boys only were admitted to the college The method of teaching was modelled on the old tol pattern. English was taught but was not a compulsory subject; as a result, it was treated with indifference by authorities and students alike. It was not part of the regular curriculum. Students had to start from the Vyakaran or grammar class, as grammar was the main approach to the Sanskrit language. After it was mastered, the students had to pass through the portals of Sahitya (literature), Alankara (rhetoric), Smriti, Vedanta and Nyaya classes to acquire the attainments of a good Sanskrit scholar. It took about twelve years to go through these stages.

Ishwar Chandra as a student was daunted by grammar: it was a desert without oases. Despite his teachers' best efforts to make it interesting, he had to grapple with its formidable rules till late hours in the night in spite of his frail health. At last the desert was crossed in an effort spread over three years and more and when he had won many scholarships and prizes. One of the first tasks which he undertook as an educational reformer was to reform Sanskrit grammar thoroughly and to make it easier for the students to learn, through the medium of their own language, Bengali.

Elementary lessons in English were then given to students in the grammar class. Iswar Chandra did well in the subject and won prizes, but his English education ended abruptly in 1835 when the authorities decided to abolish the English Department in the College. As he had won the battle of Sanskrit grammar with considerable credit, he was promoted to the Sahitya class in 1833. Pandit Joygopal Tarkalankai, an eminent Sanskrit scholar, was then a protessor of Sanskrit Literature in the College. He was greatly liked by his students for his studious ways and charming personality Some of his old students have told us in their reminiscences that after reciting a Sanskrit sloka from a kavya, and reading out a passage from a prose text in the class, he used to close his eyes in appreciative meditation and, like a dreamei but half-awakened, explain its literary excellence in rapturous joy, holding the students spell-bound, and lifting them from the drab class-room to the cloud-land of literary imagination. Iswar Chandra was fortunate in getting initiated into classical Sanskrit literature by a profound scholar like Joygopal. He stood first in the final examination of Sahitya in 1834-35 and won prizes. These two years of Sahitya class were perhaps the happiest of all in Ms long student life.

As early marriage was the prevailing custom, he was married when barely fourteen to Dinamoyi Devi, who canto of a middle-class Brahmin family of Khirpai village near Birsingha.

After getting creditably through Alankara, Vedanta and Smriti classes, he appeared for the Hindu Law Committee's examination in 1839 and qualified himself to hold the office of Hindu Law Officer in "any of the Established Courts of Judicature "His name was mentioned as "Iswar Chandur Vidyasagur" in the Certificate awarded to him in May, 1839, by the President and Members of the Committee. It is evident that sometime in the middle of 1839 he qualified himself for the title Vidyasagar, and not after the completion of his full course of study in 1841, as is usually supposed.

After he had passed the Law Committee's examination, the post of the Judge-Pandit of Tripura district in East Bengal was offered to him. He was very eager to accept the post for financial reasons but his father was not willing to let him do so before he had completed his studies. He had to decline the offer and enter the crucial Philosophy class of Nyaya to complete his education. He was again, fortunate in having as his teachers two outstanding Nyaya scholars of that time—Pandit Nemai Chandra Shiromam and Pandit Jayanarayan Tarkapanchanan.

In the final examination in 1840-41 he stood first in Nyaya philosophy, winning a cash prize of Rs. 100, He also won Rs. 100 for the best poetical composition in Sanskrit, Rs. 8 for the best Dcvana-gan handwriting Rs. 25 for proficiency in the Company's Laws, as also a monthly scholarship of Rs. 8.

He handed over to his father the cash prizes and scholarships, which he had gained in his student life, to help his family. His father set apart a certain portion of it for buying a suitable plot of land for a tol in Birsingha village and advised his son to spend the rest in buying rare and valuable Sanskrit manuscripts. This he did earnestly and was able to collect several good Sanskrit manuscripts as also to get some of them copied by scribes These may still be seen in his magnificent library, which was the talk of the day and which has been preserved partly in the Bangiya Sahitya Parishad in Calcutta.

After about twelve years' study in the Sanskrit College he was awarded the Final Certificate of Proficiency in Sanskrit Language and Literature on December 4, 1841 The copy of this Certificate has been recently acquired and is preserved in the Bangiya Sahitya Panshad collection. He was also awarded an additional Certificate by the learned professors of the College for his extraordinary merit and achievements during his student career. This is dated December 10, 1841. His student life, for all practical purposes, ended on this date, when he was twenty-one years and a few months old It was time now for him to pass out of the temple of learning into the world to make headway there also.

A Long Fight

In fact Vidyasagar had to fight every inch of his way in the strange society of the city. Progressive reforms, social and educational, were his watchwords as with his great predecessor Rammohan Roy; but he also possessed a strong sense of national heritage and tradition.

Some important events in his life were his first appointment in the Fort William College as Sheristadar or Head Pandit of the Bengali Department in December, 1841, as Assistant Secretary to the Sanskrit College in April, 1846, his subsequent resignation from the post in 1847, and his reappomtment in the Fort William College as Head Writer and Treasurer in March, 1849. During the fifties of nineteenth last century his activities were directed towards educational and social reform when he was Principal of the Sanskrit College. His resignation from the Principal's post in November, 1858, marks another turning-point in his life, after which we find him gradually fading out from the social scene in ever-deepening isolation. Although he lived till 18MI, he was never again to the fore. Perhaps he was tired and worn out with many disappointments in his long life.

The years 1841 to 1850 led to his rise to eminence in the succeeding fifties. It was clear by the end of the decade that he had finally taken his stand and that there was no turning back from it He was appointed Head Pandit of the Bengali Department in Fort William College in December, 1841. This College had been established at Calcutta on November 24, 1800, by Marquis of Wellesley for giving training in the Oriental languages to the Junior Servants of the Company on their first arrival in India During the iorty-one years of its existence, many Bengali and Hindustani Pandits and Muslim Maulvis, appointed as teachers of Indian languages in the College, had come in close contact with some of the best English minds of the time. A suitable atmosphere had been created in an educational institution in which the mutual exchange of European and Indian ideas could take place freely. The Pandits were imbued here with the new liberalism of the West; the young English rulers grew acquainted here with the catholicity of our cultural tradition.

When Vidyasagar entered the College, the atmosphere and the standards of the College were fast deteriorating. Still his direct contact with talented young English civilians of the post-Industrial Revolution era in the College served to form his modern outlook.

While Vidyasagar was the Head Pandit, the affectionate patronage of Captain Marshall, Secretary to the College, afforded him an opportunity to learn English and Hindi simultaneously. He engaged a Hindi teacher, and being a good Sanskrit scholar, he learnt it quickly For learning English, of ^course, he had to work hard. Among his English teachers were Durgacharan Banerji, Rajnarain Basu, Nilmadhab Mukherji and Rajnarayan Gupta, a student of Hindu College. He gave up his mathematical studies after some time and studied Shakespeare with Anandaknshna Basu, grandson of Raja Radhakanta Dev of the Sovabazar Raj family. As he had to visit frequently the Sovabazar Rajbari, he was one day introduced to Raja Radhakanta Dev, the great Sanskrit scholar and the most influential leader of the orthodox section of the Hindu community of his time. It was Radhakanta Dev who led the movement against Ram-mohan's social and religious reforms as also against Vidyasagar's. Widow Remarriage, Anti-Polygamy and Anti-Child-Marriage reform activities. But the orthodox Raja was very much impressed with the brilliance of young Vidyasagar, and he often used to say that the bright Brahmin boy was destined to play a very significant role in India's social and cultural life. Vidyasagar did not know then that the Raja would shortly be his duel opponent in the social reform movement. Radhakanta Dev was a moderate in his social outlook and was not opposed to reform, provided it was induced from within and not imposed from without. The goodwill of such a powerful person at the outset of his carrier was undoubtedly inspiring to Vidyasagar; his respect for his great opponent never diminished in later life.

Learning English himself, Vidyasagar was teaching Sanskrit at the same time to others. He adopted a novel technique for teaching Sanskrit to Bengali students, and its success encouraged him to write a Sanskrit grammar in Bengali He was thus occupied in the Bengali Department of the College of Fort William, In 1846 the post of Assistant Sccrctaiy to -the Sanskrit College fell vacant Dr F. J. Mouat, the Secretary to the Council of Education, sought Marshall's consent for appointing Vidyasagar to the post. Marshall agreed gladly and requested Vidyasagar to apply for it. After stating his qualifications and the nature of his duty in the Fort William College, Vidyasagar mentioned in his application that he had devoted much attention to acquiring piofi-ciency in the system of Sankhya philosophy and the Puranas, which did not fall within the regular course of education offered by the Sanskrit College. "This," he wrote, lfcto-gether with my long connection with the College as a student has given me an intimate knowledge of the system of education pursued there, and inspires me with confidence that in case my services are accepted, I shall prove useful to the Institution. In the certificate sent along with the application, Marshall enumerated almost all the unique traits of Vidyasagar's character. His scholarship was then known to many, but little was known about his "freedom from all bias or unworthy motives" and his "industry, good disposition and high respectability of character".

Vidyasagar's desire to reform the system of education pursued in the Sanskrit College was clearly reflected in his application. He set about reforming the whole system without delay, after taking over charge of his new office in April, 1846. As he entered upon this work, serious obstacles in his way led to a clash with the Secretary, Russomay Dutta, resulting in Vidyasagar's resignation.

The stoiy of this encounter may be gathered from the unpublished manuscript Records of the Sanskrit College. It has a great bearing on the subsequent reform activities of Vidyasagar in the field of education. It is the earliest instance of the clash of his views with those of others, and it showed that he was the last man to bend to any authority if convinced, of the correctness of his stand. It is evident from the Records that after taking over his charge as Assistant Secretary on April 6, 1846, he applied himself immediately to drafting a plan of reform and formally sent it for consideration to the Secretary on September 19. Within about six months from that date, in April, 1847, he had to resign.

The resignation was formally accepted on July 16, 1847. The Pandits of the Sanskrit College and other teachers submitted a "Memorial" on April 10, 1847, to the Secretary and also to Dr Mouat, the Secretary to the Council of Education, to persuade Vidyasagar not to sever his connection with the institution. In a letter, dated April 21, 1847, Russomay Dutta requested Vidyasagar to give the reasons for his resignation. Vidyasagar replied on May 3, 1847: "I studied the Sanskrit Language and Literature in the Government Sanskrit College and there imbibed my respect and zeal for these subjects. Impelled by these feelings and without any other strong motive, I applied for this appointment. I had hopes that I might be enabled to remove the impediments which I knew existed to the pursuit of effectual study, and that I might be instrumental in intio-ducmg new and efficient methods, but finding iny hopes of being useful frustrated and that there were circumstances of disgrace superadded, I thought it high time to resign". He proceeded to explain in detail the principal reasons lor his resignation. By regrouping the subjects, revising the syllabi, changing the textbooks, laying stress on the regularity of attendance of both the teachers and the students in the classes, he tried his best to introduce a new climate into the Indian classical educational system which was admirably suited to the time. The new system, with its new order and discipline, was not so much disliked by the students as it was resented by the old Pandits and teachers. Vidyasagar himself had been their student hardly five ycais carlici, but he did not feel in the least embarrassed to make his lormer gurus submit to the new discipline for the improvement of the College. It was really difficult for the staff, the senior Pandits particularly, to come punctually to College.

It was no easy matter to modernise the outlook of the veteran Pandits completely at short notice. But the students, as also a few Pandits, did not resent much the new discipline, They adapted themselves to it without fuss, a fact which Vidyasagar did not leave out in his reply. He added; ult cannot however be denied that the method of instruction has in the course of last year greatly changed for the better and that I have spared no exertions on my part in effecting this object. Every Pandit and student can bear testimony to these points".

The Secretary was not willing to put through his Assistant's plan of reform. The object of the reform, as stated by Vidyasagar in his reply, was to facilitate "the acquirement of the largest store of sound Sanskrit and English leafmng combined, under the impression that such a training is likely to produce men who will be highly useful in the work of imbuing our Vernacular dialects with the science and civilisation of the Western world". (italics ours)

This attempt at East-West synthesis, this "work of imbuing our Vernacular dialects with the science and civilisation of the Western world" was the greatest, perhaps the dearest, ideal of Vidyasagar in the field of education. He first broached it when he was Assistant Secretary to the Sanskrit College, and was only 25 years old. His first effort, it is true, was not crowned with complete success, but he did not abandon his project at the first set-back. He left the College, only to return later with more authority and power, almost dictatorial, to put into effect his ideals in the field of education more vigorously.

4

Great Educationist

Educational Reforms

"I would rather sell vegetables in the market to earn my bread than serve any institution against my principles". This was Vidyasagar's blunt reply to some friends who earned him against the economic consequences of quitting the Assistant Secretary's job. He remained unemployed for about a year and a half, and applied himself to learning the English and Hindi languages thoroughly. He re-entered the Fort William College in March, 1849, as Head Writer and Treasurer, on a salary of eighty rupees a month. His second term of office lasted for about two years only, he soon had an opportunity to get back to his favourite Sanskrit College in December, 1850, as Professor of Literature. In January, 1851, he was made the Principal of the Sanskrit College.

In the preface to the eleventh edition of his Bengali book: Betala Panchavimsati, Vidyasagar himself has given us the story of this appointment: "When Pandit Madan Mohan Tarkalankar accepted the post of Judge-Pandit of Murshidabad district, his place in the Sanskrit College as Professor of Literature fell vacant. Dr. Mouat, the Secretary to the Council of Education, offered the post to me. For many reasons, I was not inclined to accept the offer, but Dr. Mouat insisted on my acceptance, I told him at last that I was prepared to accept the situation if the Council would give me the executive authority of a Principal. Dr. Mouat readily agreed and made me enter into an agreement to that effect. I was then installed as Professor of Literature. Shortly after this, Babu Russomay Dutta resigned his office as Secretary and I was directed to submit a report on the present condition of the College and suggest ways and means that may be adopted for its improvement. My report was highly appreciated by the Council of Education and I was made Principal of the Sanskrit College Hitherto the function of the Principal had been performed jointly by the Secretary and the Assistant Secretary. The two offices were now combined into one. The post of Principal was newly created and by the end of January, 1851 (January 22, 1851) I was appointed Principal".

The report submitted by Vidyasagar for the improvement of the Sanskrit College covers ten printed pages of the General Report on Public Instruction, etc. 1850-51. It is dated December 16, 1850. The points raised by him in reply to Russomay Dutta's letter in May, 1847, are considerably enlarged here and treated in detail. His first target of attack was the Grammar Department As he put it. "Sanskrit is in itself a very difficult language, and to begin its study with a difficult Grammar seems, in my opinion, not to be a well, chosen plan "He pointed out that Vopadeva's Mugdhabodha, "with all its voluminous commentaries, is an imperfect Grammar," and the first five years of a student's study of it were almost wasted. He therefore proposed that the boys should learn some of the fundamental rules in Bengali, after which they should go through two or three Sanskrit "Readers". After this the students should begin with Siddhanta Kaumudi, and this should continue to the highest class of the Grammar Department According to Vidyasagar, "of all the Sanskrit Grammars, this is decidedly the best and the highest authority on the subject".

He was not for much change in the literary studies of the Sahitya class but he did mention some better textbooks for Alankara or rhetoric. With regard to Ganita or mathematical studies, he suggested some significant changes.

"Great changes are required in this branch of study. For the present, complete treatises on Arithmetic, Algebra and Geometry should be compiled from the best English works. The higher branches of Mathematics should be attempted to be translated afterwards, and, when ready, should be adopted as class-books. I would propose that a popular treatise on Astronomy, such as Herschel's, be compiled in Bengali and be read in the Mathematical class". Vidyasagar clearly was in favour of introducing Western methods in mathematical studies, but as far as possible through the medium of the Indian language concerned.

With regard to the Smriti or Law Class, he suggested that the twenty-eight Tatvas should be discontinued as "though they are of use to the Brahmins as a class of priests, they are not at all fitted for an academical course". The other works like Manusamhita, Mitakshara, Vivada-Chintatnani, Dayabhaga, Dattakachandrika, etc. were to keep their place in the course But his unfavourable opinion about the Tatvas, as of use only to the Brahmins as a class of poets, should be rioted.

Then he took up the Nyaya class and its system of philosophy. After criticising the texts and their authors, he pointed out: "True it is that the most part of the Hindu Systems of philosophy do not tally with the advanced ideas of modern times, yet it is undeniable that to a good Sanskrit scholar their knowledge is absolutely required". He suggested that by the time the students came up to the Darsana or Philosophy class their acquirements in English should enable them to study the modern philosophy of Europe. "Thus they shall have," he said, an ample opportunity of comparing the systems of Philosophy of their own with the New Philosophy of the Western World, Young men thus educated will be better able to expose the error of ancient Hindu Philosophy than if they were to derive their knowledge of Philosophy simply from European sources One of the principal reasons why I have ventured to suggest the study of all the prevalent systems of Philosophy in India is that the students will clearly see that the propounders of different systems have attacked each other and have pointed out each other's errors and fallacies Thus he will be able to judge tor himself. His knowledge of European Philosophy shall be to him an invaluable guide to the understanding of the merits of the different systems "These comments on the ancient Hindu philosophy by Vidyasagar attracted most unkind criticism and ridicule from the orthodox Pandits of that time He stuck to his opinion, however, and made the Council accept his proposals for reform.

Of all subjects, English was most poorly treated in the Sanskrit College till his time. There was no rule as to what students were expected to study, it being left to their option They commenced the study when they pleased, left it off when they chose, and resumed it when it suited them. It was suggested by Vidyasagar in the Report that the students should not be allowed to begin English till they had acquired some proficiency in the Sanskrit language, and that the study of English should be made compulsory after that.

Vidyasagar stood forth as an educational reformer in the Report. He set out his views quite boldly and clearly, although he knew that it would set the orthodox Pandits, particularly the old Brahmins, against him The authorities approved of the Report and highly commended it Russomay Dutta tendered his resignation but was requested by the Council to hand over charge to Vidyasagar, "pending the sanction of government to the permanent changes proposed and adopted by the Council "Within a fortnight Vidyasagar took over charge of the College as Its first Principal.

He then directed his efforts whole-heartedly to the improvement of the College. The restriction of admission to students on the basis of caste was first removed by him. When the matter was brought to the notice of the Education Council, he was asked to submit a report, which he did on March 20, 1851. His contention was that the Brahmins and the Vaidyas were no better than the Sudras and that there was no reason therefore why boys of all castes should not be admitted to the College. He frankly stated that the Pandits of the College were almost all averse to this liberal measure. But he urged the Council to relax the rule, at least in favour of the Kayastha boys, as the first step towards the complete removal of all caste restrictions. The Pandits, most of whom had been Vidyasagar's teachers, rebuked him for his move and tried to resist it. Vidyasagar argued his case well, citing the example of some great non-Brahmin Sanskrit scholars. He also told them that if they were so willing to teach Sanskrit to Englishmen for remuneration, he failed to understand why they should be reluctant to teach the language to sons of the soil, irrespective of caste. He was determined to open the College to all boys, and he warned the Pandits that if they were equally determined to resist it, he would resign his office. But he had not to go that far as the authorities allowed him to admit Kayastha boys to the College, Some time later boys of other castes were also admitted to the College and permitted to study all branches of Sanskrit learning except theology.

Vidyasagar then sought to remove the anomalies in Sanskrit education. The Departments were reorganised, textbooks were changed, and teachers and students were told to abide strictly by the rules and regulations of the College. The new scheme proved fruitful and the College made satisfactory progress in all directions. The Council noted the progress with pleasure, and in May, 1853, expressed their desire to get the new method of Sanskrit education, introduced by Vidyasagar, approved by Dr. L. R, Ballantyne, Principal of the Banaras Government Sanskrit College Invited by the Council, Dr. Ballantyne visited the Calcutta Sanskrit College in July-August, 1853, and submitted his observations in a letter to the Council. One of his main points was that what was good for the Bengali boys in Calcutta might not be so for the boys of the Upper Provinces in Banaras. "Calcutta is so far inoculated with Anglican feeling, consciously or unconsciously," he wrote, "that an argument from Calcutta to the Upper Provinces is very apt to mislead. This holds also conversely". It was better, according to him, to leave the two institutions, in differing local circumstances, to differ in several respects. It is clear from his letter that he did not favour the idea of offering simultaneous Sanskrit and English courses to boys, as "the two courses may end in persuading the learner that 'truth is double.'" This danger, he pointed out, was "no chimerical one". He was acquainted with Brahmins who, being well-versed in both Sanskrit and English, were aware that the European theory of Logic was correct, who knew also the Hindu theory, while at the same time they could not grasp the identity of the two in such a way as to be able to represent the processes of the one in the language of the other "If this be the case," he wrote, "with the very best of those who have studied both Sanskrit and English independently, it is not likely that the case will be different with the general run of pupils similarly trained". He made suggestions for obviating this danger and recommended some textbooks in English, with notes, to indicate the points in the Hindu system of philosophy which corresponded with points in European Science.

Vidyasagar criticised Ballantyne's observations in a letter to Dr. Mouat, dated September 7, 1853 It is perhaps the most important letter that he ever wrote on education He could not wholly agree with Ballantyne on the adoption of textbooks Ballantyne recommended the adoption of his own Abstract of Mill's Logic in place of the original, and one of the principal reasons for doing so seemed to be the high price of Mill's original work. Vidyasagar rejected this suggestion saying, "Our students are now in the habit of piu-chasing standard work at high prices, so we need not be deterred from the adoption of this great work," Ballantync recommended three textbooks, printed with English versions and notes, for each of the three systems of Philosophy—Vedanta, Nyaya and Sankhya—of which except Vedantasara, those on Nyaya and Sankhya were, in Vidyasagar's opinion, "very poor treatises in their own departments". With regard to Ballantyne's suggestion for the introduction of Bishop Berkeley's Enquiry as a class-book, his comment was incisive. He remarked that it "would beget more mischief than advantage". He was bold enough to state that they were obliged to teach in the Sanskrit College the Vedanta and Sankhya only because they commanded unbounded reverence from the Hindus, It was necessary, therefore, to teach students philosophy through the English course also. Out Bishop Berkeley's Enquiry he pointed out, "which has arrived at similar or identical conclusions with the Vedanta or Sankhya and which is no more considered in Europe as a sound system of Philosophy, will not serve that purpose. On the contrary when, by the perusal of that book, the Hindu students of the Sanskrit College will find that the theories advanced by the Sankhya and Vedanta systems are corroborated by a philosopher of Europe, their convenience for these two systems may increase.

About the danger of the fallacy of "double truth" Vidyasagar said, "I believe, the danger that Dr. Ballantyne apprehends is not so inevitable in the case of an individual who has intelligently studied both English and Sanskrit sciences and literatures Truth is truth, if properly perceived To believe that 'truth is double" h but the effect of an imperfect perception of truth itself, the effect which I am sure to see removed by the improved courses of studies we have adopted at this Institution".

As regards Ballantyne's attempt to discover parallelisms between the Hindu Shastras and Western Science, Vidyasagar remarked with characteristic forthrightness: "It is not possible in all cases, I fear, that we shall be able to show real agreement between European Science and Hindu Shastras. Even if we take it for granted that we shall be able to point out agreement between the two, it appears to me to be a hopeless task to conciliate the learned of India to the acceptance of the advance of Science in Europe "By "learned" he hinted at the class of old Pandits. He said: "We need not hear the opposition of a body declining in their reputation. Their voice is gradually becoming more and more feeble There is little chance of their regaining their former ascendancy "To be the head of an institution named Sanskrit College and to hold this language about the old Sanskrit-educated intelligentsia was nothing short of being heretical in those days. But Vidyasagar never minced matters, in social or educational fields Fear of opposition or criticism was unknown to him.

His reply to Ballantyne's observations, as was expected, did not receive the favourable consideration from the Council that it deserved. In their Proceedings, dated September 14, 1853, the Council put on record that the Principal of the Sanskrit College in Calcutta was expected and directed by the Council to continue the course of study recommended by Ballantyne. The Principal was also directed to avail himself freely of the Abstracts and Treatises compiled by Ballantyne, "the use of which must be in the highest degree valuable in explanation and illustration of the subjects of his own Lectures and those of the Instructors under him". It was also the desire of the Council that "the Principal will be In frequent communication with Dr. Ballantyne on the progress of his classes". A copy of these Proceeding was forwarded to the Principal for information on September 22, 1853.

Vidyasagar was deeply hurt by this communication. It was couched in language to which he was not accustomed. The College was then going to be closed for the Puja holidays and he was in a hurry to go home. But he wrote in reply to the Council that their orders "if carried out in their entirety will involve a degree of interference with the scheme of study lately adopted" by him and "make his position in the College somewhat unpleasant." He had no objection to introducing the works of Ballantyne which he considered good and suitable, but he added, "If compelled to adopt all his compilations without any reference to my own humble judgement as to their utility and value, or to their adaptation to the peculiar wants of the Institution over which I have the honour to preside, my occupation is gone.'

Happily for him and for the cause of education, his occupation did not go. The Council had to give up their stand in view of Vidyasagar's sound reasoning. He was given a freer hand in formulating and executing his policy of education in the Sanskrit College. It proved wholesome to the cause of Sanskrit learning, and to English as we!!. It gave a new lease of life to the institution which had been fast declining before he was appointed Principal. The College grew in strength and reputation.

The first battle which Vidyasagar fought in the field of education as Assistant Secretary to the Sanskrit College in 1847 was lost. The first round of the second battle with the Council of Education he won as the Principal of the College. But it was a temporary victory, the peace that followed was not a lasting one. It was disturbed within a few years, and he differed from the Council in regard to the method and policy of education. It happened in 1857-58, and it led to his resignation in November, 1858.

The importance of the Ballantyne-Vidyasagar episode lies in the fact that it enables us to assess Vidyasagar as an intellectual humanist of the modern age. While Ballantyne, the European Sanskrit scholar, remained a happy hunter of resemblances between the Western sciences and the Hindu Shastras, it was left to Vidyasagar, a thoroughbred Bengali and Indian classical scholar, to discard the very idea of such resemblances as something puerile and pernicious.

The arguments put forward by Ballantyne place him in the company of the scholars who hold that there is nothing in the world of science and literature which cannot be traced to the Vedas. This view attracted sympathisers among European

Orientalists like Wilson and Jones. Vidyasagar exploded Ballantyne's myth of "double truth," and exposed the hollowness of Ballantyne's favourite philosopher, Bishop Berkeley, by stern materialistic reasoning. He went to the length of criticising the Hindu Idealist Philosophies, Vedanta and Sankhya, not so much for condemning them as such, as for demonstrating the worthlessness of their European counterparts Both Vidyasagar and Ballantyne were profound Sanskrit scholars, but the scholarship of Vidyasagar generated the spirit of the renaissance in him In the words of Symonds, "It was scholarship, first and last, which revealed to men the wealth of their own minds, the dignity of human thought, the value of human speculation, the Importance of human life regarded as a thing apart from religious rules and dogmas". (italics ours) Vidyasagar's scholarship was homocentric, and not theocentric He was a true intellectual humanist.

Medium of Instruction

Vidyasagar was greatly exercised over the languages in which the Indian people were to be educated. It could be either Sanskrit or English. In his letter on Ballantyne's observations, he wrote to the Council. "What we requite h to extend the benefit of education to the mass of the people. Let us establish a number of Vernacular schools, let us prepare a series of Vernacular class-books on useful and instinctive subjects, let us raise up a band of men qualified to undertake the responsible duty of teachers, and the object is accomplished The qualification of these teachers should be of this nature: they should be perfect masters of their own language, possess a considerable amount of useful information and be free from the prejudices of their country. To raise up such a useful class of men is the object I have proposed to myself and to the accomplishment of which the whole energy of our Sanskrit College should he directed". In a later letter he fervently appealed to the Council to allow him freedom of judgement in the matter of policy; he wrote: "Leave me to teach Sanskrit for the leading purpose of thoroughly mastering the Vernacular and let me super add to it the acquisition of sound knowledge through the medium of English, and you may rest assured that before a few ears are over I shall be enabled, if supported and encouraged by the Council, to furnish you with a body of young men who will be better qualified by their writings and teaching to disseminate widely among the people sound information than it has hitherto been possible to accomplish through the instrumentality of the educated of any of your Collects, whether English or Oriental. To enable me to carry out this great, this darling object of my wishes I must (excuse the strong word) to a considerable extent be left unfettered".

His aim, it is clear, was to carry the torch of education to the people through their language. He has himself called it a "great object," a "darling object" of his Me. "If I may be so fortunate as to be permitted to carry out the system introduced," he added, "I can assure the Council with great confidence that the Sanskrit College will become a seat of pure and profound Sanskrit learning and at the same time a nursery of improved Vernacular literature". He stood for the principle of making the people's own language and literature the medium of all instruction, including the Western sciences.

The famous controversy between the Anglicists and the Orientalists- about the medium of instruction has already been noted. When the General Committee of Public Instruction was appointed in 1823 with men like Prinsep and Wilson, it set about founding Oriental Colleges and publishing and translating works in the Oriental classical languages. This policy of the Committee was subjected to severe criticism by Rammohan Roy in a letter to Amherst in 1823. In the thirties the controversy rose to a climax, it finally resolved itself into the question of whether education should be imparted through the Oriental classical languages or through English. The case for the Indian languages was set aside lightly The "'filtration theory," the theory that education would filter down from the upper and the middle classes to the masses gradually, was also then gaming ground commanding support from both wings of the Committee This led to an impasse, when three persons appeared on the stage—Lord William Bentinck, Macaulay, and the well-known missionary, William Adam.

Adam was asked to make a survey of education in Bengal with a view to taking "measures for its extension and improvement," and to submit reports. Macaulay was called upon to resolve the controversy, and this was the occasion for the celebrated Minute which he wrote on February 2, 1835, violently attacking the

Orientalists and supporting the Anglicists. Hastily, without waiting for Adam's report, Bentinck accepted Macaulay's opinion, and on March 7, 1835, passed a Resolution in favour of the promotion of European literature and science among the natives of India stating that "all the funds appropriated for the purpose of education would be best employed on English education alone.' That Adam was asked to go ahead with his survey, in spite of this Resolution, indicates that whatever might have made Bentinck introduce English education, he was also conscious of the existence and weight of a widespread indigenous system of education with all its implications Adam's reports were subsequently published, but they were relegated to the State archives while English education scudded the monopoly of official patronage.

Bentinck's Resolution did not set the controversy at rest In three open letters addressed to Auckland in 1841, as well as in his evidence before the Select Committee of the House of Lords in 1853, the Rev Alexander Dull railed at the Orientalists. Auckland admitted the necessity of education in the Indian languages; but the demands of a higher type of education to be imparted to the upper and the middle classes through the English language, he felt, were more urgent and important The Committee scathingly condemned Adam's proposals and offered to open twenty rural schools only as an experimental measure. This offer was turned down by the Government, In 1844, during the Governor-Generalship of Hardinge, an attempt was again made to give some effect to Adam's recommendations, and 101 "Hardinge Schools" were established in the rural areas. For lack of adequate support from the local government these schools proved a failure.

Adam's proposals, however, bore fruit in a different climate. The Lieutenant-Governor of the North-Western Provinces of Agra and Oudh, Thomason, made a laudable attempt to introduce education "through the medium of Vernacular language and not through that of any foreign tongue". He was much influenced by Adam's reports and had portions of his Third Report reprinted and circulated. Books for the village schools were prepared and introduced. His experiment was highly successful and it attracted the notice of the Governor-General, who asked the authorities in Bengal if something like it could be done there too. In 1853-54 experiments were made in Bengal for advancing the cause of education in Indian languages, not directly on the basis of Thompson's scheme but on the basis of a plan put forward by Vidyasagar to the Council of Education.

There is a note preserved among the manuscript records of the Sanskrit College, drafted by Vidyasagar and dated April 12, 1852, with the caption "Notes on the Sanskrit College". The first five paragraphs of the note in which he summed up his views are extremely important in the history of Indian national education. These are:

- The creation of an enlightened Bengali literature should be the first object of those who were entrusted with the superintendence of education in Bengal.
- Such a literature cannot be formed by the exertions of those who are not competent to collect the materials from European sources and to dress them in elegant, expressive, idiomatic Bengali.
- An elegant, expressive and idiomatic Bengali style cannot be at the command of those who are not good Sanskrit scholars. Hence the necessity of making Sanskrit scholars well versed in the English language and literature.
- Experience proves that mere English scholars are altogether incapable of expressing their ideas in elegant and idiomatic Bengali. They are so much Anglicised that it seems at present almost impossible for them, even if they make Sanskrit their after-study, to express then, ideas in an idiomatic and elegant Bengali style.
- It is very clear that if the students of the Sanskrit College are made familiar with English literature, they will prove the best and ablest contributors to an enlightened Bengali literature.

The next question discussed in the "note" is the kind of instruction needed in the Sanskrit College for the purpose. It is clear that the creation of an enlightened Bengali literature was his primary aim as an educationist This note, it appears, was drawn up by him at the request of F. J. Halhday, a member of the Council of Education at the time, who submitted it to the Council in June, 1852, with the accompanying note. It is the result of several consultations I have kid with the Principal and I lay it before the Council as deserving, in my humble judgement, of very careful consideration. Halhday set out in a Minute his views on the proper course to be taken for the betterment of education in the Indian languages: "In the Province of Bengal we have a vast number of indigenous schools... Our object should be, if possible, and as far as possible, to improve these schools and we cannot do better than follow the excellent example of the late Lieutenant-Governor of the North-Western Provinces, and establish a system of Model Schools as an example to the indigenous schools, and a regular plan of visits by which indigenous schoolmasters may gradually by stimulated to improve up to the models set before them".

He thus commented on Vidyasagar's "note": "I append a memorandum on the subject, drawn up by the energetic and able Principal of the Sanskrit College who, as is well known, has long been zealous in the cause of Vernacular education, and has done much to promote it, both by his improved system in the Sanskrit College and by elementary works which he has published for the use of schools. I approve generally of the plan which is contained in the Principal's memorandum, and would wish to see it carried into effect.

Halliday became the first Lieutenant-Governor of Bengal in May, 1854. ' As one of the greatest admirers of Vidyasagar he actively helped to shape his policy in the right direction But there was much opposition in the Council to entrusting Vidyasagar with the supervision of the model schools. His ability was not questioned; the opposition argued that one man, however capable, should not be saddled with such heavy responsibility. Halliday knew that the opposition was not based on this consideration alone, and pursued his own point to the end.

In 1853-54 certain important educational matters were engaging the attention of the Council and the Government. They were busy reforming the Calcutta Madrassah and making preparations for the establishment of the Presidency College. On the publication of the great Educational Despatch of July, 1854, from the Court of Directors, a department of education was created and the Council of Education was dissolved in January, 1855. William Gordon Young, a civilian, was appointed the first Director of Public Instruction, The Despatch led to the grant-in-aid system, During the years 1855 and 1856 a scheme for the establishment of a university was prepared and this was incorporated under Act No. II of 1857.

In a period of turmoil and transition, the cause of regarding the Indian languages as the chief object of education might have been lost. But lost it was not owing to Halliday's insistence and Vidyasagar's encouragement. In a letter dated November 16, 1854, Halhday's scheme, "Vernacular Education for the Lower Provinces of the Presidency of Bengal," was communicated to the Government of India by Hodgson Pratt, the Under-Secretary. It was proposed by him that Vidyasagar was the fittest man to be placed in charge of this scheme in certain districts of Bengal Cecil Beadon, Secretary to the Government of India, wrote in reply to this on February 13, 1855: "His Lordship in Council does not object to the employment of Pandit Ishwar Chandra Sharma in occasionally inspecting the Vernacular Schools in Bengal, if on full consideration you continue to think that his important avocation, as Principal of the Sanskrit College, will not thereby be detrimentally affected.

But the terms of Court Despatch will not allow of his being made a Superintendent of Vernacular Education, the functions of such an office having now to be performed by the Director and by the Inspectors whom it is intended to employ under his orders". Halhday was not satisfied with the reply. The new Director of Public Instruction was informed that it was impossible to do anything for Vernacular education in Bengal without the whole-hearted cooperation of Vidyasagar. He desired therefore that he should ask him for this cooperation.

The Director of Public Instruction proposed that the Pandit might be appointed Inspector of Schools temporarily, to which the Lieutenant-Governor seriously objected He knew full well that the Pandit was a man of strong will and principles and that he would not accept such a great responsibility just for the sake of filling a temporary gap He would not also tolerate any interference from above and would not work for a good cause half-heartedly.

It would be a tragedy indeed, he pointed out, if the government neglected its duty to seek and enlist the cooperation of a person like Vidyasagar in a cause to which he had dedicated himself.

The Director of Public Instruction changed his mind, and Vidyasagar became an Assistant Inspector of Schools on an additional monthly salary of Rs. 200 from May, 1855. For about a year after this, in addition to his regular duties as the Principal of the Sanskrit College, Vidyasagar toured the districts of Bengal—Nadia, Burdwan, Hugh, Midnapore, 24-Parganas. He established about 20 Model Schools in 20 villages. It was soon found, however, that these did not take firm hold of the people's minds. The people were indifferent, and in some places where the middle classes were dominant, this indifference even grew into distrust and opposition.

Various reasons may be assigned for this conspicuous failure of a great attempt. One was the tepid support given by the government. The chief reason undoubtedly was the reluctance of the middle class Bengali parents to send their children to these schools and to pay fees for a purely Indian education. Not only the urban middle class in Calcutta, but the rural middle class also had grown conscious, by this time, of the social and economic potentiality of English education. As for the rural masses, they could not be made, at this tune, aware of the need of having any education at all—in any language, Indian or English.

Vidyasagar, therefore, could not pursue his scheme for long. There were other public issues like women's education and social reform to claim his attention and to which also he had to devote his limited time and energy He had to abandon the "darling object" of his life for the time being. English education had strongly entrenched itself, in Bengal at any rate, by holding out a new social status and economic prospects to the upper and the middle classes; Vidyasagar felt that it was well-nigh impossible to go ahead with any project of Indian education. Vidyasagar was far ahead of his time, the time was not yet ripe for such projects.

Advocate of Women Education

Women's education in India attracted official attention long after definite measures had been undertaken for the education of boys; women's education was left solely to the care of a few individuals and private societies. Neither the Court of Directors nor the local government referred to women's education even in a single despatch on educational matters in the first half of the 19th century. Lacking official patronage, local efforts on the part of individuals as well as the zeal of the foreign missionaries in this field were almost wholly lost.

In his evidence before the Select Committee of Parliament in July, 1832, Rev. James Hough spoke of the progress of the girls' schools in Tinnevelly: "One very important feature in these schools remains to be noticed; it was for many years considered impossible to prevail on the Hindus to allow their women to be educated". Rev. J. Tucker of Madras, in reply to the question, "What attempts have been made by Indians themselves in that direction?" said, "None whatever; they are as a body rather opposed to the education of women "In reply to a similar question William Jacob of Bombay said, "None on the western side of India I do not think as yet a single woman has come under the government system of education in Western India".

In fact, one searches vainly for any notice of women's education as a recognised part of the government scheme prior to 1849-50 in any part of India. It is undeniable that there did exist a strong prejudice against the education of Indian women amongst both Hindus and Muslims, and that this prejudice stemmed from an age-old tradition. It is true that there is evidence in the ancient literatures of India that women took part in religious and philosophical discussions with men, shared in the affairs of the State, participated in heroic acts, and were taught to read and write. But this does not establish the social truth that the women of India had enjoyed the blessings of education as a matter of right in ancient and medieval times.

The Indian ideal of women's life, particularly the Hindu one, was one of pristine purity, social seclusion and the quiet domestic duties of an affectionate mother and a devoted wife. And the Company's government was at that time reluctant to impose any policy which might interfere with ancient social customs and traditions This indifferent attitude of the authorities was one of the reasons why the efforts of the early pioneers failed in this direction.

We give a brief summary of the attempts for promoting women's education in Bengal up to the foundation of the Bethune School at Calcutta in May, 1849, and with which Pandit Ishwar Chandra Vidyasagar was associated from the beginning. As early as 1819 the Female Juvenile Society was founded at Calcutta in cooperation with the Baptist Missionaries "for the promotion of female education in Bengal". In 1821, Miss Cooke (better known as Mrs. Wilson) was deputed by the British and Foreign School Society to open a girls' school at Calcutta. In 1824 the "Ladies' Society for Native Female Education" was formed for the purpose of coordinating the activities of the girls" schools scattered in Calcutta, and starting a Central School. The foundation-stone of the Central School for girls was laid by the Society's patroness, Lady Amherst, on May 18, 1826. Other schools were also established by the London and the Church Missionary Societies, but nothing had yet been done by the government to encourage the pioneers.

The efforts of the missionaries tailed because they wanted to use the school for religious propaganda. Even the so-called Zenana and Select School Scheme proved a failure because the European governess employed by wealthy Bengali families to teach their wives, sisters and daughters, was found more anxious to teach Christianity than reading, writing and arithmetic. A three-tier system was envisaged in this scheme, of which the first was private tuition in zenanas, that is, in private houses; the second stage was several neighbourly families meeting in a central house for instruction; and the third was a step forward to a school. The scheme was only partly successful.

More important than these schemes of the missionaries were the efforts of some pioneers in this field like Raja Rammohan Roy, Raja Radhakanta Dev, Raja Baidyanath Ray, and of the young men educated in the Hindu College The establishment of the Bethune School at Calcutta in May, 1849, may be regarded as the turning-point in the history of women's education in India. Henceforward, not only the authorities in India, but the educated and influential members of Hindu society began to take a genuine and active interest in the cause. Raja Radhakanta Dev of the Sovabazar Raj family, a conservative moderate in social outlook, started a girls' school in his own house at Sovabazar within a fortnight of the opening of the Bethune School. In August, 1849, the Council of Education received a communication from Joykissen and Rajkissen Mukherji for the establishment of a girls' school at Uttarpara. Other girls' schools were started at different places.

The opposition of the orthodox Hindus grew violent as the schools grew in number Scandals and calumnies were deliberately spread against those who ventured to take an active part in this noble cause. Some of the enthusiasts were even assaulted publicly. But both Bethune and Dalhousie were determined not to indulge the opposition any further but to foster women's education.

Few Englishmen have come to India with a more sincere desire to do good than J. E. D. Bethune Having taken part in the great movement in England for the education of the people, he naturally directed his attention to educational matters immediately on arrival here, before long he was appointed President of the Council of Education In a letter to Dalhousie he requested the Government of India to issue a circular expressing public sympathy with all private endeavours connected with girls' schools. Dalhousie responded quickly to the request, and the historic circular, a kind of a charter in the history of women's education in India, was issued on April 11, 1850. It was made known to the people that the Government of India sympathised with those engaged in promoting women's education.

Bethune found in Vidyasagar a great fellow-fighter in the cause of women's education from the beginning. He had known the Pandit as a highly talented man during his Presidentship of the Council of Education He induced the Pandit to accept the Honorary Secretaryship of the Bethune School in December, 1850 Bethune was now convinced of his institution's success as it had been placed under the care of a man whose moral courage, honesty and singleness of purpose were beyond question.

The "Derozians" popularly known as "Young Bengal," the students of Derozio, the famous young radical teacher of the Hindu College, took an active interest in the progress of women's education It is interesting to note that some of the Pandits of the Sanskrit College too were ardent supporters of the cause This is evident from the famous letter of Bethune to Dalhousie of March

29, 1850. Bethune wrote: "It is known to your Lordship that in the month of May last year I established a Native Female School in Calcutta I explained to your Lordship at that time my reasons for making this experiment on my own responsibility and was honoured by your approval of the course I adopted. I considered that my station in the Council of India and as President of the Council of Education afforded me peculiar advantages in endeavouring to discover whether my belief was well founded that the time has come when this important step in the system of education of the Natives can be taken with a reasonable hope of success. I wished the discredit of failure to rest with myself alone, if my expectation had proved abortive, and that the credit of the government should not be pledged to the measure until its success was assured.

"The failure of every attempt to induce respectable Natives to send their daughters to a Missionary School, and the conviction which I have that the system of the government schools is best calculated for producing a rapid and salutary effect in the country induced me to establish my School on the same principle of excluding from it all religious teaching, though I was well aware of the additional difficulty which this restriction would cause to me for procuring efficient female teachers English was to be taught to those only whose parents wished it, all were to be instructed in Bengali and in plain and fancy work.

"Great excitement was caused, as I expected, by the opening of my school which at first numbered only 21 pupils, and it was vehemently opposed by many of the most influential natives of Calcutta, chiefly however as I believe on the ground of mortified vanity because they had not been consulted in the matter. I had refrained from doing so, after carefully weighing all the arguments for and against that course. On the other hand, I was not left without encouragement by those who were favourable to my plan my gratitude for their assistance are Baboo Ram Gopal Ghose, the well-known merchant who was my principal adviser in the first instance and who procured me my first pupils, Baboo Duckmarunjan Mukherji, a Zamindar, who was previously unknown to me, but who, as soon as my design was published, introduced himself to me for the purpose of offering me the free gift of a site for the school, or five beeghas of land valued at Rupees 10,000 in the Native quarter of the town, and Pundit Madan Mohan Turkalunkar, one of the pundits of the Sanskrit College, who not only sent two daughters to the school, but has continued to attend it daily, to give gratuitous instruction to the children in Bengali, and has employed his leisure time in the compilation of a series of elementary Bengali books expressly for their use. Every kind of annoyance and persecution was set on foot to deter my friends from continuing to support this school and with such success that at one time the number of enrolled pupils dwindled to seven, and on some occasion not more than three or four were present in the school...

"I am of opinion that the time is come when all that is needed to secure their complete success is a declaration on the part of government that it looks on them with a favourable aye. It may seem incredible, after all that the government has done in the cause of education, that such a declaration should be thought necessary in order to convince the people of this fact, but among the shameless expedients to which the opponents of female education have resorted to has been an unblushing assertion that the government is not merely indifferent but actually hostile to it. I am convinced that the bold misrepresentation will not be without its effect, if some encouragement is not given to those who have put themselves forward in advancing this work; otherwise I could have wished, in order to demonstrate more unquestionably the success of my experiment, to have continued for some time longer without endeavouring to enlist the influence of government on the side of the schools, but I am already in a condition to assure your Lordship that the step I recommend may be taken with full confidence of carrying with it the sympathies of a great body of the people, and I believe that discouragement may follow, if it is not taken forthwith No opposition to the declared wishes of government is to be apprehended. The feeling excited has never been, even at the worst, so violent as on the occasion of the establishment of the Medical College, and the good to be expected from the full development of the scheme cannot be surpassed by that of any institution in the country".

Ramgopal Ghose, whom Bethune mentioned as "the well-known merchant" and his "principal adviser" in his letter, was one of the leading Derozians He was known as the King of Bengali Intellectuals, the great "Edu-Raj" or "the Rajah of the Educated Bengalees" He was also a master in the art of oratory, and a public man of his time. There was hardly any institution—educational, commercial or political—with which his name was not associated He took a particular interest in education. "In fact," observed Dr. Mouat, late Secretary to the Council of Education, "I can look back upon no part of my early career in connection with education which is not associated with him (Ramgopal)". Dakshinaranjan, "a Zamindar," was also one of the most prominent Derozians, and a staunch supporter of all progressive reforms. Pandit Madan Mohan was a close friend of Vidyasagar, and he was no less enthusiastic in social and educational reforms than his great friend. In a Bengali periodical Sarvashubhakary Patrika Madan Mohan contributed a comprehensive article in support of women's education in September, 1850 He mentioned in the article that Bethune was spending out of his own pocket something between seven and eight hundred rupees a month on the girls' school.

The patronage of Lord and Lady Dalhousie was a great help to Bethune and his friends. But Bethune did not rest content with official patronage. He, in cooperation with English-educated Bengali intellectuals, and radical Bengali pandits like Vidyasagar and Madan Mohan, took positive measures for the propagation of women's education. As President of the Council of Education he had to visit different centres of education in the districts of Bengal, and deliver instructive addresses to the students. In almost every address he emphasised the urgent need of women's education, and called upon educated young men to fight for the progress of the noble cause with all their might.

But Bethune did not live long to see the progress of the cause for which he had fought and sacrificed so much He passed away on August 12, 1851. From October, 1851, however, Dalhousie had borne all the expenses necessary for keeping the institution going, and on his retirement in March, 1856, the Bethune School became a recognised government institution, supported by the State, and was placed under the supervision of Mr. Cecil Beadon In August, 1856, Beadon proposed to the Bengal Government a scheme for the appointment of a managing committee for the School, with some prominent members of the Hindu community, and also for securing the services of Pandit Ishwar Chandra Vidyasagar as the secretary to the School. He remarked in his letter: "It may be thought by his honour no less than justly due to the past services and distinguished position of Pandit Ishwar Chandra to appoint him Secretary to the Committee". Vidyasagar was made Honorary Secretary of the Bethune School Committee in August, 1856, and a committee with prominent members of the Hindu community was constituted. With Vidyasagar as Secretary and the Constitution of the new committee, the Bethune School entered a new phase of its career.

Vidyasagar had his own way of taking up and fighting for a cause. His boundless energy and will were not confined solely to the Bethune School or to the limits of the city. They sought a wider field—the rural areas of Bengal.

In the Education Despatch of 1854 the Court of Directors recognised for the first time the need and importance of women's education in India. The Directors communicated in their despatch that they had observed with pleasure the evidence which was now afforded "of an increased desire on the part of the natives of India to give a good education to their daughters". They admitted further that by women's education more might be done for the educational and moral tone of the people than by the education of man. The girls' schools were included among the schools to which the new grants-in-aid scheme could be extended. The local Government, by 1857, found it feasible to offer grants to girls' schools.

Early in 1857, Lieutenant-Governor Halhday, enthusiastic in the cause of women's education, sent for Vidyasagar, at that time Principal of the Calcutta Sanskrit College and an Assistant Inspector of Schools, South Bengal, and discussed with him the subject fully They appreciated the difficulty that they might have to encounter in trying to establish girls' schools in the villages. Women's education had not made much headway in the city itself. Undaunted, Vidyasagar told Halliday that there was nothing that could not be achieved, given determined will and sincerity.

The inexhaustible energy of the Pandit found full scope immediately, file reported to the Director of Public Instruction on May 30, 1857, the opening of a girl school in the Burdwan district: "It is with great pleasure that I have the honour to report that the inhabitants of Jowgong in Bturd-wan have, at the suggestion of the Head Master of the Model School at the village, established a female school there. It was opened on April 15 last and now musters on its rolls 28 girls from 4 to 11 years, the majority of whom are daughters of respectable Brahmins and Kayasthas of the place... Having however visited it during the week I have been led to hope that there is every chance of its flourishing within a short time. Not only do the inhabitants take the liveliest interest in its success, but the girls themselves appear to prosecute their studies with great delight and attention".

Between November, 1857 and May, 1858, Vidyasagar established thirty-five girls' schools with an average total attendance of 1,300. The government was requested to modify the grants-in-aid rules in favour of girls' schools, so that whenever a suitable school building was provided and the attendance of not less than twenty girls was promised, all expenses for maintaining the school were defrayed by government. The government, however, refused to modify the rules, holding that unless girls' schools were really and materially supported by voluntary aid, they had better not be established at all.

The order, of the government had its effect on Vidyasagar's activities in the field of girls' education. He had established quite a number of girls' schools on the understanding that the local people would provide suitable accommodation, while the maintenance charges would be defrayed by the government. After the government order, it now appealed to him that all his efforts in this direction had been in vain and that the schools set up by him would have to be closed without delay. He had already to bear part of the running cost, including the teachers' salary.

The authorities were informed of this awkward situation, and after a spate of correspondence the government of India agreed to pay the amount and free the Pandit of all worries. Although Vidyasagar was disappointed by the indifferent attitude of the government towards women's education, he pursued the cause vigorously. He took the initiative in opening a Fund for rendering financial assistance to girls schools and collected money for it from persons of means in Calcutta.

Meanwhile, after the formation of the managing committee of the Bethune School he issued a circular to prominent Hindu families in Calcutta and its suburbs in December, 1856, giving the method and purpose of education to be followed in the School. "None but the daughters of the respectable Hindus are taken in, and Reading, Writing, Arithmetic, Natural Science, Geography and Needle-work are taught. These subjects are taught through the medium of Bengali, and lessons in English are given only with the consent of parents and guardians. No fee will be charged from the girls, and books will be supplied free. Those who live at a distance from the school and cannot afford the cost of conveyance, will be allowed free use of the carriage and palanquins of the school".

The learned Pandit selected a suitable saying from Manusamhita and got it painted on the doors of the carriage and Palaquin of the School, its meaning was that daughters too, like sons, can claim equal attention in training and education. This passage from one of the oldest Shastras would surely better serve to convince the Hindu householder of the need of giving education to his daughters than tons of arguments based on reason.

Vidyasagar was doing all this besides his other regular strenuous duties as Principal of the Sanskrit College. He continued to serve the Bethune School as Secretary even after he had resigned his principalship of the Sanskrit College In November 3, 1858; and he held the post till the Bethune School Committee was dissolved in January, 1869.

How far the School progressed during the secretaryship of Vidyasagar can be gleaned from his report of December, 1862- "As regards the number of admissions the Committee beg to observe that there has been a steady increase from 1859. The number at present on the rolls is ninety-three. It would have exceeded 100 ere this if the Committee had not been obliged for some time from want of the means of conveyance. The inconvenience has since been removed by the provision of a third carriage and it is hoped that the anticipated increase will soon take place... In cases where girls are admitted at an early age and permitted to remain at school till the age of eleven or twelve, they attain a fair amount of knowledge in the different subjects taught.

> "From the manner in which the number of admissions has recently gone on increasing, the Committee trust that the institution is rising in the estimation of those classes of the community for whose benefit it was originally established. The Committee are happy to believe that home education for females is being resorted to by many families amongst the wealthier classes; and this result, they believe, is in a considerable degree owing to the beneficial influences of the Bethune School"

It is evident from this report that women's education was making but little headway against strong social prejudices. It is true that by the year 1866-67 the number of girls' schools under the Department of Education increased to about 300 and the number of students to about 6,000, but owing to early withdrawals by guardians, very few girls were able to prosecute their studies up to a general standard Elementary reading, writing and arithmetic, with some needle-work, were perhaps all that the girls were allowed to be taught by their parents in the school. Usually they were withdrawn at the age of nine or ten. It is clear that the custom of early marriage stood in the way of good education.

The pull of custom on the upper classes was much stronger than on the middle or the lower. For their daughters they preferred antahpur strisiksha, or home education, to public school education. Woodrow's Report of 1863-64 confirms this impression. "The children (girls) do not seem to be drawn from the rich classes of society; for the recent order that the children should pay for their books excited much opposition, and the hint that I gave of the expediency of imposing a small fee was unanimously opposed. The bhadra lok (the respectable), not the dhani lok (the rich), send their children to the Bethune School".

The little progress which the women's education was making at that time was mainly due to the influence and exertion of a number of young men who had received University education in Bengal. Most of them belonged to the new urban middle classes and one of the new symbols of their social status, other than "money" was "education. This educated urban middle class was the most active supporter of women's education in Bengal in the second half of 19th century.

In the middle of the sixties a new impetus was given to the women's education in Bengal by Miss Mary Carpenter. Her name is well known as a philanthropic worker and friend of the Indian people. She reached Calcutta on November 20, 1866, and came in direct contact with such sincere advocates of women's education as Vidyasagar, Keshab Chandra Sen, and others. She proposed a Normal School for the training of female teachers and prepared a scheme for it, which was sent to the government. Vidyasagar's opinion was sought by the authorities.

Vidyasagar in a letter to the Lieutenant-Governor on October 1, 1867, gave the reasons for his opposition. "Since we met last, I have made careful enquiries and have thought over the subject, but I regret to say that I see no reason to alter my opinion as regards the difficulty of practically carrying out Miss Carpenter's scheme of rearing a body of native female teachers either in connection with the Bethune School or independently, such as may be acceptable to the bulk of the Hindu Community and worthy of their confidence.

Indeed, the more I think about it the more am I convinced that I cannot conscientiously advise the government to take the direct responsibility of setting in motion a project which, in the present state of the native society and native feeling, I feel satisfied will be attended with failure. You can easily conceive whether respectable Hindus will allow their grownup female relatives to follow the profession of tuition and necessarily break through the present seclusion, when they do not permit young girls of ten or eleven years to quit the zenana after they are married. The only persons, whose services may be available, are unprotected and helpless widows, and apart from the consideration whether morally they will be fit agents for educational purposes, I have no hesitation in saying that the very fact of their dispensing with the zenana seclusion and offering themselves as public teachers will lay them open to suspicion and distrust and thus neutralise the beneficial action aimed at...

"I need hardly assure you that I fully appreciate the importance and desirableness of having female teachers for female learners, but if the social prejudice of my countrymen did not offer an insuperable bar I would have been the first to second the proposition and lend my hearty cooperation towards its furtherance. But when I see that success is by no means certain and that the government is likely to place itself in a false and disagreeable position, I cannot persuade myself to support the experiment".

He, however, did not fail to point out in his letter the necessity of keeping the Bethune School going, and said in conclusion: "As regards the Bethune School, I entirely go with you that the results are not proportionate to the amount expended upon it, but at the same time I cannot recommend its abolition altogether. As a memento of the services to the cause of female enlightenment in India of the great philanthiopist whose name the Institution bears, it has, I submit, a claim to the support of government. In the next place, it is very desirable that there should be a well-organised female school in the heart of the metropolis, to serve as a model to sister institutions in the interior. The moral influence of the present institution in native society has been undoubtedly great. It has, in fact, paved the way 10 female education in surrounding districts and this, in my humble opinion, is no mean return for the large sums which have been annually expended upon it".

Although Vidyasagar was not very hopeful about the success of Miss Carpenter's scheme, he gave the authorities every assistance and cooperation, as will be clear from Mr. Woodrow's letter to the D.P.I of March 2, 1869: "I have the honour to report that Pandit Ishwar Chandra Vidyasagar made over to me the documents relating to the Bethune School... He also spent a long time in going with me over the school and its grounds and discussing the means necessary to make it suitable for the residence of Hindu ladies. He kindly offered to give me every assistance in his power in the establishment of the Normal School, though he entertains but slight hopes of its success".

The government was in favour of giving a fair chance to Miss Carpenter's scheme. The Bethune School Committee, under Vidyasagar, refused to take part in the scheme, and was dissolved by an Order of the Government of January 27, 1869. The Normal School for training female teachers was opened in the Bethune School buildings, and an annual expenditure of Rs. 12,000 was sanctioned by the government for its maintenance. It proved a failure. The Report on Public Instruction for 1869-70 admitted its failure with this remark: 'The attempt that has been made to get together a class of adults to be trained as teachers in the Bethune School has at present met with no appreciable success "The Report of the following year was also disappointing "The adult classes established in the Bethune School, Calcutta, for the training of female teachers, has not attracted pupils, and can scarcely be said to exist". The government in a letter to the D P I on January 24, 1872, passing orders for the abolition of the Normal School, observed "On a general review of the whole subject, it is clear that after a three years' experiment the Female Normal School has unquestionably failed". Vidyasagar proved a true prophet.

After Vidyasagar's dissociation from the Committee, the Bethune School soon lost the leadership in women's education in Bengal to Hindu Mahila Vidyalaya, founded in the eastern part of Calcutta in November, 1873, and later renamed and reorganised as Banga Mahila Vidyalaya from 1876 This Institution was sponsored by Miss Akroyd, with the active support of some young progressive educated Bengalis like Monomohan Ghose, Dwarkanath Ganguli, Durgamohan Das, Anandamohan Bose, and others.

The government admitted in its Report on Public Instruction for 1876-77 that the Banga Mahila Vidyalaya was "in every sense the most advanced school in Bengal". It was found that the government-patronised Bethune School was lagging far behind the Vidyalaya in matters of teaching, administration and organisation. A suggestion was, there-foie, put forward by Mr. Justice Phear, President of the Managing Committee of the Bethune School, that the two institutions should be amalgamated and brought directly under the supervision of the government. This was eventually done on August 1, 1878, and it was from this reorganised Bethune School that Miss Kadambini Bose was sent up for the first time to sit for the Entrance Examination of Calcutta University in 1878. Kadambini came out successful and was placed in the second division. It was a great event in the annals of women's education in India. It was in this year, April, 1878, that the Senate of the University of Calcutta resolved for the first time that "female candidates be admitted to University Examinations subject to certain rules".

With the passing of the Entrance Examination by Miss Kadambini Bose, a new career opened out for the Bethune School, and a new phase of women's education began. "In consequence of the success of Miss Kadambini Bose, and in accordance with her desire to continue her studies to the First Arts examination, the Lieutenant-Governor consented to the proposal to raise the status of the school by appointing a Lecturer qualified to teach the First Arts course.'

It was only in the beginning of the eighties of the last century that the dream of women's education, which Vidyasagar and a few of his contemporaries had dreamt for decades, came true. The Report on Public Instruction for 1883-84 took note of this progress in the higher education of women in Bengal. "Of the young ladies who have taken the lead among the more highly educated women of Bengal, Kadambini Bose (now Mrs. Ganguli), who took the BA, degree in January, 1883, is studying medicine in the Calcutta Medical College; and Chandramukhi Bose, who has taken the M. A. degree with honours in English, has recently been appointed a teacher in the college classes of the Bethune School".

The ailing Pandit was then in the last stage of his life, pondering over the failures and frustrations in the struggle for social reform. It was perhaps a consolation to him that at least one of the noble causes for which he had fought so hard—the education of women—had made hopeful progress in his lifetime. He presented a copy of Cassell's Illustrated Shakespeare to Miss Chandramukhi Bose, after she had passed the highest examination of Calcutta University and got her M. A. degree.

On July 29, 1891, Vidyasagar passed away. In a fitting tribute to the memory of one of the greatest fighters for women's education and emancipation in India, educated Indian ladies founded a Memorial Committee and raised Rupees 1,610 from among themselves which they made over to the authorities of the Bethune School for the foundation of a scholarship in the name of Vidyasagar. The Bethune College Committee noted this in their Annual Report for 1894: "The late Pandit Ishwar Chandra Vidyasagar was the coadjutor and fellow-worker of Mr. Bethune, when the school was founded, and since then continued, so long as he lived, to take the keenest interest in its welfare It is, therefore, a source of great gratification to the Committee to find that a body of Hindu ladies in Calcutta should have interested themselves in this manner to perpetuate the memory of the late Pandit Vidyasagar who, during his lifetime, in addition to the philanthropic work to which he devoted his whole life, had done so much to promote Female Education.. ".

Vidyasagar's Own Experience

Arriving at Calcutta, Thakurdas took Ishwar Chandra to the house of his former host, Bhagabat Charan Singha, at Burrabazar, After Bhagabat Singha's death, his son Jagatdurlav, a young man of twenty-five, lived in that house with his mother and widowed sister Raimoni. Thakurdas and Ishwar Chandra were cordially received by them. Raimoni treated Ishwar Chandra with the affection of a mother, a fact Ishwar Chandra never forgot in his life. "The image of this noble woman," he writes in his autobiography, "has been indelibly impressed upon my mind. She was a goddess to me as my mother had been, and there was something divine in her affection which I can never forget Even at this old age whenever I recollect her loving care for me, I cannot resist my tears". It has been said that Ishwar Chandra's profound love and respect for Raimoni and his sympathy for her early widowhood made him fight for the cause of widow remarriage and monogamy.

Within a few days of his arrival at Calcutta, Ishwar Chandra was sent to a Bengali pathsala for a check-up of his elementary education. The teacher of this pathsala, Swarup Chandra, was a better teacher than Kalikanta. For about three months he studied in this pathsala and completed his elementary lessons He was now quite fit to take up higher studies in a standard school. But what was to be the medium of his higher education—English or Sanskrit?

This was a difficult problem for Ishwar Chandra's father, teachers and other well-wishers Discussions ranged over the prospects of English and Sanskrit learning In his autobiography Ishwar Chandra sums up the problem thus; "The education that one could have had at that time in a gurumahasay's pathsala, 1 had from my teachers Kalikanta at Birsingha and Swarup Chandra at Calcutta. After that, my relatives began to put forward their suggestions and advice to my father in regard to the kind of education 1 would be benefited to receive. Our hereditary caste-occupation had been teaching in *tols and chatuspati s*, but my father, pressed by unfavourable circumstances, had to give it up He was therefore determined that his failure should be made good by me. I should learn Sanskrit, be a good Pandit and take to our traditional occupation of teaching in a tol, preferably of my own, and in my own village. He told his friends that he did not at all like the idea of giving him English education for its economic utility, as it would convert me to a money-earning machine. He would be rather pleased to see me become a good Sanskrit scholar and a humble teacher in a village tol. In his words:

> "Our relative, Madhusudan Vachaspati, was then a student of Sanskrit College, He told my father that his desire would be fulfilled, if I was admitted into Sanskrit College. Besides, he said, there were many opportunities in store for the brilliant students of that College. For instance, the post of 'judge-pandit' or legal adviser on Hindu Law to the District Judge in Civil Courts was then reserved for scholars who, after completing a certain stage of education in Sanskrit College, passed also the Law Committee's examination Madhusudan's arguments appeared quite convincing to my father and he readily accepted his advice. It was decided that I should have a sound Sanskrit education in the Sanskrit College of Calcutta".

It was in 1829 that this discussion over the respective merits of English and Sanskrit education took place between Thakurdas and his relatives. It was the time when a fierce controversy raged between the promoters of English education—the Anglicists—and the patrons of classical Sanskrit education—the Orientalists. It raged for about twelve years, beginning from 1822-23, rising to a climax between 1829 and 1835, and ending with Lord William Bentinck's famous Resolution of March 7, 1835, which was adopted on Macaulay's recommendation in favour of State patronage of English education.

There are certain well-marked stages in the progress of education in India under the East India Company's rule. During the earliest stage the Company had no recognised territorial or political authority and the education of the Indian people was not looked upon as a part of its administrative policy. The second stage was marked by the encouragement of Oriental studies from 1781 to 1791, when the Calcutta, Madras and Banaras Sanskrit Colleges were founded. The object of this policy was to train Muslim and Hindu officers for suitable posts in the Company's Administrative and Judicial Services. The third stage was marked by the legislative recognition of education as a duty of the State in the year 1813 and by some notable individual efforts among Indians for promoting English education. In his famous Minute of March 6, 1811, Minto criticised the indifferent attitude of the rulers to education and remarked: "It is seriously to be lamented that a nation particularly distinguished for its love and successful cultivation of letters in other parts of the Empire should have failed to extend its fostering care to the literature of the Hindus and to aid in opening to the learned in Europe the repositories of that literature. Upon this, it was laid down for the first time in the Charter Act of 1813 that a sum of not less than one lakh of rupees yearly should be set apart for "the revival and improvement of literature and the encouragement of the learned natives of India, and for the instruction and promotion of a knowledge of the sciences among the inhabitants of the British territories in India".

It was found that roughly an amount of about two lakhs of rupees was spent annually on education in the three Presidencies of Bengal, Madras and Bombay, from 1813 to 1830. But it was not a properly planned expenditure, though Committees of Public Instruction had been appointed for the purpose of planning in 1823 at Calcutta and in 1826 at Madras, and an Education Society had been organised in 1823 at Bombay. Meanwhile, it was resolved by the Governor-General-in-Council on August 21, 1821, that a Sanskrit College, like the one at Banaras, should be founded at Calcutta, and for it an annual grant of Rs. 25,000 was to be sanctioned. It was stated in the Resolution that although "the immediate object of the institution'—the Sanskrit College of Calcutta—is the cultivation of Hindu literature," yet in the judgement of His Lordship in Council, it was a purpose of much deeper interest to seek every practicable means of effecting the gradual diffusion of European knowledge". In pursuance of this

Resolution the Sanskrit College was founded in Calcutta in a rented house at 66, Bowbazar, on January 1, 1824, wherefrom it was removed to its new buildings (where it still stands, at College Square) on May 1, 1826.

It is obvious that the educational policy of the Company did not take a final shape till the middle of the thirties. In the meantime, some prominent Bengalis, in cooperation with the famous educationist David Hare, the watchmaker, and Mr. Justice Edward Hyde East, established an institution at Calcutta in 1817 for the promotion of English education among Indians. This institution was known by different names—Hindu College, Maha Vidyalay, and Anglo-Indian College. The present Presidency College of Calcutta is its direct successor. The Hindu College was sponsored by a group of upper-class orthodox Bengali Hindus, and it is noteworthy that the name of Rammohan Roy, the great pioneer of Western education in India, was not associated with its origin or development.

The reason is not far to seek. Settling down in Calcutta in 1815-16, Rammohan set about demolishing the age-old practices of Hinduism, such as polytheistic image-worship, the custom of sati or of concremation and post-cremation of widows. The campaign enraged the orthodox Hindus, and it is quite likely that their leaders refused to cooperate with Rammohan in sponsoring an educational institution exclusively tor the Hindu boys. 'Rammohan, therefore, established a separate English school at Calcutta in 1822. He wrote his famous letter to Amherst against the Orientalist policy of the government in regard to education in India. In this letter he strongly criticised the proposal for establishing a Sanskrit College at Calcutta, and pleaded for the promotion of a more liberal and enlightened system of education in "India, embracing "Mathematics, Natural Philosophy, Chemistry, Anatomy and other useful sciences, which the Nations of Europe have carried to a degree of perfection that has raised them above the inhabitants of other parts of the world".

There were many Orientalists among Englishmen at that time, but very few Anglicists among Indians. Rammohan Roy was the first outspoken Anglicist in this land and it was he who led the movement in its behalf from about 1816 till his departure for

England in 1830. A new generation of young men, educated in the Hindu College sprang up in the meantime, and strengthened the hands of the Anglicists. This was in 1829-30, when the question of the kind of higher education which Ishwar Chandra should receive, posed a problem. The Orientalists were gradually retreating when the government resolved on the policy of English education.

This was in the year 1835, the mid-period of Ishwar Chandra's student life. When Thakurdas decided in favour of giving classical Sanskrit education to Ishwar Chandra. The Orientalists were still holding the field, and the English rulers were hesitating between the two courses. The rulers could afford to wait and see, but the fate of a boy of nine years could not be kept in suspense. The decision was therefore quickly translated into action. On the first day of June, 1829, Ishwar Chandra was admitted to the Sanskrit College of Calcutta. He thus set out on his voyage of learning in the stirring thirties of 19th century.

5

Great Social Reforms

Advocate of Widow Remarriage

The movement for the remarriage of Hindu widows advocated by Vidyasagar set the people of Bengal speculating why the learned Pandit had launched it.

Two or three stories may briefly be given here to indicate their speculative and romantic nature. One story is that Vidyasagar had a girl playmate widowed in her infancy, at his native village Birsingha. He had been fond of her and mutual attraction had developed between them as they had grown up When Vidyasagar had come to know of her widowhood and of the lifelong celibacy to which she had been condemned by the injunctions of the Shastras, he had resolved to fight for the right of remarriage of Hindu widows. Another story is that in his youth Vidyasagar had heard the story of a woman who had committed suicide for not being able to stand the socially ostracised life This tragic end of a helpless widow's life inspired him to take the vow of securing the right of remarriage for Hindu widows and getting it sanctioned by society and government.

The biographers of Vidyasagar have all committed the mistake of looking for the motive for this great attempt to reform this hoary social custom in some accidental circumstance or other in the middle of the last century. A "social attitude" takes time to shape itself to the point of decisive action The attitude to social reform, which took concrete shape in favour of widow-remarriage and against polygamy in Vidyasagar's time, had a long history behind it. It originated in the days of Raja Rammohan Roy in the first quarter of the nineteenth century. The Atmiya Sabha organised by Rammohan Roy in 1815 had been discussing these social problems since its foundation. A report of the meeting of this Sabha in 1819 says: "At the meeting in question... the necessity of an infant widow passing her life in a state of celibacy, the practice of polygamy and of suffering widows to burn with the corpse of their husbands, were condemned". Rammohan Roy, to whose exertions are to some extent indebted for the prohibition of the inhuman custom of sati, as constantly spoken of in almost every home of Bengal, as having sailed to England with the avowed purpose of bringing about the remarriage of Hindu widows. It is said that the old widows often jocularly talked of their marriage on the return of Rammohan Roy from England. There is no doubt that the remarriage of Hindu widows engaged the attention of Rammohan Roy, but he could not find time, after the abolition of sati, to earnestly take up the problem.

This problem, along with others, was taken up earnestly for discussion and for influencing public opinion by the young Derozians in the thirtics of the last century. The Derozians discussed it also in their press, mainly in the columns of their English periodical The Enquirer and the Bengali Jnananweshan That they were able to create some impression by these discussions is evident from the fact that the Indian Law Commission took up the matter for consideration. Mr. J P Giant, Secretary to the Commission, addressed a circular calling for information on the subject and for the opinion of the Sudder Courts at all the four Presidencies. It is interesting to note that most of the British officers attached to the different Courts rejected the idea of legislation for enforcing the remarriage of widows and thus preventing infanticide. Mr. R. Macan, the officiating Registrar of the Calcutta Sudder Court, wrote in reply to the circular on July 24, 1837: "In reply I am directed to intimate that the Court with a perfect understanding of the evils resulting from the prohibition now existing against remarriage of Hindu widows, have no hesitation in stating it as their unqualified opinion that a law of the nature contemplated could not be passed without a direct and open violation of the pledged faith of the Government". Mr. H. B. Harrington, Registrar of the Allahabad Sudder Court, wrote in reply on August 11, 1837: "The object of the proposed enactment is doubtless a most humane one; but being directly opposed to the Hindu Law, and calculated from the great importance attached to the due observance of that law, to be exceedingly offensive to the feeling of the people, the Court see great reason to question the expediency and policy of passing it". Mr. W. Douglas, Registrar of the Madras Sudder Court, wrote in reply on July 31, 1837. "The Judges are of opinion that any such law in this part of India would not only prove a dead letter for the purpose intended, but would unite the whole of the superior classes in maintaining with increased bigotry the established custom against which it would be levelled".

It is evident from these replies of the Sudder Courts that they were not at all in favour of enforcing widow remarriage by legislation for fear of direct intervention in the social customs of the Hindus, when the question was raised in the thirties of last century. The agitation of Young Bengal had this much effect: the authorities concerned took up the matter earnestly and went to the extent of seeking expert opinion in the matter of legislation. The discussion, led by the progressive section of the Bengali educated middle class, went on with renewed vigour in the forties. Such famous Associations of middle class Bengali intelligentsia as the Society for the Acquisition of General Knowledge; the Tattwabodhini Sabha and the Bethune Society discussed the matter frequently at their meetings. These ceaseless discussions and agitations, through press and platform, led to the formation of a positive attitude towards social reforms in Bengal in the middle of the fifties when Vidyasagar gave it concrete shape by launching a movement for legislation for permitting widow remarriage and prohibiting polygamy.

The ground was prepared for it in the middle of the 19th century. Its chief promoters and supporters, the educated middle class, had by that time grown into a social force in Bengal The vanguard of the educated Bengali middle class had hotly discussed and debated child marriage, polygamy, and the enforced celibacy of the widows since the beginning of the twenties of the last century, in various cultural societies and through the press, pleading for their reform. The demand lose to a climax in the forties. The Bengal Spectator, an English and Bengali periodical of the leaders of Young Bengal, was wilting zealously about it since the beginning of the forties. In the very first issue of the periodical in April, 1842, we find that the subject of "Widow Remarriage" was reviewed thoroughly. Even the evidence which Vidyasagar adduced in his famous essay on Widow Remarriage in 1854-55 was fully utilised by the writer of the aforesaid article in the Bengal Spectator. The idea of sending a petition to the government signed by the leading members of the, Hindu community was also sponsored by the writer of the article. A suggestion for restoring the right of remarriage to Hindu widows, by legislation if necessary, was put forward in it Sometime in 1845, the British Indian Society corresponded with the Dharma Sabha and the Tattwabodhini Sabha on the remarriage of Hindu widows. "The latter association made no reply. The correspondence with the Dharma Sabha was carried on for sometime, but it led to no practical results". After about ten years Vidyasagar resumed the discussion with renewed vigour and courage in the middle of the fifties. The discussion, as we have seen, leached its climax in the beginning of the forties and had spent itself by the end of the forties.

A new social situation was created in the fifties, mainly by the efforts of the Tattwabodhini Sabha and the Tattwabodhini Patrika, founded by Maharshi Debendranath Tagore in 1839 and 1843. The Tattwabodhini Sabha commenced its career with only ten young men as its members. It used to hold weekly and monthly meetings in which papers on different social and religious subjects were read and discussed The beginnings were very small, but "so great were the energy and enthusiasm with which its proceedings were conducted that in the course of two years the number of members lose to 500, and in the course of a few years more, it attracted many rich and influential men into the ranks of its members and sympathisers: It became the most representative and powerful organisation of the educated Bengali middle class in the middle of the last century. Vidyasagar was closely associated with this Sabha and was a member. In the closing years of its existence, before it was merged with the newly organised Brahmo

Samaj, Vidyasagar became its Secretary (1858-59) Vidyasagar was also a member of the Editorial Board of Tattwabodhini Patrika and one of its regular contributors. He found in the first editor of the Patrika, Akshay Kumar Dutta, one of his great friends and collaborators in the cause of social reform. Akshay Kumar was an invincible rationalist and materialist of his time, and like Vidyasagar, one of the most powerful Bengali prose writers who pioneered in the field of historical and scientific dissertations through the medium of Bengali. With his unbending will and clear outlook, he stood beside his friend Vidyasagar and supported his every move for social reform, for widow remarriage and abolition of polygamy, through the columns of the Tattwabodhini Patrika. Vidyasagar himself put forward his proposal for widow remarriage in an article in the Tattwabodhini Patrika of Phalgun 1776 Saka (1854). In the next issue of the Patrika Akshay Kumar gave it strong editorial support.

A new spirit began to manifest itself in the activities of the young members of the Sabha in their debates and discussions on controversial social topics This was also manifested in the columns of the Tattwabodhini Patrika, where articles appealed regularly advocating women's education and widow remarriage, denouncing polygamy, child-marriage and intemperance.

It was in this situation that Vidyasagar stepped into the field of social reform. He was not the originator of the idea of widow remarriage, as has been wrongly given out by some of his biographers; nor was he the discoverer of the oft-quoted slokas of the Parasar Samhita which prescribed the remarriage of Hindu widows under certain specific conditions.

It is true that he passed many sleepless nights in the Principal's room in the Calcutta Sanskrit College reviewing and searching out the ancient Hindu Shastras for some evidence in support of his contention, it is not, however, true that he suddenly stumbled in ecstasy upon the "Nastey Mritey" sloka of Parasat Samhita and cued out, "Oh ! I have found it at last". This story does scant justice to Vidyasagar's profound scholarship in ancient Sanskrit literature. But the credit of carrying through the movement for widow remarriage to its logical conclusion, against all opposition, is due to him. He fulfilled this historic mission, with rare courage and determination.

We need not suppose that Vidyasagar worked hard for getting some prescriptions of the old Shastrakars in support of the thesis on widow remarriage The saying of Parasar Samhita, on which he built up his case, has been reiterated by ancient sages like Baudhayana, Narada, and supported by Puranas like Agmpurana. Baudhayana describes "paunarbhava" as the son of a woman who after abandoning an impotent or outcaste husband marries another. This could not have happened in a society where widow remarriage had been rigidly prohibited by custom.

Narada, Parasara and Agnipurana have, in fact, the same verse in support of widow remarriage—"another husband is ordained for women in five calamities, viz, when the husband is lost (not heard of), is dead, has become a sanyasi, is impotent or is patita. It is unlikely therefore that a profound Sanskrit scholar like Vidyasagar would lose much time in finding out such prescriptions for widow remarriage in ancient Indian sources, Though widow remarriage had been prohibited for centuries among the Brahmins and similar castes in the caste hierarchy, it was never forbidden among the other castes.

Among the Sudras and similar castes, widow remarriage had been allowed by custom, and is still allowed, though it is held to be somewhat inferior to the marriage of a maiden Among these castes, remarriage is allowed after the death of the husband, or during his lifetime with his consent—he has to give a writing called fatkhat or sod-chitti (deed of release). Such marriage are called pal in Maharashtra, natra in Gujarat, udki in the Kanarcse districts. In Bengal, Bihar and Orissa, among the people of lower castes, and among the Santhals and other tribes, widow remarriage has been allowed by custom It is commonly called nika.

These lower castes and tribes predominated in the villages and its surroundings (formerly in the Hooghly district of West Bengal, now in Midnapore district) in which Vidyasagar was born and brought up. It may be, that he derived his inspiration in his early youth from the custom of these people living around him. It might have dawned on him, when very young, that widows presented a serious social problem after sati had been prohibited by law by Bentinck in 1829. As polygamy, wedded to the cruel practice of Kulimsm, was still prevalent in Bengal, and the inhuman practice of self-immolation by the widows in the funeral pyre of their husbands was prohibited, the number of widows grew alarmingly Most of these widows were young By the middle of the century the crisis had deepened "to such an extent that it was realised by serious-minded people that the moral foundations of society could hardly survive, Vidyasagar also realised it deeply, but, unlike others, he began in right earnest to translate his ideals into action.

Vidyasagar published his first pamphlet in defence of widow remarriage in January, 1855. The famous sloka of Parasar Samhita on which he erected the main structure of his thesis, he interpreted thus: "On receiving no tidings of a husband, on his demise, on his turning an ascetic, on his being found impotent, or on his degradation—under any one of these calamities it is canonical for women to take another husband".

His comment on the passage was: "Thus it appears that Parasar prescribes three rules for a widow marriage, observance of brahmacharya, and burning with the deceased husband. Among these, the custom of concremation has been abolished by the order of the ruling authorities, only two ways, therefore, are now left for the widows; they have the option of marrying or observing brahmacharya. But in Kali Yuga it has become extremely difficult for widows to pass their lives in the observance of brahmacharya; and it is for this reason that the philanthropic Parasar has, in the first instance, prescribed marriage. Be that as it may, what I wish to be, clearly understood is—that as Parasar plainly prescribes marriage as one of the duties of women in the Kali Yuga under any one of the five above calamities, the marriage of widows in Kaliyuga is consonant with the Sastras".

Great controversies raged round the interpretation of this verse. Some pandits offered the easy explanation that the verse in question refers to the state of society in another yuga (age) and has therefore no application to Kaliyuga or the modern age. Pandits from ancient centres of learning in Bengal like Navadvip and Bhatpara assembled in conference in the house of Raja Radhakanta Dev in north Calcutta. Radhakanta Dev, the great scion of the Sova-bazar Raj family, was not only an eminent Sanskrit scholar but also one of the richest and most influential leaders of the

Hindu community of his time. This leader of the orthodox Hindu community was gracious enough to invite Vidyasagar to take part in the conference. In the first day's debate the young scholar and reformer Vidyasagar presented his case with such force and ability before the veterans that Raja Radhakanta was profoundly impressed, and though he could not agree with him on many points, he, rewarded Vidyasagar as the best debater of the day with a pan of shawls.

The leaders of the orthodox community thought that their grand patriarch, Raja Radhakanta, had been won over by Vidyasagar. This created an unprecedented commotion in the Hindu society of Calcutta, and people rushed in hundreds to the Raja and wanted to know what his actual opinion was about Vidyasagar proposal for widow remarriage. The Raja met the leaders and pacified them by assuring them that he was not at all in favour of widow remarriage and that he was not convinced by Vidyasagar's arguments; Vidyasagar had been rewarded by him only for his unrivalled powers of reasoning and scholarship.

To remove the misunderstanding completely from people's mind, a second meeting of the pandits was called in his house, in which, among others, Pandit Brajanath Vidyaratna of Navadvip, a great scholar in Smriti (Hindu Law) of his time, was present. The Raja presented a pair of shawls to Pandit Brajanath, who emphatically denounced and rejected Vidyasagar's arguments. Vidyasagar soon realised, after these conferences of pandits in Raja Radhakanta's house, that he should have, to face a violent storm of protest against the cause of widow remarriage.

Many pamphlets were issued from different associations of pandits and orthodox Hindus. Many individuals also took part in the protest by publishing books and pamphlets. Strong protests were issued from the Dharma Sabha of Calcutta, the Hindu Dharma Rakshmi Sabha of Jessore, and other associations.

The occasion yielded a rich crop of satirical poems, dramas, domestic tales and sketches in Bengali literature. Ishwar Chandra Gupta, a leading satirist of the time, composed some entertaining poems in Bengali on the theme of widow remarriage. Dasarathi Ray, one of the most popular singers and composers of that time, wrote some songs on the theme which people in every village and town, fair and festival, started singing for the sake of fun. Even the famous Bengali weavers of Santipur, Dacca and other places in Bengal wove songs about the remarriage of widows in the borders of saris worn by women ! In all this spate of popular poems, songs, dramas and tales, it was not the anger of people which found its outlet, but a kind of awe and wonder, mingled with deep love and reverence for Vidyasagar.

The common people never gave vent to any ill-feeling against Vidyasagar; but the leaders of the orthodox Hindu community and the majority of the pandits of the old school indulged in diatribes and invective against Vidyasagar.

In the second pamphlet on widow remarriage, published in October, 1855, Vidyasagar refuted the arguments of his opponents in sober and elegant language. But it produced no effect whatsoever on his opponents; rather it added fuel to the fire. So he decided to act and avoid further deliberation and discussion.

On October 4, 1855, Vidyasagar sent the Government of India a Petition praying for an enactment in favour of widow remarriage. The Petition has been preserved in the National Archives of India. It carried the signatures of 987 persons, besides his own. It was forwarded to the Council with the following letter of Vidyasagar:

To
W. Morgan, Esquire,
Clerk to the Honourable the Legislative Council of India

Sir,

On behalf of the petitioners, I have the honour to forward herewith the Petition of certain Hindu Inhabitants of the province of Bengal which I beg to request you will do me the favour to lay before the Honourable Council at their next sitting.

I have the honour to be, Sir,
Your most obedient Servant,
Sd. Ishwar Chandra Sharma.

Calcutta,
Sanskrit College,
the 4th October, 1855.

Paragraphs 8-11 of the Petition ran as follows:

"8 That, in the humble opinion of your petitioners, it is the duty of the Legislature to remove all legal obstacles to the escape from a social evil of such magnitude which, though sanctioned by custom, is felt by many Hindus to be a most injurious grievance, and to be contrary to a true interpretation of Hindu Law.

"9 That the removal of the legal obstacles to the marriage of widows would be in accordance with the wishes and feelings of a considerable section of pious and orthodox Hindus, and would in nowise affect the interests, though it might shock the prejudices, of those who conscientiously believe that the prohibition of the marriage of widows is sanctioned by the Shastras, or who uphold it on fancied grounds of social advantage.

"10. That such marriages are neither contrary to nature nor prohibited by law or custom in any other country or by any other people in the world.

"11. That your petitioners, therefore, humbly pray that your Honourable Council will take into early consideration the propriety of passing a law (as annexed) to remove all legal obstacles to the marriage of Hindu widows, and to declare the issue of all such marriages to be legitimate".

On November 17, 1855, a draft Bill of "An Act to remove all legal obstacles to the Marriage of Hindu Widows," was introduced in the Legislative Council by Mr. J. P. Grant, one of the members of the Council. Doing so he said: "It is said that this custom (restriction of Hindu Widow marriage), cruel and unnatural in itself, is highly injurious to the morals, and is otherwise most mischievous to society From these premises, it argues that a law having such effects ought not to be forced upon anyone who disapproves of it; and it prays that, as the petitioners are of opinion that the custom is not in accordance with a true interpretation of Hindu Sastras, they and those who agree with them may be relieved from the legal restriction of which they complain".

When the Bill was being piloted in the Council it roused great interest all over India, and the controversy was not confined to Bengal. All over India, a great controversy raged round Vidyasagar's thesis on widow remarriage. Reactions to it were ventilated through petitions to the Government of India, and they stated pointing in from all corners as the debate went on in the Council.

In the Widow Remarriage Papers preserved in the National Archives of India, petitions from Poona, Vinchoor, Secunderabad, Satara, Dharwar, Bombay, Ahmedabad, Surat, and from different parts of Bengal are found to contain arguments both for and against widow remarriage. The Mahratta Chief of Vinchoor wrote in his petition, dated January 12, 1856:

> "...It seems unnecessary for us to enter into details connected with the proposed enactment We merely wish to express our cordial approval of the principle on which the proposal is based, and to solicit that the Legislature will remove any bar, which may exist in the eye of the Law, to the remarriage of the Hindu Widows".

A petition from Poona, bearing about 46 signatures, dated November 7, 1855, stated: "We understand that there is a movement in Bengal, headed by the enlightened portion of the Hindu community, which has for its object the removal of all legal objections to the remarriage of Hindu Widows. Such a laudable movement cannot but be seconded by those who take a real interest in the welfare of India.

We are far from thinking that the removal of legal disabilities will be followed by the immediate abolition of a practice, which not only entails innumerable hardships and misery on hundreds and thousands of innocent but unfortunate females, but lies at the very bottom of many of the existing social evils, and too much of the crime which at present has to be deplored.

That which bears the stamp of ancient custom can only be dedicated from the Hindu mind by the steps which are being taken in every direction, to, diffuse knowledge, to explode erroneous ideas, and thus undoubtedly to effect a gradual reformation in the state of Hindu society".

The Brahmin Pandits and the "Gentoo Hindus" of Secunderabad wrote in their petition of March 2, 1856, "that we truly concerning in the spirit and letter of that Petition and Draft submitted by certain Hindu inhabitants of Bengal for legalising the marriage of Hindu Widows, beg leave to submit a copy thereof, and to second this prayer".

Their were also petitions strongly protesting against any interference by the British Government with the traditional socio-religious customs of the Indian people. From an analysis of the material available it is clear that outside Bengal the widow remarriage movement created considerable interest in Maharashtra and also in some parts of South India. Bengal was sharply divided into two hostile camps— the Vidyasagar and the Dharma Sabhaites. Casual conversations and discussions at last settled into opinions; no less than a hundred tracts were published, and twenty petitions bearing a total of at least 50,000 signatures were sent from different districts of Bengal to the Government of India. If the number of signatures is taken into account, it must be admitted that the overwhelming majority of the petitioners from Bengal was against Vidyasagar and any such reform, Only about 10 per cent of the petitioners supported Vidyasagar and pleaded for passing a law removing all bars to widow remarriage.

The most formidable petition against Vidyasagar's reform was sent at the initiative of the veteran leader of the orthodox Hindu community in Calcutta, Raja Radhakanta Dev, with 36,763 signatures, on March 17, 1856. Among other things, it was stated in the petition that the followers of Vidyasagar constituted a very small minority, and that it would not be prudent and just to enact a law in the interest of this negligible minority and thereby interfere with the rights of the majority. Another petition, signed by about one thousand pandits was sent from Bengal against the proposed Bill.

Among the petitions sent from Bengal in support of the Bill, the following were important: petition from Maharaja Snshchandra, Zamindar of Nadia, his Dewan Kartikeya Chandra Roy, father of D. L. Roy, and 26 other eminent persons of Krishnanagar, in December, 1855; petition from Krishnanagar and its neighbourhood, signed by about 129 persons, in December, 1855; petition from Santipur, the famous culture-centre of the Bengal Vaishnavas, Ishwar Chandra Ghosul sent a petition signed by 531 persons in favour of the proposed Bill in 1856—the Head

Gossains or the leaders of the Vaishnavas signed this petition; a petition was sent from the district of Murshidabad by Sureshchandra Vidyaratna, signed by eminent pandits like Madan Mohan Tarkalankar—Tarkalankar was a close collaborator of Vidyasagar in his educational and social reform projects; from the district of Midnapore, Rajnarain Bose, the venerable leader of the Brahmos and the father of modern nationalism in Bengal, sent a petition in support of the Bill, with the signatures of a number of important persons of that area, in March, 1856; a large number of persons from the districts of Burdwan, Bankura and 24-Parganas sent petitions in support of the Bill; from the remote district of Chittagong in East Bengal a petition was sent by the Hindu inhabitants in support of the Bill in February, 1856.

The most interesting petition found among the Widow Remarriage Papers is the one sent by the leading Derozians of Bengal, Rasik Krishna Mullick, Radhanath Sikdar, Peary Chandra Mitra, and others, which while supporting the main contention of the Bill, sought to modify it drastically in the light of the equality of status of men and women in modern times. This has not been brought to light before. The reasons laid down for the modification of the proposed Bill were: "It does not lay down what shall constitute valid widow marriage. Such definition appears to be absolutely necessary, since widow marriage, when it comes to pass, will be a new fact in the Hindu social system, and it may be naturally expected that different men will employ different modes of solemnising it, and also it may be apprehended that such marriages will often be disputed in a Court of Justice". A very reasonable point, perhaps, this was the most important lacuna in the draft Bill for Widow Remarriage which the Derozians wanted to fill in before the Bill was passed into law. It was proposed by Young Bengal that the bride and the bridegroom should separately sign two declarations before they married. The marriage formalities were:

Declaration

> "I... widower or bachelor, and I... widow or spinster, do hereby jointly and severally declare that of our own free will and accord we have solemnised our marriage with each other on this day of...".

Agreement

> "I...have taken...as my wedded wife on this day, do hereby bind myself not to contract a second marriage during her lifetime, and in breach of this engagement on my part, to pay to her the sum of Company's Rupees... on the date of any second marriage".

It was also suggested in the modified proposal that a Marriage Registration Clause should be inserted in the Bill, "under which marriages of Hindu Widows in whatever manner performed, will be held valid provided they are registered by the contracting parties before public officials appointed by the government for the purpose". In fact, this amended proposal for the Widow Remarriage Act was incorporated into the Civil Marriage Act III of 1872, passed mainly at the initiative of Keshab Chandra Sen after a great controversy over the form and procedure of Brahmo marriage.

This vitally important amendment was, of course, not incorporated into the Widow Remarriage Act when it was discussed on July 26,1856. Neither Vidyasagar, the inspirer of the Act, nor the legislators recognised its importance at that time. Vidyasagar was on good terms with the Derozians, and it is unlikely that they had not communicated their views and suggestions for the proposed reform. It seems likely, therefore, that Vidyasagar was not in agreement with their views on the registration of such marriages, for some reason or other.

One may guess the point of difference between Vidyasagar and the Derozians He was not in favour of introducing any drastic changes in the institutional pattern of Hindu marriage Within its framework he wanted to fit in his widow remarriage scheme. This limitation produced some inevitable contradictions, which he had to face when the Act was passed, the gap in the Act pointed out by the Derozians grew evident as the Act was translated into practice. Most of the widow remarriages proved tragic in the end, as a large number of those who came forward to marry the widows were found within a short time to be the worst of opportunists and cowards Taking advantage of the situation they extracted money from the patrons of widow remarriage. Even Vidyasagar himself lost a considerable sum that lie had secured for carrying out his reform. In the last days of his life, it may be noted, he had to accept indirectly the proposal that had been put forward by the Young Bengal group. He himself drafted a sort of a contract form of agreement and compelled the parties to sign that before marriage. Keeping the institutional pattern of Hindu marriage as also the practice of polygamy permissible up to any extent, it was inevitable that mere restoration of the legal right, to remarriage to the widows would end in a fiasco.

The Widow Remarriage Bill was read for the third time on July 19, 1856, and passed into Act XV of 1856, "being an Act to remove all legal obstacles to the marriage of Hindu widows "It received the assent of the Governor-General on July 26, 1856, and became law. It declared that "no marriage contracted between Hindus shall be invalid and the issue of no such marriage shall be illegitimated by reason of the woman having been previously married or betrothed to another person who was dead at the time of such marriage, any custom and any interpretation of Hindu - Law to the contrary notwithstanding".

After the Act was passed, Suhrid Samiti (the Association of Friends for the Social Improvement of Bengal), one of the leading organisations of the progressive reformers in Bengal, commented in its second Annual Report of 1856-57: "It is, as it should be, permissive law, but unfortunately it prescribes neither registration nor any other mode for establishing the validity of marriage in this land of false accusations, where it is so liable to be disputed by interested parties. The Committee cannot, therefore, help repeating their conviction that it must be soon followed up by a more catholic Marriage Act like that contemplated by the Association on the defective Marriage Act of 1856".

But nothing could deter Vidyasagar from translating the Act into practice. For about four months after the Act was passed none was found to come forward to marry a widow. The first marriage under the Act took place on December 7, 1856—a memorable day in the history of the social rights of women in India. The bridegroom was Pandit Shrischandra Vidyaratna, son of the famous kathak (village bard), Ramdhan Tarkavagish of Khantura, in the district of 24-Parganas in Bengal The bride, Kabniati Debi, a child-widow of 10 years, hailed from the village Palasdanga in Burdwan district. The marriage day was fixed earlier but, as reported in the Bengali periodical Sambad Bhaskar and the Englishman, November 27, 1856, Shrischandra, out of fear of social persecution, wanted to back out.

But the bride's party was adamant, and as the news was already circulated, they were determined to perform the marriage. A suit demanding adequate compensation was instituted against the bridegroom in the Supreme Court. Sambad Bhaskar and the Englishman tauntingly criticised the pusillanimous attitude of Shrischandra and praised Lakshmimani Debi, the bride's mother, for being firm on the marriage. Later on, the bridegroom changed his mind and decided to marry. Possibly he was persuaded to do so by his friends, particularly Vidyasagar. He was a colleague of Vidyasagar's and a lecturer in the Sanskrit College and was subsequently promoted to the rank of judge-pandit of Murshidabad district.

Newspaper reports of the marriage and the accounts of it given by some fortunate eyewitnesses bear testimony to the unprecedented interest roused by the occasion The marriage was celebrated in the house of Rajkrishna Banerji, an intimate friend of Vidyasagar's at Sukea Street in north Calcutta Most of the social leaders and intellectuals, sympathetically disposed towards the reform, were present on, the occasion to cheer up the marriage parties and to stand by the side of Vidyasagar in the hour of his first great trial.

Among others, Ramgopal Ghose, a leading Derozian, Rama Prasad Roy, son of Raja Rammohan Roy, Raja Digambar Mitra, an eminent Derozian, Peary Chandra Mitra, the first novelist of Bengal and a leading reformer, Kaliprasanna Sinha, a powerful satirist and a progressive thinker, and Pandit Goun Sankar Bhattacharya, editor of Sambad Bhaskar Patrika were present on the wedding day. At about 11 in the night the bridegroom's Palaquin, amidst thunderous cheers and jeers, reached Rajkrishna Babu's house at Sukea Street. Vidyasagar with some of his friends and supporters like Ramgopal Ghose walked by the side of the Palaquin and escorted it through the crowds, apprehending trouble and attack on the bridegroom's party by the Dharma Sabha's men.

Pandit Sivanath Shastri, a great leader of the Brahmo Samaj movement in the latter half of the 19th century, has left the following account of the first widow remarriage in his book Men I Have Seen, He says: "Things went on like this when in the cold season of the year 1856 took place the first remarriage of a Hindu widow, celebrated in the house of Babu Rajkrishna Banerji I shall never forget that day. When Vidyasagar Mahashay came with his friend, the bridegroom, at the head of a large procession, the crowd of spectators was so great that there was not an inch of moving space in the whole street, and many fell into the big drams which were to be seen by the sides of the Calcutta streets of those days. After the ceremony it became the subject of discussion everywhere the bazaars and the shops, in the streets, in public squares, in students' lodging-houses, in drawingrooms, in offices, and in distant village homes, where even women earnestly discussed it among themselves The weaver of Santipur issued a peculiar kind of women's saris which contained woven along its borders the first line of a newly composed song. 'May Vidyasagar live long. Thus was an agitation kicked up, the like of which has seldom been witnessed in this country".

The second widow marriage was held on the very next day The bride and the bridegroom belonged to Kulm and high-caste Kayastha families. Commenting on this second marriage Tattwabodhini Patrika wrote: "We are very happy to learn of the progress of widow remarriage in our country. It proves that where there is a will, there is a way, and that nothing can prevent a good cause from making progress against all opposition". After paying glowing tribute to Vidyasagar for his great sacrifices for the cause, the Patrika commented statistically on those hostile to the reform. The orthodox became in particular the target of attack of the Tattwabodhini Patrika, "One wonders how a section of people in a society, claiming to be the trustees of its best heritage, feel exasperated at the cure of a long-standing ill of a suffering society". These comments, however, could not bring round the conservatives. The voice of the Vidyasagar was drowned in the dm of the vituperation of the orthodox papers like Samachar Chandrika and Sambad Prabhakar. Tattwabodhini Patrika and Sambad Bhaskar, however, went on consistently supporting the reform.

The movement gathered strength for the time being, despite opposition. The thud and fourth marriages occurred in the family of Rajnarain Bose, the veteran leader of the Brahmo movement in Bengal. His two brother, Durganarain Bose and Madanmohan Bose, were married to widows, and this created a sensation in his native village Boial, about four miles south of Calcutta. The people of the village grew so furious that they threatened to kill Rajnarain Bose. In his Bengali Autobiography he wrote that he used to receive many threatening letters but felt comforted at the thought that the Bengalis, at any rate, were shaking off their proverbial lethargy and plucking up courage to take physical vengeance upon a perfectly non-violent Brahamo missionary like himself.

One can easily imagine, the enmity which Vidyasagar himself had to face. An account of it was published in the Bengali Hitabadi Patrika in the year Vidyasagar died, 1891. Whenever Vidyasagar came out of his house, people surrounded him and passed bitter remarks on his widow marriage activities, and often threatened him with physical assault. Stones and mud were thrown at him. It was organised violence, patronised by certain rich Hindus of Calcutta. It so happened that Vidyasagar one day came straight to the house of a rich gentleman in Calcutta known to him, and found that deliberations were going on there with the heads of the city's underworld criminals about how to break his head one dark night. The gentleman in question was shocked to see Vidyasagar suddenly appearing on the scene then He stammered, "Absurd! absurd! how could you come here?" Vidyasagar replied with characteristic humour. "I have come to know that you are planning to teach me a lesson by the hired goondas of north Calcutta. I have come to you personally to save you the trouble and to give you an opportunity of doing whatever you like with my frail body right here in your house "The conspirator could not but hang his head in shame.

Vidyasagar was for challenging his enemies, and never tried to bypass them During the widow remarriage movement when his life was in danger, his father sent him an expert lathial (club-man) to serve as his bodyguard. Although this club-man was loyal to Vidyasagar, he was never allowed to walk by Vidyasagar's side in public with a big lathi in his hand. When he insisted on going with Vidyasagar, the latter used to tell him that although he had nothing but a few thinly covered bones in his body, each bone of his was at least hundred times more powerful than the bodyguard's lathi.

Vidyasagar treated his opponents with good humour and magnanimity Many amusing stories are related in this connection. Once when he was coming to Calcutta by tram, a pandit got into his compartment from a wayside station and started raving against Vidyasagar and widow marriage in a discussion with his fellow-passengers That Vidyasagar himself was one of them, he did not know. When he got down at Howrah station, someone told him that the man to whom he was talking most eagerly was none else but Vidyasagar himself The pandit fell down on the platform at the sudden shock of the news When he regained consciousness, he found that the "awful man" was nursing him.

One day, during the peak period of the widow marriage commotion, Mr. Pratt, an Inspector of Schools, asked him whose protest was best against his widow remarriage "paper" Vidyasagar at once told him the name of a person who had vilified him most, Mr. Pratt could not catch the humour of it and immediately sent for the man and offered him the post of a Deputy Inspector of Schools. When the man came to know the cause of his good fortune, he called on Vidyasagar and requested him to see that he did not lose the chance, Vidyasagar smiled and reassured him.

The stories may be exaggerated, but they indicate how Vidyasagar was unruffled in the midst of all kinds of provocation.

Widow remarriages continued to be performed sporadically by the scattered followers of Vidyasagar. It was not gaining momentum, but gradually losing ground before the slow but steady advance of Hindu reaction after the sixties of the last century. Hindu revivalism was on the march and this fact grew clear as the decade neared its end. The Brahmo Samaj movement gathered strength and dynamism under the able leadership of Maharshi Debendranath Tagore in the forties and fifties, and of Keshab Chandra Sen in the sixties and seventies; but schisms, resulting from ideological differences led to its weakening hold by the end of the 19th century About this reaction, Bipin Chandra Pal writes in his Memories of My Life and Times. "Many things contributed to this reaction. The revival of medievalism in the Brahmo Samaj was certainly by no means the least powerful of these". One of the most important reasons for the rapid advance of reactionary Hinduism in the last three decades of the 19th century was this historic dispersal of the progressive forces in Bengal which followed the split in the Brahmo movement A section of Brahmos, under Keshab's guidance, largely influenced by Ramakrishna Paramahansa, swung over to Pauranic Avatarvad and Bhaktivad leaving the fortress of Brahmo rationalism and monotheism. The widow remarriage movement naturally could not gather strength in this social situation. It began to weaken after the sixties.

But the interest of Vidyasagar in the cause of widow remarriage did not slacken. Here are instances of Vidyasagar's abiding interest in it from the reminiscences of Pandit Sivanath Shastri. He writes: "In the year 1868 one of my classfellows, the late Pandit Yogendranath Vidyabhusan, lost his first wife, and sought my advice as to the course he should follow, because his friends and relations began to press him for a second marriage We two friends held consultations together and as the cause of the remarriage of Hindu widow was uppermost in our minds, we decided upon a widow remarriage. A young Hindu widow was soon found, and I approached Pandit Vidyasagar seeking his aid in getting up that match The Pandit threw himself heart and soul into the affair, and materially helped us in going through the ceremony. He procured the Brahmin priest who was to preside at the ceremony; made material contributions, towards feeding a pretty large number of guests; made valuable presents to the bride; and personally graced the ceremony with his presence.

There was a little incident in connection with that day's gathering which was characteristic of the great Pandit's habitual good humour. A friend of his, one of the guests, came there with his little daughter, a girl of nine or ten. This friend made his daughter bow at the feet of Pandit Vidyasagar, whereupon the latter blessed her with the following benediction, 'May you live long, my little daughter, may you be united to a suitable bridegroom, but then become a widow, and may I have the opportunity of getting you married again.' This curious benediction naturally gave rise to general laughter, the great Pandit also laughed heartily saying, if the daughters of his friends did not become widows how was he to carry out his pet idea? It was so unpopular amongst his countrymen.

"After this ceremony we, the promoters of the remarriage, were put to very severe persecution. My friend who had married the widow was boycotted not only by his friends and relations but even by the ordinary class of Hindu servants. None would serve under them. At this extremity, finding my friend and his wife altogether deserted and solitary, I went to reside with them. When we were thus living together, Pandit Vidyasagar made it a rule to pay us visits almost every other day to cheer us up by his company. His visits were sources of great pleasure to us. He would tell us delightful little stories about his past experiences, and make funny observations about men and things which made us laugh heartily and in a manner forget all our trials and sufferings...".

Mr. Shastri writes about another "memorable incident" in this connection: "One day the Pandit called, and found a little girl of seven or eight seated on my lap, and calling me her dada or elder brother. He had never seen that girl in our house. She was a neighbour's daughter, belonging to the barber caste. That little girl was a widow and we were trying to persuade her widowed mother to consent to her remarriage. Hence our interest in her and she had by that time become partly naturalised in our house. She became a little companion to my friend's wife, and specially took to me as her kindred. She was a handsome little girl... When the Pandit saw her on my lay he was startled and asked me who she was. When apprised of her history and of her condition, he was greatly moved. The fact that the little girl was a widow roused all his old emotions; big tear drops began to trickle down his cheeks; he took her on his lap, clasped her in his arms; and when leaving, ordered me to get her; admitted to the Bethune School, himself agreeing to pay her fees, and to send her and her mother in a palanquin to his house so that he could present them to his own mother. The next day they were sent to his house and when the mother and daughter returned we heard of the warm reception they had received at the hands of Vidyasagar and his mother. The great Pandit turned up next day and held a conference with me about her education and her final remarriage. But alas! before these plans could be carried out, my friend's wife fell ill and died".

Vidyasagar's interest in widow remarriage never flagged till the last day of his life. The followers of Brahmo Samaj in Bengal had all along been the staunchest supporters of his reforms; they remained so even in the dark days of Hindu revivalism, when progressive reforms of the Vidyasagar-Young Bengal variety were the midst of this gloom of reaction, the young however, kept the torch of reform, alight. Bipin Chandra Pal testifies to this in his autobiography.

He says: "In those days the Brahmo Samaj actively threw itself into the cause of social reform, particularly of widow remarriage. Many a young Hindu widow found shelter in Brahmo families from where they subsequently got married. We also sometimes helped young Hindu widows to run away from home and the protection of their families, and gave them shelter and education, and, if possible, opportunities of remarriage in the Brahmo Samaj". He also narrates a memorable incident: In the middle of 1884 he received an application for help of this kind from a young highly connected kayastha widow of Konnagar. Arrangements were made immediately to help her run away from home. This was done, and the girl was brought to the house in Calcutta where Bipin Chandra lived with his young friends. The girl's elder brother came next day, saw his sister and pressed her to go back with him which she refused to do. The brother returned with a number of rowdies with a view to Intimidating him and taking away the girl from his custody. This Mr. Pal could not do, and in the course of a few minutes he found himself surrounded by a couple of hundred young men, threatening to take the girl away forcibly. Bipin Chandra writes: "I stood firm. And standing at the door leading to the inner apartments, I told them that if they wanted to take the girl by force, let them clearly understand it that they would have to do so by walking over my dead body, and there were my friends behind me who would not submit to any violence of this kind without breaking heads. They were not prepared for this. Some of them declared that they would beat me with their shoes into submission. I went forward singly and advancing to the very middle of the threatening crowd I took off my own shoes and placed them in the hands of my opponents, saying, 'Here are my shoes, if you dare, beat me into submission with these, why should you injure your own shoes for so small a thing' This took them aback". Gradually they melted away This girl was subsequently married to Mr. Sitanath Datta, better known as Pandit Sitanath Tattvabhushan, one of the foremost intellectuals of the Brahmo Samaj in the last days of the 19th century. "This incident," writes Mr. Pal, "deserves record as one of many that occurred in those.. days in connection with the social reform propaganda of the Brahmo Samaj".

Vidyasagar lived to see the ideal of social reform spread across Bengal and all over India Although Bengal gave the lead in the social and religious reform movements in the first half of the 19th century, they gradually spread to other parts of India when Bengal was caught in the swamp of a revivalist ideology of an out-of-date Hinduism. It undoubtedly helped in the growth of nationalism, but at the very heavy cost of inter-communal integration. In Bengal the pendulum swung from one extreme to the other in the course of the 19th century. In its closing years, the lead of the reform movement passed to Maharashtra.

The mantle of Bengal's Brahmo Samaj fell upon the Prarthana Samaj of Bombay, which concentrated on the movements for interdining, intermarriage and widow remarriage. The Satya Sodhaka Samaj, founded in 1873, carried on vigorously social reform propaganda, and men like Ranade, Phule, Malabari and Vishnu Shastri Pandit turned uncompromising crusaders against all outmoded customs in the Hindu social system. Vishnu Shastri Pandit translated into Marathi Vidyasagar's widow remarriage tracts. He was one of the founders of the Widow Marriage Association in 1861 in Maharashtra. He led the movement so energetically that the first widow marriage took place in Maharashtra in 1861, he himself participating in the wedding ceremony, defying the threat of excommunication by the conservatives. He became the life and soul of the Sarvajanik Sabha founded in 1870 in Poona by Ganesh Vasudev Joshi, and exerted a tremendous influence on the social and political reawakening of the people of Maharashtra.

The name of Dhondo Keshav Karve deserves mention in this connection, especially with reference to the widow remarriage movement. Having become a widower, Karve remarried in 1893 a Brahmin widow. This happened just two years after Vidyasagar's death. Karve writes in his My Twenty Years in the Cause of Indian Women: "The remarriage of a widow in Poona, the stronghold of orthodoxy at that time, was not without apprehended difficulties; but every thing passed off well". This event set him firmly on the path of Hindu widows' uplift. He revived, and became the Secretary of, the Widow Marriage Association in 1893, In 1899 Karve opened a Hindu Widows' Home in Poona which he shifted later to a lonely spot some ten miles off the city. The home is a humble cottage preserved to this day. Any Indian visiting the spot will remember not only Karve, Vishnu Shastri and other social reformers of Maharashtra, but also the great Vidyasagar of Bengal and his widow marriage movement.

Such facts indicate that the widow marriage movement sponsored by Vidyasagar had not spent itself out by the end of the 19th century or at the beginning of the 20th century. But the robust optimism with which Vidyasagar had set out on his reform movement gradually waned in the last days of his Me for various reasons An important reason was the dubious attitude of a large number of advocates of widow remarriage. They took advantage of the institutional pattern of Hindu marriage in which polygamy is sanctioned for men, and came forward to marry widows, not for the sake of any "principle" whatsoever, but mainly lured by the money offered by rich patrons of widow remarriage as rewards.

All this profoundly shocked Vidyasagar. Within a short time of the passing of the Widow Marriage Act, Vidyasagar resigned his appointments in November, 1858, carrying a monthly pay of Rs. 500, without any pension or gratuity for all the work he had done, owing to his serious difference of opinion on educational policy with the British officers of the Public Instruction Department. He wrote to Mr. W. Gordon Young, the Director of Public Instruction: "I feel I can no longer devote the assiduous attention to my duties which their due performance necessitates. I need repose, and in justice to the public interests, as well as to my own comforts and happiness, can only secure that repose by retiring into private Me". He took this momentous decision of his life just in the wake of the Indian War of Independence of 1857 at a time when he had need of money most for his widow remarriage reform He had to seek assistance and borrow from his friends and admirers. We can imagine his profound disappointment when he found that he had been cheated of a considerable amount of his money by persons who came forward to marry widows.

Overburdened with debt and disillusioned with the integrity of people, he once wrote a letter to his friend Dr. Durgacharan Banerji, father of the eminent nationalist leader, Surendranath Banerji, which may be translated: "I am very sorry to have to tell you that in spite of my best efforts I have not been able to find out any means of clearing your debt. In the present situation I am also unable to give you any assurance about its repayment in the near future. You are well aware of the fact that I have not incurred this debt for personal reasons, I had borrowed it for meeting the expenses of widow marriages; you are not my only creditor, there are many others also. I expected that the promised sum of the patrons of widow marriage would be received soon, and that I should be able to clear my debts. Unfortunately, most of the rich people who wanted to patronise it had not kept their word On the other hand, the expenses of widow marriages are daily mounting and I am helplessly getting into debts without any hope of discharging them. If the gentlemen had been good enough to keep their promise of financial help, I would not have been landed in this crisis. Like others, you also promised to help me with monthly donations and lump contributions... I shall do my best to get out of my difficulties as soon as possible If I fail to secure money from any source, I shall not hesitate to sell all my belongings to free myself from debt. But at the moment, when you are badly in need of money, I am really very sorry for being unable to offer you anything. If I had an idea of the worthlessness, dishonesty and lack of integrity of the big people of our country, I might perhaps not have ventured on this widow remarriage. I am not speaking of my opponents, but of my so-called friends and supporters who miserably failed me and thereby the cause. I have been condemned to suffering and ignominy for the fault of believing in the sincerity of those who professed high idealism.

Far from giving me any help or cooperation, none of them now even cares to know whether I am alive or dead".

There is no denying the fact that Vidyasagar's frustration was deep, and he almost lost his faith in the goodness of people, particularly of "big people.' Not only abuses and slanders were his reward, but economic distress also was the price of his perseverance in the cause. But he was steadfast in the cause of widow remarnage till the last days of his life, and his face lighted up whenever he heard of any widow marriage.

The letter he wrote to his younger brother Sambhu Chandra on the occasion of his own son Narayan's marrying a widow unmistakably reveals the depth of his attachment to the cause and the invincible integrity of his character It is also one of the best letters ever written by Vidyasagar to his relatives and friends Written, in Bengali, the letter ran as follows: "I am writing to you to inform mother and others that Narayan has already been married to Bhabasundan on Thursday, the 27th Sravana (1277 B S.) last. You informed me earlier that if Narayan was married to Bhabasundan, our relatives may forsake us, and it is wise therefore to dissuade him from marrying a widow What I have to say in the matter is this: that Narayan himself has selected the bride and decided to marry her; he did not seek my opinion about it, nor did I offer it myself. When I came to know of his decision to marry a widow, I did not consider it right on my part to put any obstacle in his way How could I do it? I have myself set in motion the widow marriage movement, pleaded for its legislation and arranged for many widow marriages. Now if my own son wants to marry a spinster or is persuaded by me not to marry a widow, it will bring disgrace upon me and I shall have to hang my head in shame. Narayan has given me a spiritual uplift by willingly agreeing to marry a widow and has proved himself the worthy son of his father. The starting of widow marriage movement has been the noblest work of my life and I do not think that I shall ever be able to achieve anything nobler than that. I have staked everything on it, my health, wealth, peace and comfort, and I shall not hesitate to stake my life even. The threats of relatives or friends are nothing compared to this. If I had submitted to the threat of excommunication and desertion of my relatives and objected to Narayan's widow marriage, I would have been the most ignoble person on earth I need hardly say that I have been highly heartened by this decision of my son. I have never been a slave to custom. And what I shall think best in the interests of my countrymen, rest assured, that I shall do against all conceivable odds, and shall never yield to the threats of people or so-called relatives, or bother about the consequences.

"In conclusion, I wish to make it clear to you that those who would excommunicate us and would not dine or mix with us socially are at liberty to do so... I think every individual should have liberty to act according to his own conscience and discretion and should not allow others to impose their will on him".

We need add only a few words in reply to those who objected to Vidyasagar's reform movement as being something like putting the cart before the horse. Some of the leading Bengali intellectuals thought that a custom like the lifelong celibacy of widows could not be changed without a change in the social situation where it had been the practice for centuries: that required the spread of good education among the people and the careful fostering of a rational and scientific outlook. Logically the argument is flawless, but historically it is definitely wrong. The history of all progressive reforms, since the dawn of human civilisation, had been like putting the cart before the horse, that is, they were introduced before the people were mentally prepared to act up to them. If the reforms had waited for the situation to ripen, there would have been no progress at all It is difficult to break the cake of custom; it takes time. But this does not mean that a bad custom, blocking all social progress, should not be eradicated. Vidyasagar thought and acted much in advance of the times to which he belonged.

Crusade against Polygamy

Simultaneously with the widow remarriage movement Vidyasagar set on foot an agitation against the evil practice of Kulmist polygamy in Bengal. He himself was a Kuliti (high caste) Brahmin, and he was therefore well-acquainted with the abuses attending the practice of polygamy. A large number of his relatives had become the miserable victims of the practice It was responsible for increasing the number of widows in Bengal and creating a serious social problem. Polygamy was thus closely linked to his widow marriage movement.

Within a few months of his Petition to the government for an enactment in favour of widow remarriage, he sent a separate petition for prohibiting polygamy on December 27, 1855. It was signed by 25,000 persons, among whom were Maharaja Mahatab Chand of Burdwan and a number of other influential persons of Bengal. The following excerpts from the petition are interesting "The Coolins many solely for money and with no intention to fulfil any of the duties which marriage involves. The women, who are thus nominally married without the hope of ever enjoying the happiness which marriage is calculated to confer particularly on them, either pine away for want of objects on which to place the affections which spontaneously arise in the heart, or are betrayed by the violence of their passions and their defective education into immorality. That the remedy, though obvious and perfectly consistent with the Hindu Law, cannot in the present disorganised state of Hindu society be applied by the force of public opinion or any other power than that derived from the Legislature".

To appreciate the italicised statement above we have to consider briefly the social background of Kulinism and polygamy in Bengal. In Bengal, there is an extensive literature known as kulaji or kulasastra. It deals with the history of the Brahminas and some other principal castes in Bengal in a general way, and also gives a detailed genealogical account of the notable families belonging to the Kulin caste. The kulajis of the Radhiya Brahminas ("Radhiya" from "Radh," which means the western division of ancient Bengal) hold that the Kulin Brahmins are the descendants of the five Brahminas brought by King Adisura sometime in the 8th or 9th century. The identity of this Adisura has not yet been established. The kulajis of the Varendra Brahminas ("Varendra" means northern division of ancient Bengal) regard the Sena King Vallalasena (1158-79 AD) as the founder of Kulinism in Bengal. It is related that the King laid down nine virtues as the criteria of Kulinism and assigned the top rank to those Brahminas who possessed all of them. Those who possessed eight or seven of these virtues were respectively called Siddha-srotriya and Sadhyastrotriya and the rest Kashta-srotriya. The kulaji texts, however, do not prescribe any such test for Kulinismu. The kulajis are unanimous that the rank of Kulin was a personal distinction and that Vallalasena placed all Kulins on the same footing, without any bar to their marriage with non-Kulin girls. It was his successor Lakshmanasena who made the system a complex one by introducing restrictions of marriage and by the classification of the Kulins into different grades according to their adherence to marriage rules.

The historical truth to be gleaned from this account is that after the end of the reign of the Pala Kings of Bengal, who were the patrons of Buddhism, a revival of Hinduism followed during the reign of the Sena Kings from the 12th century onwards. There was need for reorganising the social structure of Hinduism based on the caste system, and some rigid rules were formulated to maintain the purity of the higher castes, particularly the Brahmins.

What was a social distinction in the beginning, associated with caste virtues, became within a few generations a social privilege to be exploited and Kulinism became a hereditary rank in the course of a century or two. The Muslim invasion gave an impetus to the enforcement of this rigidity of caste rules, and in the situation that followed Kulinism became an easy handle for social exploitation to the upper castes, especially to the Brahmins in Bengal. Subsequently, Kulinism in Bengal led to the notorious pattern of hypergamy, the inevitable corollary of which was polygamy. The practice of hypergamy, that is, of seeking a bridegroom in a higher caste or subcaste than that of the bride, led to a surplus of unmarried girls. This surplus, together with the duty incumbent on high-caste Brahmins of getting their daughters married before puberty, resulted in the mischievous practice of Kulinist polygamy, by which a man of Kulin subcaste often married a large number of brides, whom he had never intended to support economically, but solely for the purpose of saving their parents the disgrace of failure to get their daughters married in time. Thus, marriage itself became a gainful occupation. Among the Kulin Brahmins, even septuagenarians and octogenarians, with two or three dozen of wives, were considered good matches by the helpless parents of Kulin Brahmin girls, A kind of marriage fee, ranging from Rs. 5 to Rs. 500, was usually charged by the Kulin Brahmins for marrying a Kulin girl. Even teenagers were married to dying octogenarian husbands. The old man's gain, before his death, was a few rupees.

Many Kulin Brahmins of Bengal, who took part in the anti-polygamy movement, have left behind some harrowing accounts of the tragic condition of their families. One of the most prominent among them was Rashbehari Mukhopadhyay, the leader of the anti-Kulinism and anti-polygamy movement in East Bengal (now East Pakistan). Under tie guidance of Pandit Ishwar Chandra Vidyasagar, he started and led the movement from Dacca in the sixties of the last century, and the movement spread over the other districts of East Bengal within a short time. He was advised by Vidyasagar to write an account of the movement and he did so with a brief autobiographical sketch. It was published in Bengali in the year 1881. It is an important document of the anti-polygamy movement in Bengal.

He says: "My father died when I was a child. I was brought up under the care of my uncle Mr. Tarak Chandra Mukhopadhayay. As we were very poor, he insisted on my early marriage, and I was married to eight girls in quick succession, for the economic relief of my family. As orthodox Kulin Brahmins my grandfather, father, and uncles were married to scores of girls, and I was born and brought up in a family atmosphere where nothing but hatred for Kulinism and polygamy could grow. Even in my boyhood I could understand that marriage, to a Kulin Brahmin, was nothing but a sordid means to monetary gains. Whenever a Ghatak (marriage-agent) was called in for negotiating my marriage, I ran away from the house for days together, till I was caught, rebuked and chastised to submission. If I had expressed my willingness to marry, I would have been forced, in the midst of the economic distress we were then put in, to marry at least one hundred girls within a few years. My uncle Tarak Babu was not pleased with me for this attitude of mine towards marriage He therefore compelled me to break away from the joint-family When I was thus forcibly separated, with the load of a loan of Rs. 300 shifted on my shoulder by my uncle, I was put in great difficulties. With starvation staring me in the face, I had to take recourse to the easy means of solving it by marriage. I had already eight wives, and I decided to add six more to it to meet my immediate economic needs. All my debts were paid and with the security of a minimum subsistence thus obtained, I became free to choose an independent livelihood. Soon I got one, a very humble one of course, the job of a Tahsildar in a Zammdar's cutcherv."

All this justified the statement made by Vidyasagar in his petition to the Government of India that the Kulins "marry solely for money and with no intention to fulfil any of the duties which marriage involves".

The movement for the prohibition of polygamy launched in 1856-57 fizzled out for the time being, owing to the outbreak of the Great Rising of 1857. Although J. P. Grant promised in 1857 to introduce a Bill on polygamy, the Rising stopped all further action. It is recorded that no less than 127 petitions against polygamy, very numerously signed from all parts of Bengal, and one from Banaras, were sent to government. Raja Radhakanta Dev, the leader of the orthodox Hindus, sent a petition as usual, in defence of polygamy. In a note to the Government of India on the subject, the Bengal Government wrote: "It is known that a Draft Bill was prepared by the late Baboo Ramaprasad Roy, in communication with Sir J. P Grant, and that it was about to be introduced into the Council, when the Mutiny of the Bengal Native Army, and the events which followed, put a stop for a time to further action in the matter. The movement did not die out in the turmoil of political revolt. Within five years after Mutiny the problem was again brought to the fore by agitation. In 1863 about 21,000 Hindus from Bengal presented a petition to government for enacting a law with the aim of restraining the abuses of polygamy.' One of these petitions stated: "Your Memorialists have ample grounds for believing that the almost unanimous feeling of the native community is against an usage which has destroyed the domestic happiness of Hindu women to a far greater extent than the doom of perpetual widowhood"

On February 1, 1866, Vidyasagar again submitted a petition to government, signed by 21,000 persons, among whom were such influential leaders of Bengali society as Maharaja Satischandra Ray Bahadur of Nadia, Raja Satya Saran Ghoshal of Bhukailas

(Kidderpore, Calcutta) and Raja Pratapchandra Singha of Kandi (Murshidabad). The following is an important extract from the petition: "...It is the fervent hope and prayer of your petitioners that before your Honour laid down the responsibilities of your office, your Honour might signalise the close of your long and successful career by emancipating the females of Bengal from, the pains, cruelties and attendant crimes of the debasing custom of polygamy".

On March 19, 1866, a deputation, consisting of, among others, Pandit Ishwar Chandra Vidyasagar, Mr. Justice Dwarkanath Mitter, the great educational reformer Peary Churn Sarkar, and the well-known political leader, Kristodas Pal, waited on the government. The leader of the deputation read out the petition, and the Lieutenant-Governor, Mr. Cecil Beadon, said in reply: "I have great pleasure in receiving this numerously signed memorial, and in assuring you and the other highly respectable gentlemen who compose this deputation that I shall gladly use my best endeavours to procure the enactment of a law to restrain the abuses attending the practice of polygamy among Hindus, and to impose upon a custom, which I cannot but regard as altogether demoralising, the utmost degree of restriction consistent with the reasonable opinions and wishes of the intelligent Hindu public".

Referring to this revival of the movement, Hindu Patriot, the leading organ of the English-educated Bengali middle class, wrote on March 26, 1866: "After the lapse of a decade a fresh agitation has been organised under the auspices of the ardent advocate of social reform, Pandit Ishwar Chandra Vidyasagar, for the restriction of the abuses of the Kulin Polygamy. The appeal which he has initiated has been endorsed by all sections of the Hindu community of Bengal, the wealthy, the learned, the orthodox, as well as the enlightened. The petition ...it will be observed, bears the signatures of the representatives of all classes of the community and all shades of opinion. We notice in it the names of the great Zamindars of Bengal, men who in the aggregate may be said to own half the country, of the most eminent Pandits of, Calcutta, and other places, the expounders of the Sastras, the custodians of our ancient learning, of the representatives of the strongholds of orthodoxy in town and in the mofussil, of the acknowledged leaders of the educated class, and last, though not the least, of the head and other members of the reformed party of the Brahminic faith. The petition does not attempt to argue the question of the abuse of Polygamy in Bengal; it avoids a discussion of the subject, simply because the thirty-two petitions, which have been presented in 1866, were replete with it.

But a repetition of the arguments and considerations, which led to the movement ten years ago, would not have come amiss at the present time. There are now many able persons to form an independent opinion, who were at school ten years ago, while there might be others who might have forgotten what they had subscribed to in former petitions. Such being the case, we do not wonder that the brevity of the petition has been misunderstood in certain quarters, that it has been construed to be a prayer for the total abolition of Polygamy while it only seeks to correct the abuses of that custom".

A section of the educated Bengali middle class had shifted its position in the ten years between the first and second movements (1856-66) in regard to the prohibition of the Hindu custom of polygamy. According to it, a process would spontaneously set in motion with the spread of modern education among the people.

When the government found that a considerable body of educated opinion in Bengal was in favour of taking the middle course regarding restraint of polygamy, it refused to go in for any legislation. The Governor-General-in-Council desired that no Bill should be immediately introduced, but that further investigations should be carried out. The Governor-General, in a letter, dated August 8, 1866, communicated to the Bengal Government: "It must be remembered that polygamy, as it exists in India, is a social and religious institution... and the Governor-General-in-Council doubts whether the great difficulty of dealing with the subject in India, or even in Bengal, has been fully considered. As regards the latter Province, there is nothing in the papers before government which, in the opinion of the Governor-General-in-Council, would lead a calm and unbiased enquirer to the conclusion that a large majority of even the more enlightened people of the Province will be found to be heartily against polygamy, apart from the special abuses practised by the Kulin Brahmins".

Acting under the directions of the Government of India, the Lieutenant-Governor of Bengal appointed a Committee consisting of some leading Bengalis, associated with C. Hobhouse and H. T. Prinsep, with instructions to conduct an enquiry into the feasibility of enacting any law for the prohibition of polygamy among the Hindus, without, of course, affecting the liberty enjoyed by the Hindus of taking more than one wife The report of the Committee was submitted on February 7, 1867. The Committee gave in outline a history of the origin of this denomination of Brahmins and of the various grades of Kulins existing at the time. They analysed the customs from which stemmed the abuses of polygamy. Some of the results of the customs, pointed out by them, were:

In addition to the presents usually given among all classes of Hindus on the occasion of the marriage, a Kulin always, except when he gives his own daughter to a brother Kulin and takes in exchange that brother Kulin's daughter, exacts heavy consideration for marriage from the family of the bride.

In addition, a present is often given on the occasion of any visit made to the house of the father-in-law. This renders marriage a very lucrative profession A Kulin Brahmin, having about thirty wives, may find it immensely profitable to pay a monthly visit to each father-in-law's house and spend the whole year, enjoying good foods and presents, without any effort on his behalf for earning a livelihood. Hence it is a fact that Kulinist polygamy was making the Brahmins a class of unproductive parasites, and the socio-religious institution of marriage a perennial source of demoralisation.

Polygamy, therefore, is said to be resorted to as a sole means of subsistence by many Kulin Brahmins Marriage is said to be contracted quite in old age, and the husband often never sees his wife, or at best visits her once in every three or four years or so

As many as three or four marriages are known to have been contracted by one person in one day.

Sometimes all the daughters and unmarried sisters of a man are given in marriage to the same person.

As it is very difficult to find husbands for Kulm girls, quite a large number of them remain unmarried. These married and unmarried girls, and also the wives of Kulins, naturally live a very miserable life; and is said that crimes of the most heinous nature, "such as adultery, abortion, infanticide and prostitution, are the common results of his system of Kulin marriages.

Cases are known of men who have married 82, 72, 65, 60 and 42 wives, and have had 18, 32, 41, 25 and 32 sons, and 26, 27, 25, 15 and 16 daughters. Facts from Burdwan and Hooghly districts have been collected showing the existence of a plurality of wives on the above scale, and also in numerous other cases. The evils of Kulinism and polygamy were briefly summed up by the Committee: "The practical deprivation of the indulgence of natural ties and desires in the female sex in a legitimate manner; the virtual, sometimes the actual, desertion of the wife by her natural and legal protector, the husband; the encouragement of the practice of celibacy amongst the female sex; the non-maintenance of the wife by the husband; the suppression or abandonment of the wife at the mere pleasure of the husband; the formation of the contract of marriage for merely money considerations; the denial of nuptials except upon special monetary consideration given; the ruin, from a property point of view, of families; the contraction of the marriage tie avowedly without any intention even on the part of the husband of fulfilling any one of the duties of that tie, the binding down of the female sex to all the obligations of the marriage state, whilst yet withholding from that sex every one of the advantages of that state; prostitution, and, lastly, the encouragement of the actual crimes of adultery, abortion and infanticide, and of the habit and practice of the concealment of such crimes".

The Committee further proved very clearly, by quoting relevant extracts from the Hindu Shastras, that these customs had for the most part no warrant among the approved authorities of Hindu theology. So far, in the opinion of the Committee, the part for legislation was smooth enough, as a declaratory Act might be passed setting forth the law on the subject of polygamy and making infraction of it penal. But the Committee pointed out that, owing to the limitation imposed upon them, they regretted their inability to recommend even the passing of a declaratory Act of any kind. Among the Bengali members of the Committee, Ramanath Tagore, Jaykrishna Mukherji and Digambar Mitra expressed the opinion that there was no need of imposing any legal bar on the Hindu custom of polygamy, and that the Kulin Brahmins would settle to monogamous habit in due course by the force of education and social opinion. But Pandit Ishwar Chandra Vidyasagar signed the report with the following note of dissent: "I am of opinion that the evils alluded to... are not greatly exaggerated, and that the decrease of these evils is not sufficient to do away with the necessity of this legislation...

> "I do not concur in the conclusion come to by the other gentlemen of the Committee. I am of opinion that a declaratory Law might be passed without interfering with that liberty which Hindus now by law possess in the matter of marriage".

That the Lieutenant-Governor of Bengal was in favour of passing at least a declaratory Law for curbing the excesses of Kulinist polygamy, and was more sympathetic to the view of Vidyasagar expressed in his note of dissent, can be gleaned from his note on the Committee's report to the Government of India, dated February 23, 1867: "The Lieutenant-Governor cannot share the sanguine anticipations entertained by the three Native Members of the Committee who have recorded a separate paper on the subject, that Kulin Brahmins will settle into a monogamous habit only by the force of education and social opinion. It is satisfactory, however, to receive their testimony that the opinion of Hindus on this subject has undergone a remarkable change within the last few years, and that the custom of taking a plurality of wives as a means of subsistence is now marked with strong disapprobation; and it may be hoped that with the further progress of these enlightened ideas the necessity for legislation as the only effectual means of giving them full effect will at no distance be realised".

But as a considerable section of educated Bengalis subscribed to the views of the three concurring "Native" members of the Committee, the Government of India could not agree to the proposal of passing any declaratory Act against the practice of polygamy. Meantime a despatch was received from the Secretary of State in which he objected to any measure of a legislative character being adopted at present, as it did not appear to him that a large majority of people even in Bengal were against the practice of polygamy, apart from the special abuses which the Kulin Brahmins indulged in.

But Vidyasagar was undaunted. Although by that time, after the bitter experience of fifteen years of widow remarriage movement in practice, he should have been completely pessimistic about shaping people's opinions about social reform, he was found vigorously carrying on a campaign, mainly literary, against polygamy, even in the seventies of the last century. In 1871 and 1873 he published two important Bengali tracts on polygamy, in which he rebutted his opponents' arguments exhaustively by quoting numerous extracts from different Shastras against Kulinism and the particular type of hypergamy practised by Kulin Brahmins in Bengal. He collected some important statistical data about the nature of Kulinist polygamy, as practised in the Hooghly district of Bengal, which is nearest to Calcutta He also included a long list of names of polygamous Kulins in his Bengali book, giving the number of their wives and their age.

Some Kulin Brahmins did not even know how many girls they had actually married Some of them used to keep a sort of diary with them, in which the marriages and an account of presents received in cash and kind were recorded. The accounts of presents received, during visits to the houses of different fathers-in-law by rotation, were also kept in detail. All these facts were given besides the statements forwarded to the government by the anti-polygamists, but the British Government was overcautious, after the great Rising of 1857, in enacting any law that might hurt the sentiments or interfere with the socio-religious customs of the Indian people.

But Vidyasagar campaigned ceaselessly against the practice of Kulinist hypergamy and polygamy, fervently appealing to his countrymen to abjure it by all means for the good of society. In his first book on polygamy, published in 1871, he wrote: "One of the root causes of our social disintegration is the prevalence of the custom of polygamy in Hindu society. It has been eroding the moral foundations of our society for centuries, and breeding many evils and vices. Thousands of married women are being daily thrown into the hell of untold sufferings for the continuity of this inhuman custom. It has let loose all conceivable vices and uprooted the moral anchors of society. It is encouraging all sorts of vices—adultery, debauchery, infanticide and prostitution. I feel that it is not possible to get rid of this vicious custom by our own efforts alone. If we could do anything ourselves, there would have been no occasion for applying to government for prohibiting a custom like polygamy by law. Now either we should seek the help of government in this matter or we should desist from doing it tor fear of a foreign authority's interference in our socio-religious institution and accept it as something that cannot be changed, regardless of its moral or social consequences. Those who are witnessing the tragedies of this cruel custom, they are rather eager to eradicate it by all possible means, and that also without any further delay.

The earlier this abominable custom is abolished, the better for society. If that is done by government, well, I do not understand how can that be harmful. To cry down those who have sought the help of government in putting down polygamy is an easy task But such denunciations do not carry any sense. It is childish to argue that we are asking the government to do for us that which we could do ourselves. We have, of course, plenty of energy at our disposal to waste in criticising a limited few who happen to possess the will and strength. This is really a strange phenomenon. We can only hope that the number of these critics will gradually dwindle, and thereby the cause of our social progress will be strengthened". The appeal fell on deaf ears. Invective and abuse were hurled at him, and these were from the pen of eminent pandits Vidyasagar was then suffering from various physical ailments, and was fifty-two years old.

The energy and strength of a young man, which he had possessed in abundance during the Widow Marriage Movement of 1855-56, "had ebbed away, and his load of debts and frustrations was heavy. But when his cause was at stake, and he was attacked by all sorts of critics from all sides for advocating the abolition of polygamy, he raised his head high, defended his cause with all his might and hurled back the thunderbolt at his opponents indignantly, without sacrificing the dignity of language like his opponents. This was done in his second book on polygamy, published in 1873. But it was soon drowned in the noise of Hindu revivalism which reached its crescendo in the eighties. Vidyasagar was in his last years and his clarion call for reform was almost the last in the battle between Reaction and Progress, which raged afresh in the closing years of the 19th century, with the forces of Progress temporarily on the defensive.

Other Social Reforms

Vidyasagar, who fought for such great social issues as widow remarriage and prohibition of polygamy, could also find time to look into the problems of organising an independent educational institution, a Hindu Family Annuity Fund for the protection of helpless widows and dependants, and the reforming of a Wards Institution for the security of minor estate-owners. He also joined the Temperance movement; even a few months before his death, he examined the Age of Consent Bill and sent his opinion to the government. There was no rest for him till death.

Sometime in 1859 a school under the name of "Calcutta Training School" was founded and maintained in North Calcutta by some local Bengali gentlemen. The object of the founders was not profit but to impart English education to the middle class Hindu young men at lower fees than those charged in the government and missionary schools. Vidyasagar and his friend, Rajkrishna Banerji, joined the Managing Committee, and under Vidyasagar's guidance the School prospered steadily. In 1861 Vidyasagar took over complete control of the School under a new Managing Committee, of which he became the Secretary In the beginning of 1864 the name of the institution was changed to "The Hindu Metropolitan Institution," and in April, 1864, an application was made, for the affiliation of the Institution to the Calcutta University for higher instruction in the arts subjects.

The application was rejected as most of the European members of the Syndicate were not in favour of granting affiliation to any institution for higher English education: exclusively owned by the "natives". But Vidyasagar was not accustomed to take such reverses lying down. In 1866, after the death of the Patron-Chairman, Pratapchandra Singha of Paikpara Raj family, the sole responsibility for the management of the Institution fell on Vidyasagar's shoulders—a great burden for him indeed, particularly after the debts incurred in widow marriages. But he bore it for the sake of the Institution.

In 1872 an application was made for the second time to the University for affiliation of the Institution up to the First Arts examination This time Vidyasagar did not rest content with the formal application alone, but addressed a personal letter to E. C. Bayley, one of the most influential members of the Syndicate. The letter, dated January 27, 1872, said, among other things: "If it should be urged at the Syndicate that the character of the instruction to be imparted in the Institution would be inferior inasmuch as the instructive staff would enlist exclusively of natives, I would take the liberty to remind you that the Sanskrit College, which teaches up to the B. A. standard, has an exclusively native staff, and that our Professors, if selected with care and judgement, would be found quite competent; but should we from experience feel the necessity of enter-taming an English Professor for instruction in the English language in which alone English aid might be necessary, we would certainly employ one. It will be our aim to combine efficiency with economy, and as I have spent, I may say, my whole Me in managing schools, I hope you will allow me to exercise my own discretion in selecting Professors and regulating their pay.

"The high rate of schooling charged at the Presidency College is prohibitory to many middle class youths, while their parents, being opposed to their boys being sent to missionary Colleges, they are obliged to give up academic education after Matriculation, This Institution would be a great boon to them.

"The managers of the Institution are myself, Mr. Justice Dwarkanath Mitter and Babu Kristodas Pal. We are satisfied that the means at our command will be quite sufficient for all the purposes of the Institution. But should any deficiency arise, we will be prepared to supply it from our own pockets. 1 trust our assurance for the maintenance of the Institution on the proposed footing for five years will be deemed satisfactory by the Syndicate".

Application was granted and permission given to teach students for the F.A. examination. Most of the distinguished scholars of Bengal joined the Institution as Professors The question of emoluments was secondary to them. Their primary attractions were Vidyasagar's personality and the independent national spirit which urged him to undertake the responsibility of the Institution. The Institution recorded brilliant successes in the final University examinations. The Europeans and the missionaries were amazed at this success in English education imparted by a "native" institution. Mr. Sutcliffe, Principal of the Presidency College and the Registrar of Calcutta University, admitted that the Pandit had really done wonders. After Vidyasagar's retirement from active service, the foundation and successful running of this Institution may be looked upon as one of his lasting achievements. Rabindranath Tagore in his Bengali Vidyasagar-Charit speaks of this achievement We may translate it. "This is the first national Institution of its kind, founded for the purpose of giving higher English education to Bengali boys, maintained and guided solely by the efforts of the Bengalis Thus the foundation of English education was first laid on a national basis in our country by Pandit Ishwar Chandra Vidyasagar. The man, who was born poor, became the greatest benefactor of our country. The man, who was born in a tradition-and-custom-ridden Brahmin family, became one of the most valiant fighters for freeing society from the bondage of such tradition and custom. And the man, who had profound knowledge of our classical Sanskrit literature, laid by his efforts the foundation of English education on a national basis".

When English education thus blended with the national spirit, its result was far-reaching. It became an Institution where the budding nationalists of our country were nurtured. Our great nationalist leader, Surendranath Banerji, testifies to this in his recollections A Nation in Making. He was dismissed from the Indian Civil Service and he could not even join the bar, whether as a vakil or a barrister. All professions were closed to him when he came back to Calcutta in June, 1875, after his second visit to England. He writes, "There was no industry to which I could turn". But suddenly a door was opened to him. He adds: "Soon after, Pandit Ishwar Chandra Vidyasagar offered me an appointment as Professor of English in the Metropolitan Institution, which I accepted. My speeches had already made me popular with the students, and helped me, I think, to get the appointment.

The salary was small, Rs. 200 a month, less than half of what I had been getting as Assistant Magistrate, but I was glad that I had something to do and that it afforded me an opportunity of which I took the fullest advantage. I sought by every possible means in my power to kindle in the young the beginnings of public spirit, and to inspire them with a patriotic ardour, fruitful of good to them and to the motherland". (italics ours)

Within 12 years, from 1881 to 1892, the latter a year after Vidyasagar's death, 498 students of the Metropolitan Institution obtained the B. A. degree, and 33 students the M. A. degree. In 1882 the affiliation of the University was extended to the teaching of law in the Metropolitan Institution, and in 10 years 513 students of this Institution obtained the B L degree. Lawyers constituted the most important section of the educated Bengali middle class who assumed the leadership of the nationalist movement in the last quarter of the 19th century. It is no exaggeration to say that a large number of these Bengali nationalist lawyers was produced by the Metropolitan Institution, and this Institution was a nursery of the budding nationalists of Bengal.

Did Vidyasagar visualise any such development when he founded the Institution? Perhaps he did, for he picked up men like Surendranath Banerji, who had a distinct political bias, for appointment to the teaching staff of the college. There must have been some method in this policy of selection Whatever might have been his intention, there is no doubt that he wanted to transplant the sapling of English education on the soil of our country The need for this transplantation was indeed great at the time, as the products of the Hindu College, or for that matter of the missionary colleges, were not becoming "national" in the true sense of the term There was the social need for stopping this process, and if there was any educational institution which consciously fought against this process, it was the Metropolitan Institution under Vidyasagar's guidance After Vidyasagar's death, the name of the Institution was rightly changed into "Vidyasagar College" and it stands now as a monument of Vidyasagar's contribution to the cause of national education.

To turn to another cause taken up by Vidyasagar in the 19th century the social structure of the Hindus was mainly based on the joint-family system When the head of the joint-family died, his wife, children and other dependants suddenly faced a grave economic crisis, almost insoluble. It was a disaster which shattered many middle class families.

Being himself the son of a lower middle class family, Vidyasagar was fully aware of this haunting fear of economic insecurity. His efforts in solving this problem materialised in the founding of the Hindu Family Annuity Fund on June 15, 1872.

Life Insurance and Annuity Funds were not in vogue at the time. Vidyasagar's main concern was to provide the minimum economic security to the helpless dependants of poor middle class families after the death of their breadwinners. With this object in view the Fund was organised: if one, wished his wife or any other dependant to have a monthly allowance of Rs. 5 after his death, he had to pay 25 per cent of this amount monthly till his death. The limit was a monthly allowance of Rs. 30 For making a provision up to this maximum limit, a monthly premium of Rs. 7 and annas 8 was to be paid. In fixing these limits, Vidyasagar thought of providing the minimum economic security to the lower-income and the middle-income groups of families in Bengal.

In the premises of the Metropolitan Institution the first meeting for the organisation of the Fund was held, with ten subscribers only, besides the donations of a few wealthy persons. Among the notable trustees of the Fund, besides Vidyasagar, were Mr. Justice Dwarkanath Mitter, Mr. Justice Ramesh Chandra Mitter and Maharaja Jatindra Mohan Tagore. Vidyasagar was associated, with the Fund till the end of 1875. He communicated the reasons for severing his connections with the Fund in a long letter to the Board of Trustees on February 21, 1876. As usual in the matter of such Funds, there was irregularity in its management, and a scrupulously honest man like Vidyasagar naturally did not want his name to continue to be associated with it He charged the Directors with disregard of the rules and with neglect of the interests of the Fund.

"In the letter he said: "At your special meeting you have expressed a wish and request that I should retain my connection with the Fund; but it has become very difficult for me "to comply with your request. Numbers of people come to consult me whether they should subscribe to the Fund. I am then put to a great dilemma. Under the present state of the Fund, I think, it would be wrong to advise any one to subscribe to it; while it would be equally wrong to deter anybody from, subscribing to it The reason is, that it would be deceiving a man to induce him to subscribe to it, when a conviction has grown upon me that in future the Fund might be in a state of disorder, while to deter him would be acting in opposition to the Fund To deceive a man wilfully, and to act in opposition to it while continuing in its connection, both are equally very wrong. If I keep any further connection with the Fund, I must commit either of the wrongs. It is this dilemma that disables me to comply with your request, for which I crave your indulgence".

Soon after his retirement some other Directors also decided to withdraw their names from the Fund. But considering the humanitarian objects of the founders of the Institution, and the considerable number of middle class people connected with it, it was ultimately taken over by the government.

Sometime in 1854-55 the Wards' Institution was founded by government for the training of the minor heirs of the Princes and Zamindars of Bengal, and it was placed under the direct control of the Board of Revenue. Dr Rajendralal "Mitra, an eminent scholar of the time, was appointed its Director. Vidyasagar was nominated a Visitor of the Institution by the Board in November, 1863. After paying four or five visits, he submitted a Memorandum to the Board, in April, 1864, suggesting some changes in the existing arrangements of the Institution On receipt of this Memorandum the Board called on him for a full report on the working of the Institution. Vidyasagar submitted the report in January, 1865, followed by a later supplementary one. His main recommendations were:.

> that the Institution be turned into a Boarding School, instead of being merely the residence of the Wards as at present;
>
> that a separate course of instruction, especially suited to the needs of the Wards, be framed for them,
>
> that the requisite staff of efficient teachers be entertained for their instruction.

There was another point in the report which is also important. One of the rules of the Institution prescribed for the Wards corporal punishment in "aggravated cases "But the instances of such punishment which Vidyasagar found in the Order Book could hardly be classed as "aggravated cases". "But, irrespective of the nature of the offences committed," remarked Vidyasagar in his report, "I would beg leave to observe that corporal punishment should be discarded altogether as a part of the training of the Wards. This punishment is strictly prohibited in all Educational Institutions on account of its banetul influence Hundreds of pupils are managed in them without the use of the cane, its necessity in the Wards' Institution is scarcely perceptible In my humble opinion, such barbarous and harsh treatment by no means becomes the inmates of that Institution I have some experience in the training of boys and my firm conviction is that corporal punishment, from its degrading effects, spoils more than mends the recipients I would, therefore, beg leave strongly to recommend that this rule may be rescinded at once."

This is one of the most important social and educational reforms introduced by Vidyasagar which is usually overlooked. Even in the twenties of the present century, corporal punishment, including caning, was resorted to in schools in a city like Calcutta. Vidyasagar was greatly against this method of punishment and he banned it in all the institutions he was in charge of, directly or indirectly. He was not even in favour of inflicting any punishment on students, like making them stand up on the bench, shaming a student before others. He once compelled the Head Master of his Metropolitan Branch Institution to resign for having punished a boy by making him stand up on the bench. This system of punishment was changed in accordance with Vidyasagar's suggestion and the Ward's Institution was later conducted on the basis of more liberal and humane principles.

We take up another issue. The Hindu Wills Act was introduced as a Draft Bill in the Legislative Council in the year 1869. The problem of Indian succession had hitherto been served by the Indian Succession Act, which was enforced with equal authority on Indians and non-Indians. Since the establishment of the Supreme Court, the wealthy families of Bengal used to leave their Wills at their own option. This led to serious litigation, complicated and endless. Some modifications of the Act were needed. Hindu public opinion was considerably agitated during the introduction of this Bill. The government asked for the opinion of all the leading members of Hindu society, particularly of the learned Sanskrit pandits; Vidyasagar's opinion was sought. He opposed two points in the Bill: in the first place, according to the Hindu Shastras, the gift of something to any person yet to be born is unlawful, but in the Act such gifts had been considered lawful in certain cases; secondly, what is termed as Rule against Perpetuity is also opposed to the Hindu Shastras. Vidyasagar's arguments were based on the sound footing of Shastraic evidence But the government did not pay any heed to these suggestions, and the Bill was passed into law in September, 1870. That the great reformer of our society was not always non-conformist in his views about Hindu society, can be judged from his observations on the Hindu Succession Act.

We now come to Vidyasagar's efforts in the cause of temperance. Since the beginning of the 19th century, the Bengalis, particularly the upper and the middle classes living in a city like Calcutta, were fast becoming addicts of alcohol, owing to direct contact with Europeans. Entertainments and parties in European and aristocratic Bengali houses were held almost everyday, in which various kinds of imported wines flowed freely. From the upper class Bengalis, the English-educated middle class caught the habit. It spread so much that by the thirties of the 19th century, in the days of Young Bengal, one of the catchwords was that drinking was a sign of progress and that those who did not drink were reactionaries. So said the Hindu College students, the torchbearers of Western education in Bengal. Very soon, addiction to drinking was rampant among the Bengali urban middle class. Educationists grew alarmed at the situation, and earnestly considered the effective steps necessary for arresting this development.

The Temperance movement was started by some of the leading educationists and reformers of Bengal in the sixties of last century. The name of Peary Churn Sarkar, an eminent educationist, will ever remain associated with this movement. He was an ardent supporter of all social reforms, and was a great friend of Vidyasagar. It was mainly on his initiative that the Temperance movement was started, and in the beginning of 1864 the Bengal Temperance

Society was founded in Calcutta. On its foundation Vidyasagar joined the Society, and took a leading part in its organisation. The movement made great strides within a decade, and even after Peary Churn's death it did Hot lose its momentum. A letter of Vidyasagar, of November 27, 1875, addressed to Dr. Bhooban Mohun Sarkar in this context, may be given: "I regret exceedingly that in the present state of my health, of which you are aware, I am unable to attend this evening's meeting of the Bengal Temperance Society. No one knows better than yourself the profound grief with which the lamented death of my beloved friend Babu Peary Churn Sarkar has filled me. We knew each other from early youth, and we were so closely attached that in him I have lost a dear and affectionate brother.

To the public the loss cannot be easily replaced. His great ability, high character, and single-minded zeal in work of humanity rendered him highly useful to society at large, whilst his devotion to the cause of temperance which was manifested in the foundation of the Bengal Temperance Society, in the publication of very many valuable tracts in English and Bengali and in other acts will doubtless be long cherised in grateful remembrance by all lovers and promoters of temperance in this country".

The particular meeting referred to in this letter was attended by Surendranath Banerji, and in this meeting the great nationalist orator of Bengal delivered his first public speech before a large audience. He writes in his autobiography, A Nation in Making: "Soon after my return to Calcutta (in June, 1875), a meeting was held in the theatre of the Medical College to promote the Temperance movement. It was a crowded meeting. The Temperance cause excited much interest in those days. The labours of Peary Churn Sarkar, the apostle of the Temperance movement in Bengal, were bearing fruit. It was a living' movement; for the dangers of intemperance spreading among the rising generation were real and ominous".

Soon after, Surendranath Banerji became Professor of English in the Metropolitan Institution of Vidyasagar. Writing about it he says: "My speech had already made me popular with the students, and helped me, I think, to get the appointment. I delivered lectures in Calcutta, Utter-para, Kidderpore and other places, upon such subjects as Indian Unity, the Study of History, the Life of Mazzini, the Life of Chaitanya, High English Education, etc. I was in great demand as a speaker and never spared myself". This statement of his proves that the Temperance movement in the sixties and seventies of 19th century, of which Vidyasagar was one of the promoters, provided a training-ground for the budding nationalists.

Age of Consent Bill

We turn to the Age of Consent Bill in 1890, a Bill was introduced in the Legislative Council for the amendment of certain sections of the Indian Penal Code and the Criminal Procedure Code relating to the Age of Consent of child wives in India As on all important social matters, the government sought Vidyasagar's opinion. Vidyasagar was then seriously ill, and dying. But the flame of passion for social reforms, for the good of the country, was burning bright in him. From his deathbed he consulted the relevant Shastras and sent his opinion to the Government on February 16, 1891. He criticised some major provisions in the Bill, which went against the religious usage of the Hindus. Nevertheless, he supported the Bill in so far as it was framed to give "an adequate protection to child wives, without in any way conflicting with any religious usage". He also strongly supported the penal clause in the Bill, as in his opinion, "the punishment which the Shastras prescribed for violation of the rule is of a spiritual character and is liable to be disregarded. The religious prohibition would be made more effective if it was embodied in a penal law".

Some have given a wrong interpretation of his Note on the Age of Consent Bill, "by suggesting that in the last years of his life Vidyasagar's attitude towards traditional Hinduism and its usages and customs was less uncompromising than in his youth. This is to misunderstand altogether the social outlook of the great reformer. He had no love or respect for any usage or custom, simply because it was traditional, or because the people were rigidly attached to it He was also not an iconoclast in the sense that the young Derozians were. He was not in favour of breaking the bond of tradition so long as it was not positively harmful to society It has been already noticed that in making legal provision for the remarriage of widows he did not accept the suggestion of those who wanted to change the Hindu marriage system into a system of contract, although he knew well that to keep the system of Hindu marriage as it was then, his scheme of widow remarriage was bound to fail, even under legal protection in the Age of Consent issue also, while he was not in favour of introducing measures in flagrant violation of Hindu usage, he strongly supported the provision of a penal law, instead of ineffective religious Shastraic injunctions for those who violated the rule He stressed the necessity of having a penal law in the last line of his Note: "I may be permitted to press this consideration most earnestly on the attention of the government".

This was his last recommendation to the government for the protection of the unfortunate child wives of India. A few months later, in July, 1891, Vidyasagar died. As became his life and character he wrote this last Note on the Age of Consent from his deathbed for the welfare of the women of our country. No cause was nobler and dearer to him than this, and against nothing else did he fight so intrepidly as he did against the subjection of women.

Services during Famine

In the middle of 1866, Raja Pratap Chandra Sinha of Paikpara was severely ill at Kandi, his ancestral home. When the news reached Vidyasagar, he hastened to Kandi, accompanied with the best native medical practitioner, Dr. Mahendra Lal Sarkar. But the illness grew more serious every day, and at last his life was despaired of. He was removed to Paikpara, where he expired at 3 o'clock in the morning of the 19th July, 1866.

The deceased Raja was a great friend of Vidyasagar. Before his death, he had requested his friend to be a Trustee of his estate, but Vidyasagar declined. The newspaper, the Hindu Patriot of the 23rd July of the same year thus spoke of the Raja:— "He (i.e. Raja Pratap Chandra) was one of the principal supporters of the female schools established and managed by Pandit Ishwar Chandra Vidyasagar". Vidyasagar was heartily grieved at the untimely death of his dear friend.

On the death of the Raja the state of his family and estate was most deplorable. For arrears of land revenue the estate was about to be put to auction. At the request of the deceased Raja's grandmother (father's mother), Rani Katyayani, Vidyasagar, accompanied with the Raja's-minor sons, interviewed Sir Cecil Beadon, the then Lieutenant-Governor of Bengal. At his earnest solicitation, Beadon saved the estate from revenue sale and placed it under the management of the Court of Wards. It was at the instance of Vidyasagar, that the minor sons of the Raja were saved from the hands of the Wards' Institution, They were placed under the care of Rani Katyayani, and several European and native gentlemen were appointed their guardians, among whom Vidyasagar was one.

He had thus to visit the *Rajbati* often. One day on his way thither, he was confronted by a poor shopkeeper, by name Ramdhan, an old acquaintance of his, who saluted! him, and asked him respectfully to step over to his shop. Vidyasagar followed him to his place, which stood by the wayside, and there took his seat upon the grass in front of the shop, and began smoking a hookah offered by Ramdhan. In the meantime, some officers of the Paikpara estate saw him in that situation. At last, when Vidyasagar called at the *Rajbati,* the officers winked at him, and some of them even ventured to remonstrate with him on the impropriety of his mixing with such vulgar people. Vidyasagar smiled, and said with great emphasis, that the rich and the poor were all alike in his eyes.

On another occasion, as he was sitting in the *Rajbati,* a beggar approached the gates and asked for alms. The Darwans drove him away. Vidyasagar was deeply afflicted at the sight. Some say, that henceforth he scarcely visited the *Rajbati.* But we have been informed from a reliable source, that there arose a graver cause, which made Vidyasagar cease his visits to the Raj-house. Some of the Kumars (sons of the Raja) had grown wanton, and Vidyasagar was afraid of the loss of his respect. But the Kumars' respectful demeanour towards him never diminished for a moment. Kumar Indra Chandra often paid him respectful visits. If any one ever advised him to put a Darwan at his gates, he would at once point to the Paikpara *Rajbati.* He was generally heard to say: 'If I place a Darwan at my gates, the beggar shall be deprived of his handful rice, and the visitor shall be prevented from having an easy interview with myself. Death is by far preferable to that.' Sometimes he warned his grandsons,—' If I ever hear that a visitor has been prevented by any one of my house from coming up to me, I shall at once drive the offender out, I have witnessed inconveniences caused by the placing of Darwans at rich men's gates and I do not wish to bring those inconveniences into my own house.

He never put the slightest obstacle in the way of a visitor's easy entrance into his house. On one occasion, as he was sitting one day at about noon-time with a *hookah* in hand after dinner, a man with a very irate appearance appeared hurriedly before him, and enquired for Vidyasagar. It is needless to say that the man did not know Vidyasagar in person, but only in name. The man was an inhabitant of East Bengal, and had come to Calcutta on business. He had, that day, tried 'to have an interview with two or three wealthy persons of the city, but had failed to see them, and hence had lost his temper. Vidyasagar asked him to take his seat. But the man said, not until he could see Vidyasagar. He also said that he had been baffled in his endeavours to have interviews with some other great men of the city, whose names he had heard before, and he now wanted to see if Vidyasagar was also a great man of that nature. Vidyasagar then asked the man if he had eaten anything that day.

The visitor answered in the negative, and said that he was too intent on having an interview with Vidyasagar to give heed to the demands of nature. He repeatedly insisted on instantaneous visit with Vidyasagar. In the meantime, refreshments were ready for the man at Vidyasagar's hints. He then said to the man,—'You shall have your intended visit, as soon as you have partaken of the refreshments. When the visitor had been made to refresh himself, he was somewhat pacified. Vidyasagar then disclosed himself, to the utter amazement of the visitor, who now acknowledged that Vidyasagar was really equal to his great name'.

But this unrestricted admittance caused him now and then no small amount of inconvenience and annoyance. Once on a time, several residents of Uttarpara came to his residence to see him with the object of securing his recommendations for employment. It so happened at that time, that his youngest daughter was critically ill. He was on the upper floor tending the sick girl. He was very anxious for the child's life; his mind was in a most perturbed state. The medical attendant, Dr. Amulya Charan Basu, who was sitting in a room on the ground floor, informed the visitors of the state of Vidyasagar's, mind, and told them to come some other day. They would not listen to him, and sent word to Vidya-sagar by a servant The domestic returned and said that he was instructed by his master to in form them of the serious illness of his master's daughter, and to request them to call another day, as his master was quite unable to leave the bedside of his dear girl. The men would hear of no denial. They began to ascend the stairs, Vidyasagar was now compelled to come down, but he was somewhat annoyed, and thus addressed the intruders; I see, you understand your necessity best. You have not the slightest pity or mercy in you Please, leave me alone for this day, and call same other day. The impudent trespassers hung down their heads in shame, and precipitately left the house.

In 1866, a Bill was introduced into the Legislative Council for legislation on the Alienation of *Devatra* property. The Board of Revenue asked Vidyasagar for his opinion on the subject based on Hindu Law. Vidyasagar communicated his opinion by a letter, which speaks for itself, and is therefore given below:

"To

"R. B. Chapman Esquire

"Secretary to the Board of Revenue. "Sir,?With reference to the correspondence forwarded to me under docked No. 656 B. dated 13th ultimo, I beg to state that there do not appear to be any texts in the Books on Hindu Law which either permit or prohibit the alienation of *Devatra* property. But the general practice of the country does not sanction the disposition of such property in any shape. In fact, when Endowments of this description are made by Hindus, they make them with the sole object of securing the property endowed from any sort of alienation, and attach conditions accordingly. Trustees are consequently prohibited from disposing of the property. Though no distinct ruling on the point is traceable in any of the Text Books, no alienation can be permitted in accordance with the principles of Hindu Law. According to that Law, alienation cannot take place except with the *express consent* of the owner, and as in the case of *Devatra* property the Idol, to which it is consecrated, is the owner, it cannot be disposed of except with its consent, which, as a matter of course, can neither be given nor extorted, *Hence, Devatra* property has become inalienable.

"2. I am fully aware of the difficulties which may occasionally be felt by trustees in the execution of the trusts in connection with Religious Establishments. Circumstances may arise, which may compel them to incur liabilities, which the fixed income of the Trust will never enable them to meet; because, in many cases, the endowers appropriate the income in such a way as to leave little or no margin for any extraordinary or unforeseen expenditure connected with the endowments, such as repairs of temples, payment of government Revenue in cases when it is not realised from the Ryots in consequence of draught, inundation or other causes &c. It cannot be expected that Trustees will meet this expenditure from their own funds or from subscriptions. Some provision must therefore be made by Law for the purpose, and on this consideration, I see no objection to section I of the Bill No 8 of 1866, if it be so worded as to express distinctly that the funds raised by the disposition of the property are to be appropriated solely to meet extraordinary or unavoidable expenditure connected with Religious Endowments. Disposal of Devatra property for such purposes would not, in my humble opinion, be inconsistent with the principle of Hindu Law. The chief object of all endowments is to guard against misappropriation, and as the extra expenditure referred to is solely and entirely required for Devatra purposes, it can, on no account, considered in the light of misappropriation. Nay, if the Idol could be made to speak, it would certainly not only have given its consent, but would have also insisted on the disposition of its property under such contingencies.

"3. Alienation being allowable only under the circumstances above set forth, section 11 of the Bill appears to me to be objectionable, as it confers undue powers on Trustees, and prescribes that it is not necessary for purchasers or mortgagees of Devatra property to enquire into the necessity or expediency of the sale or mortgage or to see that on more than is absolutely required is raised. With such unlimited powers on the part of Trustees, and freedom from all responsibility on that of the purchasers or mortgagees, the property may probably be liable to misappropriation against which it is absolutely necessary to guard. I believe that the Law in regard to the disposition of other Trusts enjoins upon purchasers or mortgagees to make reasonable enquiries about the immediate necessity for the alienation. The benefit to be conferred or the danger to be averted by alienating a portion of the Trust property must be the criterion by which the validity of such alienation is to be judged of. With such provisions in cases of other Trusts it is not clear why similar conditions should not be attached to transfers of Devatra Trusts. I would therefore take the liberty to suggest that section II may be so modified as to guard against any possible chance of misappropriation. With such modifications, the Bill would, I believe, be opposed neither to the spirit of Hindu Law nor to the general feelings of the Hindu community on the subject.

J (Sd.) Ishwar Chandra

The government saw the soundness of Vidyasagar's arguments, and the Bill was ultimately rejected.

In the beginning of 1867, Vidyasagar visited Birsingha. About this time, the relations of a helpless widow were endeavouring to misappropriate her landed property. The widow came to Vidyasagar, and with tearful eyes besought his help. He sent for the widow's relations, and requested them not to meddle with the helpless woman's affairs, but they would not listen to him. They brought a suit against the widow; but when they heard that Vidyasagar was determined to help the poor woman by all means, they desisted from their unlawful attempts, and never more appeared in court.

At this time, he made arrangements for separate boarding of his second and third brothers, and of his only son, Narayan Chandra, and provided for their monthly allowances in proportion to their respective needs. The main cause of this disruption was intermittent quarrel among the members of the large family, which disturbed now and then the tranquillity of the household. Separate houses had already been built for his two sisters, some time before this. Servants were engaged and provisions made for the separate boarding of the boys of other places, who lodged in his house and read in his free school. Shortly afterwards, a separate house was erected for his son, and arrangements were made of keeping his mother with himself in Calcutta.

Form this, it is apparent that Vidyasagar was not well disposed towards the Hindu system of joint family. It was not his innate fault. It was his English education that produced in him this failing, It was his want of insight that led him to meddle with the customs of Hindu Society, which is self-evident from the dismemberment of his joint family. The practice of the Hindu in his own household, in his dealings with Society, and in everything else is conducive to the attainment of spiritual knowledge. Every usage, every custom, every practice has been prescribed by the saintly *Rishts* with a view to enable the common laymen to begin to learn the secrets of the Hindu religion. Joint family is a prominent member of Hindu Society—the principal means of the realisation of Yoga-the royal road to salvation. What is *Yoga*? It is nothing but union or communion—complete absorption—in Divinity. It is nothing but the combination of one with the other—the conversion of duality into unity. The union of self with the whole world, the annihilation of the universe in self, the feeling of the existence of every external thing in self, this is the high way to redemption for the Hindu. This idea begins in one's own family. It begins between one and one—*vis.* between preceptor and disciple, or between husband and wife or between parent and son, or between brother and wife; the wife, her husband; the brother, his sister, the sister, her brother; and fled to towns in hopes of getting something to put into their burning stomachs. But many of them could not reach their destinations. They were reduced to mere skeletons, and, what with faint and what with continued want of food and consequent illness, lay dead in numbers by the wayside. The small space at our command will not permit us to enter into a detailed account of the state of the country at that time. We will confine ourselves to that portion only, with which our benevolent, heroic Vidyasagar was connected.

He was at that time in Calcutta, and had no information of the great scarcity that raged fearfully in his own native village and its neighbourhood, till he saw some correspondence on the subject in the Hindu Patriot and shortly afterwards received a letter from his own home bearing the horrible news that people were dying in numbers from want of food. The news gave him, tender-hearted as he was, a terrible shock, and he was moved to a flood of tears. He at once informed the government of the fatal calamity and requested for speedy succour. They listened to him and instituted immediate enquiries. They opened feeding camps in the different parts of the country, but these were not amply adequate to meet the urgent demands. The correspondent of the Hindu Patriot said, that Babu Hem Chandra Kar, Deputy Magistrate of Garbeta was taking much pains to visit personally the villages under him and provide for the relief of the poor villagers, hut that Babu Isan Chandra Mitra, Deputy Magistrate of the Jehanabad Subdivision of the Hooghly district did not attend to it seriously. It may not be out of place to mention here that Birsingha and its neighbouring villages were at that time under the Hooghly district, but were subsequently transferred under Midnapur in the time of Sir George Campbell.

Vidyasagar then hurried to the scene of occurrence, and was glad to find that his kind mother had already begun feeding the hungry people. She cooked the food with her own hands, and fed on an average one hundred persons daily. As was the son, so was the mother ! But Vidyasagar was not content with this. He opened feeding houses at his own cost for Birsingha and the surrounding villages. The number of hungry people increased every day; from one hundred it finally rose to one thousand. As the number increased daily, Vidyasagar raised his scale of expenditure. On this occasion he wrote to his third brother, Sambhu Chandra, who had been charged with the management of the feeding houses, not to show stint of expenses on this account, however large the amount might be.

He had returned to Calcutta after completing all arrangements, but visited Birsingha often. Provisions were at first made for supplying the hungry with *Khecharanna* everyday; but on the occasion of his second visit they applied to him for plain rice now and then. Vidyasagar granted their application and made provisions for the supply of plain rice with fish and curd once a week. But unfortunately on the very first day of this new arrangement, a sad incident occurred, which grieved the tender-hearted, benevolent reliever most seriously. A poor, hungry fellow in his eager desire for food, thrust a handful of the dry, plain rice into his mouth, which choked him to death, Vidyasagar took up the unfortunate man's corpse into his lap, and lamented bitterly that a fellow-creature should thus die a miserable death from want of food.

We have said that Babu Isan Chandra Mitra was a little indifferent at the outset. But subsequently he felt the severity of the situation, and visited the different villages under him, in company with Vidyasagar's second brother, Dinabandhu Nyayratna. He requested the government for feeding camps, which were opened in some important villages, where the hungry were fed up to the month of October.

It is said, that Vidyasagar anointed the heads of the poor females of the lowest classes with his own hands, and thus set an example to his son, brothers and other relations, to emulate him in taking tender care of the poor sufferers. He also opened nurseries for the pregnant, hungry females, and provided for their safe delivery and supply of milk to the newborn babies.

The poor people in gratefulness changed his name from Vidyasagar to *Dayar Sagar* (an ocean of kindness). Gradually the number of the hungry rode to such a height that the 12 cooks engaged for preparing the food and the 20 men employed to distribute it felt quite used up with their work. As the hungry sat to their meals, they rent the air with repeated loud cheers for their "ocean of kindness".

These people were fed by him up to the close of the year, when the new corn being ripe, they left the feeding camp one by one and returned to their respective houses, blessing with all their heart their benevolent protector, and praying to God for his long life.

He was not content with merely feeding the hungry people in his camp, but he visited the houses of his neighbours one after the other, and enquired after every one of them. The poor of the upper classes felt a great humiliation *in* resorting to the feeding camps. He helped them with money and articles of food, supplied at their houses. In fact, the unbounded kindness of Vidyasagar, who was by no means a man of money, put the great millionaires of the country to shame, Even the government was obliged to acknowledge his generous bounty for the relief of the sufferers. The Commissioner of the Burdwan Division wrote to him as follows:

"To
"Pundit Ishwar Chandra Vidyasagar,
"Beetsingha

"Sir,

"I have been instructed by the Secretary to the Government of Bengal under order of the 20th instant to express to you the warm acknowledgment of government for your generous exertions in relieving the poor during the recent scarcity in the Hooghly District.

"I have the honour to be,

"Sir,

"Your most obedient servant (Sd.) "C. T. Montrisor "Commissioner, Burdwan Division". Vidyasagar's third brother, Sambhu Chandra, says:—

"In the meantime, Babu Hem Chandra Kar, Superintendent of the feeding Camp at Garbeta, and his brothers appealed to my eldest brother (Vidyasagar) for help. He sent through my hands 100 rupees,—50 rupees for food, and 50 rupees for cloth. Besides this, some gentlemen came to him praying for aid towards the celebration of the *Sraddha* of their deceased parents. He gave to some of them 50, to some 100, and to the rest 200 rupees. A separate feeding camp was opened on the 28th Sraban, which was closed after the feed-ing on the 1st day of Paush. But the helpless poor of distant places stopped there up to the 8th Paush. Consequently, about 60 feeble and help less persons had to be fed for a few days more.'

Services during Disasters

About the time, of which we are speaking, Vidyasagar had to encounter disasters and troubles of different kinds. He had to mourn over the loss of many of his sincere friends and coadjutors. The Hon'ble Sambhu Nath Pandit, the first native Judge of the Calcutta High Court, breathed his last on 6th January 1867. He was a friend and fellow worker of Vidyasagar in many of his acts. He was an advocate of widow-marriage and female education. At the prize distribution of the Bethune School in 1865, when

Vidyasagar presented a gold necklace, Sambhu Nath also gave a valuable prize of a pair of gold bracelets. Vidyasagar was deeply afflicted at the death of such a worthy friend.

In its train, followed the demise of Raja Radhakanta Dev Bahadur, which sad catastrophe before on the 13th April of the same year. The reader is aware that the Raja was an advocate of female education. Though he was against the remarriage of Hindu widows and had petitioned the government opposing the legislation, yet he cherished a fond regard for Vidyasagar on account of his attainments and spiritedness, Vidyasagar also had a great esteem for the Raja, and was sincerely grieved at his death.

About this time, notices appeared in the Hindu Patriot and some other papers for starting a Widow Marriage Fund for the clearance of Vidyasagar's heavy debts on that account, appealing to the general public to come forward to help Vidyasagar with liberal contributions, Vidyasagar knew nothing of this appeal, being absent from Calcutta at his native village, Birsingha. When he returned to the city and heard of what was being tried to do for him, he was extremely picqued, and at once contradicted the appeal in the columns of the Hindu Patriot Among other things he said, that though the sixty widow marriages consummated upto that day had actually cost 82,000 rupees, yet his debts on this account would not come up to half of the 45,000 rupees accounted for by the appellants, who had no knowledge of the real state of things. He also said that he was quite ignorant of this appeal, having never even entertained the remotest thought of ever calling upon the public to help him in this matter, that he would not have cared to protest against the measure, if the proposers of the movement had not made mention of his debts in this affair, and that he therefore requested the movers to keep back from their uncalled-for intrusion. 11th July, 1867, Vidyasagar married his eldest daughter, Hemlata Devi, to Gopal Chandrapati of village Aismali in the Nuddea district As Hemlata was a girl of accomplishments, so her husband was also a young man of very good attainments, and to Vidyasagar's mind.

Sometime after this, a great misfortune befell our noble hero. His greatest friend and coadjutor, Ram Gopal Ghosh, expired at about 11-30 a.m. on the 21st January, 1868. The deceased was a great orator and staunch advocate of widow marriage. The loss of such a sincere friend gave our hero a great shock, and moved him to a flood of tears. Speaking of Ram Gopal Ghosh, the Hindu Patriot of the 27th January of that year said:—"He was a warm advocate of widow marriage and assisted the noble cause with money as well as personal labour". The Hon'ble C. E. Buckland, in his 'Bengal under the Lieutenant-Governors says:—" In politics, Babu Ram Gopal Ghose was a zealous and indefatigable reformer. He was a leading member of the British Indian Association, which was established in 1851, and took the most prominent part in every political movement of the day: such subjects as the admission of Natives into the Legislative Council of India and the Civil Service, the extension of reproductive public works, were agitated, largely at his instigation. It was he who first matured a plan and established a Society for political agitation in England, with the assistance of Mr. Adams, for the purpose of drawing the attention of the British public to Indian questions.

"But, above all, Babu Ram Gopal was distinguished for his great oratorial powers. When the government of Bengal, on 26th February 1864, desired to remove the burning *ghat* from Nimtolla, though he felt personally no religious scruples against the proposal, he identified himself with his orthodox countrymen and made an eloquent speech setting forth their grievances. His speeches on the renewal of the Charter Act of 1853, on the memorial of Sir Henry Hardinge, and on the administration of Lord Canning are also famous, the former being praised by the *Times* as a masterpiece of oratory".

A little farther on, Buckland says:— "As a promoter of education, a patriot, a politician, a speaker, a social reformer, as a successful merchant, and in force of character, Babu Ram Gopal Ghose was one of the foremost men of his time: and did much for the advancement and enlightenment of Hindu Society".

In fact, when in the beginning of 1864, the announcement of the desire of government to remove the burning *ghat* from Nimtala and to set up an engine crematorium outside the town was made public, a great excitement prevailed among the Hindu community, and Vidyasagar was determined to oppose the measure, which was so repulsive to the religious feelings of his countrymen. It was at his goading instigation that Ram Gopal Ghosh delivered his eloquent speech at a meeting held in the Calcutta Town Hall for the purpose, which made the government throw up the project, In this connection, the following story is current in the country.

When Vidyasagar heard of the measure projected by government, he was very firmly resolved to thwart it. Many leading native gentlemen had also sided with government. Vidyasagar saw that there was only one man who was competent to oppose it vigorously and effectively. That man was Ram Gopal Ghosh, Vidyasagar called on him and gave out his mind, but he, having no scruples of his own on that account, declined to interfere. Vidyasagar now set himself to think of some means whereby his friend could be persuaded to stand against the proposal. It suddenly struck him, that Ram Gopal was highly filial to his mother, and never disobeyed her. He decided upon persuading her to induce her son to take up the cause.

Accordingly, early in the next morning, he again called and seated himself in the outer apartments of his friend's house. As Ram Gopal's mother returned from her bath in the Bhagirathi, she saw Vidyasagar seated alone with a very melancholy face, and asked him the cause. He replied.—'Madam, perhaps you are not aware that government have resolved upon removing the burning *ghat* from Nimtala and setting up an engine crematorium, for the cremation of the dead bodies of the Hindus. The law on this subject is going to be passed very shortly.'

The old lady was taken by surprise. She asked him if there was no means to prevent it. Vidyasagar said,—'There is only one means. Tomorrow the matter will be decided at the Town Hall meeting. If your son should attend the meeting and speak against the measure, the legislation may be averted. The matron replied,—'I will at once ask Ram Gopal to do so.' She went into the inner apartments and told her son to oppose the proposed legislation. Ram Gopal promised to obey. He then came out and said to Vidyasagar,—'O! You have told mother. There is no help now; I must' obey my mother. Very good, come tomorrow at 3 P. M.; I will attend the meeting.' On the next day, Ram Gopal, accompanied by his friend, went to the meeting and made a highly eloquent speech strongly opposing the proposed measure, which made the government abandon the project. Shortly after this, Vidyasagar had to encounter the loss of another great friend. Sarada Prasad Ray, a Zamindar of Chakdighi in the Burdwan district, died on the 18th March, 1868. The deceased had a great familiarity with Vidyasagar. He consulted the latter on all points. He had no issue of his own, and he, therefore, had a great mind to take an adopted son. But Vidyasagar prevented him from that step and advised him to establish charitable institutions and to do other useful works. Sarada Prasad acted up to this advice. In 1853, he opened a charitable dispensary, and on the 1st August, 1861, established a free school, both at Chakdighi. It was on a poor family of this village that Vidyasagar had settled a monthly allowance of fifteen rupees. A few years subsequent to the death of this Zamindar, there was a suit instituted with respect to his will. In this case, Vidyasagar had to appear in Court as a witness, of which hereafter.

Although Vidyasagar was heavily embarrassed with debts on account of his widow marriage movement, he never stinted his charities. We have already said, that he never refused a beggar or supplicant. He always contributed very liberally to the aid of such works, as in his opinion were useful to the country.

About the middle of 1868, some respectable residents of Ghatal in the Midnapore district appealed to him for aid towards the establishment of a High English School at Ghatal. Vidyasagar was a warm supporter of English education, and he very generously responded to the appeal. He, contributed as donation the whole amount of 500 rupees which they wanted.

The reader may recollect the name of Rani Katyayani of Paikpara Raj, and how much indebted she was to Vidyasagar. The Rani was now grown too old. She breathed her last on the 17th day of August, 1868.

In the course of this year, appeared his *Akhyanmanjari, Parts* II *and* III. The language of the two books is equally excellent and very well adapted to the purpose intended. Both of them are very nice school books.

Hara Chandra Ghosh, with whose name the reader is already acquainted, was one of the native, judges of the Calcutta Small Cause Court. He died on the 3rd of December, 1869, He too was a staunch supporter of female education. A condolence meeting was held on the 4th January next when a Memorial Committee was formed to perpetuate his memory. Vidyasagar was on this committee.

In 1868, he had to enter into a very disagreeable family dispute. His second brother, Dinabandhu quite unexpectedly laid claim to a share of the Sanskrit Press and the attached Depository. He was so eager about it, as to be ready to bring the matter into Law-Court. When Vidyasagar saw, that his dear brother was zealously intent on going to court, he advised him to have the question settled; out of court by arbitration, Dinabandhu assented! Accordingly, the Hon'ble Justice Dwarka Nath Mitter, the second native Judge of the Calcutta High-Court, and Babu Durga Mohan Das, one of the ablest pleaders of the bar of the said court were chosen by them to be their arbiters.

The two brothers then entered into an agreement executed on a one-rupee stamped paper binding themselves to abide by the decision of the umpires. Their third brother, Sambhuchandra, cousin Pitambar Bandyopadhyay, who was the Printer of the Sanskrit Press, and Vidyasagar's friends, Raj Krishna and Shyama Charan, and Giris Chandra Vidyaratna were cited as witnesses. Vidyasagar had at this time two more brothers living, besides Dinabandhu, namely, the third Sambhuchandra, and the sixth Isan Chandra, the fourth, fifth, and seventh brothers having already died; but they laid no claim to the property in dispute.

It is said that for fear of appearing and deposing in the witness-box, Sambhuchandra requested his second brother to surrender his title. However that might be, Dinabandhu at last renounced his claim. On the 17th day of October, 1868, he submitted to the arbitrators a deed of relinquishment to the following effect:

"On the 11th October current, I filed an agreement and a plaint with a list of witnesses; but I see that it is quite unjust to enter into dispute with a brother on account of a small property. I therefore hereby declare that I relinquish the claim that I laid to a share of the Sanskrit Press and the Book Depository attached to it. In future if I myself or my heirs should lay any claim to it, that shall be null and void. 17th October 1868.

Sd. "Dinabandhu Bandyopadhyay". The umpires passed the following judgement: — The *plaintiff,* Dinabandhu Bandyopadhyay, having filed an agreement relinquishing his title and claim to a share of the Sanskrit Press and the Book Depository connected with it, and having declared that any such claim in future either on his own part or on the part of his heirs should be considered null and void, further investigations and proceedings are unnecessary. In the presence of both parties, it is therefore, 'Decreed

'That the plaintiff's claim be dismissed and a copy of this judgement and decree be supplied to each party. 18th October 1868.

Sd. 'Dwarka Nath Mitter

Sd. 'Doorga Mohun Dass,'

When Dinabandhu first gave out his mind to lay his claim to the property, Vidyasagar expressed his willingness to divide it into six equal shares among the four living brothers and their parents; but Dinabandhu would not be content with such a small share. It is said, that having failed in his attempts to substantiate his claim to the property, Dinabandhu was greatly displeased with his elder brother, and refused to receive monthly allowances from him, Vidyasagar saw the pecuniary difficulties of his brother, and used to pay the money to his sister-in-law (brother's wife), cautioning her, at the same time, not to let her husband know it. Vidyasagar was a lover of mankind; he loved his brothers and relations very dearly, and always tried to make them happy. He had to spend a deal of money on their account, but unfortunately they did not reciprocate the same feelings. He was often heard to say with tearful eyes, that like the old man of the fables, in trying to please everybody, he had been able to please nobody.

Long before this dispute, Dinabandhu one day requested his elder brother to recommend him to the Lieutenant-Governor for a Deputy Magistracy. Vidyasagar was in great difficulty as to how he should request the Governor for his own brother. He called on the latter several days, but could not give out his mind. At last, he said one day,—'I have been trying for several days to request you for something, but bashfulness always stands in the way, and

I cannot express my mind. The Governor was very curious to hear it. The more he pressed Vidyasagar for the request, the more he grew shy and could not give utterance to it, and on different pretexts left his friend's august presence. When he called again the next weekday, the Governor said to him,—'I will confine you today, unless you tell me your mind. Vidyasagar was now obliged to give out his brother's prayer. The Lieutenant-Governor said,—'Why have you been so much shy about it? Had you told me before, I could have given him one; there was a vacancy at Hooghly, *Very* good, I will see if there is still a vacancy, and let you know ere long." In the next week's Gazette appeared Dinabandhu's appointment as a Deputy Magistrate; he was posted to Barisal. About this time Vidyasagar was favourably disposed to Homoeopathic mode of treatment. He had had a great aversion for it before. In 1866, the illustrious homoeopathist, Dr. Berigni, had arrived at Calcutta. Doctor Rajendra Nath Datta of Bowbazar had already begun to learn the principles of Homoeopathy.

The two medical men, one a European and the other a native, being of the same turn of mind, formed an intimate friend-ship. The latter obtained great help from the former in the acquisition of his knowledge in the new mode of curing diseases, and soon rose to eminence. By this new method of treatment, doctor Rajendra Nath relieved Vidyasagar of his painful head-disease. The latter saw the wonderful curative properties of the homoeopathic drugs in the case of his friend, Raj Krishna, who had had a great costiveness of the bowels. Enema had had to be injected at short intervals, and even then the bowels would move very slowly, and eject bolus formed stony discharges; the rectum bled profusely. Allopathic and other modes of treatment had been tried for a long time, but without any effect Such a painful, incurable disease doctor Rajendra Nath cured marvellously by his new method. These two reliefs convinced Vidyasagar of the superiority of the efficacy of Homoeopathy over that of Allopathy.

Besides, he saw that. Homoeopathic medicines were cheaper, and their application far easier. He therefore devoted him; self to the study of the new science, and soon acquired a tolerable knowledge in it. He then began to treat simple cases himself according to this mode and experienced good results. He induced his second brother, Dinabandhu, to learn the new science and to relieve the sufferings of the diseased poor. It was he, who persuaded the famous Dr. Mahendra Lal Sarkar, the greatest Indian homoeopathist of the day, to try the efficacy of the new medicines. Dr. Sarkar was an eminent allopathist and had had a great aversion for the new science. One day, when he and Vidyasagar called together to see the Hon'ble Justice Dwarka Nath Mitter, who was confined to bed through illness, their conversation turned to Homoeopathy, and a great debate ensued between the two friends as to which of the sister sciences was superior. At last, Dr. Sarkar was obliged to say that he would *no* more condemn Homoeopathy, but would try and see if there was anything in it. He was a great scientist and had good inquisitive faculties. He soon found out the superior curable properties of the new medicines, and became a staunch follower of Homoeopathy. In a short time, he rose to great eminence, and surpassed in practice even Dr. Berigni, the founder of the homoeopathic treatment in India, who had consequently to return horns with an empty pocket.

About 6 or 7 years after this, Vidyasagar's youngest daughter was cured of a serious illness by homoeopathic treatment. Allopathy had been tried for a long time, but without success. Vidyasagar thus grew more zealous to learn the new science perfectly. He knew that medical science could not be acquired thoroughly without a knowledge of Anatomy. He therefore purchased a set of human skeleton, which he subsequently presented to his friend, Raj Krishna's son. He procured many homoeopathic, works, which are still to be found in his library. Besides these, his Library' contained a collection of a good many valuable books all beautifully bound and nicely arranged. He never allowed anybody to take away any book from his Library. Babu Nilambar Mukharji once asked him for some historical works to compile a history of India; Vidyasagar would not lend him the books from his Library. He purchased a newset and presented it to Nilambar Babu.

Some say that formerly the friends and acquaintances of Vidyasagar had free access to his Library, and they were at liberty to take away books to their homes occasionally. But subsequently, his mistrust arose from the conduct of one of his so-called friends, which compelled him to withdraw his permission to remove books from his Library. The so-called friend, alluded to above, once borrowed a valuable Sanskrit work from Vidyasagar and took it to his own home. After a time, when Vidyasagar asked him to return the book, the unscrupulous fellow at once replied, that he had returned it long since. The book was missing, and the owner was at a loss to account for its loss. It was a rare and valuable Sanskrit work procurable only in Germany. It was at that time out of print, and consequently there was no possibility of procuring a new one until it was reprinted. Fortunately, in a few days, a hawker of books, whom Vidyasagar had known for some time, came 'to him with the very missing book to sell. Vidyasagar was quite surprised to find it in the possession of the hawker, and asked him where he had got it from. The innocent peddler replied, that he had purchased it fromBabu (the name of the man who had borrowed the book`from Vidyasagar's Library). Vidyasagar was startled to hear the name, but he said nothing, and purchased the book from the hawker, giving him the price he demanded. From this time forward he was determined not to lend his books to any body.

It is said, that on one occasion a wealthy man of the city called on him when he was in his Library. The visitor was quite amazed at the sight of the beautiful binding of the books, and remarked;—'Sir, you must be crazed to spend so much money in getting these books bound from Europe?' Vidyasagar smiled, and after an interval of a few minutes said to the visitor;—'Your shawl is very nice, indeed; how much did it cost you?' The man quite forgetful of his own remarks and unconscious of Vidyasagar's tactics, replied most innocently, that the shawl was of real Banaras make, and cost him 500 rupees, and at the same time began admiring the qualities of the texture. Vidyasagar smiled and said:—'Why have you spent so large an amount on this shawl, when an ordinary blanket might keep you equally warm? What is the good of the valuable gold chain to fasten your watch with, when the purpose might be sufficiently served by a piece of strong thread? You are no less crazed than myself. The visitor was dumbfounded and could make no reply.

On his recovery from the injuries of his fall at Uttarpara, Vidyasagar first went to Chandernagore for a change, but the place being found to be uncongenial to his improvement, he left it for Burdwan, Burdwan was at that time one of the best sanitoriums in Bengal. The dangerous Malaria, which subsequently ravaged it, had not then set in, and people from different quarters resorted to it for renovation of their damaged health. At Burdwan, he put up with Babu Pyari Chand Mitra, who was then the Serishtadar of the local Judge's Court-office. Pyari Chand had married a sister of Vidyasgar's intimate friend, Syama Charan. Although he took a second wife after the death of the first, his love for his former brother-in-law did not lessen. He often visited the tetter's house, as formerly during the lifetime of his first wife. On one of these occasions, Syama Charan had introduced him to Vidyasagar, and the two had since formed a great friendship.

The people of Burdwan had already heard his name before, and some of them had knows Aim on his previous visits. The poor and the needy gathered round him, and he gave away his alms to the supplicants without distinction of caste and creed. A good many Musalmans are known to have been rescued by him from peril. During the period of his stay at Burdwan, he used at intervals to pay visits to Birsingha, and on those occasions, numerous poor and hungry children of the lower classes crowded about his palanquin. He gave alms to all of them; to some of them he presented sweatmeats; to some, pice and other coins; and to others he gave clothes. Whenever Vidyasagar's intended visit to a place was reported, people of different classes, male, female and children, crowded in the streets he was to pass through, to catch a glimpse of the face of the renowned, kind and benevolent Vidyasagar. In this connection, we will take the liberty to relate here an incident of his former life.

As Inspector of Schools he had once an occasion to go to a village in the interior of the Hooghly district to visit the school of that place. The local people had already heard his name, and were eager to get a sight of the great man. From ten o'clock in the morning, the houses near the school building began to be filled in with women. Every door, every window was crowded to suffocation. Those females who were rather advanced, in, age took their stands on the roofs of the houses; some of them even stood by the way side. Vidyasagar was a little late that day. It was past noon; the sun shone very hot on the heads of the spectators, but they did not mind it; they were too eagerly anxious to catch a glimpse of the Mysterious hero. At last, they were relieved of their suspense by a cheerful cry of 'There comes Vidyasagar.' The schoolboys sat in their places quietly; the teachers looked to their dresses, and heaved a deep breath. Vidyasagar passed by the way, but the female spectators could not see him, that is, could not distinguish him from his companions. We have already said, that our hero had acquired very simple habits of life. He was clothed in plain *Dhoti* and *Chadar,* his usual dress. At length, one of the aged women ventured to advance forward, and ask the foremost of the company;—'Where is Vidyasagar? Is he not come? The man replied,— Here is he of whom you speak,' pointing to Vidyasagar. The woman looked for a while at our hero's face with eyes dilated with wonder, and then said;— Ah! Indeed! Pooh! To see this Uriya bearer with a coarse *Chadar* we have scorched ourselves to death! He has neither a coach nor a watch, neither *Choga* nor *Chapkan*!' In fact, it was very difficult to distinguish him from ordinary poor people.

To resume the thread of our narrative. The reader has already been told that Vidyasagar was at this time heavily embarrassed with debts. His letter published in the Hindu Patriot, referred to above, showed that his debts amounted to some-thing between 20 and 22 thousand rupees. To clear some of these debts, he asked for a loan from the estate of the munificent Maharani Swarnamayi of Cossimbazar. We have said before, that Vidyasagar was intimately connected with the Cossimbazar Raj family, and used to borrow monies from the estate now and then, which he repaid at convenience. On the 4th November, 1869, he addressed to Rajib Lochan Ray, the Maharani's Pewan, a long letter to the following effect:

You are aware that I have been encumbered with debts on account of the widow marriage, movement, and I am clearing them by degrees. I owe somewhat heavy debts to two persons, who are unwilling to be paid off by instalments. They demand repayment of their entire amounts at a single instalment. I have no means, at present, to pay them off. I therefore ask the Maharani for a loan of 7,500 rupees. If she should be pleased to lend me the amount, I will execute a hand-note, agreeing to repay it in three years. I have not an iota of doubt that I shall be able to liquidate the debt Otherwise I would not have asked for the loan. Without your help, there is no chance of my success in this affair. You may assist me freely. Do not think that if you should aid me in this matter, you will have to meet with any inconvenience. I am not so mudi devoid of respect and worth that I should not care to liquidate the debt So long as Raja Pratap Chandra Sinha was living, I borrowed from him now and then, and paid him off by instalments. For the present, I happen not to have so much familiarity with any of the rich men here, that I may ask him for a loan. If you had not been where you are, i would not have ventured to request the Maharani for the loan. You must, please, be "kind enough to do your best for the success of my prayer. Other-wise I shall be put to great shame and humiliation. Please, consider this and do as you think proper. Unless I had been put to great inconvenience, 1 would not have vexed you and the Maharani. I want the money in the course of one month. If I am favoured with this debt, there will exist no necessity of awarding the regular annual grant-in-aid, I have received many benefits from the Maharani, which are always fresh in my memory. I shall show shortly that I appreciate her merits and that I bless her always.

'I am somewhat better now. I shall be glad to hear your own welfare and that of the Rajdhani. The Maharani gave the loan as prayed for, and the debtor repaid it at the end of his promised three years. When he sent the if they, Rajib Lochan had already been dead, an Vidyasagar remitted the money to the creditor herself with a covering letter to the following effect:

'To Maharani Swarnamayi,

C. I. E. Madam,

'It is long since that on account of a pressing necessity for money, the late most generous Dewan Rajib Lochan Ray very kindly favoured me under the permission of the Maharani, with a loan of 7,500 rupees, on condition of being repaid at convenience without any interest on it.

'Words cannot express how much I was benefited by this loan. This benefit will remain ever fresh in my memory. The Maharani is born to do good to humanity. Undoubtedly there are plenty of wealthy persons in the country, but none of them has been able to win the sincere gratitude and heartfelt blessings of the general public.

'I was much ashamed that I could not repay the debt for a long time, I have now got an opportunity of clearing it. I beg to enclose herewith Currency Notes for 7,500 rupees. Please, accept the money and release me from the debt.

Yours.

'Ishwar Chandra Sharma.'

It was not from Maharani Swarnamayi alone that he took loans. He borrowed from many other wealthy persons of the time. On one occasion, he took a loan of 25,000 rupees from a female member of the Paikpara Raj family. In 1876, he acknowledged this debt in the course of his deposition in the Chakdighi Will Case Dispute in Kumarganj,

These debts were incurred by him mostly on account of persons connected with widow marriage in the interior of the country. Vidyasagar himself admitted this in his letter to the Hindu Patriot. Not only was he heavily embarrassed for them, but he had also to encounter difficulties of different-sorts. In village Kumarganj under Thana Chandrakona in the Jehanabad Sub-Division of the Hooghly District, there was once a very disagreeable friction-between two parties, the 'one for, and the other against, widow marriage. Vidyasagar noted down in his own handwriting statements of the case. Some of these papers, which speak for themselves, are quoted below for the edification of the reader:

(A)

"A portion of the inhabitants of Comergonge, Thannah Chundrakonah in the Sub-Division of Jehanabad have formed themselves into a party to support the cause of the marriage of widows. This party having come to know that their opponents in the village would not permit them either to join with them in the worship of the idol *Shiva* or to offer a separate pooja themselves on the occasion of the Churrukpooja and apprehending a breach of the peace if they followed the latter course petitioned the Deputy Magistrate on the 25th Chait last for the aid of the Police. The requisite order on the Daroga of the Thannah was passed and at the solicitation of the petitioners the Amlah were directed to issue it on the same day, as the interval between that day and the date of the pooja was very short, namely 5 days. Enquiry was made at the Thannah every day whether the order in question had reached and a reply in the negative was invariably returned. On the 28th the applicants, being impatient for the arrival of the order, went again to Jehanabad, and the Deputy Magistrate being absent enquired of the Nazir about it and were told that the order had been duly despatched. They came back to the Thannah and learnt that it had not reached up to that time. Despairing of any assistance from the Police they began to negotiate with the leaders of the opposite party and it was settled that the former would be allowed to offer their pooja separately without any molestation. Relying upon the faith of their opponents they went to the Temple on the 30th to make their pooja and were beaten back with great violence. They came to the Thannah to lodge a complaint, but the Moonshee, the Daroga being absent, paid no attention to them, used harsh words and referred them to the Deputy Magistrate. They accordingly went to Jehanabad and lodged their complaint before that officer who made it over to the Moonsiff of the station for trial. The case is still pending.

"It has since been learnt from the Daroga that the order came to the Thannah after the 30th when the evil had already been done".

"The leaders of the opposite party observing the course taken by the widow marriage party became exasperated against them and waited upon the bona fide Zamindar of the village Baboo Shib Narain Roy who sent his men to apprehend and bring before him the men of the latter party. Those who were apprehended were at first severely beaten before the village community in all the public places of the village. They were next taken to the Zamindar, beaten again and fined and then dismissed on their promising to renounce all connection with the marriage of widows. Some of these men have returned to their homes, some have left them with their families, while others, afraid of the harsh treatment dealt out to their brethren in the cause, have followed the example of the latter and left their homes also.

"Two of the oppressed bolder than the rest repaired to Jehanabad and laid their complaint before the Deputy Magistrate, who for 4 days successively refused to take their petition.

It is notorious that Baboo Shib Narain Roy often calls on the Deputy Magistrate at an advanced hour of the night,"

(B)

"You may have by this time received the note I sent through Jamadar. After he left, I was writing to the Mooktear of Jehanabad, while Damoo, Sriharee, Nilcomal and Gopal were with me. Sreenibass Doss and his brother of our party rushed in and reported that the *Goallas* of the opposite party had severely beaten them. I told them to prepare to go to Jehanabad in order to lodge a complaint They accordingly went home and the 4 others followed them. When about to enter their house, the Goallas beat Sreenibass on the head with a *lattee.* The wound was deep and bleeding profuse and he fell senseless on the ground. His brother was also very severely beaten, Nilcomal's head has been fractured with a *lattee* and his side where there was a pain before was struck with 3 or 4 *lattees.* He lies insensible, frequently vomits, and does not open his eyes. His stomach is distended and his pulse flattering and there is very little hope of his life. Another has also been very severely beaten on the head. Nemaee, Prem Chund and Satrooghun have each received 10 or 12 strokes of the *lattee.* On receiving the news of the affray I went to the spot and saw a stream of blood. I have reported the matter to the Daroga through the Farreedar and the Barkundaj especially appointed for the preservation Of peace and I expect one of the officers of the Thannah by evening. Three of the Goallas have been apprehended and the rest have absconded".

(C)

I have not yet succeeded in getting any more widows married. Nor do I expect to succeed at all, if things do not mend. Baboo Shib Narain Roy of Jurul has been oppressing with impunity those of the Royots of his Talook Comergonge who belong to the widow marriage party. This news having reached the inhabitants of Pergonnas Burda and Chandrakona, those among them who are willing to marry their sons and daughters have fallen back, through fear of con-sequences, Shibnarain send, 10 or 12 Durwans to his Talook Comergunge with the order to bring before him forcibly, men of the widow-marriage party and while they are ushered into his presence they are dismissed with 10 strokes of shoes and a fine of 10 Rs. each. He also exacts a promise from them that they would in future renounce all connection with widow marriage. Several of them have left the village with their respective families. If a complaint is laid before the Darogah and Moonshee they do not perform their duty but on the contrary ridicule and abuse the complainants. When a complaint is made before the Deputy Magistrate, he issues orders against the repetition of the oppression but no subordinate officer moves in the matter, "I am intimate with a Police Amlah, who, on being hard pressed by me to explain this state of things, stated that he would do so on being assured that his name would not be made known. On my consenting to this condition he said you must not make any complaint before the Khan Bahadoor who has privately directed us not to render any- assistance to the widow marriage party but to endeavour to give them trouble if possible.

The party at Comergunge consisted of about 66 families, who with the exception of 4 or 5 families have been obliged to leave the party. If those, Who joined the cause at my solicitation and are suffering from their act, are not relieved and if the oppressors are not punished, I must leave the world, for what is the good of my remaining in it when there is no chance of success of the cause. I have resolved to devote my existence to it and if it fails, life would have no charm to me and existence would be useless".

Social Work in Burdwan

We have said before, that latterly Vidyasagar had to seek healthy places for renovation of his impaired health, and that he generally resorted to Burdwan, which was one of the best sanitoriums of the day. Vidyasagar had an old cook, by name Harakali Chaudhuri, who used to accompany his master in his sojourns. It is said, that one day, while at Burdwan, this Harakali reprehended a beggar woman, who had received alms from Vidyasagar in the shape of coins and cloth several times, for her impudence in coming to his master often for help. The kind-hearted Vidyasagar overheard this, and at once ordered retirement of the old servant on a monthly pension of two rupees. It is also said, that though the cook implored his master's dying from want of medical help. He heard that the Civil Surgeon in charge of the district had lent a cold ear to the pitiful cries of the poor. He informed government of the terrible state of things. He was not content with mere writing. He returned to Calcutta and interviewed Sir William Grey, the then Lieutenant Governor of Bengal on the subject, and caused temporary hospitals to be opened in different parts of the infected area, under the charge of able medical officers. He also caused the apathetic Civil Surgeon of Burdwan to be removed, and a sympathetic man posted in his place. He then came back to Burdwan, and applied himself in right earnest to relieve the afflicted of their miseries.

In his own private dispensary he made provisions not only for the supply of medicines and diet to the sufferers but also money in cash for the food of the convalescent and the unaffected poor, without distinction of caste or creed. He provided them also with clothes, which cost him nearly 2,000 rupees. He was moved to all these acts of benevolence not by any desire for a name or fame, but simply by the impulse of his naturally kind heart. Yet the Hindu Patriot and other leading periodicals of the time spoke of him in highly complimentary terms and gave him loud cheers.

In this work of love and charity, he was greatly aided by doctor Ganga Naryan Mitra, a medical practitioner nephew of Pyari Chand Mitra. Ganga Narayan was placed in sole charge of Vidyasagar's OF dispensary. The fearful epidemic grew every day more and more serious and caused a great havoc among the people. The number of patients attending Vidyasagar's dispensary daily rose by leaps and bounds, as here they ever supplied with food and pice, besides free medicine. Latterly, the number of patients rose so high, that Ganga Narayan asked his principal to be permitted to give Cinchona instead of pure Quinine, as the latter was much more costly than the former. But Vidyasagar did not approve of the plan. He said that the lives of the rich and the poor were equally valuable, and should be taken care of equally. He insisted on the use of Quinine, however costly it might be. He looked after the poor sufferers from hut to hut, and when he saw that the diseased was too feeble to walk to the dispensary, he made the medical officer attend the patient at his own hut, and he himself carried the medicine for him. He thus saved numbers of poor people from imminent death, who, but for his kind care and charities, would certainly have died. We have said before, that Pyari Chartd Mitra and Vidyasagar were intimate friends. On the former's death, the latter treated his family with the same tenderness and affection. Pyasi Chand's first son, Babu Khetra Nath Mitra is at present a Munsiff, and his youngest son, Avinas Chandra Mitra, is Serishtadar of the Judge's Court at Bard wan. His son-in-law, Babu Giris Chandra Basu, is the managing proprietor of the Bangabasi College at Calcutta. Vidyasagar loved Giris Chandra most dearly. The two families are still in very good terms of friendship.

Although Burdwan had lost its former salubrity of climate, it was all these attractions and his former love of the place that made Vidyasagar visit it now and then. The people of Burdwan knew him too well to forget him. Whenever he alighted at the platform *pi* the Railway Station, the poor surrounded him on all sides, as they were sure to get from him something. On one of these occasions, a poor, ragged, little boy with a pale countenance approached our noble hero and begged him for a pice.

The lad's fleshless body and wan face moved him to compassion. Besides, the sorrowful, pale countenance of the beggar boy had something of a peculiar illumination in it. Vidyasagar was a little curious about him, and began to talk with him in rather familiar tones. He said,—' Suppose, I give you four pice.' The boy did not know Vidyasagar personally, and he thought naturally that the man was jesting. He said,—'No use of joke, sir; kindly give me a pice.' Our hero replied, 'This is no joke; if I do give you four pice, what would you do?' The boy said.—' I would lay out two pice in buying something to eat, and give the other two pice to my mother. Vidyasagar then said,—'And if I give you two annas?' The bay now thought, that the man was really making fun of him, and was about to recede, when Vidyasagar caught hold of his arms, and said,—'Now tell me the truth, what would you then do?' The poor boy's eyes were now full of tears, which trickled down his breast; he said,—'In that case, I should buy rice for four pice and give the rest to my mother, for that will defray our expenses for an-other day.' Vidyasagar again asked him,—'And if I give you four annas?' The boy was still in the hold of our hero; he had no means of escape, unless and until he answered the question. He there-fore replied,—'I would reserve two annas to cover our expenses for two days, and the other two annas I would lay out in purchasing mangoes. I shall sell them for four annas; that will again defray our expenses for two days and serve me to have a capital of two annas, which I might lay out *in* dealing in mangoes, and thus manage to feed my mother and myself for some days.' Vidyasagar was greatly touched by the tale, and gave him a rupee. The boy bounded away highly de-lighted. About two years after this, Vidyasagar again went to Burdwan. As he was about to enter the shop of a former acquaintance near the Station, a stout and strong boy advanced and saluted him, and then said,—'Would you please, sir, come and take your seat in my shop.' Vidyasagar was taken by surprise, and he asked the youth,—'Who are you; why should I go to your shop?' The boy said with tears in his eyes,—"About two years ago, I begged you for a pice; you kindly gave me a rupee. Out of that rupee, I bought rice for two annas, and laid out the remaining fourteen annas in dealing in mangoes. I made a little profit by selling them. By degrees I had a small stock, and I have now, turned a chapman of petty miscellaneous articles. Would you, please, come and have a look into my shop". Vidyasagar then recollected the little incident of two years back. He blessed the youth and accompanied him to his shop, to his great satisfaction.

Even when so busily engaged in his labour of love at infected Burdwan, his own health completely broken down, he never forgot his literary work. Here he composed his *Bhranti-Vilasa,* compiled from Shakspeare's "Comedy of Errors". The language of the book is sweet, melodious, and humorous. What wonderful powers of translation did Vidyasagar possess. How beautifully he has clothed foreign language and ideas in his native dress, and made them peculiarly his own! The plot of the Comedy of Errors is rather complex. In spite of this difficulty, he has so nicely narrated it in his *Bhranti- Vilas,* that the excellent humour displayed in the original has not lost its force in the translation. To say the truth, *Bhranti- Vilasa* is an excellent novel in Bengali. The readers of Lamb's Tales of Shakspeare are well aware how difficult it is to turn a play into a novel. This difficult task has been very nicely accomplished by Vidyasagar, He has displayed the same skilfulness of attractive express-Jon in his compilation of the *Bhranti- Vilasa,* that he has displayed in compiling the *Sitar Vanavasa* from Bhababhuti's excellent drama, the "Uttara-Charita". If Vidyasagar had favoured us with some more translations of Shakspeare's plays, the Bengali language would surely have attained far greater improvement.

It is said, that Vidyasagar finished the composition of this book in 15 days, during which he wrote for a quarter of an hour every day before going to dinner. It must be said that fortunately for the country Vidyasagar gave up Mathematics as a dry subject, and applied himself to the study of Shakspeare with his friend, Arianda Krishna. If he had not done so, how could the readers of Bengali ever expect to get such an excellent translation of the great poet of the world? The same was the case with Macaulay, He also thought Mathematics dry and insipid, and paid greater attention to Literature. Had he not done so, most probably the world would have been deprived of his numerous excellent literary works. It may consequently be deduced that God opens to men of talents their ways of work according to their respective natural propensities.

The *Bhranti-Vilasa* was the last of his schoolbooks. All such books that he wrote were printed and published in his lifetime, with the exception of two, the *Basudeva-Charita,* noticed before, and the *Ramer Rajyabkisheka* (Corronation of Rama). The last-named book was under print in 1869, and only six forms of It had been printed, when Vidyasagar was told that another book bearing the same name by Sasi Bhushan Chattopadhyay had already appeared. He, therefore, stopped the publication of his book. Sasi Bhushan once said to one of his friends:—"After my *Ramer Rajyabhisheka* had been published, Vidyasagar one day personally called at the Press where the book had been printed, and purchased a copy of it. I was not then present at the Press. When I came to the Press and heard of it, I at once ran to the Sanskrit Press Depository with a copy of my book. I met Vidyasagar there. I saluted him, and presented him with the copy. He smiled, and said;—'I have already bought a copy of your book. Very good, I accept your present. The book has been nicely got up".

The six forms already printed show that the language of Vidyasagar's book is more concise and refined. The same beautiful language, the same vigorous flow of style, and the same nice arrangement of thoughts and expressions are found here as in his "Sitar Vanabasa". Of course, it must be admitted that the Bengali language has nowadays taken a different course; but there was a time, when Vidyasagar's language was the best-model—when writers of Bengali imitated his style.

Pyari Chand Mitra, under the pseudonym of Tek Chand Thakur, wrote his books in an easy, provincial style, and tried to turn the course of the Bengali language into a different channel; but he failed to leave a standing landmark for the succeeding generation of authors to follow. It was the talented writer Bankim Chandra Chatarji that succeeded in giving the Bengali language a new shape, which he formed by a combination of the styles of Vidyasagar and Tek Chand. *As* the chemical combination of two substances of different attributes produces quite a new substance, so by the combination of the two different styles of Vidyasagar and Tek Chand, Bankim Chandra has given birth to a new style. At the present time, this style is imitated in most cases, though endeavours are being made in some quarters to give it a still newer shape, by casting it in Bankim Chandra's mould, but, at the same time, adding to it something more. The language of the Tagores of the present day might be mentioned by way of illustration. The Bengali language is, no doubt, under change, and there is no certainty what form it will ultimately take; but whatever shape it may take, it will always recall Vidyasagar with sentiments of profound veneration, and the writers of Bengali will ever be under a deep debt of, obligation to him and pay homage to his feet, in as much as the Bengali language, however shaped, must bear some shade of the elegance and beauty of the great writer's style.

The Bengali *laxigitage* has its origin in Sanskrit. As a matter of Consequence, the inflexion of gender and other changes are formed in accordance with the rules *of* the mother tongue. But in most cases, the practice is at present being deviated from. Banking Chandra's language Shows that in sortie cases he has strictly followed Sanskrit in the inflexion of his words, while in others he has quite deviated from it.

This deviation is almost general with most of the authors of the present day, with the honourable exception of the very able and thoughtful writer, Kali Prasanna Ghosh of Dacca. Some are still of opinion, that Bengali should follow its mother language in the inflexion of gender and other changes, and a deviation from it would make it incorrect. Its the correct use of the inflexions, Kali Prasanna Ghosh has no equal.

But the modern writers of Bengal do not like to bind themselves to follow Sanskrit in every respect. In fine, *the* Bengali language, like the English, is under change. But we must repeat again, that however alteration it might undergo in shape, beauty, or *melody*, it most always remain deeply indebted to Vidyasagar. It will not be an easy thing to discard him altogether; his framework most unavoidably be taken up.

6

Contribution to Literature and Journalism

Ishwar Chandra Vidyasagar was an innovator in the fields of literature and journalism also. His original contributions to Bengali literature were not many; he was mainly a maker of modern Bengali prose. He was never directly in journalism, but he actively helped in promoting and running many important Bengali and English periodicals of his time. Of these the most notable were the Bengali Somprokash and the English Hindu Patriot. He also took a keen interest in modern press and printing, and many will be surprised to learn that the great Pandit, as a printer and publisher, modernised Bengali printing typography and composition. In all this he showed the qualities of a typical renaissance scholar and man.

Most of the Bengali works of Vidyasagar are translations, adaptations and textbooks. The type of work chosen reveals the purpose of his writing. A maker of Bengali prose, he was naturally concerned much with the raw materials of a written language still in its infancy. The father of modem Bengali literature, Bankim Chandra Chatterji, wrote of Vidyasagar's contribution to Bengali language and literature (translated from Bengali): "It is said that Rammohan Roy is the first maker of modern Bengali prose. After

Rammohan, Bengali prose set out developing differently from the spoken language of the people In course of time these two streams of development took on different names. One was called Sadhu bhasa or the pure language, and the other. Kathya bhasa or the spoken language. Sadhu bhasa means the language of 'puritans' or the 'pandits.' This pandit's language was obviously more Sanskritic, and it was used first by our great Pandit Ishwar Chandra Vidyasagar and Akshay Kumar Dutta. Its first modern orientation came from these two great scholar-writers of Bengal. Their prose, though Sanskritic in quality, was not very stiff and incomprehensible, specially, the language that Vidyasagar wrote was as sweet a's it was charming. As far as I knew, no one before Vidyasagar, and none even after him, could write such elegant and graceful Bengali prose as he did".

Rabindranath Tagore's tribute to Vidyasagar on this point was more eloquent than that of his great predecessor. He says in his Vidyasagar-Chant (translated from Bengali): "Vidyasagar's greatest achievement is the Bengali language. If Bengali language is ever enriched with literary wealth and beauty, if it can command equal respect with the other great languages of the world as the eternal fountainhead of noble thoughts, then alone this great achievement of Vidyasagar will be crowned with the glory it deserves.

"Vidyasagar was the first creative artist of modern Bengali prose. It is true that Bengali prose set out on its literary career before him, but he was the first writer who showed us the way of using the Bengali language artistically. Before him our language was like an undisciplined mob, beyond the writer's control. He brought it under control and imposed a new discipline on it by properly arranging the words, classifying them into different orders, relating sound with sense, making their movement easy-flowing and enhancing considerably their usefulness. After the great pioneering work of Vidyasagar, many a commander of Bengali literature is now able to lead the disciplined army of words triumphantly into ever-new realms of knowledge. But the glory of these innovations should be first ascribed to him who made them possible by bringing the language under the control of the artists.

"Vidyasagar was the first Bengali prose-writer to introduce marks of punctuation, like the comma and the semicolon into the Bengali language. When this was done, a new era dawned in the life of the language, which had been nothing before but an inarticulate mass of incoherent words. The language, static before, became dynamic.

"Vidyasagar freed Bengali prose from the shackles of Sanskritic influence Bengali words were given new shapes and meanings by adding appropriate prefixes and suffixes to them and changing their pattern of composition A new syntax emerged, and the language, by a sudden stroke of magic, as it were, became easily susceptible to all forms of expression Its usefulness grew immensely. Many Bengali words were purged of their colloquial impurities, as well as of superfluous Sanskritic ornamentation He tried to bring in a harmony of sound between the words in a sentence, to give it a cadence and make it flow uninterruptedly. Thus Bengali prose was made elegant and graceful, and a suitable vehicle of modern thought. It was Vidyasagar who rescued the Bengali language from the clutches of uncultured scholarship and folk-vulgarism, and lifted it to the level of the most civilised Aryan languages of the world This work alone can be given as one of the noblest achievements of Vidyasagar, and as something calling forth a man's whole-hearted effort and energy in this direction".

We shall add to the above another passage from Rabindranath Tagore's Jivan Smriti (recollections). Vidyasagar wrote a Bengali Primer, Varna-parichay, in 1855 —the first primer of its kind in Bengali based on modern methods of teaching This Varna-parichay has ruled Bengal for about one hundred years, when every Bengali child, on his first initiation into reading and writing has had to read it. Vidyasagar is known to everyone in Bengal as the writer of this Vcona-parichay priced about two annas, and then only as a great social reformer. It is about a primary lesson in this Vatna-parichay that Rabindranath has given his impressions as a child He says:

> "It was the first verse of the First Poet that I came across in my life. I had then just swum across the sea of simple spellings like kara and khala and reached the shore Then I read Jal pathay, pata narhay. I can

> still vividly recollect what a delightful sensation these two simple rhyming words produced in my mind' I felt, and also realised for the first time in my Life, the tremendous potentiality this rhyming had in poetry. It is for this rhyme that a poet s 'say' does not end with his 'words. The words vibrate, and through the ears react on the mind. This strange experience I had when I read these two lines, and I felt their throbbing in my consciousness. I was feeling within myself the atmosphere of it and it seemed as if the rams were falling and the leaves were rustling around me".

With the opening of the 19th century and the Fort William College in 1800, it may be said that the beginnings of modern Bengali prose could be discerned. The English civilians sent from England to rule this country were required to learn the Bengali language at this College (Bengal being then the chief centre of the British administration). Under the celebrated Baptist Missionary, William Carey, the Head of the Department of Bengali Language and Literature, in the College, a group of Bengali pandits was appointed to teach the language to foreigners.

But suitable textbooks for beginners were hardly available at that time. Mr. Carey wrote in 1801 to Dr. Ryland of Serampore that he made Ram Basu compose a history of a King (Raja Pratapaditya Charitrd) which was "the first prose book ever written in the Bengali language". Among other Bengali pandits called on to write suitable Bengali prose texts under Carey's supervision, Mrityunjay Vidyalankar, Golokenath Sharma, Tarinicharan Mitra and Chandicharan Munshi are notable. These early attempts at prose-writing are worthy of notice only historically, and not as something of real literary value. Most of this prose stuff was an odd mixture of colloquial, spoken and panditi or Sanskritic language. One Bengali pandit alone, Mrityunjay Vidyalankar, could reach the nearest standard of readable Bengali prose, but he had not the ability to make it a suitable vehicle of modern thought.

It was left to Rammohan Roy to do the spade work for it. Bengali prose, in his hands, turned into a weapon of social controversy. He fought against the orthodox supporters of idolatry, polytheism and concremation of Hindu widows, mainly with the weapon of Bengali prose. Besides his Bengali polemical writings, he translated some Sanskrit Upanishads for the first time into Bengali. In spite of these pioneering efforts, he could not bring the prose syntax and vocabulary under perfect control. The movement, or the essential rhythm of prose, was lacking in his writings Later in the thirties, in the hands of the Rev. Krishna Mohan Banerji and others of the Young Bengal group, Bengali prose did not make much progress beyond the standard set by Rammohan. It was mainly owing to the Anglicised attitude of the Young Bengal group that Bengali prose could not make any headway.

In the forties, with the advent of the Tattwabodhini Sabha and the Tattwabodhini Patrika under the leadership of Maharshi Debendranath Tagore, the two giants of early Bengali prose, Pandit Ishwar Chandra Vidyasagar and Akshay Kumar Dutta, stepped into the field. Writings on a variety of subjects like history, philosophy, religion, ethics, science, literature, economics and sociology were encouraged and regularly published in the paper. This venture of writers into unexplored regions of knowledge gave a tremendous impetus to the development of Bengali prose in the forties and fifties of the last century. Akshay Kumar Dutta, the first editor of Tattwabodhini Patrika, made a significant contribution by his powerful prose-writings. But the most significant of all contributions in this era was that of Vidyasagar.

Whether in his polemical writings on widow remarriage, polygamy, child marriage and other subjects, or in his textbooks, translations and adaptations, the Pandit was always set on reforming the prose drastically by making it free alike from the shackles of Sanskritic conservatism and rustic vulgarism. Being the first conscious artist in Bengali prose, he was highly aware of his historic responsibility for making the language the most suitable medium of expression for the creative artists and scientists in Bengali literature.

After him, the advent of the age of Bankim Chandra and Bangadarsan was a matter of course. The writings of Vidyasagar provided the needed stimulus to modern Bengali prose-writing, which was staited simultaneously with him by Bankim Chandra and his Bangadarsan, and was later carried over by Rabindranath Tagore through the 19th to the 20th century.

Vidyasagar was never a journalist in the sense that he never took to journalism as a profession during his life. But he was directly and indirectly associated with a number of papers and periodicals, of which the most notable were Tattwabodhini Patrika, Sarvashubhakary Patrika, Somprokash and Hindu Patriot. Tattwabodhini Patrika and Somprokash were the most influential Bengali periodicals of their time, and they dominated the Bengali literary scene in the latter half of the 19th century. Sarvashubhakary, although socially important, lasted for a few months only. The Hindu Patriot was an English paper, the most important mouthpiece of educated Bengalis. Its famous editors were Harish Chandra Mukherji of anti-indigo-planters movement fame and the nationalist leader, Kristodas Pal For sometime, in the most crucial period of its existence, it was placed under Vidyasagar's guidance and management This sums up Vidyasagar's journalistic ventures and connections.

Since the commencement of the Tattwabodhini Patrika in 1843, Vidyasagar was closely associated with it till almost the last days of his life. He had been a member of the Paper Committee, which was a kind of an Editorial Board, empowered to edit and select the articles for the paper, including those of the editor himself In this Committee an opportunity arose for Akshay Kumar, the first editor of the Patrika, to come into contact with Vidyasagar and to have his prose edited regularly by him Besides his own writings, Vidyasagar's greatest contribution to Tattwabodhini Patrika was his influence on its editor. Akshay Kumar became in due course the most formidable rival of Vidyasagar in this field, and none was more pleased to welcome this fact than Vidyasagar himself for the good of Bengali literature.

Vidyasagar, in collaboration with one of his friends. Pandit Madan Mohan Tarkalankar, brought out the Bengali periodical Sarvashubhakary Patrika in August, 1850 The editor of this paper was one Matilal Chattopadhyay, but the real sponsors were the two Pandits. It appears from the contents of the paper that Vidyasagar's intention was to bring out a Bengali journal devoted whole-heartedly to the cause of social reform Only a few numbers of this periodical came out, and it ceased publication within a year. In spite at its brief existence it has a place in Bengali journalism because of its emphasis on social and educational reform.

His next venture in this field was Somprokash, published in 1858 The editor of the paper was his friend and colleague, Pandit Dwarkanath Vidyabhushan. It was first projected by Vidyasagar, and there is reason to believe that the first number was entirely written by him. After sometime he fell ill and made over the paper to Pandit Dwarkanath under those management, and with Vidyasagar's support, the paper attained the foremost place among Bengali newspapers. Tattwabodhini Patrika had many limitations, of which the biggest was its religious affiliations to Brahmoism, a considerable portion of its writings being religious in content. Somprokash had no such limitations and it was therefore freer in dealing courageously with contemporary social, political and cultural problems Somprokash proved a great success in the field of sociopolitical Bengali journalism.

As an English organ of the educated Bengali community, the Hindu Patriot commanded unique respect and exercised a tremendous influence over all sections of people in those days From the high government official down to the ordinary English-educated Bengali clerk, everyone read this paper with interest and valued its views. Although it had consistently preached the typical middle-class views of class-collaboration between English rulers and Indian subjects, between landlords and ryots, it provided a platform to the educated middle class to speak out their grievances and plead for their special privileges; as such, it helped in the spread of early political consciousness among the middle class in Bengal, particularly the educated section.

About Vidyasagar's connection with the Hindu Patriot, Mr. C E Buckland says in his Bengal under the Lieutenant-Governors: "When Harish Chandra Mukherji, the founder of the Hindu Patriot, died on the 14th June, 1861, its new proprietor Babu Kali Prasanna Sinha, after managing it at a loss for some time, made it over to Pandit Ishwar Chandra Vidyasagar, who invited Kristodas Pal to take the editorial charge in 1861, and subsequently transferred the proprietorship in July, 1862, to a body of trustees. They made over the management to Kristodas Pal, so that from 1861 to the time of his death he was in charge, and raised the paper to a position of influence and pecuniary prosperity".

Vidyasagar was intimate with Kaliprasanna Sinha, and he had love and regard for Harish Chandra, the founder-editor of the Hindu Patriot. When the charge of the paper was made over to Vidyasagar, he looked out for a talented young man who could be entrusted with the editorial task of the paper. Kristodas Pal was at the time employed as a clerk in the office of the British Indian Association. He caught the eye of the Pandit and was selected for the post. He speedily rose to eminence. We do not know for certain whether Vidyasagar had any idea of giving any positive, ideological shape to the paper when he selected young Kristodas for the editor's post. From the circumstances in which he chose the young clerk Kristodas, he would appear to have had some idea of the sociopolitical role which the paper might play in the young man's hands under his guidance. But the man chosen was found to be growing closer to the moderate upper-class politics of the British Indian Association. This disillusioned Vidyasagar about the future of the paper, and he decided to transfer it to the management of trustees.

This, in brief, was Vidyasagar's contribution to journalism in Bengal. Without being a professional journalist himself and without enacting any direct role on the stage, he rendered signal service to the cause of both Bengali and English journalism in Bengal from behind the stage. Tattwabodhini Patrika and Somprokash, the two outstanding Bengali periodicals of the 19th century, owed much of their prominence and influence to the versatility of Vidyasagar's genius. The English periodical, Hindu Patriot, commanding great influence over the educated Bengali middle class, owed its existence for some time to the Pandit's generosity, and its revival with new life and energy to his vision.

We turn to the least known and the most significant of Vidyasagar's contributions to the promotion of modern knowledge, the science and art of printing and publishing. As a true "humanist" renaissance scholar, Vidyasagar took a profound interest in the Sanskrit classics, in the hunt for old and lost manuscripts and in getting them copied, as well as in the technique of modern printing and publishing as a powerful weapon for the diffusion of modern knowledge. The great pandit and social reformer was also one of our pioneer printers and publishers.

Borrowing about Rs. 600 from a friend, he set up at Calcutta about the year 1847 the Sanskrit Press, jointly with Pandit Madan Mohan Tarkalankar. Being a writer himself, he soon set cut publishing his own books as also of some of his friends. A bookshop, the Sanskrit Press Depository, was also started, and it grew into a very profitable concern. Not only the Publishing House and the bookshop, but also the Sanskrit Press became leading concerns in Calcutta Vidyasagar had to depend almost entirely upon this press and publications for his living after his retirement from public service.

This is not all his interest in the technical side of printing was great It grew out of the difficulties in Bengal printing-typography that he had to face. The problem was the handling of the large number of separate Bengali types in the press, particularly their scientific placing in the type-case and juxtaposition in composition. Bengali composition requires about 500 separate boxes for type-setting. Vidyasagar expended much of his energy on devising the simplification of this complicated Bengali printing-typography. Bengali, press-workers have remembered this contribution of Vidyasagar to printing-craft by giving the name "Vidyasagar Sort" to his simplified arrangement of Bengali printing types, a great technical contribution of his days.

First Great Effort

Shortly after he had entered into the service of the Fort William College, Vidyasagar was asked by the authorities of the institution to write good, readable books in Bengali prose for the use of the students of the College, who were European-would-be civilians, as the reader has already been told In compliance with this request, he wrote the "Vasudeva Charita". It was compiled from the *Srimad Bhagabata,* a religious book of the Hindus in Sanskrit. It was not exactly a *verbatim* translation throughout. Some portions of the original were left out altogether, here and there the sense only was taken, and only a portion of the original text was literally translated. Considering the nice style, choice diction, and beautiful, easy, flowing language of the "Vasudeva-Charita", it must be said, that it very nearly approaches an original composition. It may be taken as a good model of Bengali prose. Unfortunately for the Hindu readers of Bengal, the "Basudeva Charita" was not approved of by the authorities of the Fort William College, and was, therefore, not published. The book treats of *Sri Krishna,* trying to demonstrate him to be a bodily incarnation of the Supreme Deity,

In the Vasudeva-Charita, the *Itlas* (sports) of Sri Krishna have been fully described. Every page, nay every line, of the book has been devoted to divine manifestation. Vidyasagar of course thought, that though the book treated of Sri Krishna as an incarnation of God, the authorities would not hesitate to accept it as a text book for the Civilians, on the consideration that it was only a translation, and not an original composition. To say the truth, although the work was the fruit of Vidyasagar's first attempts at Bengali composition, yet it was undoubtedly a good, readable book for the Bengali-reading Civilians, on account of its beauty of style, sweetness of language, perspicuity of expression, and proper arrangement of thoughts.

Prior to this, no Bengali book in prose had ever been written in such chaste, correct, easy, idiomatic language. No doubt, many Sanskrit pundits had, before this, written books in Bengali prose for the use of the students of the Fort William College, but none of them were worth realing. On the contrary, most of them were not at all readable for the worthlessness of their language.

Several of the Vernacular teachers of the Fort William College had also compiled Bengali books for the use of the College students. Of these Babu Ramram Basu had written the "Pratapaditya-Charita," a prose work, its language was quite worthless. Pandit Mrityunjay Vidyalankar had written the "Prabodha-Chanbut drika". In addition to these, Mr. Cary, a European Christian missionary, had compiled an Anglo-Bengali grammar and dictionary. The grammar is now rare, but the dictionary is still extant. Besides the above, there were many Bengali prose books written by other authors contemporaneously with, or prior to, the "Vasudeva-Charita,' but none of them could approach it in elegance of style, correctness of language, or sweetness of expression.

Such easy, chaste Bengali, as is found in sagar's "Vasudeva-Charita," is not generally to be met with in any other book written by Sanskrit pundits save Vidyasagar himself. It cannot, there-fore, be said that those, who have a knowledge of Sanskrit, must invariably write good Bengali. Raja Ram Mohan Ray, Raja Rajendra Lal Mitra, and Rev. K. M. Banerji had a considerable knowledge of the Sanskrit language. They made no small amount of attempts for the culture and development of the Bengali prose. They rendered no inconsiderable extent of help for the improvement of the Bengali language. For this, their names ought to be respectfully cherished in the memory of every native of Bengal, equally with that of Vidyasagar, But even the language of these notable authors could not approach that of Vidyasagar in easy flow, chasteness, correctness, and elegance of style.

Raja Ram Mohan Ray had died at Bristol on the 27th September, 1833, at the age of 61, when Vidyasagar was still a scholar in the Sanskrit College. Raja Rajendra Lala Mitra and Rev. K. M. Banerji, devoted themselves to the cultivation and development of the Bengali language, contemporaneously with Vidyasagar. Both of them 'were well versed in English. K. M. Banerji had ' forsaken the religion of his forefathers, and converted himself a Christian. The devotion of these two men to Bengali is really admirable. K. M. Banerji died in 1884, at the good old age of 85 years, and Rajendra Lala Mitra died in 1891, at the age of 70. For some time Vidyasagar and Rajendra Lala had been intimately and closely connected; but after a review by Vidyasagar of the working of the "Wards' Institution," of which Rajendra Lala was superintendent, they separated. Vidyasagar had only a familiar acquaintance with K. M. Banerji, but they were not intimate friends. For the sake of ready reference and comparative review of the language of these writers, we will quote a little from each of them.

The works of these notable authors surely teach us many substantial, important things, and they are mostly free from grammatical errors; but there can be no doubt that their language is some-what unintelligible for want of perspicuity and plainness. On account of the unusual lengthiness of their sentences, and improper, confused arrangement of expressions, their language has failed to be melodious and attractive. In trying to imitate the English manner of expression, it has become difficult to understand.

Of these three, the language of Ram Mohan Ray is hardly intelligible; while that of Rajendra Lal Mitra is somewhat better, but less inteligible than that of K. M. Banerji, whose language is plainer than that of the other two, though not very easy to understand. In Vidyasagar's "Vasudeva-Charita" and other subsequent works, there is an abundant use of long compound words and sentences in imitation of Sanskrit, but these words and sentences have been so nicely and properly chosen and arranged, that they never read harsh or jarring, On the contrary, they sound in the ear like sweet, harmonious music, and reach the very core of the heart, making it dance in merriment. Although his manner of expression is not much varied, yet it is not dully monotonous. It must be admitted, that he had a great command over his language. He could elevate or lower it at pleasure, according to the seriousness or otherwise of his subject. The use of useless or meaningless words is hardly to be found in his writings. He applied his epithets with distinctness and certainty. He used his words with such precision and adaptability to the subject of discourse, that it is very difficult to replace them by other words and sentences without marring the exact meaning intended to be conveyed by them. Even his first book, the "Vasudeva-Charita", abounds with illustrations of this wonderful power of Vidyasagar.

We have already noticed, that before Vidyasagar was made to write his "Vasudeva-Charita", many other writers had written books in Bengali prose, and attempted at the development of the language. Gary, Marshman, and some other notable Christian missionaries were among their number.

Besides Carey, Marshman, and other missionaries, many European civilians and talented natives of Bengal made admirable attempts at the development of the Bengali language. They wrote and published many books, newspapers, and periodicals in Bengali, Newspapers and periodicals will be dealt with afterwards. Here we will confine ourselves to the discussion of some of the easier books, that had helped the growth of the Bengali language, and, by comparison, try to show the immense superiority of Vidyasagar's composition.

In 1778, Halhead, a European Civilian, published a Bengali grammar. At that time, there was no printing press in this country. Charles Wilkins, a friend of Halhead's, cut out the Bengali letters on wood, and then moulded from them a set of types, with his own hands. Halhead's grammar was then printed with these types. In 1793, Forster, a European, translated into Bengali all the law-books, which had been collected by the then Governor-general, Lord Cornwallis. In 1799, Marshson, Ward and some other Christian missionaries settled down at Serampore, and set up a printing press there. They formed and prepared Bengali, Devnagri and other vernacular types; and, with these, they printed Bengali, Sanskrit, Hindi, Uriya and other vernacular versions of the Bible. Kirttiabas's *Ramayan,* Kasidas's *Mahabharat,* and some other ancient Bengali works also were printed at this press, and sold at a cheap price.

Vidyasagar's abilities to contribute to the development of the Bengali prose were displayed in his very first translation. He did not, in the beginning, attempt at original composition. His early writings were all translations, which served gradually to strengthen his powers of composition, and make him so famous an author. The "Vasudeva-Charita", although only a translation, is not wholly wanting in proofs of his creative genius. Vidyasagar was the first to show the way how to compose translations in chaste, plain, easy, graceful language. But, at the same time, it must be admitted, to his credit, that the language and style of his subsequent translations and original compositions are more refined and elegant than those of the "Vasudeva-Charita". It is obvious, that the difference between the language of this his first translation and that of his subsequent writings is exactly similar to the difference between the language of Johnson's first English translation, the "Voyage to Abyssinia," and that of the latter's subsequent prose works.

However much progress and development the Bengali language may attain, it must always remain highly indebted to Vidyasagar as its pioneer. His style, and arrangement of words and sentences, are peculiar by his own, and bear the appearance of newness at all times. Even when he has made a literal translation, there is no lack of beauty and grace in it.

He, who can express his many thoughts and ideas in the fewest possible words, is reckoned to be a powerful writer. He, who is expert in the choice of words, particularly suitable and determinate in their signification, and can use them properly, is admired as a good author. He, who rarely expresses the same thoughts more than once, is considered to be a skilful writer.

There can be no doubt, that Vidyasagar was an author of this class, as can be easily perceived from the language of his translations, as well as, original compositions. Babu Akshay Kumar Datta's skilfulness in translation and his manner of expression are not less admirable. Akshay Kumar Babu's language is nearly equal to that of Vidyasagar in correctness of grammar and style, but is far inferior to it in variety of expression. It is rather monotonous.

In spite of all these qualities, however, Vidyasagar's "Vasudeva-Charita," was rejected by the authorities of the Fort William College, for which we have found cause to be deeply sorry. We are sorry, not because the Europeans did not approve of it, but because the Hindus have been deprived of its invaluable instructions, in as much as it was not printed, as we have already said. We are deeply sorry, because never more did Vidyasagar exercise his powerful pen and fertile genius in that direction. He never more tried to write another book on the sound principles of Hindu religion. Had he only the inclination, he could have written many instructive books for the guidance of the Hindus in this age of degeneration. If he had had that inclination, he could easily have shown it in his "Sitar Banavas," one of his best productions. It is said, that in his later years, Vidyasagar intended publishing his "Vasudeva-Charita"; but the manuscript was then missing; he could not find it. After his death, his son, Narayana Babu found it, but quite worn out. No date or year is to be found in it. Most probably it was written sometime between 1842 and 1847.

Printing Press and Bookshop

Vidyasagar's retirement from public service was productive of incalculable good to the country. He had so long been chained down by the fetters of thraldom. As a lion when confined in a cage can not display its powers, so Vidyasagar had been incapacitated by his servitude from unfolding his abilities to their full extent. He now discovered fresh fields of action. He found ample opportunities *to* do a good turn both to his countrymen and to himself. In his resignation letter he had stated, that although his direct official connection with the education and enlightenment of his countrymen would cease with his retirement, yet he would devote his remaining days to the advancement of the sacred cause in which his deep and earnest interest could only close with his life. He now applied himself in right earnest to the fulfilment of that sacred promise.

When Vidyasagar resigned his appointments under government, his friend, Sir James Colvile, the Chief Justice of the Supreme Court at Calcutta, advised him to pass the Law examination and enrol himself as a pleader of the Sadar Adalat. He had, from his early years, a great aversion for the legal profession, and therefore, expressed his unwillingness to follow the advice of the Chief Justice. Yet when Colvile repeatedly goaded him to it, he visited for a few days his friend, Dwarka Nath Mitter, one of the best pleaders of the said Court, to have an inkling of the manners of the legal professionals. But from what he witnessed on those days, his aversion for the bar waxed tenfold, and he gave up that forced project once and for all.

Shortly after his retirement from public service he had to face a most heart-rending calamity in the death of his dear grand-mamma (father's mother). According to the custom of the Hindus she had been brought living to the shores of the Bhagirathi (the river Hooghly) at the Salkea Ghat, where she lived for 20 days, and then breathed her last in the bed of the holy river. These 20 days she had lived simply on the sacred water of the Bhagirathi. Her Sraddha ceremonials made a large hole in Vidyasagar's purse. His Widow Marriage movement had turned most of the inhabitants of his native place to be his enemies. They now found an opportunity to revenge upon him. They tried their best to dissuade the Pandits and the Brahmins of the locality from joining the ceremonials and eating in his house. But Vidyasagar had won a great reputation from his universal philanthrophy, and had done immense good to his countrymen in different forms. The reader has already been told that he had established a free English School, a night school, a girls school, and a charitable dispensary at his native village, Birsingha. He had provided for board and lodging of upwards of 60 school boys, sons of Brahmins and Pandits, who were residents of the neighbouring villages. He was always eager to help and succour the distrest. Whenever anybody was in danger and in need of help, and sought for Vidyasagar's assistance, he would run at all risks to rescue the man, without at all considering whether he belonged to the high, middle, or low station of life, or whether he was a friend or foe. Besides the establishment of the charitable institutions in his own village, he had contributed largely to the opening of schools and other useful institutions in the different villages of the neighbourhood. He had secured employments to many young men of the locality. In short, he had endeared himself to all classes of people. Most of his neighbours were under deep obligations to him. How could then they be so ungrateful and impudent as to boycott him from Society and refuse to eat in his house for the only offence that he was the father of the Widow Marriage agitation and had associated himself with those who had formed such alliance? He had given no member of his family in such marriage. Many Pandits, other Brahmins, and lower class people, numbering in all nearly three thousand, feasted in his house for two days; *Paka Phalahar* (Bread fried in Ghee with sweatmeats of different kinds) was given on the first day, and rice on the second day.

Vidyasagar also spent a good sum of money on the occasion of her *Sapindana* (first annual Sraddha). We have no means of ascertaining exactly his religious faith, but this much has been known for certain that he did not observe the forms and rites of modern Hinduism. He was never seen to tell *Mantras* or to worship a Hindu god or goddess. But he, nevertheless, never objected to the members of his family following their own beliefs or acting up to the rites of their respective faiths. On the contrary, he rather encouraged them and helped them in the performance of those rites, and he was often heard to say that it was improper to throw obstacles in the way of one's acting up to one's faith.

Vidyasagar was very deeply afflicted at the death of his beloved grandmother, who bore a most tender affection for him. We have seen with what haste she ran down to Calcutta on the occasion of her dear grandchild's illness and attended his sickbed with watchful care. In *his* childhood whenever Vidyasagar was refractory or naughty (as he usually was at that time) and any of his parents wanted to chastise him, he fled for protection to his grand-mamma, who never, in her life, upbraided him for even a grave offence. Vidyasagar too was fondly devoted to her, and felt a great filial veneration for her. Even when he was a young man and had entered into service, the grandparent and the grandchild reciprocated the same feelings of affectionate attachment. It is no wonder, therefore, that he should be so sincerely grieved at the loss of such a dear, old grandmother.

Sanskrit Press

The reader is aware that Vidyasagar had established in Calcutta a printing press, called the Sanskrit Press. He had also started, in connection with this Press, the Sanskrit Press Depository, where he kept for sale all the books that were printed in his Press. By degrees this Depository was converted to a regular Bookshop, where not only his own publications but those of other authors also were deposited for sale. On his retirement from service, he had to depend for his maintenance mainly on the income from the Press and the Depository. It is needless to say that *in* this business he had to employ a number of men who thus found means of their livelihood. When he freed himself from the bonds of thraldom, and found leisure to look into its affairs, he was highly dissatisfied, with the working and conduct of his chief officer. The accounts were not kept properly, and everything was in disorder. He, therefore, requested his friend, Raj Krishna, to supervise the business of the Depository. Raj Krishna was, at this time, employed as Head-Assistant in the Fort William College on a monthly salary of 80 rupees, as the reader is already aware. He took six months' leave of absence, and engaged himself in superintending the management of the Depository. "These six months he applied himself closely and diligently in examining and clearing the accounts, and after much efforts succeeded in so regulating method and order in every respect, that the business soon prospered, and a glance at the accounts would at once show the state of affairs.

Vidyasagar's father was so pleased with Raj Krishna's management that he requested the latter to resign his office in the Fort William College and employ himself permanently as Superintendent of the Depository. Vidyasagar also urged him to it. Accordingly Raj Krishna was permanently appointed as Manager of the Sanskrit Press Depository on a pay of 150 rupees a month. The Depository soon rose to be a very prosperous and profitable business. But Vidyasagar was by nature excessively charitable, and the income from this business could not meet all the demands of his charity. As a matter of consequence, he had to meet them by loans, and slowly his embarrassments grew so heavy, that he was ultimately obliged to dispose of this profitable business, of which hereafter.

We will try to notice here, in passing one or two instances of Vidyasagar's gratefulness and benevolence, and the ungratefulness of the world. The reader has already had some inkling of Vidyasagar's and Raj Krishna's intimate friendly attachment to each other. The former often ate and slept in the house of the latter, whose mother loved Vidyasagar as dearly as if he was her own son. The other members of Raj Krishna's family, both male and female, looked upon him as if he was one of them. He also reciprocated the same feelings towards them. Raj Krishna had a little girl, who was named Prabhabati. Vidyasagar loved this girl exceedingly. Her babblings were a source of great delight to him. He was so much grieved at the untimely death of this little child of three years, that he gave up food and sleep for some time, and at last wrote a booklet, *Prabhabati - Sambhashana,* full of laments for her. Its language is very heart-rending and beautifully attractive. It was not, therefore, very strange that a man of Vidyasagar's stamp should look to Raj Krishna's welfare, and employ him in his own business on a handsome remuneration.

Vidyasagar was so benevolent that he secured appointments to many persons quite unconnected, or only very distantly connected, with him. But unfortunately, some of these men, who through Vidyasagar's exertions had risen to high posts, behaved towards him most ungratefully. On one occasion, there was a post vacant under a certain Babu, who was at this time a high official of government, but had originally secured the service through Vidyasagar's exertions. A candidate for the vacant situation came to Vidyasagar for a recommendation to this high official. Armed with Vidyasagar's recommendation, the candidate waited upon the Babu at his residence. The Babu was, at that time, reclining upon a sofa, enjoying his hookah and chatting with some of his friends. The candidate handed over to him Vidyasagar's letter. The Babu read it, and smiled. On his friends enquiring the cause of his smile, the Babu replied that Vidyasagar had opened a business of securing situations for others. The candidate was thunderstruck to hear the Babu, and left the place in utter disgust.

Shortly after this, there were five vacancies in a government office under Babu Priya Nath Datta of Bagbagar, who was the Head Assistant of the department. The aforesaid candidate again came to Vidyasagar for a recommendatory letter to Priya Nath. Vidyasagar did not know Priya Nath personally, and he, therefore, declined to give him the letter. But, at the urgent importunities of the man, he very reluctantly gave him a note of recommendation. The authorities had directed Priya Nath to fill up the vacancies by an examination of the candidates. He, therefore, requested Vidyasagar's man to appear at the examination. The man stood seventh. There were only five vacancies. Priya Nath was in great peril. He then devised a plan. He reported to his superiors that two more hands were required for the efficient working of his office, and thus provided the man with one of the newly created posts. When Vidyasagar heard this, he was greatly amazed at Priya Nath's noble conduct He expressed himself thus:—'How wonderful is this world ! He who was benefited by me, slighted my recommendation; but one, who was quite unknown to me, has been eager to comply with my request.' With this, he at once ran to Bagbazar, and made an acquaintance of the noble Priya Nath.

On another occasion, a situation fell vacant under a European. A man came to Vidyasagar for a recommendation. But he was not known to the European, and, therefore, declined. He was then told that a friend of his, whom he had made Editor of a newspaper, was intimately familiar with the European. Vidyasagar called on the Editor, and asked him for a recommendatory letter to his European friend for the man. The Editor plumed himself up and said that he was now Editor of a journal, and that if he should go to recommend others to Europeans for situations, he would be under obligations to them, and in consequence would not be able to review their actions freely. Vidyasagar was startled, and at once left the presence of the mighty Editor. While this conversation was going on, the Head Mate of a European mercantile firm was sitting there, and heard everything. No sooner did Vidyasagar leave the place, than he followed him to the street, and enquired of him very politely if a post of 20 Rupees would suit his man. He also said that a situation of that value was lying vacant at his disposal, and he was prepared to offer the post to Vidyasagar's man, if it suited him. Vidyasagar smiled, and admired the magnanimity of the Mate. The man was accordingly sent to his office, where he was provided with the situation.

There are plenty of such instances in Vidyasagar's life. Whenever he was told that a certain person had condemned his conduct, he would at once say,—'Why should that man go to abuse me? I have never done him a good turn !' Vidyasagar was often heard to declare that whoever had been benefited by him the most, did him the most evil.

Immediately after his retirement from service, he, had given no less than fifteen widows in marriage in different parts of the Hooghly district in the course of one year. We have already said that he had to bear all the expenses of these marriages. He had, besides, to provide for the maintenance of the, married couples and their families. His income from his business, alluded to before, was not sufficient to meet these demands, which made him contract debts. Though he was thus highly embarrassed, yet he could not economise his outlays. He was always liberal and charitable. He even went so far as to borrow money himself on his own account to liquidate the debts of other persons. He was, no doubt, a very wise and prudent man, but the overflows of his charitable disposition found the uppermost place in his heart and drove away his wisdom and prudence, whenever an occasion presented itself. May be, he thought that these debts contracted solely for benevolent and charitable purposes must find their own means of liquidation. In fact, his debts had amounted to nearly 50,000 rupees, but he lived long enough to be able to clear them off before his death.

About this time, Gokulchand and Govinchand Basus, two brothers, of Bainchi, came to Vidyasagar, and said that Nilkamal Banerji intended distressing their homestead-land with premises for debts, and prayed for his assistance. Vidyasagar immediately paid 1,000 rupees to Nilkamal, and released the property of the Basu brothers. Subsequently, when Raj Krishna resigned his office of the Manager of the Sanskrit Press Depository, Vidyasagar appointed Gokulchand Basu to the vacant post on a monthly pay of 50 Rupees.

Some time after this, the premises of one Syama Charan Banerji were about to be put to auction sale for debts. Syama Charan supplicated Vidyasagar for help, who at once paid off his debts of 500 rupees and released his property.

We will notice here, in passing, an incident of his noble liberality, that happened some time after this, Baidya Nath Chaudhury, a respectable Zamindar of Radhanagar, a place not very far from Birsingha, had hypothecated his estate to Babu Rama Prasad Ray, son of the illustrious Ram Mohan Ray, on a loan of 50,000 rupees. After his death, his son had also taken from the same creditor another loan of 25,000 rupees. The debt thus amounted to 75,000 rupees. His son, Shiva Narayan Chaudhuri went to Rama Prasad to make some arrangements for clearing the debt by instalments, and died quite suddenly of Apoplexy in the creditor's office. After this, his two sons came to Rama Prasad and implored mercy, but he was inexorable. At last, they with their mother and aunt earnestly solicited Vidyasagar for help. His tender heart was moved at their tears, and he promised to aid them. He tried in various places for the money, but Rama Prasad having previously prohibited other moneylenders, no one ventured to lend so much money.

Rama Prasad was one of the best pleaders of the Sadar Adalat and he had an eager desire to grasp the mortgaged estate. Vidyasagar travelled for six months continually in different places and spent nearly 2,000 rupees of his own to procure the loan. At last, with great difficulty, he borrowed 50,000 rupees of Babu Kali Das Ghosh, a relation of Raja Pratap Chandra Sinha, and a further sum of 50,000 rupees from another moneylender. But when this one *lakh* was offered to Rama Prasad, he refused to receive the money. Vidyasagar then placed the matter in the hands of Swinhoe & Co. Solicitors, who settled the affair and cleared off the debt, thus releasing the property of an ancient respectable family. All the country admired Vidyasagar's noble, disinterested exertions. But, unfortunately, for want of proper management, the estate failed to prosper, and the debt grew heavier. At last, the property was sold at auction, and the widows of Shiva Narayan Chaudhuri and his brother were in great distress. Vidyasagar settled on each of them a monthly allowance of 30 rupees. Shortly after this, one Kasi Nath Ghosh of Monpur sued them for 800 rupees. Vidyasagar settled the debt on 150 rupees, which he paid out of his own pocket, thus relieving the poor widows of their embarrassments.

Even after the legislation of the remarriage of Hindu widows, several means were devised by Vidyasagar's friends to keep the movement alive. With this view, Umes Chandra Mitra, brother of the Hon'ble Sir Rames Chandra Mitra, one of the late native Justices of the Calcutta High Court, composed a drama, titled *Bidhava-Bibaha Natak.* The first performance of this play was opened to the public in the beginning of 1859. Keshab Chundra Sen, one of the greatest orators of Bengal, was intrusted with the management of the stage, and some of his friends and coadjutors, such as Narendra Nath Sen, Krishna Vihari Sen, Protap Chunder Mozoomdar, and others played the different parts.

Vidyasagar was always averse to dramatic performances. He had only once seen theatricals performed in the premises of the Paikpara Raj family at their urgent solicitations. Some time after, Babu Giris Chandra Ghosh, the great Bengali drama-writer and actor of the present day, compiled a play with the title *Sitar Banabas,* and dedicated it to Vidyasagar. At the first performance of this play, Giris Chandra requested Vidyasagar to be present, but he did not like to go there. But he was present at the threatricals of the *Bidhava-Bibaha Nataka* more than once.

It would be better to quote what P. C. Mazoomdar, the author of "The Life and Teachings of Keshab Chunder Sen," says on this point: "In the splendid structure at Chitpore Road, to which the Brahmo School was removed in 1859, Keshab found a somewhat unexpected occupation. He was entrusted with the management of an institution very different from the Brahmo School. It was a dramatic club to put on the stage *Bidhava-Bibaha Natak* (widow marriage drama), written with the object of reforming the cruel custom of the forced celibacy of young Hindu Widows. Since the inauguration of the widow marriage reform in 1856, Keshab, though then a very young man, wished well to the cause, and did what he could to contribute to its success. He therefore cheerfully accepted the management of the Widow Marriage Drama. The plot of the drama was the miserable life of a Hindu widow shut up in the zenana who, in her solitary friendless condition, formed an attachment to a young neighbour, by whom she was led to a course of sin. The concluding scenes depicted her sufferings, her suicide, her confessions, with appeals to all patriotic men to put an end to the cruel celibacy of Hindu widows.

The performance was first opened to the public in the beginning of 1859, and produced a sensation in Calcutta, which those who witnessed it, can never forget. The representatives of the highest classes of Hindu society were present. The pioneer and father of the widow-marriage movement, Pundit Ishwar Chandra Vidyasagar came more than once, and tender-hearted as he is, was moved to floods of tears. In fact there was scarcely a dry eye in the great audience. Undoubtedly the most wholesome effect was produced. Keshab, as stage manager, was warmly complimented on his energy and intelligence, and we, his friends, as amateur actors, who had done our best, also received our humble share of praise".

7

Interesting Anecdotes

Rich Crop of Stories

That a man of Vidyasagar stature and character, in the days when the traditional art of storytelling had not yet declined, should have called forth a rich crop of stories, factual and imaginary, is not to be wondered at. Most of the stories narrated here are based on facts, partly shaped for entertainment But the "man Vidyasagar" is revealed in these stories as nowhere else.

Tit for Tat

We begin with one or two stories about the famous chati (pair of Bengali slippers) which Vidyasagar used to wear on all occasions. One story relates to his rebuff to the English Principal of the Presidency College, Mr. Kerr. Vidyasagar, Principal of the Sanskrit College at the time, called on the other Principal to discuss an urgent official matter. When he stepped into his room, he found that the Principal did not stand up from the chair to welcome him, but sat on, stretching his feet over the table with shoes on. He had not the courtesy even to ask Vidyasagar to be seated. Without waiting much time talking to him, Vidyasagar left the room and returned to his own college. Now it was the turn of Mr. Kerr to come to him for discussing the matter. When Mr. Kerr stepped into his room, Vidyasagar sat on stretching his feet over the table with his slippers on. The Principal was not even shown to a chair. This behaviour of the Pandit, and an Indian pandit at that, openly insulting as it was, hurt Mr. Kerr's vanity as a member of the English ruling class. Furiously agitated, he left the room and sent a letter to the Secretary of the Council of Education, complaining against the uncivilised manners of the Bengali Pandit. The Secretary, Dr. Mouat, could immediately guess what had happened, as he had known the Pandit quite intimately. Without calling for any explanation, he just made a formal enquiry about the matter to the Pandit. Vidyasagar wrote to him in reply: "I, being a humble native, am not acquainted with the civilised European manners. The other day when I called on Mr. Kerr's room, I found him sitting on the chair in that peculiar posture, and talking with me without asking me to sit down. At first I was shocked and surprised, but on second thought I took it as a kind of civilised European manner, which half-civilised people like us should certainly try to imitate. I did that only when he paid a return visit to me, and nothing else with the intention of offending him". Dr. Mouat understood the situation and thought it wise to drop the matter.

Heated Controversy

There was another incident, which caused a heated controversy, in which Vidyasagar's slippers figured. Sometime in 1874 Vidyasagar was invited to visit the library of the Asiatic Society, and the Indian Museum, which was then located in the same building. Vidyasagar went accompanied by his friend Harish Chandra, the celebrated Hindi poet of Banaras, who wanted to see the Society and the Museum. The Pandit was clothed as usual in his typical white dhoti and chadar, and wearing a pair of native slippers. His friend Harish Chandra was dressed in Indian choga-chapkan-pagri, but fortunately he had on a pair of English shoes. When they arrived at the gate of the Society's buildings, Vidyasagar was prevented by the porter from entering the room and was told to leave his chati behind. His companion was, however, permitted to go in with his English shoes. Vidyasagar at once went back home. His friend could not also swallow the affront, and followed him. Returning home, he wrote a letter to Mr. H. K Blanford, Honorary Secretary to the Trustees of the Indian Museum, as follows: "Having had occasion to visit the library of the Asiatic Society of Bengal, I called on the 28th January last (1874), and as I wore native shoes, I was not admitted, unless I would leave my shoes behind. I felt so much affronted that I came back without an expostulation.

'"Whilst I was in the compound, I saw that native visitors, wearing native shoes, were made not only to uncover their feet, but also to carry their shoes with their own hands, though there were some people moving about in the Museum rooms with their shoes on... Besides, if persons wearing shoes of the English pattern, though coming on foot, could be admitted with shoes on, I could not make out why persons of the same status in life and under similar circumstances should not be admitted, simply because they happened to wear native shoes".

The Secretary, Mr. Blanford, was for dropping the matter, to avoid controversy. But the incident raised a controversy, the contemporary press taking a lively part in it. Even a large section of the English press criticised harshly the haughty attitude of the Society's authorities. We quote below a few lines from the Englishman on this "great shoe question": "We understand that the great 'shoe question' has again come to the front and is occupying the attention of no less distinguished a body than the Council of the Asiatic Society of Bengal. Pandit Ishwar Chandra Vidyasagar, a native gentleman of learning, modesty and merits, who has rendered inestimable services to his fellow-countrymen and whose reputation extends far beyond the bounds of Asia, complains that he is not allowed to enter the rooms of the Asiatic Society with his shoes—native shoes—on, and the Council does not know precisely how to act in the matter. We can see but one course sufficiently dignified for the successors of Jones and Colebrooke, viz. to abstain from laying down, or in the remotest degree countenancing, a petty regulation which will letter the usefulness of the Society, discourage the resort to it of eminent persons of the Pandit's stamp, render it the laughing-stock of Europe But if there is a mark of respect attached to the leather, it is immaterial as to what turn the leather may take. We hope the Council of the Asiatic Society and the Trustees of the Museum will have the good sense not to make native gentlemen feel that to enter their rooms is to court insult".

Vidyasagar's shoes were a simple and traditional pair of slippers, but they were, as has been suggested by Rabindranath Tagore, the symbol of his indomitable individuality. Pandit Shivanath Shastri, a great Brahmo reformer of the post-Vidyasagar period, has mentioned a small story about this great chati of Vidyasagar in his reminiscences. Vidyasagar had always a very soft corner in his heart for Shivanath and treated him very affectionately. One day Shivanath raised the topic of his chati and the incidents connected with it.

Following a brief discussion, Vidyasagar calmly said: "Yes, yes, my dear little friend, this is my country-made slipper and I am proud of wearing it. It has great moral courage and power, you know With this slipper on, I can kick right at the face of any of your big Princes in India, if situation calls for it "Shivanath closes the topic with this comment: "As I felt then, and I feel it even now, what he said was perfectly true. Before his towering mental strength and moral courage, his strong individuality, the Kings and Princes really seemed nothing but nonentities".

This story relates to Vidyasagar's attitude to orthodox Hinduism and religion. It is extracted from Pandit Shivanath's book. He writes: "Within a few years after my joining the Brahmo Samaj my father left my village home in despair and went to spend his remaining years in Banaras. Vidyasagar Mabashay did not quite like this proceeding, as will be manifest from the following incident. During his residence in Banaras, my father once visited Calcutta, and as his usual practice was, called at the house of his friend Pandit Vidyasagar.

The latter, who had scant regard for the forms of orthodox Hinduism, taunted my father for settling down in Banaras. The following is the substance of the conversation that took place between them, as reported to me by a third party present on that occasion. Vidyasagar: 'Well, Haran, you have settled down in Banaras; but have you learnt to smoke ganja?'

My father: 'What connection is there between settling down in Banaras and smoking ganja.

Vidyasagar: 'Don't you see, according to popular belief, as soon as you die in Banaras, you are to become god Shiva. But

Shiva is a notorious ganja-smoker. Is it not the wiser course then to habituate yourself to ganja-smoking? Otherwise the first experiment may be a sore trial to you.'"

Pandit Shivanath adds: "Soon after my joining the Brahmo Samaj, my father expelled me with my wife and my infant daughter and we came to reside in Calcutta. Vidyasagar Mahashay did not lose sight of us, but went on making kind enquiries about us and giving me such advice as he thought necessary".

Making Fun of a Preacher

Here is another story about the Pandit's practical attitude to religion Once when Shivanath was a boy, he visited, with some of his young friends, the house of an ailing friend. There they met Vidyasagar and what followed is given in Shivanath's "Men I Have Seen" "Finding it more agreeable to sit in the open verandah of the house by the side of the street, we were all seated there, when the great Pandit arrived. He was delighted to find so many of us there, a great treat for his social instincts. He requested us to stay on till he had finished his feeding business (with the ailing patient) and returned. We did so. He came and began his stories, which kept all of us in roars of laughter. At last he requested his friend to send for a few pice worth of muri (a kind of fried and puffed rice, used by the poor of Bengal), When the muri was brought he requested us to eat it, and he also began to make his tiffin out of it. Just fancy the picture of Pandit Ishwar Chandra Vidyasagar sitting with his friends in the open by the side of a public street and chewing muri! Just at that moment there came a Bengali Christian street-preacher, who knew me personally. He drew right unto me, was struck to find me chewing muri and began conversation by asking me what I thought about my salvation. He plainly told me that my Brahmoism would not do and that I had come only half way and halting on the road. Pandit Vidyasagar was immensely amused by his talk and wanted to make fun of him.

The Christian had never seen the Pandit, it seemed, for otherwise he would have been more respectful towards him. The Pandit said, 'Leave those young fellows, sir, they have yet enough time to think of their salvation; come to us, old rogues, who are about to depart this life. That mode of address should have been enough for the Christian preacher to find the spirit in which the invitation came. But he did not see it. Full of enthusiasm he went to the side where the Pandit was sitting and began his preaching. A few witty remarks of the former convinced him that the tone and temper of the old man was quite different from what he wanted. Within a few minutes he left Vidyasagar's presence in a rage, saying 'What an old reprobate sinner you must be to treat such things thus. You are sure to rot in hell.' There was hearty laughter after the man left. The Pandit said to me, 'Don't let him know my name; for if you do, he will be further shocked. I only wanted to make a little fun over these men's habit of preaching to others in season and out of season.'"

Life beyond Life

Radhaprasad Roy, eldest son of Raja Rammohan Roy, had a grandson Lalit Mohan Chatterjee, who was peculiarly susceptible to all kinds of spiritual and supernatural beliefs. Vidyasagar knew this Lalit Mohan intimately. Vidyasagar had never aired his thoughts on religion to anybody, not even to his most trusted friends. Nobody knew for certain what actually his attitude to theism was, or to religion as such. He even used to avoid controversies about it, except on very rare occasions. Seeing Lalit helplessly drifting towards supernaturalism, one day he asked him affectionately, "Well, Lalit, do you really believe that there is life beyond death? We do not know much of our life here in this world. You are really fortunate that in addition to knowing this life you know much of another beyond its extinction. Can you give me some clue to this knowledge?" Lalit Mohan had almost filial regard for the Pandit, and he began to fumble before him. Vidyasagar cheered him up and said, "Never mind Lalit, I wish you all success in your venture. Now please tell me if I have any life beyond death, and, if I have any, what sort of life it is expected to be". To this Lalit replied, "Yes, Dadu (grandfather), you have another life after this as everyone has. It cannot be imagined that a man like you, who has done so much good to humanity, will not have another better life in store for him after death. After all, you have suffered much for all the good you have done to men, and certainly you will have your proper rewards in the life beyond this". Vidyasagar burst into laughter, saying, "That's really fine and flattering, if not funny. It is a great consolation to this worn-out old man to know that he has something as reward in store for him in future".

Annoyed with a Friend

Ramprasad Roy was the youngest son of Raja Rammohan Roy. Vidyasagar and Ramprasad were very good friends, but unfortunately there was some misunderstanding between them regarding widow remarriage It is said that on the occasion of the first widow remarriage after the Act was passed on July 26, 1856, Ramprasad did not want to take part in the function directly. A few days before the marriage, Vidyasagar called on his friend and reminded him of his promise to contribute to the marriage-fund and to attend the function personally. To this Ramprasad replied, "I am no doubt in favour of the cause, and you may count also on my contribution. But suppose I do not join the wedding party, is there any harm?" Vidyasagar thought that Ramprasad had not the moral courage to be present at the wedding, and wanted merely to lend his support to a great cause indirectly This pusillanimity was unbearable to him, particularly as it was quite unworthy of 'a son of Rammohan Roy. After a brief silence he pointed to the portrait of Raja Rammohan Roy on the wall in front of Ramprasad's table, and said, "What is the use of hanging the portrait of this man on the wall? Throw it away at once". Saying this, he left the place Ramprasad lived six years longer, but Vidyasagar never called on him again.

Refusing a Gift

Some time in 1847 Vidyasagar paid his first visit to the house of the Maharaja of Burdwan. Burdwan town is located about sixty miles west of Calcutta He stayed with a friend there, and not as the Raja's guest He was interested in seeing Burdwan town and its surroundings, and not in meeting the Maharaja. The Maharaja called on him one day and invited him to visit his palace. When he visited his palace the Maharaja, according to traditional custom, presented him a pair of costly shawls and Rs. 500 as a mark of respect. Vidyasagar humbly refused to accept the gift, and said, "It is very kind of you to offer me such valuable presents, but I regret very much my inability to accept them. Usually I do not accept gifts from anybody. I am now working in a Government College, and the remuneration I get is, I think, good enough for my maintenance I will be glad if the poor pandits of our tols and chatuspatis receive liberal gifts from you That would be really doing a great service" The Maharaja was neither surprised nor shocked to hear this reply from Vidyasagar, as he had heard about the Pandit before. Since making this personal acquaintance, the Maharaja held the Pandit in the highest regard, and he consistently lent his moral and financial support to the social reform movements launched by Vidyasagar. A few years later, the Maharaja wanted to offer him Birsingha village (where Vidyasagar was born) as his taluk. This offer, too, was rejected by Vidyasagar, who said, "I have no ambition to be a talukdar I may think of becoming one when I shall be able to pay from my own purse the Zamindar's rent of all the ryots living in the taluk". This time the Maharaja was really surprised to get this reply from Vidyasagar.

Society above Self

There is a very interesting story about the first meeting of Vidyasagar and the great saint, Sri Ramakrishna Paramahansa. Hearing highly of him for some time, one day the Paramahansa decided to meet the Pandit and went to his house Vidyasagar received him with due warmth and regard. After the formal exchange of greetings, the Paramahansa said, "At long last, after wallowing through many swamps, I have been able to reach the shore of the unfathomable sagar (sea), which I now see before me. You are that great sagar, and I have come to collect some precious pearls from you I hope I would not go back with empty hands "Vidyasagar replied smilingly, "I thank you very much for your kind visit But the sagar you have come to, I am afraid, is not the real sea you have been looking for I am sure there are no pearls in it, you may have just a handful of ordinary shells. You may have to return satisfied with that". The two great men understood each other through this brief conversation. Later, the Paramahansa said to the writer of *Leelamrita,* "Vidyasagar is a great sanyasi. Who else is a greater sanyasi than he? He has sacrificed his fortune, his pleasures and everything for the good of humanity. Above all, he has even refused to bother about his personal salvation by devoting himself to the contemplation of God. That is perhaps the greatest sacrifice he has made. He has not done good to his 'self' for doing good to others".

These, are simple words and the Paramahansa always used simple language The words are a judgement of Vidyasagar and the truth embodied in it is unassailable. He spoke highly of Vidyasagar's material and worldly sacrifice, but that was something he was not much concerned with. His supreme concern was with Vidyasagar's negation of self, in the spiritual sense, and his complete indifference to it There are men who can renounce all worldly things in the quest for personal spiritual salvation. Vidyasagar did not belong to men of this type His greatest concern and pursuit in life had been the redemption of society. He sacrificed his own material and spiritual interest for the sake of the greater interests of society.

Tributes of a Poet

It is now possible to estimate the "essential man," or the "authentic individual," in Vidyasagar, as also some of his human qualities. We may now judge him, in the perspective of the 19th century Bengali renaissance, as a typical "humanist," "intellectual entrepreneur" and "social reformer". Sociologically speaking, the Bengali renaissance in the 19th century produced two men, Rammohan Roy and Pandit Ishwar Chandra Vidyasagar, who symbolised almost all the historical characteristics of the Indian renaissance. That renaissance represents the dawn between the passing of the medieval age and the advent of the modern age.

The first poet representing the true spirit of the modern age in Bengal, leaving aside a minor poet Ishwar Chandra Gupta, was Michael Madhusudan Dutta. Vidyasagar was one of his greatest friends, in the sense that had there been no Vidyasagar, Michael Madhusudan might not have been able to live to prove his life as a poet. In times of utter distress in a foreign country, far away from his own, Michael found refuge in the generous heart of only one man in Bengal, Pandit Ishwar Chandra Vidyasagar. In a series of letters to his friends, including Vidyasagar, the poet expressed his own feelings about the Pandit. Of course there was poetic exuberance in the letters, but the emotion expressed therein was genuine. We give, from his letters, a few of his remarks about Vidyasagar "... I look upon him In many respects as the first man among us". (Letter to Rajnarain Bose, January 10, 1862) ".. You most go to work with that great energy, which is the companion of your genius and manliness of heart. (Letter to Vidyasagar, June 2, 1864.) "...I shall live to go back to India to tell my countrymen that you are not only Vidyasagar, but Karunasagar also" (Letter to Vidyasagar, June 18, 1864.) "...the man to whom I have appealed has the genius and wisdom of an ancient sage, the energy of an Englishman, and the heart of a Bengali mother," (Letter to Vidyasagar, September 2, 1864.) "as you are one of Nature's noble men' a Bengali, you will (unless I am greatly mistaken), feel for me, and sympathise for me... you are the greatest Bengali that ever lived and people speak of you with glowing hearts and tearful eyes". (Letter to Vidyasagar, 1867.)

We had had occasion before to notice the judgement of another poet, Rabindranath Tagore, on Vidyasagar as a man, and if we compare the two, we shall find that there is little difference between Michael's and Tagore's viewpoints None else has been able to plumb the depths of Vidyasagar's character more truly and deeply than Rabindranath, or to surpass even the casual reflections of Michael in his letters.

Of all remarks of Michael, the most popular and oft-quoted one is that Vidyasagar was a man who had "the genius and wisdom of an ancient sage, the energy of an Englishman, and the heart of a Bengali mother," Many Bengalis could boast of possessing the genius and wisdom of our ancient sages, as also the heart of a mother. A few Bengalis could boast of possessing the energy of an Englishman. But a few harmonised all these elements in their character. Of these "very few" Vidyasagar was undoubtedly one, a very great one in modern Bengal. Michael has called him "the greatest Bengali that ever lived". That is why many "great" Bengalis since Vidyasagar have wondered how the damp and humid soil of Bengal could produce the granite personality of Vidyasagar's stature. He was a noble creation of Nature, and through him the Bengalis, and other Indians, too, felt ennobled.

The most important, and the most significant, of all the remarks of Madhusudan about Vidyasagar was the one he made to

Rajnarain Bose in his letter of January 10, 1862, that he looked upon Vidyasagar as the "first man among us". There is the, hard core of truth in it. In every country "man" in the past had been an infinitesimal part of the multitude. He has emerged as an "individual man" with the dawn of modern age, that is, in the period of the Renaissance. In this sense Michael spoke of Vidyasagar as the "first man among us". There had been Rammohan and a few others before him, but it is certain that he ranks foremost among the very few "first men" in modem India.

Humanist Intellectual

Vidyasagar's magnanimity of heart and his zeal for social reform were great, but the historic role of Vidyasagar in the shaping of the national destiny cannot be understood if he is not judged as a true "humanist intellectual" in the philosophic-historical sense of the term We have to define, therefore, "humanism". The word "Renaissance" etymologically means rebirth or renewal, and it is applied to a specific period of human history in Europe (15th-16th centuries) when arts and letters, and to some extent philosophy, were modelled on classical antiquity. Symonds, an eminent authority on the history of the Italian Renaissance, says: "Men found that in Classical as well as Biblical antiquity existed an ideal of human life, both moral and intellectual, by which they might profit in the present". The revival of interest in the arts and thoughts of ancient Greece and Rome was a powerful factor in the intellectual life of the Renaissance only because ancient forms provided convenient vessels for new needs and meanings.

The concept of humanism also derives from the philosophers of classical Greece, and this has been enlarged to contain the needs and values of modern men. Humanism is homocentrism. Renaissance humanism appealed explicitly to the maxim of the Greek philosopher Protagoras: "Man is the measure of all things," Rammohan and Vidyasagar were true humanists of the modem age in India in the sense that each of them in turn initiated the fundamental homocentrism in modern India.

Both Rammohan and Vidyasagar looked back to classical Sanskritic tradition, to the Golden Age of India, to lend the halo of authority to their socio-religious ideas and reforms. Rammohan

Roy sought the authority for his anti-idolatrous monotheism in the ancient Upanishadic sources, and support for anti-sati in the Shastras. Vidyasagar too sought the authority for his social reforms like widow remarriage in the ancient Samhitas and Shastras. This authority of the Shastras was sought not because Rammohan and Vidyasagar were great believers in the Shastras, or because they had any lack of faith in reason and intellect, but because they thought that a convincing and venerable authority was needed for the people. This authority was required, as it was required in Europe, to lend weight to their new secular outlook, and to give to their socially progressive ideals the halo of age, and to sanction and legitimise their reformistic aspirations.

The humanism of Vidyasagar manifested itself, in the true spirit of Renaissance, in the revival and restoration of classical Sanskrit learning, alongside the new Western learning. Speaking of the Italian Renaissance, Symonds says: "It was scholarship, first and last, which revealed to men the wealth of their own minds, the dignity of human thought, the value of human speculation, the importance of human life regarded as a thing apart from religious rules and dogmas... The Renaissance opened to the whole reading public the treasure-houses of Greek and Latin literature... Manuscripts were worshipped, as relics from the Holy Land had been worshipped a few generations ago... The text and the canon of Homer, Plato, Aristotle, and the tragedians had to be decided. Florence, Venice, Basle, Lyons and Paris groaned with printing presses. The Aldi, the Stephani, and the Froben toiled by night and day, employing scores of scholars, men of supreme devotion and of mighty brain, whose work it was to ascertain the right reading of sentences, to accentuate, to punctuate, to commit to the press, and to place beyond the reach of monkish hatred or of envious time that everlasting solace of humanity which exists in the classics".

The spirit of these words can also be traced in the lives of many a nineteenth century Bengali pandit and scholar. These scholars opened to the whole reading public the treasure-houses of Sanskrit literature. Manuscripts were hunted, recovered and worshipped with greater regard than religious icons. Quite like the Stephanis and Frobens of Italy, the Tagores, the Mullicks, the

Seals, the Singhas, the Debs and many other big families of" ""Calcutta patronised classical learning and employed scores of Sanskrit scholars, who were undoubtedly men of supreme devotion, and mighty intellect and whose work it was to edit, annotate, translate into a living language, and to commit to the press the treasures of our classical literature.

Here lies the significant difference between the early European and the 19th century Bengali humanists: their attitude to the local language and literature. The European humanists were very proud of their Latinism and looked down upon living languages and literatures. The Bengali humanists, like Rammohan and Vidyasagar, had no such pride of classical learning or Sanskriti. Rammohan translated the Vedanta and some Upanishads for the first time into the Bengali language and had them printed for circulation among the people.

Vidyasagar edited many Sanskrit classics, translated and adapted several of them into Bengali, and printed and published most of them from his own Sanskrit Press. The remnants of Sanskrit manuscript collections which are still preserved in his Library in the Bangiya Sahitya Parishad, are worth seeing. Vidyasagar also laid the foundations of Bengali literature and education in Bengal. He wrote the first scientific Bengali primer, and also a simplified Sanskrit grammar in Bengali—Upakramanka and Byakaran Kaumudi —to break the monopoly and the esoteric clique of the conservative priests and pandits.

We know that Rammohan directed his energies mainly towards religious reforms. He wanted to purge our religion of all its priestly growths and external rituals and to make it predominantly subjective. The realisation of Brahmin was mainly to be sought in one's own self, and not in any idol worship The chief aim of his reform movement was to make religion "subjective," rather than "objective "He founded a Church—the Brahmo Samaj—where his followers congregated to listen to Vedic hymns, songs and readings, and to meditate upon Brahmin. But the Samaj was an objective something, needed at that time for propagating Rammohan's faith in subjective religion among his countrymen Vidyasagar's attitude to religion can be explained by reference to his "humanism". Vidyasagar took an interest in the Brahmo Samaj and its religious reform movement He was the Secretary of the Tattwabodhini Sabha in the closing years of its existence, and he also subscribed regularly to the Brahmo Samaj fund. Some of his distinguished friends and collaborators were leaders of the Brahmo Samaj, and his personal attachment to such eminent Brahmo leaders as Keshab Chunder Sen and Shivanath Shastri was proverbial in those days. Everybody knew that his heart lay with the Brahmos. But in spite of all this love, regard and sympathy for the Brahmos, he did not join the Brahmo Samaj, or attend its weekly congregations even once.

Why did he not join the Brahmo Samaj? It would have perfectly suited his temperament and outlook. What was his attitude to religion, Jacob Burckhardt, the author of "The Civilisation of the Renaissance in Italy" has explained this attitude thus: "These modern men were born with the same religious instincts as other medieval Europeans. But their powerful individuality made them in religion, as in other matters, altogether subjective".

Vidyasagar was born with the religious instincts of our people, but his powerful individuality made him "in religion altogether subjective" The religious ideal of Rammohan was truly realised and practised in life by Vidyasagar. He had never allowed himself to be drawn into any religious controversy, and had never publicly spoken against any religious belief or prejudice, however antiquated or regressive that might have been. Mere talk about religious views, as we see in his snub to a Bengali Christian missionary, was repugnant to him the only manifestation of his personal belief in God was found at the top of his letters, and in nothing else. But none among his friends had the courage to ask him anything about his idea of God, Whom he used to invoke in the beginning of his letters. In fact he maintained so rigid a silence about anything relating to the subject that people almost used to think of him as an "atheist". But for this small evidence in his letters, he would have been easily taken by all for a confirmed atheist.

What may be called the "core personality" of Vidyasagar was constituted of hereditary traits, and it was essentially an aggressive, masterful, masculine type of personality. These were the traits of his grandfather, Ramjoy Tarkabhushan, too, and, as pointed out by Rabindranath Tagore, that poor man could be bequeath nothing of material value to his grandson except these traits.

The "social personality" of Vidyasagar was acquired through his assimilation of the socio-historical situation, his keen sense of the trend of the times and his social experiences. This was a charming, magnetic personality, adaptive, assimilative and responsive, with the push and drive of the aggressive, masculine core behind it. From many incidents of his life it is evident that the core very often asserted itself and his socially acquired personality retreated before it Here lies the root of his tragic isolation and the deepening sense of frustration in retired life. But it should be remembered that, in his times, the drive of the aggressive, masculine "core" was needed essentially for the full expansion of the "social personality" and its fulfilment in the social milieu of the 19th century. That was the time of great men and great deeds, and Vidyasagar was a great man with great achievements to his credit.

8

Important Letters

To Giris Chandra Vidyaratna

I do not know whether you are aware that Babu Jogendra Nath Bandopadhyay, M. A. late scholar, Sanskrit College, has recently issued a biography of Madan Mohan Tarkalankar. In this book, the author writes–' Into Vidyasagar's Vetala-Panchavingsati many new ideas and sweet sentences were introduced by Tarkalankar.

It was so far corrected and revised by him, that it might be said to be the joint production of the two friends, like the works of Beaumont and Fletcher.' The Vetala-Panckavingsati is again under print. I think it necessary to say something, in the present edition, about Jogendra Babu's insinuation. You very well know what hand Tarkalankar had in the correction of the Vetala-Panchavingsati.

I shall feel obliged, if you will write to me what you know. It is needless to say, that I intend publishing your letter along with my explanation.

Yours &c.

Ishwar Chandra Sharma

To F. J. Mouat

F. J. MOUAT ESQ. M. D.
Secretary tc the Council of Education;

Sir,

I have the honour to submit for the information of the Council of Education a report on the Sanskrit College, drawn up agreeably to the instructions conveyed in your tetter No, 3538, dated the 5th instant.

I beg leave to remark that it has long been in my contemplation to submit a report of the nature now furnished, but circumstances deterred me from such a step. I am now, however, happy to have an opportunity of carrying out my wishes as a matter of duty, under the sanction of the Council.

To Lieutenant-Governor of Bengal

"My dear sir,

"When I had the pleasure of waiting upon you last, you were pleased to allude to the resignation of the officiating Principal of the Sanskrit College. But as I was not aware of all the circumstances connected with the affair, I could not tell you anything regarding the matter. I have since made myself acquainted with the facts of the case, and am inclined to think that the treatment of the Principal by has been unnecessarily and unbecomingly harsh, as will, I believe, appear to you also on perusal of the papers enclosed.

(SD). "ISHWAR CHANDRA SHARMA".

"My dear sir,

'As I am inclined to suspect that he may have also represented the matter to you in the same light, I beg to assure you that I had no hand whatever in inducing Babu P. C. Sarbadhicari in forming his resolution. On the contrary, as I was under the impression that the severance of his connection with the Sanskrit College would be injurious to that institution, I tried my best to make him withdraw his resignation, though without the desired effect.

(Sd.) "Ishwar Chandra Sharma"

To Halliday

Calcutta, Sanskrit College,
May 1857.

Sir,

"When I had the honour to wait on you on Saturday last and solicited your permission to make a few suggestions regarding the appointment of an Inspector for South Bengal, you were pleased to direct me to submit a written memorandum upon the subject. I have accordingly availed myself of the permission and beg respectfully to suggest that if you should feel inclined to transfer me to that post, the appointment of my successor in the Sanskrit College may be made in consultation with me, as from an intimate personal know-ledge of the several parties from whom the selection may be made, I think I will be best able to recommend the most proper person for the place. If however it should be thought inexpedient to place the division under my charge on account of the Government English colleges and schools in it, I would earnestly solicit that at least the districts in which there are model schools, viz, Hooghly, Midnapur, Burdwan and Nuddea may be placed under me, the colleges and schools being without Inconvenience in charge of the person who may be appointed Inspector of the Division,

I have so often troubled you with the subjects connected with the Vernacular Education that I really feel ashamed to intrude any further on your valuable time.

Your most obedient servant, (Sd)
Ishwar Chandra Sharma

To W. Gordon Young

Director of Public Instruction

At the same time, he wrote a letter to the Lieutenant Governor, intimating his determination of early retirement. The letter ran as follows:—

"Calcutta, Sanskrit College, "31st. Aug. 1857,

"My Dear Sir,

"Sometime ago while talking on the subject of education you were pleased to ask me for a memo, on the state of Vernacular

Education in Bengal under the present system of management and I agreed at the time, though with reluctance, to submit it. On subsequent consideration however, I feel the task a very delicate one in as much as the required memo, cannot but reflect on the actions of my brother-officers and others. I therefore earnestly beg to be pardoned for not submitting the memo, as I had promised,

"I may here be permitted to state that I have made up my mind to retire from the public service from January next and that I have intimated my intention to Mr. Young in a demi-official note of which I venture to enclose a copy for your information also.

"I remain, My dear Sir, "With every sentiment of respect and esteem.

Yours most faithfully,

(Sd). Ishwar Chandra Sharma

To W. Gordon Young

Director of Public Instruction.

Sir,

The unceasing mental exertion required by the discharge of my public duties has now so seriously affected my general health, as to compel me to tender my resignation of the Education service to the Honourable the Lieutenant Governor of Bengal.

- I feel that I can no longer devote the assiduous attention to my duties which their due performance necessitates. I need repose, and in justice to the public interests, as well as to my own comforts and happiness, can only secure that repose by retiring into private life.
- The moment my health is restored, it is my intention to devote my time and attention to the composition and compilation of useful works in the Vernacular language of Bengal. Thus, although my direct official connection with the education and enlightenment of my countrymen will have ceased, I venture humbly to hope that my remaining years will still be devoted to the advancement of a great and sacred cause in which my deep and earnest interest can only close with my life.
- Among the minor causes that have led to my taking so serious a step, are the absence of all further prospects of

advancement and the want of that immediate personal sympathy with the present system of education, which every conscientious servant of the Department, should possess.

- With regard to the former, I can occupy my time more profitably and with infinitely less strain upon mind and body, than in my present position. It would be idle to deny that such considerations must have weight with one who has not yet been able to make any permanent provision for his family and who fears that failing health will prevent his doing so, if he delays longer the severance of his connection with the arduous and onerous duties that belong to the offices he holds.
- With respect to the other, I feel that I have no right to obtrude my views and opinions upon the government; yet I could not conceal from those I serve, the fact that my heart is not in my work, and that Hereby my efficiency is, and must be, impaired. More I am unwilling to say, less I could not express, with the maintenance of the honesty of purpose which I deem to be an essential quality of a conscientious public servant.
- I retire with the conscious gratification that I have always laboured earnestly to discharge my duties to the best of my humble ability and I trust that I shall not be deemed presumptuous in tendering my most sincere and heartfelt acknowledgements for the unvarying kindness, indulgence and consideration, which I have always experienced at the hands of the government.

"I have the honour to be..

Your most obedient servant
(Sd.) Ishwara Chandra Sharma

To Halliday

My Dear Sir,

After mature deliberation I find that I cannot either with consistency or propriety omit the parts of my letter which appear objectionable to you. It is true that ill-health is one of the principal causes which have induced me to resign. But I cannot conscientiously say that that is the sole cause. If it were so, I could have applied for a long leave and renovated my health. I had often represented to you, that I frequently felt it disagreeable and inconvenient to serve government under existing circumstances and that I considered the present system upon which the Department of Vernacular Education was conducted, was a mere waste of money. You are aware that I often met with discouragement in my way. I saw besides no prospects of advancement and more than once I felt my just claims passed over. Thus I hope you will be pleased to admit that I had reasonable grounds of complaint: but I would nevertheless have continued in my present post for sometime longer, if I were not forced to take the step I have taken by prolonged ill-health, which has made me unfit for my responsible duties, and when the above considerations had such a considerable share in the decision to which I have come, their omission in my letter would certainly have made me liable to the charge of disingenuousness. For the same reasons, I feel it very difficult to alter it now.

Further the contents of my letter, since it left my hands, have become known to a great many people and there is as much chance of the fact of the alteration becoming equally known, in which case I shall not only be lowered in the estimation!

Of my friends, but of the public generally.

Nothing can exceed the deep regret which I have felt since I have heard from you, that the passage in question may possibly put you to some inconvenience; but words cannot express my feelings of distress when I think that unwillingly 1 should have given you the least cause for trouble and inconvenience. I should certainly have felt it a great relief if circumstances had permitted me to retract with any degree of consistency; but I humbly hope that you wilt be pleased to admit after a due consideration of circumstances I have explained at length, in what an awkward position I have been placed and how delicate and difficult it is for me now to make any alteration in my letter.

With much deference and respect and with many apologies for troubling you in a matter so purely personal to myself.

Yours most faithfully
(Sd.) Ishwar Chandra Sharma

To a Friend

My Dear Sir,

"I am very glad to learn from your note that the retention of the para in my letter of resignation therein alluded to, will, in no way, put you to any inconvenience. As far as I can remember I was led to believe from the tenor of our conversation of the other day that the para might occasion such inconvenience, and were it not for that idea, I would never have alluded to it, in my letter of the 15th instant. I feel now, however, a great weight removed from my mind. "There is only one point upon which I would wish to say a few words. I regret I did not sufficiently explain it in my last. I never for a moment meant to say that I was ever discouraged by you. On the contrary, I am fully sensible of the encouragement which I often received from you, and I think I have given vent to my feelings on this point at the conclusion of my letter of resignation. In referring to the discouragement I met with, I meant to say, that obstruction, I often met with, in my way to remove which I was frequently obliged to trouble you. You were always pleased to lend an attentive ear to my representations and very often those obstacles were removed by your kind interference. I always felt it very disagreeable to my feelings thus frequently to trouble you. But it was merely from absolute necessity that I did so.

"I would not again have troubled you, if I did not think it my duty to offer an explanation upon 'So delicate a point concerning myself.

18th Sept. 58.

I remain

With great respect and esteem

Yours most faithfully
(Sd.) Isvar Chandra Sharma.

To Gordon Young

Monday, 20th Sept. 58.

My Dear Sir,

After a mature deliberation I find that I cannot consistently make any alteration in my letter of resignation, Hoping to be excused for the delay in replying to your note.

I remain, Yours truly Sd,

Isvara Chandra Sharma,

To W. G. Young

5th. Oct. 1858

My Dear Sir,

I received your letter No. 2461 yesterday noon communicating the acceptance of my resignation. "I am already in a very disagreeable position for not having yet been able to pay the Pundits of the Female schools, and I am afraid that I will be more so, as soon as I leave my post. And though it is very desirable, in consideration of the present state of my health, that I should cease from work as soon as possible, yet I would wish on the above account to defer making over charge, if you see no particular objection, till the decision of government on my application for the payment of the bill of the Female Schools is ascertained.

Yours very truly

Sd. Ishwar Chandra Sharma.

9

Golden Words of Vidyasagar

- The indiscriminate practice of polygamy is shameful and is a source of many evils; hence, should be dispensed with. It hardly requires a logical proof.
- Oh poor India!...you think the woman whose husband dies immediately turns into a stone; she does not have sorrow anymore, cannot feel pain any more and all her senses of passions and sensualities disappear without trace suddenly! But you well know that such notions are based on false pretences as evidence to the contrary abounds. Just think how these erroneous notions are poisoning this world. How sad! The country, whose male population is unkind, unreligious and unaware of the distinction between the good and the evil and don't care about justice and fairness and where abiding the rituals is the chief preoccupation of religion, should not give birth to girls!

10

Great Life at a Glance

1820, Sep. 26: Ishwar Chandra Vidyasagar was born at Birsingha, Midnapur to a poor religious family. His parents were Thakurdas Bandyopadhyay. The childhood days of Vidyasagar were spent in abject poverty. After the completion of elementary education at the village school, his father took him to Calcutta.

1828: Eight year old Ishwar Chandra Vidyasagar walked with his father, from the village of Birsingha in Midnapur district to Calcutta to seek admission in an English language institution. The fees at Hindu college were too high for his father to pay, so Ishwar Chandra Vidyasagar was enrolled in Sanskrit college. While studying in Calcutta, he lived at the home of a friend, whose sister was a child widow.

1839: To support himself and the family Ishwar Chandra also took a part-time job of teaching at Jorashanko.

1846: Following the death of Ram Manikya Vidyalankar, a distinguished academician, Pundit Ishwar Chandra Vidyasagar took over charge as Assistant Secretary in 1846. After the retirement of Rassomoy Dutta, the secretary, the Council of Education proposed to place the Sanskrit College on an equal footing with the Calcutta.

1849, May: The need of a girls' school for imparting non-sectarian and secular education was widely felt for a long time and it was at last removed by the foundation of the Hindu Balika Vidyalaya in May 1849, on the initiative of IE Drinkwater Bethune, Legal Member of the Governor-General's Council and President of the Council of Education.

1851: Pundit Ishwar Chandra Vidyasagar was appointed Principal of the Sanskrit College. After taking charge, he made radical changes in teaching methods.

1853: Ishwar Chandra Vidyasagar, now an eminent educationist of Calcutta, who brought many Sanskrit and English classics home to common Indian readers through a very lucid translation, was the first to speak of Goethe's epigram on Sakuntala in 1853.

1855: The first important step towards the removal of the restrictions against widow- marriage was the publication in 1855 by Ishwar Chandra Vidyasagar of his work on widow-marriage in Bengali. Vidyasagar's efforts at reformation did not stop with exegetic disquisitions. Under his lead a memorial signed by two thousand Hindus was presented to government.

1856, Jul. 26: Ishwar Chandra Vidyasagar attacked on early marriage, polygamy and illiteracy among females. He was instrumental in passing Hindu Widow's Remarriage Act on July 26,1856.

1857, Jan. 24: Vidyasagar College, named after Pandit Ishwar Chandra Vidyasagar, became a government-sponsored day and evening college, affiliated to the University of Calcutta in Kolkata, India. Vidyasagar may refer to: Ishwar Chandra Vidyasagar, the Bengali scholar (1820-1891).

1860: He wrote his "Maths of Orissa" in English. His next work was his Bijangram written in Bengali blank verse. This is the first work ever written and published in blank verse in the history of Bengali language and literature.

1866: At the prompting of Ishwar Chandra Vidyasagar, the Government of Bengal appointed, in 1866 , a committee to enquire into and report on Polygamy. A brief and readable report was produced by the Committee within six months.

1868: Ishwar Chandra Vidyasagar, Dwarkanath Vidyabhusan and other liberals supported the Girls School for twenty years but the institution did not receive wide public support. Miss Piggot, the headmistress was forced to resign because she had brought in Christianity, considered a dreaded alien faith in India at that time, into the teaching programme.

1891, July, 29: Vidyasagar died at the age of 70.

Bibliography

Amales, Tripathi: *Vidyasagar: The Traditional Moderniser*, Punascha, 1998.

Ashton, S. R.: *Indian Independence: Living Through History*, Batsford Academic and Educational, London, 1985.

Asok, Sen: *Iswar Chandra Vidyasagar and his Elusive Milestones*, Riddhi, Kolkata, 1968.

Bakshi, S. R.: *Indian Freedom Fighters: Struggle for Independence*, Hardcover, 2002.

Banerjea, Surendranath and Jadu Nath Kanjilal: *An Explanatory Analysis of the Law of Criminal Procedure in India*, Olympian Press, Calcutta, 1918.

Banerjee, Bani: *Surendranath Banerjea and History of Modern India, 1848-1925*, Metropolitan, New Delhi, 1979.

Benoy, Ghosh: *Vidyasagar O Bangali Samaj*, Orient Longman, Kolkata, 1962.

Bhagwan, V.: *Indian Freedom Movement and Constitutional Acts*, Atma Ram, 1999.

Bhattacharya, B. K.: *India's Freedom Movement: Legacy of Bipin Chandra Pal*, Deep and Deep, New Delhi, 2007.

Chakravarty, Shachi: *Quit India Movement: A Study*, New Century Publication, 2002.

Chandra, Bipan: *India's Struggle For Independence*, Penguin Books India (P) Ltd., New Delhi, 1989.

Chandra, Shailesh: *90 Years of India's Struggle for Independence: 1857-1947,* Alfa Pub, 2008.

Dhar, Shailendra Nath: *A Comprehensive Biography of Vidyasagar,* Kendra Prakashan, 1976

Ganjoo, S.: *Muslim Freedom Fighters of India,* Anmol Publication, New Delhi, 2002.

Ghosh, Ratna: *Netaji Subhas Chandra Bose and Indian Freedom Struggle (2 Vols-Set),* Deep and Deep, 2006.

Gopal, Haldar: *Vidyasagar: A Reassessment,* People's Publishing House, New Delhi, 1981.

Goyal, P. K.: *Battle of India's Freedom Movement,* Vista International, 2005.

Gupta, Shantinath: *Great Freedom Fighters of India,* Anmol, 2006.

Hari Hara Das: *The History of Freedom Movement in India (1857-1947),* National, 1998.

Indramitra: *Karunasagar Vidyasagar,* Ananda Publishers, Kolkata,1970.

Indu Dave: *Indian Personality in Its Developmental Background,* Himanshu, 1991.

Iyengar, A. S.: *Role of Press and Indian Freedom Struggle: All through the Gandhian Era,* APH, 2001.

Kailash Khanna: *History of Indian Freedom Struggle,* Commonwealth Publication, 2004.

Kaushik, A. S.: *Great Freedom Fighters of India,* Indian Publication, 2007.

Khairul Anam, Md.: *Indian Freedom Movement and Murshidabad District 1905-1947,* Bagchi, K. P., 2008.

Krishan Mohan: *Encyclopaedic History of Indian Freedom Movement (4 Vols-Set),* Book Enclave, 1999.

Kumar, Prafulla Pattanaik: *The First Indian War of Independence: Freedom Movement in Orissa, 1804-1825,* APH, 2005.

Kumar, Raj: *Essays on Indian Freedom Movement,* History and Culture Series, Discovery, 2003.

Kumar, Ravindra: *Champaran to Quit India Movement*, Mittal, 2002.

Kumar, Sirisa Shadangi: *The Prisons of South Orissa and the Freedom Fighters in Incarceration, 1900 - 1947*, Punthi Pustak, 2005.

Kumar, Ujjal Majumdar: *Bankim Chandra Chattopadhyay: His Contribution to Indian Life and Culture*, The Asiatic Society, Calcutta, 2000.

Lion Agrawal, M. G.: *Freedom Fighters of India (4 Vols-Set)*, Isha Books, 2008.

Majumdar, R. C.: *History of the Freedom Movement in India (3 Vols-Set)*, Firma KLM, 1997.

Malhotra, Sumiti: *Thoughts of Great Personalities in 20 Century*, Raj Publishing, 2003.

Manju Verma: *The Role of Women in the Freedom Movement in Punjab (1919-1947)*, Abhijeet, 2003.

Maulana Syed Mohammad Mian: *The Prisoners of Malta (Asira'n-E-Malta): The Heart-Rending Tale of Muslim Freedom Fighters in British Period*, Manak, 2005.

Mazhar Kibriya: *Gandhi and Indian Freedom Struggle*, APH, 1999.

McLeod, John: *The History of India*, Greenwood Press, Westport, CT, 2002.

Mohan, Jag and M. Chalapathi Rau: *Twenty-five Years of Indian Independence*, Vikas Publication House, Delhi, 1973.

Muthaiah, S.: *Women Freedom Fighters*, The Hindu, 2004.

Nanda, S. P.: *Freedom Movement and Constitutional Development in India*, Dominant, 2004.

Om Prakash: *Encyclopaedic History of Indian Freedom Movement (12 to 21 Vols)*, Anmol, 2003.

Omesh Saigal: *Shaheed Bhagat Singh: Unique Martyr in Freedom Movement*, Gyan Publication, 2002.

Parashar, Parmanand: *Kashmir and the Freedom Movement*, Sarup, 2004.

Pradhan, K. B.: *Freedom Movement in India*, Arise Pub, 2007.

R. K. Panda: *Kavyadarsah of Dandin : Text With the Commentary of Jibanand Vidyasagar*, Bharatiya Kala Prakashan, 2008.

Rafiya, Nisar: *Shaikh-Ul-Hind Maulana Mahmud Hasan and Indian Freedom Movement*, Manak Pub, 2008.

Ram Sharma, S.: *Education of Women and Freedom Movement*, Discovery, 1996.

Ram, S. and Kumar, R.: *Encyclopaedia of Indian Freedom Struggle (10 Vols-Set)*, Commonwealth Pub, 2008.

Ramanathan, K. V.: *The Satyamurti Letters, Vol. II: The Indian Freedom Struggle Through the Eyes of a Parliamentarian*, Dorling Kindersley for Pearson Longman an Imprint of Pearson Education, 2008.

Ramu, P. S.: *Azad Hind Fauj (I.N.A.) and The Freedom Movement*, Freedom Movement Memorial Comm, 1998.

Sharma, S. K.: *Eminent Indian Freedom Fighters (2 Vols-Set)*, Anmol Publication, New Delhi, 2004.

Sundaram, V.: *Great Crusader for Women's Emancipation*, News Today, 2005.

Sundararaja, Saroja: *March to Freedom in Madras Presidency, 1916-1947*, Lalitha Publication, Chennai, 1989.

Taneja, Anup: *Gandhi, Women and the National Movement, 1920-47*, Har-Anand Publications, Delhi, 2005.

Walter, Ruben: *Indische Romane*, Akademie Verlag, Berlin, 1964.

Index

E

F

G

H

I

J

K

L

❑❑❑